Tell Me More

First Edition, Volume I
The Journey

Trebbiano

Published in the United States of America

ISBN 979-8-89395-943-7 (SC)
ISBN 979-8-89395-842-3 (HC)
ISBN 979-8-89395-843-0 (Ebook)

Hugle Publishing
222 West 6th Street
Suite 400, San Pedro, CA, 90731
www.stellarliterary.com

Order Information and Rights Permission:
Quantity sales. Special discounts might be available on quantity purchases by corporations, associations, and others. For details, contact the publisher at the address above.

For Book Rights Adaptation and other Rights Permission.
Call us at toll-free 1-888-945-8513 or send us an email at admin@stellarliterary.com.

Contents

Chapter 1

Health officials and the local government ordered me to remain home during the Covid 19 Epidemic.

The idle time given by this pandemic made me look back on my professional life. It revisited my humble beginning and the progress throughout my life.

In retirement I face the challenge to remain active, but the pandemic put it to a screeching halt.

From customers at my lodging business I was often encouraged to author a book about the life stories I told them during breakfast service. It motivated me to open the computer where I found a page of a story I had once started during a snowstorm in Vermont.

"Go and document your life's experiences. People want to hear stories! It was a constant message."

It became my call to start with my two-finger typing system.

A guest stayed with me during his grieving time when he suffered a personal tragedy and was seeking peace and healing.

As an author with several books to his credit he also encouraged me to write a book. With time on my hands, I was eager to get busy starting a project.

$$* * * * * * *$$

I woke up in the middle of the night, which was an unpleasant experience. A dream about the time I finished grade school and entered the labor force came to my memory. The details were fresh remembering every detail. It felt unusually strange. Dreams usually fade away. But why was this one so fresh and clear in my memory? It would not let go.

That night was an intense review of my past and it traced my life back, in a delirium of half-sleep and dream. My first job as an apprentice in the butcher profession, with my Father's butcher shop at the tender age of fourteen. It amazed me how I handled all that came at me at this time of my life.

Physically, I was strong, tall, and healthy but still a child inside, A teenager with dreams, emotions, ideas, and a good portion of defiance. My Father kept that element in check with his domineering personality. He was the authority, for the good of the business, and to a lesser effect, on family life.

It wasn't my choice learning the butcher trade. Father authority dictated this as the only option for my future. "You must become a butcher and support the business!" A man of status and authority, he commanded my older brother and me to enter his business and become productive workers. It would take three years to graduate from an apprenticeship and after completion I continue working as a trained butcher for about two more years at his Butchery.

I learned how to produce prime cuts of meat and produce a large variety of sausages, smoked ham, and cured meats. It was a delicate procedure that required training, refinement, and hands-on experience.

My older brother was sent to business school in preparation to take the lead and inherit the business.

During this schooltime time, my father became ill and could not lead the sausage-making process. It was not up to me to fill the void; despite the minimal skills I had so far acquired.

I made numerous mistakes and failed to produce the same quality.

Reprimands and scolding followed, and it left a lasting mark on me. It was a harsh treatment which I found it undeserving.

It became the turning point for me to seek a different career path. I realized at that moment that I was in the wrong profession.

* * * * * * *

The thought kept growing, and I eagerly waited for my older brother's return. The fear of being turned into a workhorse became unbearable. My attitude and my motivation deflated. I just had to get out!

I delayed confronting my Father until my brother completed school and returned to work.

Cooking had crossed my mind, but I was unsure if my father would agree to different profession. The image of a Chef in a tall white hat leading a hotel kitchen brigade stuck with me.

It restored my motivation and awakened excitement. A casual interest in cooking had always been with me.

I had a goal to pursue! Courage grew to confront my father.

I told him that the butcher trade would never be my profession. I was not fond of it and looked to become a cook. To my surprise, he agreed to it.

Finally, I see a way out from this dead-end job and free from his dominance.

* * * * * * *

Two more years apprenticeship followed at a chosen restaurant by him, gave me fundamental cooking skills. The owner was a Master Chef giving him the permission to educate young boys in an apprenticeship program.

The training duties fell on the senior cook, who had also jumped from the butcher trade to cooking.

We worked split shifts serving lunch and dinner under the owner's minimal supervision.

The senior cook became my mentor, serving as his backup and right-hand man.

Our common background gave us the upper hand in the kitchen. It was a simple menu that did not teach me the broad spectrum of food preparation and diverse sauces.

Basic procedures provide a foundation to grow and build experience. It was his excuse when we challenged him to upgrade the daily menu. Self-education and experimenting at my mother's kitchen gave me additional training. Cookbooks help, yet the skills my mother had acquired in her youth at a professional kitchen became my best teacher.

* * * * * * *

The owner's daughter with all the female attractions one could admire, became the object of desire by all cooks.

Whenever she arrived in the kitchen in scant clothing, she was the object of desire and brought the kitchen to a pause. The teasing fed her ego.

The conciliation price to her was the woman in her thirties who handled the beverage dispensing to the service staff. Elena was also boarding at the upper level of the restaurant designated for employee housing.

One night she knocked at my door and wanted to socialize. I was alone in my shared room, and we had a beer. One thing led to another for one of my early encounters with a woman. Her grateful age had served her well, and a secondary apprenticeship had begun for me without commitment.

It was fun and gave me a new outlook, but I realized I had much to learn.

With graduation came the time to move on and plan for my culinary future.

I typed my resume on an old typewriter that should have belonged in a museum.

In response to an advertisement listed in the regional newspaper seeking young cooks, I sent my resume to a large conference center in Zurich, Switzerland. A prompt reply with an offer came back.

With my humble bag packed, I moved to Zurich, called on the employment office, and received my work papers. Then I was given the address for a shared room at a private home in the city.

"The room is contracted by the company. We will make a deduction for your rent." I shared the room with a young cook from Berlin and took my scooter back and forth to work.

The conference center building is the size of a city block, including concert halls, conference rooms, ballrooms, a restaurant with an excellent reputation, a cafe with a garden terrace, and a nightclub featuring Switzerland's most famous band.

Professionally designed kitchen was state of the art. Sections for hot food preparation, butchering, cold food, Poultry, fish, and live trout in a chilled basin and staffed with a brigade of twenty professionals of every rank and specialty. Each station staffed with cooks; apprentices lead by a station chef.

Chef Armand leading the brigade is the highest-ranking man, projected his authority and was noted when he entered the cooking areas. One could feel his presence even prior to his arrival.

A strict code of ethics governed this operation. I quickly recognized the level of a genius in the Chef. He assigned me to aid the Chef Saucier-, also functioning as the Sous Chef. One other cook in a senior rank and an apprentice completed his staff.

The beginning of my blossoming career in this culinary world has now begun. I delivered the same skills and work ethics. Hungry for more knowledge I took in everything with an ardent desire for more.

The daily menu served as my notepad to record all the details and recipes for that day's meals. I stayed past the service time and made my notations. Something the Chef recognized at a surprise visit to my station.

There was so much to learn; a new menu every day which never repeated any of the items. I felt rich and fulfilled with what I had entered and grateful for the good luck that guided me to this place. It opened my horizon to realize the unlimited potential in this culinary field.

This kitchen serviced the restaurants, all banquets, the nightclub, and meetings. The Concert halls featured world-renowned musicians and orchestras. Sophisticated snacks were offered during intermission.

Insurance companies used the nightclub facilities to feed their employees at lunchtime.

Then came that frequent call by phone to the restaurant manager. A special request for "Emicee Honky"! Only the Sous Chef was chosen to cook this order.

Thinly sliced strips of tender veal sautéed in little butter and finished in heavy cream. Placed in a service casserole and delivered across the street to an older woman. A follow-up phone call by the Manager to inquire if the cat consumed the meal.

I was perplexed over the fuss that this order generated and promptly told by the Sous Chef that this was, in fact, for the women's cat. If not cooked meticulously right, the cat would not eat it, which prompted a re-make of the meal. I prayed that I would never be assigned for this order ever.

But it happened one day. By then, I had moved up in my ranking and was the first assistant cook (commis) to the Sous chef. The sous chef was acting chef on the chef's day off, and I was assigned to the Sauce station in the lead position. An honor and challenge, and now comes the order for this finicky cat with the veal dish!

I remembered the details and with the Sous chef looking over my shoulders, it all turned out to be accepted by the cat. The cooks gave a round of applause and a took a deep bow to the honor.

I learned the fine cuisine of France, Italy, Swiss, and international recipes. We prepared Grand gala buffets and banquets for hundreds of guests, carving inside the Ballroom and working with seafood, oysters, langouste, scampi, Dover sole, and all the meticulous preparation. It became a feast for my learning experiences.

During my time in Zurich, my strict application of the recipes, ingredients and preparation steps advanced my broad knowledge. It earned me a promotion to station Chef (Chef de partie) as the Chef tournand.

I had made up precious ground from what I been deprived during my apprenticeship.

The tournant position provided me replacing the chef de parties spot on their day off. I worked at every station on the work schedules rotation. Another learning curve too place and with it the challenges. Sink or swim, yet a fantastic learning tool. Fortunate and delighted it laid the foundation for my culinary skills and future career.

* * * * * * *

Socially I did not waste time.

Coming to Zurich as a shy German country boy and seeking friendship with girls was eagerly explored. One girl that worked in the service station and was titled Gouvernante had an eye on me.

All-female employees of the Center had been boarded in the company's employee dormitory and the building was off limited to the male gender.

We had to meet someplace outside the house, and the city's park nearby served as an alternate. Ample benches in secluded corners and privacy lead to testing one another's kissing skills and exploring the body. As exciting as it was, it never could lead to any other physical contact. I still took pleasure in caressing the female physique, the affectionate kissing, and caressing.

What if? Arises as the question!

The city offered multiple entertainment venues. It prompted me attend an opera. "Carmen" from the composer Bizet was my first opera. It remains my all-time favorite opera. I purchased a tuxedo for the occasion since formal attire was requested for this performance.

Patronizing upscale restaurants with friends and ordering food from other cultures had its appeal and expanding my food knowledge from different cultures. The Spanish restaurant in the old city quickly became one of the favorites. Paella and Rioja wine always served up a splendid experience. We also took a liking to escargot and learned that the butter-rich dish supplied a solid foundation for more significant consumption of alcoholic beverages without suffering a hangover.

I took French language classes at the Berlitz School of languages. The need to acquire a basic understanding become a pressing matter.

The late shift was part of my work shift rotation cooking the orders for the restaurant.

On banquet event nights, the servers received a small meal.

It was on August first, the Swiss National holiday, when the female bartender Janice came for her meal, But instead of taking her meal, she asked me out to dinner after work and insisting it being her treat.

She picked me up at the employee entrance and ushered me into a small red convertible sports car.

Air-dried beef and pork called Bündner Platte, with a bottle of dry wine and crusty bread was a perfect meal at this hillside restaurant overlooking Lake Zurich. I found myself in seventh heaven, this fiery black-haired woman with Romani blood, treating this simple country boy to dinner. It was delightful!

The evening was perfect and crowned with the highlight at her apartment. I made this day a personal holiday! "J.L. Day."

* * * * * * *

My learning curve in this kitchen was immense. Presumed to have more experience due to the added years over the other young cooks, I felt the pressure to perform and ramp up my skills on the fast track.

I did so by taking on bold challenges and paying meticulous attention to the procedures. The confidence placed in me was immense. Given tasks that had been way beyond my level, I managed to master the functions and came out ahead.

The skills became a confidence builder, then took me to the level I had been missing and the fine points bringing the product to the highest level.

Senior station chefs a resource. I asked questions and was gladly advised with their best answers. How can I make it better? A common question, and by now, it was expected. Ask, and you shall receive. My fear posing a burden had left me. It showed my hunger to learn and to better my skills and knowledge.

After one year, the Chef called me to his office. I presumed that something was wrong and expected the worst. When he turned around to face me, he said my last name as usual, then congratulated me on promotion to station chef.

I was stunned at first; can this be real? I then smiled and thanked him for the promotion and confidence in me.

I must have grown an inch taller when I left his office. I could see smiles and received hearty handshakes from my immediate superior, the Sous Chef, who must have made a recommendation or endorsed me for this post.

The junior cooks wished me well. The camaraderie I still treasure in my memory.

****

Unlike any Union in the U.S., the Swiss cooks Union is engaged in promoting the skill level and education of trade professionals and offers specialist skills courses in their Hotel School.

They published a periodic newspaper where the world placed "want ads" for skilled culinary personnel. It is in fact a springboard for jobs in the world and an opportunity for the adventurous individuals. I quickly learned that this character trait was dominant in this profession.

A full-page ad for a gull-winged-shaped hotel in the USA received my attention. Wow, it made an impression on me! I showed it to my girlfriend, and she said, let's apply! We mailed an application and resume to the address and promptly received a job offer.

Adventure and excitement flowed through our bodies as the prospect of going to America filled our fantasies.

For the visa and work permit, we went to the American Consulate and submitted our application. The process was paper-intensive and resulted in a ticket to enter the USA for both of us. It turned out to be a stroke of luck since my girlfriend had previously filed an application.

She had spent a year in England and had in fact filed for a visa at that time. It satisfied her waiting period.

My application was processed in record time making use of preferred quotas. We received a large envelope and instructed handing it over to the immigration officer at the entry point to the United States.

Green cards will at first be issued as a temporary Identification and mailed to the designated address. ,

We were well on the way to making our preparation for the trip. My parents took it hard, but in the end, they could not stop us.

"Off to the USA, here we come!"

Chapter 2

An ocean voyage from Southampton to New York on the Holland American lines ship *Amsterdam* took us across a stormy Atlantic.

After six-day sailing we arrived on a clear October day in New York.

During the voyage, a fellow cook from the Swiss Brigade surprised us since he was working as a cook on this vessel.

My cabin assignment in tourist class was at the aft section of the ship. The men were separated from the female gender and bunked in a group of four per cabin. My girlfriend, now referred to as fiancée, had the female section. She also had a shared cabin.

It became clear that the line catered to the rich and famous, and first-class had to be the place to be.

Our friend shows us a way to first-class dining room. My fiancé's little black dress and my tuxedo matched the dress code for dinner in first class.

Our friend put a word in for us with the Maître d'. The food was first-class with lavish dinners and fantastic beverages, and nobody ever questioned us.

After dinner, we went back to tourist class, where the down-to-earth fun took place. Drinks for fifty cents and hearty jokes had been the going routine and suited us better than the stuffy social scene at first!

* * * * * * *

When the skyline of Manhattan grew into the endless sky, we stood on deck in awe.

Looking up on these tall buildings in their grandeur, left a lasting impression on us.

We did it, something that had been a dream three months ago is now reality. A stiff neck after days of sightseeing and visiting the world's fair with the giant globe of mother earth, worked up a hearty appetite.

Our journey continued by bus to Washington, DC. A cousin on my mother's side took us in and helped us get settled. He had immigrated years earlier and worked for the US government.

My job was within walking distance from our rental efficiency. I began my first workday and reported to the Executive Chef.

As a German, the Chef had his entire kitchen staff from Europe and primarily German-speaking cooks. It helped me immensely since my English language skills had been nonexistent. I could not communicate in English and relied on my girlfriend to translate.

The job placed me in the banquet kitchen for one week and received orders from other cooks for mass-produced food for large banquets.

Then came the announcement from the top that the convention season was ending, and I would be going to another hotel, where I will continue my work.

A smaller but more luxurious hotel and also catering to affluent business travelers and politically engaged professionals, was a better suited place and more my style.

Communication moved now to the forefront as my biggest problem. Only the Executive Chef and the Sous Chef spoke German; all other kitchen staff came from the various demographics of the city, namely, people of color. Their English had a different tone, and what little I had picked up by that time was now being tested. I had asked the Sous Chef if this was a foreign language.

"No, it is slang. In time you will understand it."

The position as Chef Garde-mange made me responsible for all cold food preparations. Hors- d'oeuvres for cocktail parties, canapés, salads and salad dressings, appetizers, and fruit for the various meals. A job I learned to love and started to apply my acquired skills.

* * * * * * *

A group of European cooks from various hotels showed us to restaurants and drinking places; all had a German theme with good beer and familiar food.

We socialized and learned from their experiences, the pitfalls, and the scams. The most important information was the requirement to report to the Selective Service Board. "You must do so within ix months, no later!"

It scared me and shook me to the bones. I did not expect to serve in the US armed forces. I did not fit my plans.

We packed our bags and drove the Ford Fairlane to Montreal and beat the deadline by a week.

****

Montreal is a cosmopolitan city in the French-Canadian province of Quebec which showed us a warm welcome. The flavors of Europe came to light. Restaurants with French names and stores that carried familiar products from back home made us feel at home.

The largest hotel in town was hiring. As luck would strike again, I was offered a job on the evening shift as the Chef Saucier.

The cooks on this shift amounted to approximately twenty-five cooks. Three European cooks, two Swiss, and one German cook, completed my team on the Saucier station.

It was a challenging job producing nightly in excess of fifteen different sauces supporting the three menus.

The meal cont. would be in the 800 on a normal night and increase when the hotel catered to large conventions.

Our communication at the saucier station was handled with only hand signals, body language, eye contact, and other motions. All orders had been announced aloud by the German Sous Chef and acknowledged by eye contact. This work was fun and gratifying and gave me immense satisfaction.

We formed individual friendships and bonded. Cooks from all corners of the world delivered a variety of experiences. At the end of the shift, we often had a volunteer cook a special meal for the group. Pleased to see such harmony, the Chef joined us often and donated a case of beer. We ate Swiss dishes, German food, Chinese food, Indonesian exotic specialties, Italian dishes, and Greek food.

We socialized outside work, treasured our friendships, and stuck together as a team.

Then came a strike by the union against the hotel. The morning shift stayed out to strike, all Canadians, and immigrants from Greece. Us Europeans and other nationals had no solidarity to this union.

The call to keep operating and the kitchen open for service was going out to the evening shift. Everyone from the evening crew came to work and split up to cover the essential posts keeping the kitchen producing food

* * * * * * *

Formidable entertainment venues throughout the city attracted the young and old.

On my way home to the apartment, I overheard loud singing and laughter. An Irish pub with a piano player led the public to sing Irish songs. Good enough, let me check it out.

Winter approached. Wow, I never felt such bitter cold with icy winds from the north cutting into the skin like a knife. I realized that my winter cloth was too light for this climate. A bearskin fur coat served me, then good mittens and a fur hat completed the essentials for that winter. However, despite the highly desirable job, I would not relish repeating another winter.

Walking home from work often made me feel the razor-sharp arctic winds.

Blowing through the Northbound streets serving as a wind tunnels became unbearable. Seek the wind shadow side or you will freeze to death.

I passed the Tavern just around the corner from my apartment building. Let me get a drink and warm for a short while.

This place was packed with a drinking crowd and a sing-along theme lifted the spirit.

Charming young females graced this city. The elegant walk with posture and a stride that turned the hip movements into a rumba dance caught my attention.

They have it together, and flirting was undoubtedly a masterful skill.

What will it take to taste the forbidden fruit? This thought crossed my mind, and my body responded eagerly to it.

What came from this I must leave to your imagination.

The opportunity presented itself to meet a Norwegian waitress after work.

It proved rewarding but remained a cold arrangement.

I looked for hotel addresses in a travel magazine in the South Seas, Tahiti, Bora Bora, and more. Nothing came of it, not even a "No, thank you".

* * * * * * *

My girlfriend who had at one time gone back to Washington DC returned and we made plans to get married.

The wedding took place in a local church. The pastor managed the ceremony.

We chose a fine French restaurant to celebrate the union.

That was just the right thing. Neither my wife nor I had the stomach for a large family wedding in the homeland. Having our moms and dads here, plus my two brothers would have been nice. We could not afford to host or pay the travel costs for all these family members. We sent a picture home and found its way into the local newspaper in Germany.

The honeymoon took us on our very first airplane ride. The thrill at takeoff and the excitement to go to a tropical island overwhelmed us with joy and anticipation.

The hotel on Saint Thomas overlooked the bay and harbor like a watchdog was our host,

An employee discount rate from the hotel company secured the accommodations. We enjoyed the warm ocean, feasting on tropical fruit, Mango, Papaya, Guava and more for the first time, and discovered rum cocktails.

The mangoes and papayas all had unfamiliar flavors but appealed to our taste quickly. Sunshine and sunburns, cheap rum drinks, steel bands, local dances, and island songs intoxicated the evenings.

We could have stayed there forever! Beautiful beaches and Caribbean food suited our tastes.

The smell of the ocean and balmy air spawned the desire for the South Seas.

Back in Montreal, I received a notification in my mailbox.

My search efforts finally produced a reply. The Intercontinental Hotel Corporation, headquartered in New York at the Pan Am Building, has sent an invitation to interview for a position.

A flight to JFK followed by a helicopter ride to the top of the Pan Am Building was way over my means, but I could not pass up the opportunity. The alternative would have been the subway and getting lost or an expensive taxi with an involuntary sightseeing detour.

Intercontinental told me I would get a job, but the exact position and location had to be confirmed with the hotel. The offer for a Sous Chef position at the Intercontinental Hotel in New Delhi, India, was in the offer letter.

The contractual employment terms over two years were a salaried position paid in foreign exchange in India, and the hotel would take care of the housing, food, transport, taxes, and uniform. The hotel pays all living expenses.

Chapter 3

We returned to Germany and waited for the visa at my mother's home.

The flight took us from Kloten Airport in Switzerland past the Middle East, and landed in Moscow, USSR, for refueling.

Servicing the plane for refueling took a long time. Stern Russin officials escorted us to a hall, where our passports received a thorough scrutiny. Eventually everybody was released and allowed back on the aircraft.

Crossing the Himalayan mountains provided a splendid view at the world's tallest peaks while the pilot was pointing out those known to him. us a

Our arrival in New Delhi hit us with a wall of humidity. The air smelled foul.

The diver took us through the outskirts of the city on the way to the hotel.

When the Intercontinental Hotel came into view, it looked like it was the only building far and near. Life surrounding the large structure looked primitive. Dusty streets and cars labeled as taxis, scooters, and bicycles filled the street. The Indian countryside revealed primitive life in sheds without running water or power.

* * * * * * *

The hotel, a modern high-rise building with fifteen stories of guest rooms stood out like a temple.

We entered the stately lobby and met the General Manager's secretary. Then the General Manager greeted us warmly and assured us accommodations in the hotel to start. His secretary will be making the arrangements. We also learned that the Executive Chef, a Swiss national, had just arrived two days prior. We received a hotel room as a temporary accommodation, and permanent arrangements would be available shortly.

The secretary was a stunning, slender Indian girl in a Sari that started below the belly button.

She exposed her skin up to the breast and gave me an alluring view. My eyes are wandering, to her enjoyment. *Take your time*!

A German Pastry Chef had been there already and dated a local girl, a natural beauty.

Two more European cooks arrived the next day; one Swiss and one German, to complete the allocation of expatriates.

This kitchen served as the main production center. We had an American coffee shop with a small, short-order cooking line as a satellite operation.

The grand restaurant with three hundred-plus seats and decorated as a dining salon with a giant bead curtain on each end signifying giant Peacocks in all its glorious colors.

An Indian restaurant with its own section in the kitchen and a Chinese restaurant on the rooftop completes the food operations.

The local beer or spirits did not meet international expectations. Barely drinkable it came as a disappointment.

For parties, the embassies supplied products from their homeland and imported them under the diplomatic umbrella. Those events became an opportunity for us, expatriates, to get supplies otherwise unavailable to us.

Mr. Wong was leading his Chinese cooks.

I spent my free time with him, seeing the Chinese way of cooking in the steel woks.

The variety of dishes required practice and impressed me.

The Chefs were fast in the ways the food is cooked, seasoned, and finished in just minutes. I tried to learn from them, but it was hard to follow.

Chef Kapoor, in charge of the Indian food, was willing to pass on his knowledge in exchange for information on our Continental cuisine.

Overwhelming spice variations, strange names, and intense flavors required a specific treatment in the cooking process.

The demands for international high-quality food placed on us Europeans bordered miracles.

Pâté en croute with Cumberland sauce! Products for the sauce needed are currant jelly, port wine, and other components that are not available. A first-class product is still expected and must be developed through improvising with ingredients that came close to the actual recipe.

One event called for clear turtle soup. I questioned Chef's sanity in accepting such an order. But in his calm, carefree, and hands-off style, he assured me that fresh products were coming into the kitchen for it. I would be okay and able to produce it. He had confidence in my ability to get it right.

I had never cooked a turtle soup from live turtles. In Europe, an order for a clear turtle soup is filled by opening a can from Lacroix, a fine food supplier.

It's ready to be heated and finished with a shot of dry Sherry.

I faced up with preparing such a product from the ground up and not knowing if I could find the essential herbs and flavoring ingredients. A small dictionary and French cookbook served me to find all the necessary items. Still, most spices and herbs did not exist, nor did the hotel carry any of the fortified wines for the finish.

Live snapper turtles arrived for the soup, and now the question was, how do I go about processing these animals? Nobody had a clue, nor could the Chef give me any advice.

For dignity, I will circumvent the procedure I used. All I will say that it was a cruel procedure.

Once killed and washed, the animal ended up in a large steam kettle with chilly water and seasonings while the cooking was managed slow and careful bringing the broth to a gentle boil. .

Everybody was eager to see how it was to turn out. The executive Chef looked at this brew with great interest and gave the all-clear signal. It looked as if it was going to come to a good soup.

The flavor matched as if by a miracle and only needed concentration.

My sherry imitation consisted of dry white wine and two local distilled whiskey varieties. It boosted my confidence to see it come to a success. Good things take time; wait and see.

The turtle soup had been ordered by an Embassy for a party. I asked a staff person of the Embassy if she would donate a bottle of Madeira to refine and finish the soup. She agreed, and now we were all perfect for serving this exotic soup.

* * * * * * *

The birth of my son in New Delhi prompted an occasion to celebrate with a good bottle of champagne. The German Embassy donated a bottle of Henkel Trocken sparkling wine when I registered him for German Citizenship. .

Another time, the Russian Embassy hosted a party, and served caviar to their guests. As a thank, you for our efforts. Each of us received a one-kilo can of caviar!

It was caviar overload, no matter the fine quality.

In the main Kitchen we had the Indian local cuisine managed by Chef Kapoor. He was a warm and friendly man and interested in my culinary training.

When I mentioned the place in Zurich, he recalled a time, when he had been the guest Chef featuring an Indian food promotion, Yes, It brought back memories since I had worked there at that time.

While he could not remember me specifically, we reminisced about the Chef in Charge and his immense skills.

The state banquet in honor of " His Highness Prince Ali Khan", the head of the Islamic congregation, was hosted at the hotel.

The prominence of government Ministers, Diplomatic Corps, and prominent Indian families had been on the guestlist.

Detailed notations of the dietary restrictions marked in the list of five hundred guests.

Became an interesting logistical challenge. No pork for the Muslims, no beef for the Hindus, and a vegetarian diet segmented to a no this and not that ingredient gave us headaches.

It looked to me as if we were serving five hundred individual orders. Chicken was the only meat acceptable to the carnivores.

The vegetarians were serviced from our Indian kitchen. Chef Kapoor was familiar with the details.

Assurances from the Caterin Director providing an accurate account of exceptions to the menu was an empty promise.

At service time, guest quickly changed their mind and abandoned their original selection.

Somehow. The party became a success.

A souvenir menu with the signature of His Highness was the reward and recognition for pulling it off.

The routine set in again to manage the unique circumstances this hotel had demanded from us.

Processing chicken, which arrived on foot and herded by the farmer and his children and walked the chicken into the loading dock are, was an unusual delivery.

The hotel set up a production line to process the live birds and made them ready for the kitchen. A team of Nepalese chicken butchers took on this work daily. Short in stature, the first man chopped off the head, bled the carcass, and passed it on to the next man like in a production line. He, in turn, had to dip the bird into scalding water to loosen the feathers, then plug the feathers from the skin and pass it on for gutting and rinse.

With the head cut from the body, the neck stayed active, twisting, and turning, spraying blood all over the man's clothing and hair. This sticky substance attracted the loose feathers from the following man's action and turned him into a giant chicken by the end of the workday. It was hilarious to see! I regretted that I never took a picture of him.

Our son was born in a local hospital, grew rapidly with his mother feeding him her natural milk, then gradually transitioned to soft food and fruit. A blender was available to buy from an Australian family returning home. No such machine would have been available in any local store. The locals used a pestle to grind food to a flour consistency.

The hotel provided an *Amah*, a young married woman, to help with the child-rearing duties. It was less of a need but a status symbol to create a job and income. She could not conceive a child herself and took enthusiastic care of our boy as if he were her own. This young woman cared for the child and grew close to him. We had been worried she would take him away as her own and disappear into the slums of Old Delhi. Nothing of that sort. She was, in fact, the kind of person one would like to adopt. Had she not been married; I would have matched her with a German chef from our group. We helped her with food and extra money to ease the burden of her life.

She grew into our hearts as if she were family. Fond memories stay in my heart.

The seasons in India are different from our expectations. It is sweltering starting in March after a chilly winter with temperatures in the low thirties Fahrenheit and even frost. The warming comes rapidly with no rain on the horizon. The air is dry and pleasant, but the heat kicks in by late April and May. Walking with an umbrella suddenly makes sense. The windows on the taxi cars got rolled up, for the hot air was burning on the skin.

Inside the hotel kitchen, with the ventilation in full force, it only took in the air from the outside.

The kitchen temperature at fifty degrees Fahrenheit with dry air kept us from feeling the sweat on our bodies when suddenly, we were exhausted and dehydrated. "Don't drink the water" was the message at arrival. The water was not safe to drink , it needed boiling first. We resorted to hot Darjeeling tea at the advice from locals and a supplement of salt tablets, with that we managed to stay hydrated.

The house we shared had three floors.

The rooftop with a single bedroom, living room, bath, and bedroom was taken by the pastry chef.

A single man from Switzerland splits my two-bedroom floor with separate bathrooms.

Our bathroom with a shower and tub and directly connected to the bedroom as a convenience.

The water from the faucet did not needed heat[ng. In contrast, we searched to get cool water from the tab. Finally, we learned that filling the tub with water in the morning or overnight, then keeping the door open to the bathroom, and with the tiny 3 BTU window air conditioner cooling the bath water.

It was the only relief method to cool down the body.

It is also the time of the season when Indians head north to the Himalayan Mountains. Srinagar in Kashmir is the destination where a missionary couple from America invited us to join. A train ride that shared the cabins with the natives going home or traveling for heat relief held live chickens, sheep, food supplies, and children of all ages.

The train journey changed to "on foot," and they transferred the luggage onto cullies. Men of skin and bones make a living strapping the baggage with a leather strip on their back and around the forehead to carry the suitcases uphill. About a mile, we found a hotel. The beds had been like the house, a simple frame with a wooden board and thin but fluffy bedding material. Primitive open windows delivered the cool mountain breeze.

It was a welcome break from the work routine at the hotel. The visit had been short, but it broke the heat period.

Later, we took a train to Agra. The magnificent temple, the "Taj Mahal," sits in the middle of the countryside. Not much leads up to this tremendous, wonderful building. All marble and exquisitely decorated with inlaid stone, it was perfectly placed to catch the sunrise at just the right time; a reflecting pool makes for endless photo opportunities. With amazement, we thought, how could such a sophisticated construction be carried out under such primitive conditions?

Then nature announced a change in the weather. Winds picked up the red clay sand and whirled it into the air, forming a red cloud umbrella over the city. The wind threatened the population to suffocate under it.

The monsoon has arrived, and spectacular cloud formations and thundershowers pouring buckets from the clouds wash the land and flood the streets.

At the first bolt of thunder, everybody ran outside to welcome the first raindrops. Creatures came to the surface from drainage pipes. Snakes, rodents, and bugs, every creature that had been underground to survive the heat, are now taking part in the monsoon rain and have an adverse sight, for it brings every snake and rodent out of their hiding places onto the streets.

Sunsets with bursting red colors and sunrises alike are a spectacle of nature. Humidity set in, causing discomfort until the rains cooled the air to a comfortable temperature. This wet period gradually diminished and settled into the best season. The growing season is on its way, and it is the best time of the year.

The party business peaked and gave the hotel and us the command to produce the most incredible food products, buffets, sit-down dinners, and cocktail receptions. The German embassy had asked me to help them in my free time with party preparation for smaller parties staged at the embassy. The reward for this service came from German wine, champagne, or a case of beer. This reward was more precious than money since we could not convert Rupees to hard currency. We could not spend local money on meaningful investments. Gold silver was available yet challenging to obtain. A black market had set prices to such levels; it made no economic sense.

We relied on a monthly transfer permit to convert the salary to any hard foreign currency and then transfer it to a homeland account. Seventy-five percent was the allotment, but when the Indian ownership company paid us, foreigners, on the last day of the month that would fall on a Friday, it made it impossible to secure our translator to go with us to the bank. The total salary was in hand as rupees and worthless unless we found something to invest in as a treasure to take home. The ownership company controlled the finances, and the InterContinental managing company was the operating company and the shield to hang out for marketing purposes.

Hard currency was available on the illegal market and, of course, risky to deal with the dark elements in the city. Getting into this and caught by police bring severe punishment. Semiprecious gemstones looked of inferior quality and were not worth the chance.

I found a man who offered to me to custom-make handwoven oriental carpets. He described the product, which he showed us at our house, as being handmade in the villages outside the city, using Australian wool, German dyes from Bayer Leverkusen, and patterns with exclusive designs that he called his own exclusive. The knot count described to be a minimum of four hundred per square centimeter, and the color would never fade, not even from the sun or washing it with soap. His price required negotiating, if only for symbolic reasons.

He took the order without a deposit, simply on the honor system. In the countryside, the entire village worked on the selected design.

His product had been impressive with quality and accuracy in design and the assurance of a fair deal. He came with updates and samples of other orders to assure our quality. He delivered for prompt payment. Now that was worth doing and reflected a reasonable and fair price with triple the value outside India.

Every extra rupee was going for more rugs. He focused on a short-wave transistor radio we took to India from Germany. We traded it on a barter arrangement, and he would produce his most precious design yet. We made the deal to his delight. He delivered a great product in exchange for the radio. All these rugs are still in my house and look new fifty years later.

I look back at the honor this man displayed and my respect for a man like him. He does honor his country and his people.

The hotel kitchen continued to bring challenges in delivering products foreigners were asking for. With my butcher training and connection, I asked my father to ship me a device to inject salt brine to cure the boneless muscles of the pig's hind leg to create cooked ham. That worked like a charm.

****

Whenever I was cooking, I found a trusted helper by my side. It was the pot washer Anil! This young chap made every effort to be done with his duties to free up time so he could work with me. He was hungry to learn and performed every task as shown the first time. Impressive, but since he came from the lowest caste, his chances of being a cook had been nonexistent. Anil impressed me, learned very quickly, and should have received a promotion were it not for the social order in India.

The day came when we lost the soup cook. We must hire a replacement; however, the thought of promoting Anil did not leave my mind. I spoke to the Executive Chef about the possibility of encouraging him and ignoring the rule of the Indian caste system. He also saw his diligent efforts and supported my idea.

All we needed now was to have management sign off on it. The food and beverage director signed on to the plan, being an Italian national. He also had no firm commitment to this unorthodox system, and the American general manager supported it. The paperwork had to go to the Indian Ownership Management for approval. On the paperwork, we purposely omitted Anil's earlier position as a pot washer but labeled his position as *Casserollier*, the Frech term for washing the pots and pans. It made the position look as if was a skilled cooks position.

It worked! The sign-off came from the personal office and we made Anil the soup cook!

The other cooks protested and threatened to walk off the job. I assembled them in the kitchen and then called the bluff.

"Okay, go on and leave your precious job. You will lose employment as you exit the door. Tomorrow we will have hundreds of candidates in the parking lot for selection and interviews."

They thought about it, and with the realization of being unemployed or working for a local place, they realized to be better off tolerating this for now. The bluff had worked; no one left the job, and peace again restored.

We could see that Anil never received full acceptance, at time he was threatened, and sabotaged when working on a project alone. Foul language and harassment, he just shrugged it off. He was a strong young man and immensely proud of his accomplishment and job performance.

Since I was his benefactor, I received an invitation from Anil to visit his house and to meet his family. At that moment, it dawned on me just how big a deal this was to him.

He gave me his address, and we set a date for this visit. Do I bring anything? What is the custom? "Only yourself," it will be good.

I made my way by a scooter taxi to his address. A commune of twenty families lived there, occupying a single room per family in what looked like a gated commune. Two buildings with single rooms on each side and populated with a family. Anil assembled the entire family, from the youngest child to the great-grandparent.

The formal Indian hands folded "Namaste" Sahib served as the welcome greeting.

Hot tea with sugar, milk, and sweets made from milk and sugar cooked to a paste, rolled into portion balls, and soaked in sugar syrup, then finished in chopped pistachios. Delicious tasting, but my Western palate the level of sweetness was overwhelming.

To give "face," I had to accept it, eat with pleasure, and then praise the women. His wife and mother nodded with approval.

Now Anil was translating all questions directed to me and answers given back. It was a lively exchange centered mostly on my German nationality, European life, customs and traditions, and work at the hotel. At the close, Anil escorted me again to the front door of the complex. All occupants in the other rooms in the buildings had come out to see him and me and applauded him.

That was when Anil received "Face" in front of his commune. He must have grown an inch taller.

During my time in India, I stayed connected with the Chef in Zurich. Thoughts crossed my mind about the words he shared with me when I told him about the plans for America.

Should I return to Europe at the end of this contract, or is the world too small for me?

He had seen my talent and spoke about the plans he envisioned for my future.

The Chef in Saint Moritz had shown an interest in me for a unique position. He said the job would involve working in the dining room to prepare tableside dishes. Both had been friends for years, and it was a familiar gesture to hand over selected talents and create an avenue for a career. His original plans were to get me to the best hotel in Saint Moritz.

I considered this man a genius and kept sending postcards as he followed my job until he died. His wife had sent the last reply saying how he had enjoyed this ongoing contact. This thought never left my mind, thinking of where my career would have taken me if I had followed his plan.

"What if?

The Executive Chef at the hotel in New Delhi came from a Bangkok, Thailand, hotel. His wife was Ethiopian, a petite, graceful woman with very dark skin and European facial features. He had met her in her home country, where he worked in Addis Ababa.

The job as a lobbyist suited him better. He is not a culinary wizard and is not interested in getting his hands dirty. He backed his staff and stood up at times of conflict that did arise from the restaurant managers giving food away.

These Indian men had gone to an Austrian hotel school on an Austrian scholarship with the help of influential Indian families and businesspeople. They were very subdued while studying, but upon returning to their home country, they were awarded an assistant manager position in the hotel industry. The government pushed the tourist trade, so they needed good hotel professionals. If they hooked up with Austrian girls and took her back to India as their wife.

Back in India, the attitude changed, made themselves essential and arrogant toward the Europeans, and played the domineering role to the native fellow workers. "We are better now. You will listen to us."

It looked as if they worked into their pocket at the expense of the hotel's food cost. Suspicion of such dirty deals created tensions and conflict. Their arrogant attitude and pretended knowledge of food did not earn them any laurels. The need to learn management skills was clear. The short study period at a hotel school followed by an internship was not enough time to get traction from experience, while the Austrian management is applied with autocratic principles.

* * * * * * *

The end of my contract came about shortly. The green card for entry into the USA needed renewal, and travel preparation must proceed.

At the point of exit from India, the customs official wanted to deny my departure, sighting, that the goods I carried with me entering the country, was not in my luggage leaving the country. A heated dispute erupted over the allegation. He would not accept that I had packed an overseas custom-made travel crate which was holding the fine carpets and all heavy and bulky merchandise. This crate was shipped as freight to Honk Kong, for pick up at the airport when we arrive.

With tickets in hand to fly to Bangkok and then to Hong Kong and pressed for time to meet the flight , I gave him the freight ticket as proof and pressured him to drop his demands.

When he still resisted. I placed dollars into the passport and handed it to him. As if by magic, all papers suddenly checked out satisfactorily. He then cleared us for departure.

Three months before leaving India, I contacted the Chef of the Tokyo Hilton Hotel. He was seeking a sous chef and needed the position filled promptly. He was interested in hiring me, but the timing worked against me. He could not wait out the time it took for my release from the New Delhi position.

I stayed connected with a friend from Montreal all these times. Amazing, writing all these handwritten letters, then mailing them with the Indian postal service, and they all reached the destination. I had to stand at the counter to see that the stamps be applied and only this way I was assured that the stamps were not torn off and the letter discarded.

This friend who had left the ships job and ended in Montreal had followed the Sous Chef to Miami opening a luxury hotel. Through him I landed a job in Miami.

Miami became my final destination.

Chapter 4

We had tried at first to secure an ocean fare from Mumbai to Hong Kong with the French Maritime shipping line. A strike canceled that. The alternative was to fly out of New Delhi to Bangkok with a two-day layover and on to Hong Kong. Then an ocean voyage with the American President line across the Pacific to San Francisco. From there a final leg by air to Miami.

We had spent two days in Bangkok, a sinful city that offered open prostitution. Aggressive girls are hitting on men, whether they had a woman with them or not, and were not showing any restraint.

We heard much about it from tales the Chef in New Delhi had shared. My wife and I shared the curiosity to explore and see all the novelties in this city offered for money.

Our baby was now seven months and taken care of by hotel babysitting services. The humid tropical night air filled with neon lights, street vendors and all the young females or boys hired to sell whatever one's heart desired. We cruised the city by taxi and walked the streets seeing all the curiosities and nightclubs.

On the second day, I wanted to get a haircut. Great skilled cute girls started to scissor and razor-sculpture their hair with great skills. Simultaneously, the nails soaked, filed, and cuticles removed. The feet received equal meticulous care. The back received a gentle rub, and an invitation for a full-body massage with a bath for a modest surcharge. It was too good to turn down. What a treat, something I had never allowed on me. It was the entire body, and not an inch was unattended, and the end was memorable.

In Hong Kong, we found our travel case with broken hinges. Rough handling took its toll and needed a solution. The clerk offered us a rope to secure the lid. We hoped it would survive the remaining voyage.

A day spent looking around the bustling city of Hong Kong took us to giant Chinese shops selling their wares at bargain prices. Street vendors were everywhere and signs we could not read, the sounds and sights captured the attention of our boy.

Rickshaws are weaving through the street traffic, and men carrying wares on a pole across the shoulder. Indeed, this is a different world. We were fascinated by all these activities and Chinese products we had never seen; street vendors with chicken, pork, and ducks hanging on the hook offered a quickly cooked meal.

We watched the locals how this food was prepared and then mustered up the courage of something concocted by pointing fingers at the products. A boiling broth with noodles, vegetables, and meat cut from a hanging chicken, he combined it all into a bowl, and with chopsticks as the eating utensil, it tasted flavorful, hot, and delicious.

Taking in all these new surroundings, our baby son never cried and was eating the soup from a spoon. He was so busy seeing the actions on the streets: rickshaws, people with a hat he'd never seen, and lanterns and strange shop signs lit up with neon lighting. We carried him on the hip like in India or on my shoulder; either way, he had a full view of the world around him.

We dared to go to a floating restaurant. This place was vast and intimidating. We entered this place, received the menu, and realized it was only in Chinese. The food was challenging to identify as all items were bite-size pieces and stir-fried with fresh vegetables in a sauce seasoned with soy sauce and hot chilies. The only identifiable number in front of all the dishes had been the item numbers.

We had to take a chance and point to a number to place the order.

To date, I still do not know what I ate that night. My wife's dish was pork in a sweet-sour sauce, crispy fried, and tossed in this reddish sauce with vegetables. I ate mine because it tasted good, wondering what it was, a thought that had never left my mind entirely.

The next day, we reserved at a Japanese restaurant. Seated on cushions with my legs crossed, we ordered sashimi and sushi. To our surprise, this was all raw fish, rice, a spicy green paste that traveled through the sinus's channel like horseradish and sweet ginger, and all dressed up with long thin strips of white radish. The presentation arranged in meticulous taste stimulated my appetite, an enjoyable experience. I had an idea about it from a Japanese cookbook but never had tasted it before.

By taxi to the local food market in Aberdeen gave an insight into Chinese life.

The vendors displayed piles of vegetables and fruits on their stands. I had never seen such a variety.

Fresh fish, crustaceans, butchered meat, and live animals made for an exciting day.

The ship's arrival in Hong Kong Harbor early by 7:00 a.m. marked our departure from this land.

Boarding had already started, and we settled in for a long voyage across the Pacific. One-stop scheduled in Yokohama and then on to Hawaii.

I took the opportunity in Yokohama to see the executive Chef at the Hilton Hotel. He proudly showed me around and explained how the Japanese cooks needed managing. A proud profession and in high esteem, Japanese cooks have a social status equal to that of persons with higher education from universities and master's degrees. The skills I saw by any cook were far superior to that of highly trained Europeans.

I asked the Chef, "What do they need us for?" His comments referred to the hotel's image in foreign countries wanting assurance that the food preparation was in European skilled hands. It was essential to attract foreign travelers and the image of the Hilton brand. Equally, the Japanese wanted to project the same to domestic clientele, alluring a superior product.

Management was the most crucial function of the Executive Chef. Paperwork, cost containment, and labor management is keeping him busy.

The ship was now crossing the majestic Pacific Ocean. I was unsure what to expect, thinking back on the Atlantic crossing from England that had not been pleasant by riding out the storm in the aft section of the Amsterdam.

Still unbelievable, this giant body of water was smooth like a mirror. Glorious sunshine every day, the clear horizon, sunrise, sunset, it got boring. The ship served as a transport vehicle for people and freight from Asia to the USA.

Hawaii was the next stop and feverishly anticipated. Everyone made plans to spend the time on solid ground. Pearl Harbor showed the scars of World War II and the Japanese attack on the Pacific Fleet.

A day on solid ground and the chance to shake out the sea legs made us feel intoxicated. A rental car took us all around Oahu. In the countryside, volcanoes, tropical forests, and vegetation with wild orchids had our full attention. Giant waves and surfers riding it fascinating us. The day came to a quick close, and we are on the way to San Francisco.

Since the job was open in Miami, the essence of time pressed us and staying only one day in this city.

San Francisco is an attractive city. The contours and location on this huge bay with the Golden Gate bridge spanning over the bay entrance certainly capture one's attention and building anticipation. This city delivers the goods in all areas.

The vista, dynamics of the street, Fisherman's Wharf, Chinatown, fancy restaurants, and casual cafés with fine ethnic foods from around the world, Ghirardelli Square, fine chocolate, and world-famous Irish coffee showed off the diversity of the population.

The hippies gathered in the park areas and displayed the peace symbols. Long-haired men looked weird and disorderly, while the women who never combed their hair and wore funky clothing emptied Grandmother's Carnival costume closets. The guitar player chants in small groups, and strange-smelling smoke came from all areas.

We graved to eat good meat during the Indian time and now had our sights set on a great steak or beef roast. We selected the prime rib place, and we gorged on an enormous Caesar salad I had ever seen, then the massive cut of beef with the rib bone still in the flesh, served pink or medium as it was cooked at that time, and with a giant baked potato, sour cream, and fresh chives. It was overload for our stomach, but we could not reject even the last bite. It was simply too good, and wasting food is not in our genes. It did settle the craving.

Travel fatigue had set in on the mind and body, and glad to be finally arriving at our final destination.. We arranged for the trunk transported by ground freight to Miami's hotel address. Then Pan Am Airways took us on a direct flight to Miami.

A taxi fare to the hotel on Bay Shore Drive in the Brickell District and my friend Ernie and the Chef awaited us and set us up in a hotel room. A tour of the hotel's kitchen, restaurants, and banquet rooms completed the day. Food and sleep were all we needed.

The hotel consisted of four majestic towers on the waterfront of Biscayne Bay. A sizeable ground-floor garage with eight hundred cars connected the buildings "The four Senators." The building was a mixed-use complex. Studios and larger apartments served as hotel rooms and year-round rentals alike. The hotel had a bar, two restaurants, and a ballroom with smaller meeting rooms for group meetings, banquets, and convention shows.

Chef Fritz from Montreal had adapted to his new position with ease. The voyage had depleted our savins and our pockets are now empty.

I was grateful for the job and started to work at once.

Finding an apartment is now the wife's duty.

Back to punching a timecard seemed weird but was part of the procedure. I was once again an hourly employee! To be on the time clock had bothered me initially, and then I tried to rationalize it as a starting point and continued with my work.

The first payday showed the amount of taxes taken, social security, Medicare, and Medicaid all took a chunk from the gross pay. It had to last, and life had to adjust to make ends meet.

After settled[in my wife looked for employment. She landed a server's job in a club on the night shift.

It serves is by working different hours, we managed the childcare duties and generated additional income. We managed to get by and live a modest lifestyle.

Nearby beaches and parks served as low-cost entertainment turning the toddler loose to play.

This apartment building house primarily singles with a divorce record or male and female bachelors to this low-cost rental within walking distance to the heart of Coconut Grove. Coconut Grove had considerable notoriety as an assembly place for artistic people, and on the side street, one could see fancy houses owned by wealthy people.

As the year progressed and came to a full circle, I got itchy to seek a position like I had in New Delhi. Atlas Hotels had a hotel project under construction nearing completion. The ad in the paper listed various food and beverage positions and also a sous chef. The managing company of my current employer could not offer a transfer, or should I say, the regional food and beverage director casually shrugged it off and wanted nothing to do with other young talents' careers.

The Executive Chef from the corporate office for the new hotel, grilled me on skills and knowledge. Then came the ultimate question:

"Do you know why the Executive Chef works ten hours a day, but the Sous Chef works at least fourteen hours a day?"

Dumfounded, I thought about this strange question. Before I could answer, he said,

"The Sous Chef wants to become the Executive Chef!"

Of course, great answer. I acknowledged it.

I got the job and gave my resignation to the Four Senators Hotel. They were disappointed but understood my reasons, and we parted as friends.

Ernie stayed close to us and always displayed considerable affection for my wife. He had an American girlfriend now who catered to his every need. Ernie bragged to me by disclosing intimate details, boy talk, bragging, I thought of it as a way to make me envious.

However, it got me thinking back to the days we lived in Montreal and in the same building, that opportunities presented itself for a romance between my wife and Ernie may have been a reality.

I discarded the thought.

Preparations for a hotel opening were something new for me and I had much to learn. The Chef came from a company hotel in New Orleans and had considerable experience and culinary skills. His management skills, and artistic talent were amazing. As an expert at carving Ice into intricate figures out of a 200-pound block of ice, promised to teach me to add this skill to my résumé.

The Chef was also a skilled sailor and loved the ocean and windy conditions. We took every chance for an afternoon break to grab a sunfish sailor and took on the waves, wind and current.

First we shared a boat and as I became more confident, he handed me the rudder or the sail to manage.

One must have a feel for the elements, the boat's movement, the wind, and the sail that powered the boat forward. The direction and shifting of the sail kept one busy. Go on a broad reach or run ahead of the wind, tacking against the wind, and creating a vacuum effect like the one lifting airplane wings. A jibe to abruptly swing the sail from one extreme side to the other while the boat now turns to get the waves from behind was a dangerous move. Keeping a watch on all these activities to control the boat is a handful to manage.

The day came when I took a sailfish alone and now it is mine to maneuver. At first, it was a close reach, getting hard on the wind blowing strong from the ocean toward the beach. Then the tack-getting instructions jelled from behind me. So far, I am doing okay, and this modest success gave me confidence. Then a wind change caught me off guard and was hanging on to the sail and promptly capsized. He helped me to right the boat up again and said, "Now you learned how not to do it. It is an important lesson." And then he explained what I did wrong. I realized the logic, and yes, it was a valuable lesson.

After every sailing, we needed a good shower to wash off the salt. But refreshing and recharging the energies were the desired effect no matter how hard the wind and waves challenged us. Sailing became the recreation for the afternoons during our break times.

* * * * * * *

The gala buffet serves the grand opening festivities. Top brass from the company, dignitaries from the state and city, influential travel agency owners, and the travel publications industry attended the event.

Ice carvings, butter sculptures, cocoa paintings prepared by our Italian artistic Pastry Chef, and sugar worked from Pastillage are all creative culinary masterpieces.

Loaves of bread weaved like a basket, and elegantly decorated elegant meat pieces like hams, turkey, beef roasts, fish, and seafood of every kind was consumed by the attending guest's with pleasure. It was a show worthy of capturing on video by local television stations, and newspaper photographers all wanted a period before opening the doors to record this display on film for publication.

With this event being behind us, we settled into the daily service of hotel guests, local restaurant customers, banquets and social parties, weddings, and corporate promotional events. The day-to-day operation needed attention, cooks received training and menu items were tested, and adjusted to the clientele's taste.

Ten hours workday for the Chef, while I worked the rest of the day from the early afternoon until closing. The corporate Chef was not kidding!

The hours stretched past the fourteen and dictated by restaurant volume and banquets. I had fun and did my work with pleasure while looking forward to the next day. Never a dull moment to settle and always plan ahead plan, and prep for the future events! The service staff was also lovely and friendly, making for a joyful workday.

My wife was busy setting up a new apartment accepting in the south side. This rental apartment even accepted children!

It was a challenging task locating such a place to live. It made me incredibly angry when I faced the rejection of a child for the favor of a dog. "We would rather take a dog than a child," was the standard reply.

Ernie showed envy for me as he judged my position much more exciting, challenging, and fun. He began to distance himself from us.

My wife found a babysitter to allow her time to work.

My work schedule varied with the business volume while being primarily evenings. On Saturdays and Sundays, it tuned into an all day and late into the evening workday.

Anna and Amie, a team of mother and daughter from California, showed affections toward me. Sweet and gentle, this petite girl had considerable charm. Equally charming was her mother who worked the breakfast and lunch shift on weekends.

Little favors or a special request were honored as a friendly gesture and followed with a little kiss on my cheek. How sweet and pleasant it was!

One Saturday morning, I received a phone call at 6:00 AM at home.

"The breakfast cook had not yet shown up for work". Panic set in as I rushed and speeded to the hotel.

Nobody had the sense to turn on the oven, get water to boil, or make any preparation to ease the start of breakfast preparations. Arriving after a forty-five-minute drive from home, I found that every cooking devise had been cold, and the preparation was also incomplete.

I felt like I was being set up for failure by the breakfast cook.

By 7:00 a.m., the first orders came into the kitchen while I was feverishly working on a shortened selection.

I needed help desperately. Anna and Amie had been on duty and offered to help. I asked them to communicate to the other servers to suggest to the guest those items only, which I could produce with the limited preparation and still cold equipment. Use your power of suggestion and stir the guest away from items which require extensive preparation.

The bacon is not yet ready, offer ham or sausage patties, eggs to order any style are cooked on the gas flame, omelets again keep it simple and no potatoes.

The servers did their absolute best explaining and delivering the orders. It gave me a lifeline and we finished breakfast without guest complaints.

Exhausted after that dilemma, I instructed the pantry cook on all preparations should another situation arise.

The following day, Sunday morning, I was at work by 5:00 AM and prepared the full menu. The preparation the day before covered every need, leaving nothing to a chance.

I was ready for the orders to the delight of the service staff. As a reward, I prepared exceptional lunch food for the service staff. It was the least I could do for them and earned their gratitude for it.

Two days' no-call and no-show by the breakfast cook cannot be ignored and must face punishment. He claimed not feelin well! Too sick to call in with notice by you or a family member?

I termed it as a lame excuse.

"Three days suspension without pay was his punishment."

His resignation followed, and he was he was quickly replaced by a cook on the evening shift and received a wage increase.

The mutual affection between Anna and I grew while Amie drew a blindside to it. I walked her home on her request when she had to work the evening shift, and her mother was at home. An apartment on the island within easy walking distance made this a pleasant stroll. Warm and compassionate, she spoke of her life, her dreams, and eventually wanting to return to California. Ever since I visited San Francisco, California, I have had a particular desire for the state.

I wanted to go there myself and see the Pacific Ocean again, swim in the surf, afford a small boat, being near the mountains to take up skiing again. Just so many things crossed my mind with great desire. The desire awakened me to develop this relationship to the point of an encounter. Yes, the marriage was a moral obstacle, but the body's drive grew more vital inside me. We kissed casually at first at the back door of her apartment but quickly followed up with a mutual desire for hot and deep kissing. I bade her goodbye with yet another hot kiss for the affection. On my way home, I felt guilty and made sure no lipstick was on my shirt or neck and put on the face of innocence entering my home. The wife had gone to bed as usual; she was tired waiting for me, and past eleven was her bedtime.

After that, this scene repeated itself. I was unsure if Anna had changed her working schedule or had to be there for scheduling reasons, but she has now worked more night shifts.

One night, I could leave earlier. She wanted to go to a motel. Sex was on her mind. We found a motel and settled in on the second floor. In no time, we had disrobed and explored each other's bodies. Her petite frame and slender body had immense sex appeal. I was hungry to enter her, and she equally motioned her hips toward me and found the rhythm of love.

It should have lasted a lifetime, beautiful feelings physically and emotionally combined for an act of lovemaking and not just raw sex.

When I received a proposal from the corporate Chef to take the helm at another hotel as a starting position as Executive Chef, our bond broke and with it our hearts.

Accepting this promotion had given me a new career start. My personal goal had been reaching this position by age 30.With this promotion I had beaten my timeline by two years.

A small hotel in Buffalo, New York was just the right size for a first time leading the food department and forging experiences.

The departure from Florida was complicated and filled with heartbreaks and emotions. I loved this hotel, the people, the weather in Florida, and above all Anna. Large tears rolled down her cheeks and mine on the last goodbye. She knew too well that with being married and having a toddler in tow, there could not be a future without drama and hurting others. She was strong. Realistic and kept moving on.!

I have kept a special place in my heart for her just in case we would meet again under more conducive circumstances for a final union. It was not meant to be, and it never happened.

* * * * * * *

Another move! I am beginning a count and wondering where it will lead. It is number three and I knew, it will not be my last move. Will the family be strong enough, and what about our son? Will he miss the climate, the beach, playgrounds, neighbor friends, or will he adapt?

What little we had accumulated was moved by the company and paid for in full.

The hotel catered to the travelers near the NY Thruway on the outskirts of the city and apartments nearby were affordable and new. A drive into the city center left us unimpressed. An industrial city with smokestacks from heavy industry and oil refineries, chemical plants along the river leading to Niagara Falls made the air oppressive. .

One restaurant and bar plus meeting and banquet facilities for small groups termed this hotel as a transient lodging. Despite the label, the restaurant had an extensive upscale menu, white tablecloth at dinner and served as a popular local fine dining establishment.

Breakfast became casual for the travelers and lunch had its own blue collar clientele.

A new restaurant manager by the name Larry joined the team which was led by a general manager of Italian descent. His short stature had been compensated with an aggressive style but in total he was easy to work alongside.

His former position as food and beverage director helped us to solve an unusually difficult nut to crack. I needed help to harness a runaway food cost from the start.

Inventories had been checked and verified several times, yet nothing pointed to a fault in the operating procedures.

One last check of the books from our predecessor took us to inventory manipulations. There it was! Inventories had been overstated month after month and now produced a snowball effect. By carrying the inflated numbers forward, it had a devastating effect and needed correction. How?

The only way to fix it was to authorize a write off and book the loss by adjusting the past statements with ledger entries. The account required corporate approval for the loss.

A stern message came to the General Manager from his corporate superior "Inspect what you expect."

With the books cleaned up, the cost was easy to manage. I trained from the ground up not to waste products.

The restaurant had a sophisticated clientele, the service had to be right, and the menu received a facelift to satisfy the customers.

Larry had also moved into the same apartment complex. His wife from England had immigrated to the USA after they got married. They met in the old country and moved to the US. The women bonded and we all became good friends. We had fun together and dreamed up items to bring to the table.

Weather reports had not been as explicit as it is today, and for that reason, this snowfall was often a sudden surprise. It was during a cold upstate New York winter with snow generated by the lake's snow machine. Tow trucks could not come to the rescue of stranded vehicles.

Days like this brings out the craving for hot and spicy food. We cooked American chili and I shred recipes from Idia. Hot and spicy, it served the hunger and cravings.

I became adapted to spicy food from the meals the cooks in India took pride to prepare our lunch. It was always a simple meal of a bowl of rice with a red or greenish sauce, flakes of fish or chicken, onion, and garlic! The first bite brought blood, sweat, and tears to our tastebuds.

The cooks witnessed this and found it entertaining to see us suffer. We must eat it; the pastry Chef told us. We must give *face*!

On these New York winter nights, I also made Swiss dishes with veal, mushrooms, wine, and cream accompanied by homemade spaetzle, cheese fondue, pot roast the English way, and more. The relationship bonded into a close friendship.

Only the new Chevy Malibu bought in Florida would not cooperate. This car did not like the cold. AAA club help was no use when the first call made at 7:00 a.m. and service promises by 4:00 p.m. The solution! A set of jumper cables and the nearest neighbor's car to get the jump.

Within six months, the word inside the corporation was changing. The company arrived at an exceedingly difficult decision: expand the business by adding hotels or sell off the least profitable units and remain healthy. A massive debt needed to be satisfied to remain solvent.

The general manager called a meeting to announce that the hotel would be sold. It looked as if an effort was already in the works from a buyer. The buyer was interested in keeping all staff and engaged the GM to broker a deal by which the management would stay as a condition of the sale.

Losing my career tenure with the Hotel Corporation which promoted me to my first executive position was a risk. Uncertainty is dominating my thinking.

"What are we going to do? The job is secure, and I do not have an alternative but to stay and wait.

Chapter 5

Within days, I received a telephone call from Minneapolis. It turned out to be John, a man whom I helped on Key Biscayne at the neighboring Sheraton Hotel to carve the meat at the weekly buffet. He remembered me and had also been a close friend to the former hotel's food and beverage director. He knew personally and received a favorable reference on my ability.

He spoke about his new assignment and his need for a trusted man managing the hotels kitchen. It is a luxury property in downtown Minneapolis and his position as resident manager puts him also in charge of Food and Beverage. Improprieties are his biggest challenge. He must put a stop to stealing. "I need a trusting person in the back of the house." and to clean house

He made an acceptable offer including moving expenses and temporary housing until an apartment is found," A monthly bonus for reaching the food cost target became an added incentive.

My wife was relieved as we looked forward to moving.

Move number four.

* * * * * * *

It pleased us seeing the hotel on arrival in Minneapolis. As promised with the offer, we received a two-week hotel room free to live. John took me around and introduced me met the General Manager, a quiet, stately man in his sixties, then the sales staff, catering director, buying agent, and service managers in the restaurant and banquet. I looked everyone in the eyes to see if I could get a preliminary reading. Mental notes and impressions I kept to myself. After the tour, John sat down, and started to lay out an action plan. He began by asking me about my first impression of the people I had just met.

At first, I was surprised by the bluntness and directness by which he opened the talk. The straight talk was precisely right up my alley. I thought that this was my style too. I told him my impression and suspicion one by

41

one, saw his facial expression showing his agreement, and then he told me that I was on the right track. I thought we will have a great working relationship and now let us have fun.

He had prepared his plan to the smallest detail with action steps and a rough timeline. The first candidate on the front was to be the director of catering. In the back, it had to be the purchasing agent.

We set up a trap to get the cause for termination. It took less than a week, and we had solid proof of the thieves apprehending company funds and products. The catering guy sold out the hotel's events for discounted prices and, in turn, received a backdoor reward from the event organizer.

In purchasing, it was clear that the product quality and specifications had been compromised, yet the premium price remained on the invoices.

A visit to the meat packer and produce vendor showed the difference, prompting uncomfortable questions from the vendor's manager. He was not in the loop; it was through the sales associate and then internally that the accounting accomplice fudged the books. The produce manager was grateful, for he had an internal problem. The manager received the opportunity to take corrective actions.

When the director of catering was terminated from his post and the purchasing agent was let go, the housecleaning had started.

Resignations from every department showed us the scope of this organization.

How much had they embezzled?

We did not look into the past. I looked forward and rebuild my staff with honest personnel.

I took over the purchasing, hired a storekeeper, and set up procedures.

I had never run a storeroom, but I had seen how it was correctly done in the Florida hotels. Everything must be opened and checked, weights verified and rechecked on our scale, then dated and stored correctly. Common sense and dedication are all it takes. I did the ordering from a list of food items with specifications outlining the quality, size, counts, and brands. Price quotes on fresh produce that had weekly fluctuations had to be called in or mailed weekly by the vendors.

We decided who would get the bulk of the order from that list. We did not pick around every single item. Still, we looked at the volume items, whether meat or produce, and awarded the order to the one who showed a consistent price quote and was trustworthy in delivering quality on time.

The message to the vendors is clear and cost-effective. In time, this change was visible and reflected in a better price.

My food cost bonus kicked in the third month and continued until I left this employment. A $100 savings bond with a maturity of ten years only costs the hotel half the amount. It provided me with a way to create a little nest egg. I told my wife it could not be spent, and we would accumulate them for the boy's college.

The wife went to a real estate broker in search for an apartment. She quickly learned that a house purchase was within reach if we could extend the free housing at the hotel. I approached John with the question of extending for two weeks, but he had to turn me down. He decided with a nearby old former hotel building, now used for weekly rentals, and the hotel would pay for it. The hotel had sellout days during the week. Group business and the city had a convention to host.

The savings we generated not having to pay for a rental apartment plus the first and last month's sum was sufficient for the down payment and closing cost to buy a small house near the lake. She managed it all by herself and had done a superb job.

We moved into our first house with a cozy fireplace in the living room, two bedrooms, a garage next to it, and a small backyard to play and start a small vegetable garden.

It was the end of May and the right time to start planting. The soil needs help with peat moss and manure, spaded over and raked to make a soft bed for the delicate plant from the nurseries.

The street was quiet and safe for children to play.

Across the street, the next-door neighbors welcomed us to the neighborhood with freshly baked apple pie. The neighbors had two girls the same age as my boy. The welcome gesture made us feel good and at home. The wife started to set up the house, a welcome task after sitting idle except for house-hunting. I was super busy and spent long hours at the hotel.

Unpleasant habits prevailed in the production of food, and the seasoning before or during preparation seemed alien to them. Basics like salt and pepper became an ongoing slogan to remind them. Persistence finally paid off.

One of the cooks handling breakfasts on the hot side made a bold prediction. He said he would not give me one year in this job, for all former chefs could not cut it!

I looked at him and said, "I will accept this challenge." On my first anniversary, I would buy him a bottle. "What do you drink, David?"

"Scotch, Johnny Black, no ice. It gives me headaches!"

"You are on," I stated and left it as such.

Martha from Norway is expertly running the cold Pantry food preparation.

With lightning speed, breakfast, lunch, banquet salads, pancakes, waffles, stewed fruit compotes, and juices are conducted.

She was a solid foundation to run this kitchen. She liked me, and we often talked about Europe. I had the feeling that deep inside, she missed her native Norway. What would I have done without her?

The restaurant with an Irish theme and food concept left me at a loss. What exactly is Irish food? The Irish soda bread came daily from a local bakery. No real crust, which I would have expected from European bread but soft skin and medium gummy texture inside. It was not wrong, but nothing excellent either. I would not write home about it. A soup thickened with cheddar cheese and croutons and made with bitter ale got the label of the signature item on the menu. Tasty in flavor, made with beer and good stock.

The rest of the menu looked very American. Steaks, of course, pork chops, chicken dishes, local fish from Minnesota lakes called walleye and pike, and seasonally, we would get smelt and others during short intervals.

I was taken back to this San Francisco restaurant with this giant hunk of meat. Then, of course, prime rib. Baked potato and popover, a salad, and no unique items for desserts! Just pies, cakes, ice cream or, a combination of them.

Then there was something I could not grab as being correct. Hot apple pie with a slice of sharp cheddar cheese! What concoction is this? I asked.

"An American tradition. Do not touch it. It is a popular item." Okay, hands-off.

Banquets needed my full attention, and the timing coincided with the peak restaurant service. The restaurant had to run on automatic.

A Sous Chef was not on the staffing guide. Why not? How could I ever take a day off? I would have to abandon my duty for that day. The arguments yielded an adjustment to the staffing, and the search for a competent assistant began. The candidates all lacked the quality I was looking for.

Finally, I selected Gerald as Sous Chef. He was green behind the ears and with limited experience, I thought I could groom him if he wanted to learn and grow. He was young and naive, playful with the other cooks.

He was also socializing with the female kitchen staff and servers outside the job! To make him see that this would compromise his authority and that he needed to keep a certain distance from them was difficult to get across to him. He started to shape up after my talk to him, took on more responsibility, and grew into a dependable second man with time.

Absenteeism had been a sickness that plagued the performance of the kitchen. Whenever someone did not show up or called in sick, it stressed the others to fill the vacancy. The Sous Chef and I cover the shift. I finally got tired of it and placed a paper inside the Chef's office facing the kitchen.

"If you call in or fail to show up for whatever reason, you must need the following professionals.

a Doctor
a Priest, or
Undertaker or
All of the above

"Otherwise, I will expect you to show up. If you are sick, you will return home or see the doctor.

"Failure to obey this rule will have consequences."

Now the test! This notice got everybody's attention, especially those who tended to violate it the most.

One of the biggest violators did not show up.

My reaction was straightforward. His hours were taken off the schedule and left blank. Another cook covered these hours, and with overtime here and shifting the workload, I spread it around and was able to get around spending excessive overtime and, in the end, saved hours and payroll.

Upon returning, he looked at his schedule and found no hours posted. It caused an angry reaction. I pointed to the notice in the office window saying that he did not obey and now faces the consequences. "What are the consequences? Am I fired? What will happen now?" an angry voice was asking!

"No, you are not fired, you still have your job, but I assumed you would want a few days off for whatever illness to cure. How long do you wish to take off? At this point, I have your shift covered for this week, and I will not make any changes to it. Enjoy the week off and come in on time next week."

All cooks on duty overheard this dialogue. From this day on, we resolved the absenteeism.

The visit of the corporate food and beverage director is being announced. He had an authoritarian reputation, and fear filtered into the hotel management team.

Inspection: this word carries fear. Nobody knew what he was looking for.

We took extra attention to cleaning any small crevices that could be overlook in the daily routine. Otherwise, I thought he could tell me, and we would correct whatever mistake we made. I saw it as an opportunity first to meet the man, learn from him, gain the experience he was willing to share, and then do as he instructed me.

The man in his sixties is being escorted by the General Manager with the Resident Manager in tow. They entered the kitchen.

I greeted him by name and introduced myself by name and position. He looked around, checked the walk-in refrigerators, looked over all prepared items plated and chilled, and checked the salad mix. Then he turned toward me and explained the standard.

He proposed a better cover for the restaurant menu presentation.

During the warm summertime, I often took my ten-speed bicycle to work. It had a single holder for a water bottle. In my case, it became a beer bottle holder on the way home.

It was a nice ride along the banks of the lakes in this city, with bike lanes and people enjoying the outdoors. Lakeshore concerts from a stage with sound shell backing the water and transferring the sound to the audience, either sitting or standing. The Parks and Recreation Department looked after that. The quality of life was in focus about everywhere one could notice. Make it count, the summer is short!

One time I was riding through the narrow old village street with an arts festival displayed crafts and paintings. On my way home, I caught a glimpse of a particular picture capturing my attention. A closer look now grabbed my desire, and I decided I must have this painting, but I did not have money on me. I rushed home, took the money, and drove by car back to his location.

Getting ready to pack up, I came just in time to make an offer and get this painting of an Asian older adult, a thinned-out beard with a smoking a pipe. So peaceful and calming was the effect of this original painting. I could feel the roughness created by the oil paint on the canvas. Yes, an original, but no identification of the artist. I had it framed with a classic old frame. To this date, I treasure this painting as it captures my attention each time, I pass it in my house!

* * * * * * *

Two years into this job, the boss received a well-deserved promotion to the General Manager's position. Shortly after, the General Manager retired, leaving two senior managers open for replacement.

The new General Manager came from a luxury hotel in Chicago. The Resident Manager Kurt, a German-born, was hired from outside the company. *Good*, I thought that I can have an admirable working relationship; *nice to meet you, and I look forward to working with you.*

I had lost my mentor and was eager to get someone into this position to relate to. It turned out okay, for he relied on me as much as I did on him. Together we had the makings of a fine-tuned team. His earlier positions had been restaurant manager and food and beverage manager. New in this endeavor, he acted cautiously and consulted with me.

The General Manager had moved into the hotel suite as his living quarters. His experience with the corporation carried an extensive list of positions. He knew it all, or so he thought!

His wife had the privilege to requisition her family food from the hotel's provisions.

A list was presented to room service and delivered to me. It was a real thorn in my side, and I delegated it to one of the pantry staff and the Sous Chef to assemble the items on the list. Cleaning and paper goods we did not carry in the hotel. These items had to be left unfilled. Promptly, we received a complaint conveyed by Gary, the General Manager, saying that we must complete the order.

"Must we go to the grocery store to do the shopping for her or carry all these items in cases?

We are hired to run a hotel kitchen and not a babysitting job,"

I complained to Kurt. His sympathy did nothing to resolve the weekly ordeal. He was not too keen to confront this GM with a sensitive issue. She was wearing the pants, and that was all there was. I firmly said to Kurt and promised to endure.

The back of my mind kept the thought alive to find a solution for it. *How can we get this off our backs? She has a car. Why can she not go shopping in a grocery store, take herself outdoors, and then present the receipt to the controller for reimbursement?*

Meanwhile, Gary started a habit of visiting the kitchen, snooping around, and engaging me in conversation. "You know, Chef, in Chicago, the Chef there had this sauce he put on about every meat dish. It was delicious and shiny and made the dish so much more appealing."

Interesting," I said. Can you tell me more about it? What was it made from, taste, color, beef, pork, or veal?"

He did not know but promised to call Chicago to get the recipe. That never happened. The Chef there would not part with his recipe, or the relationship with his now-former GM may have been on the cool side.

It was the first but not the last time he produced his ideas. Another time he said that he did not like my bacon. *It was his wife's complaint.*

I responded that *it was not my bacon. The hotel was paying for it*, so it was my choice of bacon for the hotel.

"Okay, smart-ass. I want to see samples to select another brand."

We cooked eight samples on a large baking pan with parchment paper lining. Once fully cooked and the excess grease drained, I called him to come to the kitchen to select the bacon of his choice. They all looked slightly different in color and taste, including the bacon we had been serving.

Each one had a number marked on the bottom of the pan corresponding to a list of brands and purveyors. He scrutinized all with a stern look, tasted three or four, and then pointed to one.

The grin on my face gave away the choice of the bacon being the one we were serving. He then quickly made a second choice. I confirmed the selection and stated the purveyor and price. It was someone we had never used. Now he only delivers the bacon, and it will reflect on the cost per pound.

We switched and used his choice of bacon until the initial order from the new supplier was deleted and went back to the former product.

The delivery of the order to his wife was late one week and was totally forgotten the following week.

The thought crossed my mind to get this grocery list canceled forever. I instructed the person who usually got the list and hated the task to start making little mistakes by sending ham instead of turkey, and substitute items we had in the storeroom that did not move with proper rotation, Supplies in high demand for guest service and being called out of stock or back ordered, using terms like pending delivery, generated frustrations with the GM's wife.

We knew there would be a reaction and complaints, but we just took the blame and explained it with trivial lies.

Being consistent with these little steps turned too frustrating for her. Gary did not want to deal with it.

He assigned it to Kurt, but he was in on our game, and nothing changed.

It had now become a game of chicken.

The pantryman did a superb job, loved every minute, and savored this as a reprisal. Eventually, Madam reached the kitchen to speak to me directly.

It was a busy day with cocktail parties and a large banquet for an insurance company. The kitchen was buzzing, and the Sous Chef had to be hands-on and had no time to spare.

When she appeared from the service elevator, I knew she would make a big fuzz about it.

She acted bossy and demanded explanations for these problems with her grocery list.

I gave her a minute and then asked her to let me explain without interruptions. I stated, this was the action of a hotel kitchen, and it was like that about every day.

Do you think we look forward to your shopping list and kill precious time away from servicing paying customers?

To state it straight, your list is a pain in the rear, and we have put up with it for too long. Is it not time for you to find a grocery store and shop there? If there is a special occasion and you need an item the grocery store may not carry, but the hotel does, we will gladly make an exception. Let me get on with this party service. Have a good day!

She stood there speechless, turned around without a word, and disappeared into the service elevator. I briefed Kurt on this situation in case the boss would give him hell. Nothing ever came of it, but the list had disappeared. Hurray!

Chapter 6

We had not been back to Germany and Switzerland to visit our parents, and now they are the grandparents to our son. The child made all the difference now. The mother-in-law syndrome had vanished. The boy Martin had delighted Mom and Papa, and being the only male offspring, he would carry forward the name

Grandma bonded with the child spoiled him and catered to him. He also visited my cousin at the farm with chicken, geese, cows, pigs, and baby pigs; oh, so cute. Lil baby cows, also called calves, are so cute.

Martin had found a new playground and was given free rein at age five and a half years. Three girls looked after him as he enjoyed his newfound freedom.

The cousin in Washington is the brother of Eddy here in Germany. The other cousin on the mother's side had large tractors and harvesting machines, and they had two girls and two boys about his age.

Everybody loved our boy, and my wife found full acceptance everywhere.

My father started to press me again to return home with the promise to help me get into a restaurant in this area.

My concern was that he would be my best customer and sit there all-day holding court and getting drunk. He envisioned a simple Gasthaus geared to the drinking customer and less catering quality food to a sophisticated clientele.

I could not imagine sidelining the culinary skills I had gathered to tend to a beer hall or wine pub. I felt the need to add to my repertoire on the culinary side and add management skills.

If I were going to have a restaurant of my own, it would have to be in the right location, near a city with people who do not mind spending good money on exquisite food, service, and ambiance. I told him gently that I did not see myself ready for a solo run in a business. Give me more time, please. With that, he backed off.

Mother recited her complaints, singing the same old tune, "If you only would not be so far away, it would be much nicer. What is so special in that America?" and followed it up with "Scheiss America."

In Switzerland, my wife had cousins in Lucerne only. Her father, a Confiseur by training, had worked for the world-famous Lindt and Sprüngli chocolate manufacturer. He has been divorced for years from Margo's mother. My wife, Margo, had grown up mostly with her mother in her apartment in Zurich. Her father was kept away from her and bad-mouthed at every opportunity.

The relationship between father and daughter was that of strangers until she moved away from her mother. She could only meet up with her father and get to know him. He was a gentle person, dignified, and a giving man! I quickly noticed that the marriage between her mother and father had been a mismatch.

I had the opportunity to meet him one time just before our departure to the USA.

The mother originated from Austria, a large family in the northern mountain area. Cousins and uncles had to be visited. Not all had been too friendly, for there had been friction between her mother and the rest. One reason to seek residence in Switzerland and to marry her father must have been the ticket for her departure from home and competing siblings.

One uncle and cousin seemed the nicest and welcomed us to their house on top of the hill. He had been in the war and made it back. Stories to tell and experiences to share! Franz and his wife, Claudette, were down to earth people, genuine and trustworthy. They embraced little boy Martin, and he returned the affection. A lasting connection had just begun.

Back at my parent's home, it was time to return to the US. We selected memorabilia from her mother's estate that had been stored in the attic and made our way back to the Zurich airport. The duties at the hotel and home became routine, and the boy started kindergarten.

Sous Chef Gerald had held it together. No real problems aside from daily routine issues. The winter approached rapidly.

An early snowstorm had the city in its grips, traffic paralyzed, and hotel guests found themselves stranded. The driving condition stopped all traffic with no way home. The GM offered an overnight stay in a hotel room for all office staff and management. All the hourly employees bunked into the ballroom on cots. Others made a bed with blankets on the carpet.

Next to my hotel room on floor eleven was the secretary to the catering director. She had seen me going into the room and asked if I had any toiletry stuff she could borrow. I was caught off guard and, of course, was in the same predicament as her. She wanted to brush her teeth! I suggested getting her baking soda from the kitchen and salt. This way, she could use her index finger and simulate a toothbrush motion, and by dissolving the salt in warm water, there is now a mouthwash and water to gargle.

She was surprised at this solution and accepted the idea, so we met privately for the first time other than when she would distribute banquet orders and memos from the executive office. Being new in this job, she was eager to connect and get an ally inside this management team.

After washing up, she needed to talk! I got us wine from my little office cooler. There was always an unfinished bottle that the banquet Maître d' had saved for me.

TLC drank it fast with the clear effect of getting high but not drunk. I slowed her down a bit; I did not want to have her drunk. It became a heated session, urging her to keep the noise down, for she was turned on and going at it as if it had been a long time ago. She started to make affectional gestures, which led to the alleged encounter.

The morning arrived. She had to return to her room, make it look like she had slept there, and then go to work.

All employees pitched in to make up for the shortfall of the breakfast crew. The streets were closed until mid-morning; the hotel guests expected the standard service.

It had been a long time since I cooked breakfast. Memories from Key Biscayne flashed through my head, and off we went. A guilty feeling came to me as I saw TLC in action, helping on the pantry side preparing breakfast pancakes. Tender Loving Care is in motion!

With snow on the ground now, it would be there for the duration of the winter. The cooks suggested going skiing and invited me to join. I had bought skis in Buffalo and made a humble effort to relearn this skill. It had been too many years without practice, but it was like riding a bike, rusty at first and working to keep the balance. It all came back with tries and falls.

A ski hill near the city was the destination. Just a short run down and a very cold ride in the chairlift to the top! One spent more time on the lift riding up than carving curves downhill.

The warming lodge was busy getting fingers and toes unfrozen. To my surprise, the cooks had also invited TLC to this skiing outing. She was doing well and flirted at every chance with the cooks and especially with me. Not wanting to be obvious, I could see she had a crush on me.

Ever since the stormy night at the hotel, she visited the kitchen at every opportunity. At times it looked as if she delivered single sheets of documents or memos to have an excuse to return. The cooks liked her and treated her to goodies to win her favor.

* * * * * * *

The Chef's association in the city had a routine meeting that I had a chance to attend. An annual dinner must be planned and hosted in the next few months while the season prevails. The main agenda item was the association's "Les Amis d' Escoffier charter."

Terms and criteria are explained whereby the host property would do the planning; provide marketing and sell the ticket to attendants; buy all food, beverage, and requirements; and stage the dinner in a large ballroom with excellent service staff. We set the price at $100 per person, and the count should be one hundred people maximum, restricted to the male gender only.

Now that is a tall order! The Chef at the City Athletic Club offered to take on the task. Coincidentally, he was my predecessor at the hotel. The cooks who had worked under his baton did not have an excellent opinion of him. He must have the skills and accept the bid.

Weeks passed, and one day, the President of the association, Charles Mitterhauser, came to the kitchen with a worried expression. He went right to the point.

The Athletic Club membership turned down the dinner. Too much excitement for their membership's taste and cost concerns as well. Would I be willing to jump in to rescue the dinner? This hotel had a beautiful ballroom, and he thought from what he had learned about me, it would best suit me with my skill level.

In any case, at the dinner event, all chefs from the association would become my cooks. He then pointed out specific talents among these chefs, a world-class pastry chef, a great baker, and a garde-manger himself would handle it. He showed me his work from past dinners, so I was sold on the idea.

"A chance of a lifetime," I told my bosses to sell them on it, "and a boost for the hotel's reputation." I got the green light and signed on the director of catering, the resident manager, and the marketing director to take part in the planning and execution. Press coverage and even television could be there to capture this monumental task.

The excitement started to build as the first drafts got on paper. The rule set by Escoffier, who used to serve these kinds of dinners to royalty, was that no food ingredient could be repeated, and it had to be twelve courses. Wines to pair with each course must be perfect, from aperitifs to after-dinner digestives.

My little French dictionary that had saved my hide with the famous turtle soup gave me the structure and order in which these courses had to follow.

The food was easy, but the wine pairing had to be aided by an experienced wine merchant with a taste for decent food. I found this man quickly. The sales associate servicing the hotel account suggested the wine company's owner.

The menu planning took every free minute of my time. Gradually, a framework was on paper, going over it and over again, thinking about the ingredients needed for each item, revisions, and tweaking finally to the point to show this draft to Mitterhauser.

He was impressed, went through it with a fine-tooth comb, and made suggestions for the final menu.

Now it came to the wine choice. I produced a list of ingredients for each course to pair with the best wine. We met and discussed details, and I could tell that excitement was mounting.

Aside from all the publicity, the wine company would be credited with the wine selections that will boost its status and his company's reputation.

The marketing had gotten off to a good start. Reservations started brisking and then stalled at about fifty-five counts. Efforts to engage publicity attracted the attention of the newspaper food editors; the coverage had now begun.

I gave interviews, released recipes for publishing by the newspapers, and small tidbits of the menu to whet the appetite and hopefully served to attract the quota of one hundred. But the fifty-five number got stuck in the mud.

The numbers to cover the fixed cost had to be one hundred; the fifty-five would produce a huge loss at the end.

What if we get a variance from the charter to allow women? My question would be taken to the membership and voted on. Whom do we need to convince, but the association was us! The vote carried with a YES, and we released the result to the press.

This change had created the needed interest. Women are now breaking down the old male domination of gender exclusive clubs.

A "Yes" vote was a victory for the female gender and is now the headline in the news.

Each food item that needed wine pairing had to be cooked and consumed while various wines got opened and tasted. The town started to buzz about this event. The newspapers covered this event with extensive articles and photos. A daily report in the paper often had my picture with it.

The director of catering secured staffing from other hotels, and one of the restaurant managers received the Maître d' service duty. Interns from Holland and the room service managers received cocktails and wine service assignments.

My kitchen crew discovered that the city's Chefs would be helping with this task without pay. They wanted to take part in it to learn and receive a small slice of this notoriety. It would become a part of their résumé and career path.

Everybody signed a waiver for payment in exchange.

Each course's inventory of chinaware, service, and eating utensils needed to be verified and supplemented. Then the glassware, another segment to match the beverage, aperitif, white wines, red wines, dessert wines, cognac, and after-dinner liquors.

The silverware presented the biggest challenge. The hotel fell short of this volume, and adding new purchases was too expensive.

We decided to set up half the menu, and at halftime, the guest would leave the room and assemble in the banquet lobby. Sorbet would be served in the lobby while the elegant table was refreshed and reset with silverware, plates, and glassware for the rest of the menu.

A fast turnaround with everybody pitching in to get it washed and reset. It had to work, and now we were as ready as possible, if only by a plan!

* * * * * * *

The day arrived with great anticipation.

The chefs with artistic abilities had already worked on their pieces. It would be the showpiece during the reception on the buffet table.

The garde-manger, Mitterhauser, produced a magnificent butter sculpture, "Crazy Horse," a native Indian in full gear and feathers, sitting on a horse. One could have thought this sculpture was alive.

I had prepared three ice carvings, and a Pastry Chef contributed blown sugar fruit, a Pastillage sculpture in the form of a pavilion, and various cocoa paintings.

A large horn of Plenty held the baked goods and small savory canapés stimulated the taste buds of the guests. Careful not to let them overeat on these morsels, the reception was closed, and the dining room doors opened for seating.

The grand banquet table is set up as a U shape with a bust of Escoffier as a tallow sculpture at the head. And allowing service access through the middle.

The Maître D 'planned the seating arrangement with the utmost care. One hundred guests searched for their place cards. Males and females and, when known, he also considered good synergies.

Crisp white linen, enhanced with wide ribbons in the French colors running the table length just above the silver-plated set plate that showed the bust of Escoffier, date, and occasion etched, were used to signify the event.

The imposing amount of silverware for five courses and five different glasses intimidated participants.

The press was taking pictures of the room set up when it was still empty, and so were the television stations.

They had told me that the entire preparation and service would be filmed and asked for permission to access the kitchen and cooking process. The plan to show it at a distinctive feature program had already been decided.

57

My role in this event required me to guide, supervise, keep a schedule of the service flow. I had worked up in advance a timeline and synchronized the service and food preparation based on time allowed per course.

It was poetry in motion, and Murphy's law took a vacation for that night! I could not have wished for a smoother action.

We completed the first half of the menu, followed by the pause.

The table received fresh linen and silverware.

Glassware is needed to match the different wines to complete this event.

I could not have wished for more motivated help from the Chefs and my cooks. The Maître d' checked on timing, and the Catering Director was the liaison between the kitchen and the service. Now on with the rest! The time was right on target.

The balance of the courses is now in progress.

Every course is presented with a dramatic centerpiece. A show in itself and receiving the verbal approval of the guests.

Desserts, petits fours, followed by cigars and after-dinner drinks.

Happy faces and relief showed in all the men's and hotel staff's faces.

****

The total timing ended up five minutes over schedule. Not bad, a great accomplishment.

A toast with champagne to congratulate the team for exceptional performance, and everybody went to grab a bite to eat.

The dishwashing operation had been able to keep pace and started putting the goods away for storage. Of course, they did not get neglected by sharing in the best food they ever had in their life

"Everybody is happy?" I handed out wine to the city's Chefs, took a deep breath, and then the adrenaline drained out of my body.

Going home at 3:00 a.m. from this event, I collapsed on the bed and fell asleep until the late morning.

* * * * * * *

The General Manager had been out of town and could not attend this affair.

The following day still left much to do to secure the food and expensive beverages for future use.

The newspaper featured a full page in the food section and a headline on the front page. Rave reviews from the participants came into the executive office.

The following weekend, the television station featured the dinner on the feature of this popular variety program. The station gave nine minutes to show the activity, while the commentator described every step as best she could.

The accounting department had figured out the total cost, divided by one hundred to a total cost of $110 per person. A loss per person was $10 and it became a bone of contention with the GM.

"How could you lose that much money?" he blasted. I stated that the show plate had cost exactly $10 and became a keepsake to the guests. I managed to break even with food and beverage and still had food in-store to serve other dinners.

I was not in any mood for an argument but had to answer. "You see, I did not lose any money on food and beverages that came in at $100 or $10,000. The dinner paid for itself, the base plate being $10 each is advertising. It will sit on the mantel in each participant's house and remind them of the greatness of this hotel."

"Additionally, all the pre-event and post-event publicity, can you place a price on this. I am sure marketing can!"

My answer was unexpected, and with it, he stopped the accusation.

The television feature of the dinner had been given a distinguished award and was now shown twice more. What more could one wish?

Attendees from large corporations, scholars of the university, and people of stature and money were on the guest list.

After that event, the underlying effect increased hotel guest room bookings. Suites came into high demand, the catering director booked board of directors' luncheons and dinners with this caliber of food quality, and occupancy had marked a significant upswing.

59

The hotel was now on the map and highly desirable. "We were putting on the Ritz."

Everyone in the executive office noted it; only the GM kept silent. I did not need to have his pat on the back. I am self-confident, knew where I stood, and was satisfied to pull off a once-in-a-lifetime event. People on the street started to recognize me and gave a respectful nod or kind words; even asked me for an autograph.

I rewarded myself by taking selected wines home, a bottle of the Anniversary cognac, and bottles of champagne. I wanted to share something with my wife, for she patiently saw me work endless hours, taking time away from family life.

I thought of what I could give my cooks. They worked without pay, only to be part of it and learn from it. I wanted them to have a souvenir to show future employers when they move on in their career. The catering director suggested an elegant certificate showing the event, date, and participation in the culinary team issued to each individual and signed by him and me.

Great idea! He wrote up the language, and TLC found special paper in a stationery shop and printed it. With signatures in hand, we called a kitchen meeting and presented it as a graduation ceremony. Eyes popped, and even shed a tear. This document of achievement serves as a recognition of particular skills.

The least moved was the Sous Chef. He stood quietly on the sideline with a sad face.

I realized that he got lost in the shuffle. All these super professionals had outshined him, making him feel inferior, and thus he withdrew for the most part. He relegated himself to doing the easy and odd little tasks and regarded them as immaterial, unimportant.

Little did he realize that those small items could quickly fall by the wayside and should be part of the organization.

He was a poor manager of his finances and often broke before payday. I decided to write him a personal thank-you letter stating his contribution to his position and praising his performance. The certificate and a $100 savings bond I signed over made him happy.

"Wait for maturity, I explained." It will come in handy when you are ready to invest. First comes the pain to accumulate capital of your own, meaning sacrifices and money management."

A teaching moment was at hand. I hope that he learned this lesson for his own good.

My cooks had different postures and attitudes. The food received better preparation refinement, and the line cooks improved the plate presentation. The servers loved it; more money from higher tips created a win-win effect.

* * * * * * *

The GM found his way again to the kitchen's heart one day.

"Can you put a dinner of the kind you did for the one hundred people? I want to host my General Manager friends in the city in the presidential suite. Eight guests plus my wife and for a I total ten people.

"Okay, I will do this. Give me time and a date, hopefully not on a crazy busy day."

I wrote a six-course menu by using the delicatessen food in storage. Wines from the dinner had also still been in the wine cellar, and whatever was gone, I replaced from the hotel wine list.

Room service is needed to handle the service.

The hotel had very exquisite chinaware, glassware, and flatware with gold plating. I had never been used it during my tenure so far. I gave a list to the room service manager and his assistant, briefed them on the food and wines, and the show was on.

Course after course was sent up to the suite by service elevator.

These room service managers being old pros and serving this hotel for years past, did not miss a beat. From their point of view and mine, this party went on without a hitch. Feedback had been positive, judging by the guests' expressions.

Nobody spoke to them about anything; it was a reading of words and body language. Happy about the success, the three of us had a glass of wine reserved from the stock that had not opened.

The guests of Gary, the GM came with questions like, "Hey Gary, what are you serving us?"

I expected a call of praise and a thank you the following day. Instead, I got yelled at in the middle of the kitchen using his usual abusive language and name-calling.

What was wrong, I inquired!

"You SOB should have briefed me on this menu so I couldn't answer the questions from my buddies."

He did not know food and was at a loss for words.

"You made me look like a fool!"

What is there to say to this?

The thought came to my mind, and I remember him bragging about the exquisite food in Chicago. Therefore, I assumed that his knowledge of food would cover such a menu.

He was not prepared to answer me. He took a deep breath, swallowed, and told me he would have a second one for the rest of his friends.

But this time, he wanted to have a menu. Okay, that I will do!

The menu will be changed within two weeks since specialty food items are now depleted. We had a run of items serving them to the high-paying board of directors' dinners and raking in good profits.

I was not too keen to give this food to freeloaders and make an abusive boss look like the king of the city.

In these days, menu writing was done with French words, especially when describing the preparation. The catering secretary, TLC, wrote up half English referring to the menu item and the rest in French terminology.

Unique stationery was at hand for that! We gave the menu to the GM secretary in his absence. I was expecting to hear from him asking for explanations, but it never took place.

For dinner, all guests had a menu on the place setting. The dinner got into motion and, as usual, went off without a hitch.

There was no feedback, no questions, no thank you, nothing, total silence until the following day.

Déjà vu, a repeat of abusive language. He blamed me for setting him up.

"I gave you a menu. It listed all items, and nothing was left out or changed. What was wrong with that?"

"I do not know French or French cooking terminology. A briefing would have helped."

"Mr. GM," I announced, "you have no problem finding this kitchen when you have a beef about something, like the bacon. Why could you not spend a minute and see me on my turf or invite me to your office to go through it.

It would give you a chance to ask questions and make cheat notes, remember in school, exams? I have no desire to set you up. You do not need help for that,"

****

I stated angrily. I had it with him! I was disgusted and frustrated and thought a change would serve me well.

I broke the idea to my wife, which was ignored. She was comfortable, the kid loved the neighborhood, and staying put in the house-made good sense. I put it out of my mind for now.

The thought kept creeping up on me, and I wrestled with it constantly.

It was summertime and warm again outside. I took a Sunday off, which was a rare occasion, A Day to plan to spend the day with the family on one of the lakes.

The warm sun felt great and having my son by my side interacting with me was long overdue. It had been too long since he had seen me.

I was always going to work before he rose for school, and he was being tucked in when I finally got off work.

All of a sudden, I woke up disoriented. It took me seconds to realize what had happened. I fell asleep, and they did not have the heart to wake me. Ashamed, I apologized but needed no apology. They understood that fatigue had taken hold of me; there was no stopping it.

That evening after dinner, I sat down and counted all the days I could not take off, partly due to having short staffing, being hectic, having meetings scheduled that had to be attended, and on and on. Hours worked also came into this equation. Taking ten hours as the regular shift (remembering the French executive Chef's comment at the Sonesta job interview), I racked my brain to remember the weeks I worked a ten-hour shift.

Taking these away, I added these up to the rest of the hours past the ten hours and then converted them into days. This exercise accumulated over three months, which I had spent over a standard work arrangement.

With this calculation written down, I decided to confront the GM with this revelation.

The company policy had been to supply comp time to get compensated for the excess time worked. I presented these results to the General Manager in his office, listed my rationale, and asked for time off with pay.

He knew just too well that I had a right to it, for his facial expressions showed fear on his face.

"When do you want to take this time?" he asked.

My reply was, "Starting right now. I am exhausted and require the rest!" He turned pale, and his blood drained from his face. He stuttered. "This is unreasonable, and such an amount of time is not available just now."

I left the office without a word, letting him guess. He sent the Food and Beverage director to me to seek reason and a change of heart. Kurt understood my point and asked me what his reaction was, and we broke out laughing. His dealing with this GM who had also been on uneasy terms!

I said I knew too well that the timing was impossible, and my conscientiousness would not let me do it. He thought so too, but we shook him up, and he started considering treating his managers more congenially.

Nothing ever came of it! Again, the family discussed the situation for a move. My wife could finally see the problem from my side and carefully agreed to explore possibilities. I told her that I would ask for a transfer within the corporate properties. That way, a move was easier, tenure did not get lost, salary increases were given, and the company paid for the move.

The house would bring us a windfall profit. Real estate prices were up considerably and setting us up with a financial gain would be great.

Kurt resigned weeks later, seeking his fortunes in another company. That left a vacuum in my view since his replacement became the front office manager. He had no food and beverage experience on his résumé, and I jokingly mentioned that I hoped he would find the way to the kitchen!

Readily admitting to the void, he asked my help to guide him in his new position. I was unsure if he could be trusted or if he had a mission to spy on me and turn up material for the GM so he could either further torment me or use it for other purposes, a reason to fire me.

I was no longer comfortable in my skin and finally went to the GM with an appointment and spoke to him about a transfer within the company.

No promises, he said, but he would take it to the corporate director of food and beverage.

* * * * * * *

The man I had met during his inspection visit retired and received a life bull from the corporation for his farewell gift. Life on a farm was going to be his destination. Mr. Karpinski was the new man in charge of the company's food and beverage operations and based in Boston at the headquarters building. He had responded and set a date and time to meet me at 8:30 in Boston.

I took the red-eye flight from Minneapolis to Boston Logan Airport and a taxi to the address in a stately high-rise building.

Promptly and without secretary or fanfare formalities, he showed me to a chair. We talked casually about my life experiences. A résumé in his hand guided the conversation. He could make one at ease and open up on all subjects. After the one-hour talk, he directed me to go to the Boston Convention Hotel. "The General Manager is expecting you.".

It looked a bit strange, for this hotel was too big of an operation for my experience level. Were they looking for a Sous Chef? All sorts of questions and scenarios crossed my mind.

The secretary greeted me and showed me to a chair outside the office. It was, in fact, a hallway to guest rooms.

Mr. Duffy had not been at the office yet, but her secretary would call me once he arrived. By 10:00 a.m., Mr. Duffy had still not arrived. She apologized and assured me it would not be long now.

65

My stomach had been growling, and a dry mouth screamed for water and food. By 11:00 a.m., Mr. Duffy came out to greet me and ushered me to his office. He knew I had been sent to him. After quick and shallow questions, I was passed on to the food and beverage director.

I finally found his office near the general storeroom. A man in his thirties looked bewildered and wanted to know the occasion. I handed him a résumé. He read it casually, then asked me professional questions on food cost, food specifications, preparation methods, how to organize large banquets, and more about banquet productions.

It was clear that conventions and huge banquet functions had been the mainstay of this hotels business. I was hardly given a chance to ask questions of my own,

Mr. Duffy appeared at the open door and suggested a tour of the operation. A huge kitchen and equally large storage rooms were bustling with activities.

Were you getting ready for a banquet? "Twelve hundred people tonight. Had you done that size of banquets?"

My reply referred to the four thousand banquets in Zurich and five thousand in Montreal.

No specific details added gave them the impression that I oversaw these banquets. My eyes rolled up, and we moved on to a coffee shop. A 7UP was offered, but no food.

A little personal chat about the Minneapolis hotel: they wanted to learn about the theme of the "Tom Jones" dinner and the gory details on the outcome when all guest's had their fill of alcoholic beverages.

We had set up for twelve guests in a small meeting room, yet large enough to encase life chicken in a wire enclosure and a couple of life piglets in another area. The table had been an eight-foot rectangular table, double wide with the legs remaining folded. A riser fabricated with plywood gave enough clearance for the legs to stretch under the table.

Burlap fabric served as the tablecloth while no eating utensils had been supplied. Large banana leaves marked the eating spaces while in the center were piles of tropical fruits and flowers.

A pewter tankard was given to each guest as the drinking mug.

The service staff consisted of three tall and attractive females. Walking barefoot and dressed in long skirts and a low-cut peasant blouse, providing a view at ample cleavage. The male waiters looked like Robin Hood.

Guests took off their shoes, then sat on the carpet floor with the support and comfort of a cushion.

Generous amounts of beer and wine and served by the girls from jugs quickly stimulated a loose behavior by the guests. The room filled with laughter, raunchy jokes, and ample efforts to grab the girls under the skirt, which prompted a slap on the hand or in his face.

The guests did not need encouragement to empty their pewter tankards. Anticipation to catch a glimpse at the girls' breasts while bending to fill the container became an irresistible game,

Food came out on giant wooden planks placed within reach of the men. The guests used Fingers to feed their hungry mouths with steamed shellfish, crab, and lobster.

The main dish followed with chicken roasted in a clay enclosure, seasoned with rosemary and chili peppers , roasted potatoes, steamed root veggies, and gravy.

I had to break open the clay crust with a mallet and carve up the chicken. Legs and breasts were tossed to the banana leaves.

Carnivores went to work and eat like animals while tossing the left-over bones at each other.

Fruit cut and peeled came out as the dessert.

In the end, a large stainless-steel bowl filled with warm water and lemon slices, accompanied by hand towels served as the cleanup.

More stiff liquor drinks at the end put them in a total state of intoxication and now they had to be escorted to their rooms by hotel male staff.

With this illustration, I made brownie points with the General Manager and his F&B man in Boston.

Still, no food offered while my stomach was crawling and in pain!

I searched for a way to make a quick exit from this staged interview for which there was no position at this hotel. It had to be done for appeasement and an effort to keep me in Minneapolis.

"My flight is coming up; I better get to the airport. Goodbye and thank you for your time."

I left the hotel in search of food. Finally, an airport restaurant got my food order and a Heineken to satisfy my hunger.

On the late afternoon flight back, and heading West, I gained the time lost on the red eye and was pleased to get home in daylight.

My thoughts reflected on this day. There was no job waiting or any jobs in any other corporate hotel. A fake staged interview and why was this handled in that fashion? Anger had built up and stayed with me until the next day.

The GM wanted to know how it all went. Reciting the events, the story made him think that all went well initially.

The actual impression came out of my mouth at the very end with considerable disappointment and anger. But not to worry, I will get over this!

****

I loved this hotel in Minneapolis! It was my first luxury hotel and had a class on its own. The stature, and reputation I had helped building gave me pride of being associated with the Ritz.

An attachment had developed and if only management had better leadership, I would not have been so eager to make a change.

****

Once every year in May, the Metropolitan Opera Company came to Minneapolis and staged a one-week opera festival. Every night featured a different production.

The hotel as the headquarter housed all the stars and stage staff, musicians, conductor .

The press feverishly attempted to get a glimpse and photo of the stars around to catch a picture of the lead singers. It had created a buzz in the hotel.

I had planned and researched each opera, then developed a six-course menu daily to the opera's theme.

Sherrill Milnes gifted me an autograph, and Luciano Pavarotti and his wife dined in this restaurant. James McCracken graced us with his patronage and gave me free tickets when he learned of my desire to see *Fidelio*. He had been in the leading role.

My wife and I listened to music. Stage-setting and lyric sang in German, this being the only opera from Beethoven which made for a special evening to remember.

Still, today, his jail aria "Ach wie Dunkel hier" brings tears to my eyes.

How can I leave this place? Tossed between the love for the hotel, the precious experience gathered here, and the abusive management, it drove me finally to seek a job elsewhere.

The city of Minneapolis had few alternatives at the time All good positions had a competent man in the saddle. The colleagues in the Chef's association did not know of any jobs in the area. One Chef mentioned that Hyatt was looking for Chefs.

I contacted the corporate office and quickly received a response from the corporate Director of Human Resources.

The Vice President sent an invitation to meet him in Chicago at the O'Hara airport hotel. I received a prepaid ticket and was taken to my room. A fruit basket and a bottle of wine welcomed me to the hotel's hospitality.

I was treated as an important person. Impressed by the welcome, we met the following morning in his suite.

Hosted graciously to breakfast and strong coffee, this made a great impression.

The interview lasted two hours. His interview skills put me at ease while he listened to me, reciting my professional and life experiences. I took a lesson from him for my own benefit.

I wanted to learn this; it is a skill and, of course, in his position, a tool he applies on a routine basis.

The promise of a job taking me to San Diego, and a hotel just taken over from a regional airline, is now being described. I could hardly conceal my enthusiasm for California and San Diego.

A letter of employment listing salary, moving expenses, and benefits would follow.

"Perhaps you want to fly ahead since the position is open now, and time is of the essence."

Everything happened at lightning speed. I gave notice at the hotel, but did not disclose the destination. The meeting was short and cold giving minimal notice, while I stated the Comp time still due to me.

The GM wanted thirty days' notice. My reply referred to a three-month comp time and referring to the time worked over and beyond the norm and still due. *I think it will serve as my notice. Just send the paycheck to my address. It makes us even!.*

My wife was on her own to put the house on the market and pack all our belongings. She had grown to love this house and the neighborhood, and with Martin having grown and gotten attached to the area and made friends, it was an emotional task to end it.

I did fly ahead to start the job, and I the hotel needed leadership. A few weeks later I returned to help with the final leg and the drive to California.

The Chevy got replaced as it could not handle the snow in Buffalo and the bitter cold in Minnesota. A BMW 2001 model took its place.

The time was now filled with driving through the plains and desert heading westbound. Anticipation grew bigger until we could see the Pacific Ocean in the distance. The name California even got my son all excited.

Chapter 7

It is easy to fall in love with this city on the West coast of America. The climate is near perfect, balmy days, cool nights and little or no humidity.

A multinational population and near the Mexican border adds a flavor like no other city we had experienced.

Sidewalks, bike lanes and recreational area are in pristine condition. Balboa Park, the San Diego Zoo, beaches, mountains nearby gave us a new perspective in life.

We settled into a house in a quiet neighborhood at the end of a Cul de Sak and a pool to swim in. Our boy, who by now was almost five years old had forgotten the teary farewell in Minneapolis. He embraced his new world and Kindergarten.

The job quickly showed its challenges. A rotation of General Managers sent as interim caretakers only, was finally staffed with a former Food & Beverage Director as the newly appointed leader of the management team.

The Food & Beverage manager had been let go and the position kept vacant.

I was again without a backup Sous Chef and had to manage two separate restaurant facilities.

In the Hotel Tower with Fife hundred rooms, banquet meeting rooms and a coffee shop holding eighty seats including an old-fashioned counter seating with twelve seats.

The kitchen was an afterthought by the buildings planning Architect. No real production area and clean up facility was set up in a logical flow for production. A corner here for the dish washing, a table around the corner with a convection oven no surface stoves and space to stage the dishes for plating a banquet meal had been provides.

The coffee shop food line with two ranges and oven combination, a steam table plus a tiny cold food preparation area had the challenging task producing breakfast food .

On weekends, when Los Angeles city dwellers invaded the sleepy Nany town of San Diego, the hotel was filled with one thousand hotel guests.

Picture this! Eighty seats in a breakfast room is now handling the onflow of the weekend guests seeking breakfast.

Logistically it is an impossible task for the limited facility in the front and also in the back keeping pace with the never-ending waiting line. Eventually the people either leave to find an alternative or express their anger and aggression on the service staff.

The kitchen prepare as much as possible in advance, yet there comes a time, when advance preparation runs out.

The Chef is then the prep cook filling the need.

Imagine the dished coming to an undersized dishwashing and the one person being overwhelmed with recycling them to the servers!

By the time the restaurant seats had turned over for times, the overwhelming amount turned into a battlefield.

Now is the time, when the newly appointed General Manager makes an appearance in the kitchen.

Dishes are stacked on Banquet service carts, every surface able to place a service tray on, and as a last resort the floor, had been filled with dirty dished on oval serving trays.

His facial expression showed displeasure, followed by a rude and vulgar statement. "Why can't you clean up this F…..g mess?

It was directed at me personally.

Stunned at the vulgar language and the demand pointing to a failure of my performance, I simply replied to him and challenged him to show me how I can do better.

And with it we will follow his lead and procedure. His extensive experience in a sizable hotel may offer us a solution. He turned around and left without a word.

On Monday I asked for a time with him for plans to remedy this situation. It will repeat itself every weekend and must be generation complaints.

Suggestions for a satellite breakfast buffet in a banquet room and a coffee station in the lobby for a fast grab a coffee and pastry had been denied.

No alternative was proposed from his side.

Simplifying the menu and promoting a featured item with a fast production time and limited requirements of dishes had eased the pain. Yet, the overwhelming numbers of guests could not be accommodated on eighty seats alone. It remained a losing battle.

I threaded the weekends and kept on searching for alternate solutions.

The second restaurant was a freestanding building with a half-rounded front overlooking the water. A terrace provided outdoor seating for a total of three hundred guests.

The management for this facility was in the hands of a French lady with considerable service experience. Charming, speaking with a Frech accent and always smiling, she became a trusted college.

The restaurant enjoyed considerable popularity from the local clientele and also from the hotel guests.

Lucienne enjoyed the success and took credit for the recognition she received from satisfied customers.

We served meats, but primarily fish, when a huge swordfish was offered by the fishing boats for purchase right from today's catch.

It became a known promotional item which the customers were looking forward to on weekends.

It positioned me on a cutting table busy keeping up with orders from the servers. Five hundred portions of swordfish was a normal weekend count.

Two cooks on the hot cooking line from Mexico and one older man from the Philippines managed the flow and filled the fast-paced order flow.

One young man from Mexico did the dishwashing and also helped with vegetable preparation.

It was a well-oiled machine and highly profitable.

In contrast to breakfast, the evening service became a joyful work time. Despite the long hours, I had fun and also savored the environment.

Finally, I was awarded a Sous Chef, allowing me time with the family. We explored life at the beach, learned that Californian are making effective use of the waterfront, set up campfires and parties to socialize.

I took my boy places for kids, the zoo, and a trip to Tijuana, Big Bear Mountain and into the desert areas seeking the Spring bloom.

A Food & Beverage manager was announced and arriving within a week. He transferred from the same hotel in Chicago where he held the position as room service manager.

My hope for a solution to the coffee shop problem received a fresh wind. Discussing and showing him the disaster zone, made him realize the need for a change. My approach was nor directed to the main restaurant terrace for a breakfast "Al Fresco."

Previous conversations with Lucienne had me assured her cooperation providing staffing from the evening crew, eager to enhance their income and her willingness to organize and supervise a buffet service serving the overflow.

Mohammad, the new F&B manager was also briefed on the ideas we had been previously denied. He wanted to give this a second effort and spoke to his mentor from Chicago.

His ideas were once again declined, except the coffee station as a grab and run in the lobby.

Disappointed to hear the denial, I told him, that by this weekend I will set up the breakfast "Al Fresco" at the restaurant terrace without the blessings of the General Manager.

I am no longer asking his permission. I will leave it to the Food and Beverage manager to defend it. If it proves successful, then we do not have a problem. "Can he be so ignorant and deny a success?"

He looked hesitant, yet he agreed. Lucienne made the planning and we proceeded with the execution. One cook in the kitchen, a colorful display set up by my artistic Filipino man and the service fed three hundred hungry and delighted customers.

Rave review, thank you notes and smiling faces rewarded us with the success.

The coffee shop was still busy yet had chance. The lobby grab station with one server in attendance and cashiering made terrific tips by rounding up the money given by the people in a hurry to see the local attractions.

When the General manager discovered these changes, it left him speechless. Not a word, no scolding or praise, simply stone-faced.

The Sous Chef requested a raise in pay. When it was denied, he quit. I was back on seven days duty once more.

When family suffers the homelife changes with frictions and thoughts of making a change.

During the time working, the controller and GM never shared any financial results with me, I was kept guessing the cost of food, customer counts, statistics was accustomed to and still received negative feedback with the pressure for better performance.

Gut feeling told me that we had a successful operation. The GM's secretary, who on her routine distribution of memos and reports, came visiting and escaping the gossip at the executive office. TLC, here we go again, became attached to my sharing life in the back of the house and she enjoyed the little sweet treats we gave her. She managed to supply me the financial reports, P&L, and balance sheets from accounting.

I was grateful for it and expressed my gratitude. A Eurasian mixed blood gave her an incredibly attractive face, while she kept her body in perfect shape.

TLC also kept me abreast on the office conversations.

One day, she mentioned a caution to me. Something is going on but kept hush hush in the office behind closed doors.

The following day. I was called to the GM's office. Passing TLC, she had her fingers crossed, indicating trouble.

In front of the GM, while standing facing him, I was presented the question. "Are you looking for another job?"

I told him, the working condition forcing a seven-day schedule are creating family problems.

"We know that you are, because we have your resume you submitted to a blind ad placed by the hotel."

Is it a crime to look around?

"No, but since you plan to leave, lets call it a day, you are fired!"

I was shocked and left.

TLC must have heard the words spoken, had tears in her eyes and motioned to see me shortly.

Back in the main restaurant I had to digest what had just been told to me. Never had I been fired, and the reason was absurd. How will I explain this t my wife and my son?

TLC came with papers in her hand for future banquet events, she hugged and kissed me with tears running down her face and offered comforting words. At the end, she confessed that she will be leaving also, since her work climate was unsatisfactory.

It was tearing my heart apart. Dumbfounded, I packed my tools, said goodbye to the staff in the kitchen and looked for Lucienne who was not yet on the property. I left her a note and best wishes with thank you's for her supportive role.

It was a moment deeply embedded in my memory.

Chapter 8

Seeking a job led me to calling former coworkers and managers networking.

It yielded an Executive Chefs position at a hotel of the same company I had previously been employed with.

Strangely, they had not yet resolved the challenging task in coordinating transfers of talented managers within the corporation. Searching for a key professional like a Chef, was simply left to the General Manager or Human Resources to pursue.

My inquiry at the Hartford Hotel received a prompt reply with the invitation to an interview. A ticket was arranged at record speed and the Interview took place the morning after I arrived in the city. The GMs at his office early had welcomed me and inquired about the comfort of the room and flight.

I did not have the red eye flight and made it to the hotel at a civilized time. Dinner at the restaurant and a good night's rest had me prepared for the early morning interview,

He had already been reading my resume, found it fascinating and stated talking about a particular problem, he was facing.

The adjacent center with luxury shopping, a sports arena and home to a prominent hockey team, had also a large hall for banquets and trade shows.

The catering contract with the hotel was put on notice, because any and all food service functions ended up with serving food that had gone cold in the process of service.

We toured the way to the hall, leading from the hotel kitchen to the crossway by a skyway bridge, and down three floors to the hall level.

There he explained that the center did not find it essential to furnish a kitchen, let alone any heating cooking facilities. The hotel must provide eight-foot-long banquet tables and set up a temporary staging area for dispensing the plated food. All food must be cooked and plated in the hotel kitchen, then placed into heater carts and rolled to this staging area.

He opened one of the heating carts to show me with pride how the system was supposed to work.

I took a look at this, and I wanted to shake my head. A wire rack in the form of a carry devise holding eight plates and no room for a cover over each plate, left the food exposed to the draught of airconditioned air, and taking all the heat away. The food had to be cold or at best lukewarm.

He must have seen my facial expression and ask me my assessment.

I simply said, "This is a dead born child."

Shocked at first, I explained it further pointing to the exposed food, the cold air, distance from the staging area to the nearest and farthest table, the time it will take winding through the narrow space people leave once seated and then still expecting piping hot food on the plate.

He quickly realized the error made in selecting this kind of service system.

"Do you have a solution to this problem and what will it take?"

I said, let us talk this over at your office. We are not alone here, and these people may be listening in on us.

I noticed a sign of relief on his face.

Once we reached his office, his secretary offered coffee and closed the door.

So, you think there can be a solution and now, I want you to know, just how big this deal is.

Corporate superiors are breathing down my neck about it and I will make you a promise, if you solve this problem once and for good."

I will make you Food and Beverage Director after one year of service as the Executive Chef."

I gave him a nod and outlined the equipment need for the tableside service procedure. Trays and serving dishes with covers and capable of holding ten portion each. It will be a worthwhile investment.

The heating carts are not optimal, since they lose the built-up heat from preheating, but I know a way to make it work. There is no need to replace them.

Serving spoons and forks are oversized utensils and will be used by the servers dishing out the meat and accompaniments ads a team, completing one table, then get the next trays and continue. Teams will be assigned a maximum of three tables.

The skinny servers receive the tables at the far end.

I will personally demonstrate the technique to the servers, make them repeat the steps and send them home with the spoon and fork for more practice at home.

With the first banquet, they must first demonstrate an efficient and secure way handling these tools and only then will they receive table assignment. All others will be sent to kitchen duty.

There you have it, My plan!

A big smile illuminated his normally reddish face, and we shook hands. "You have gotten yourself the job, a deal, and a lucrative promise.

Salary, benefits, health insurance became a formality/ Moving expense will be covered by the hotel, if I am willing to do the packing and unpacking. Material will be reimbursed.

Returning to San Diego, my wife immediately put the house on the market and prepared to pack our dishes, grillware and accumulated goods.

Furniture which was marginal we donated to the Salvation army and kept the moving expenses to a minimum. It left room for one small car and the family BMW was then driven east, across the northern route via Colorado to Connecticut.

$$* * * * * * *$$

I was eager to prove to James, the General Manager my worth and skills. The kitchen staff was fair but needed to get sharp and also reliable.

I restructured various positions once I was comfortable with the skill set of each cook. A cold food lady from the Philippines and married to GI after the Vietnam war, became my trusted person. She was a keen observer, kept herself busy and at quiet moments she would give me the insights of the talking behind my back. Again, the previous Chef had been the opening Chef and was quickly promoted to F&B manager. In that position he failed.

The crew had been without an Executive Chef for one month, took liberty to show up late and create an undisciplined working climate.

Lina did not like this. She was accustomed of correctness and put in her efforts to her work.

The staffing guide showed one cook short. At first, I attempted to work without h that position, but quickly learned, that a banquet cook was indeed a dire need. Otherwise, it would fall on me. Again, I find myself without a backup person covering days off.

For that, I went to Human resources and found that the position was left open by the former Chef.

It brings to light, why he had failed as a F&B manager. He tried to juggle two position and collect two salaries.

This issue resolved; the search was now on. A candidate who originally stemmed from Washington state, but ended up in New England showed potential and was hired.

After him, I received an applicant which was a girl. Her working experience showed her working as a banquet cook at a neighboring hotel and her knowledge sold me to hire her.

On her first day of work, she came to me with a similar assessment of the other cooks lax attitude. She quickly assured me, that she will be working circles around them and making them look inferior, unless the shape up.

My plans for a shakeup meeting had now been put on hold.

Indeed, she did just that, challenged the boys to outperform her and she followed up on their work. Banquets need organizing, She took care of it. The line cooks left the food unseasoned. She straightened them out.

On the Sous Chefs day off, she filled his shift supervising and also had a profound positive effect on the servers.

In hindside, she should have been the Sous Chef.

Johanna was an attractive girl, but she kept to herself and kept the boys' advances at a distance. At work, Johanna was all work.

After a busy day with groups in the hotel and multiple banquet events, she joined me for a beer in the Chefs office. There she loosened up, told personal and family stories, and revealed her difficult childhood.

Now the time came, when the Sous Chef wanted to return to Seattle, his hometown. The love he was in hot pursuit, had given him the walking papers and bloke the engagement.

I offered Johanna the position and she accepted it.

As a cohesive team we staged food promotions helping the restaurant attract the local customer and more of the hotel guests,

A bistro of the lobby was revamped with a food selection appealing to the young professionals and also the theater patrons right across the hotel.

All this time, the General Manager pretended looking and functioning as the Food& Beverage director.

Pretend was the operative word.

In the absence of leadership, I took on more and bigger responsibly. Johanna followed my footstep taking a larger role in the kitchen.

A pencil pusher had handled the wine purchase and storage titles "Food & Beverage Controller" with the reporting line to the hotel controller. He also handled the purchasing and storeroom function.

I stumbled upon the problem, when a new menu for the restaurant was generated, and a review of the current wine list showed wines in storage since the star up of the hotel. Half liter bottles of expensive red wines had been in stock ever since and did not sell. The expectation offering the smaller bottles at a lesser rate had backfired, since the small quantity did not hold up to the normal life cycle. Many wines, when opened had been brown instead of the vibrant red color.

A substantial loss for the hotel and too many questions without answers.

The once still alive, needed to be sold quickly. But how? The F&B controller James came to me to cry the blues after receiving a reprimand from his boss.

James, I have an idea and for it we must get the Catering manager involved.

We created an appetizer and salad combination for the next sizable banquet in the center. All cold food and it will be pre-set on each place setting. I coerced James to purchase five hundred wineglasses and we assembled a list of wines targeted with the most urgent definition to sell.

Cost plus a margin for a profit, but not the customary amount. The price must be attractive.

With it, we planned our attack selling wines for the next five hundred customers at the center banquet.

An incentive of one dollar per bottle sold was offered to the servers. This and the customary gratuity from the sales price, made for a lucrative supplemental income for the server staff.

The time to execute the sale is as soon as the customer is seated, to offer wine and usually one person heading up the group of company officials will buy wine for the table.

The theory held true. In the staging area we had a rapid cork extractor opening the wine and gently pushed it back in a half inch for easy removal by the servers.

The servers caught on quickly and kept us in the back super busy pulling corks.

Now the food service commenced with the removal of the appetizer plate and setting in the hot dinner plates in time to serve the main course.

Smiling faces all over and the servers wasted no time to refill the glasses with wine ad came back with another sale.

Then the dessert and now the speeches are beginning. Time to quietly cash out the wine sales.

Empty bottles compiled in the unused space of the staging area and James was smiling from ear to ear.

On Monday, the night auditors published the revenue reports from the weekend and gave the controller and the GM a surprise.

"What happened here, these numbers and the party organizer dd not have wine on the function order."

It was an easy explanation by James to convince his boss and the GM the success of the initiative we had pulled off.

The old wine was rescued, turned into a modest profit, but the cost was recovered, therefore no write off.

A new wine list is now in place by the selection of the Chef and Banquet manager. Knowing what sells makes all the difference.

* * * * * * *

Dinner business suffered despite an increase from local customers. The hotel guest would rather seek an unknown restaurant in the city, which give the hotel's restaurant a chance. Frustration and loss for solutions took me to a logical solution.

If we can create a wow effect at breakfast, a meal every hotel gest consumes inside the hotel, we have a chance to convince the gest that this hotel has in fact a superior restaurant operation.

I called Joahnna, the controller, the restaurant manager, the Resident manager who was new on the job and a few open-minded servers and brainstormed ideas.

The premise of delivering a superior product and to make a lasting impression was the goal.

Coffee: It's the first service a guest receives. Why can't we have a far superior product, then even the best of the brands we now use.

The question came from a food server who is working the breakfast shift.

My answer to the question was as follows.

First, we must have better coffee beans from a small roaster, who caters to the premium small restaurants and possible has a limited supply. But let us first find that coffee roaster.

Second, the coffee must be brewed in small quantities and kept rotating to stay fresh. No more that 20 minutes.

For this we need several small coffee brewers,

We disassemble the large urns currently in use and put a person making coffee during the peak serving time. I can train a dishwasher fir that, He or she is not terribly busy at that time.

Then we must have our breads Danish pastries, apple turnovers, croissants, and adding a crusty roll baked fresh and just pulled out of the oven before service. No longer will we tolerate the use of these warmer drawers, who simply dry out the product. An increase of the aroma agents is also a requirement. I want to smell the cinnamon, vanilla, caramel, and butter from these products.

Oven fresh, but not oven hot.

The menu will receive new breakfast items, and also cater to the female customer, who now eats in room service.

Invite them with fresh berries, Swiss muesli, yogurt, and the list goes on.

The breakfast menu must be displayed in each guest room, but not hidden inside a directory binder.

Service being prompt and unintrusive will place the check on the guests table once service was rendered.

No more waiting and calling for the check.

A captain's table using the large round family table will be preset with juice, coffee in thermos containers, dairy products, fruits, and breads in baskets.

Newspapers from the front desk will be on this table, which is now ideal for the single business traveler. The hostess will greet the guest with a cheerful good morning, n may I get you a seat at the captain's table, where we will another single traveler have joining you. Your server will be here for your hot food order.

This became a hit, since we had them taken care of, given the news and companions for conversation.

It also freed up the tables for two and not tie up the table with a single lonely traveler.

The plan is agreed and ready for implementation.

A sense of excitement flushed through my staff, and everybody contributed. The hot food orders were no longer mixed up, or stolen and causing decent, the cooks made efforts with garnishing the plated enjoying autonomy in that part, the front door no longer used the cliché" One for breakfast" instead had a big smile and a daily changing greeting with a positive message.

The effects was not lost on the hotel guest, and as we had hoped, we saw a massive increase at dinner with guests signing the tab to the room. After dinner, the lounge filled up with hotel guests and locals and we had just turned the corner on a tricky situation.

Two weeks later the General Manager called the Chefs office and spoke to me with instructions to come to work in a suit tomorrow morning.

It must be the day when he will fulfill his promise.

Stay in the kitchen until I call you to my office had been the instruction.

At home, I asked my wife to freshen up my only suit and f give it a pressing with the iron. Will it still fit me?

I did not gain weight while working in the kitchen, To the contrary, I was this as at the time when I was a teenager. It fit like a glove and a new white shirt had me ready for the promotion.

My cooks wondered what was going on. Only Johanna knew the details to which she added, not to be burdened with the Executive Chef's position. She wanted to grow and add more experience. It will only prepare me for a future promotion when I am certain to succeed.

I assured her to protect her and whenever we had time, to sit and teach her the management skills, she felt she was still short on.

* * * * * * *

Arriving at the GMs p office, the staff gave me a standing ovation. The news had been leaked.

He gave me a firm handshake, praise my accomplishments and entrepreneurial spirit and handed me the appointment letter.

"Read it, I added something extra to it."

In it was the formal appointment with a job description, imminent goals he wishes to be accomplished and to keep life interesting. You can take over the director of catering job. I had to dismiss him.

Wow, two for the price of one?

"not so, I added to the salary, and you will receive the full share of the hotels catering incentive program. It amounts to 12% of gross sales of food and beverage. I know you will make hay out of this, best of success."

The catering secretary will work exclusive for you.

* * * * * * *

I had by now already left the kitchen and been fully engaged in the food and beverage director's role.

The catering manager's job was added.

These two jobs took all my energy, both being new and much to learn, and yet I had to prove and produce in this new position.

Any day will starts at breakfast service and every task handed to me demands the utmost energy and concentration.

My secretary, Maya, became my lifesaver.

I had little clue about the office protocol. My poor English language skills and grammar required an overhaul.

The structure proved to be in reverse. Long sentences are the norm in German, but English is different and to the point and in fact in the reverse order.

Maya came in early each weekday, took my notes, and formulated my handwritten letters into a remarkable and ready for signature work. She tuned into my right-hand support. I would not have survived without her expert assists.

The efforts received my gratitude and were rewarded with an ample supply of chocolate. Swiss chocolate from Lindt, or Toblerone which had become her favorites.

She helped me schedule sales, call for appointments, wrote memos from simple notes taking my message, and kept the kitchen informed much like a personal assistant on a secretary's wage.

She took no interest in chatting or socializing with the other female clerical staff and was often labeled being unsociable. She received the smallest of all when earning a wage increase. This decision bothered me, and I knew it also bothered her. She knew what kind of high-quality work she performed and was worthy of equal or better.

My protest to the GM had fallen on deaf ears as he referred to the ranking. I had no clue that such a hierarchy did exist but suspected that the GM's secretary was the driving force behind it. She was a gossiper and backstabber.

I decided to give Maya a share of my bonus. The controller had to be convinced to instruct the payroll person, but he understood my reasoning and made the arrangements. Maya was thrilled and was now assured of a nice increase in her weekly pay.

* * * * * * *

Tensions increased at home since I learned how much my wife she had gotten involved with this religious group. The day of reckoning arrived when I returned home at about 9:30. It had been a long and stressful day.

Greeted by my wife and the son, who was waiting for me before his bedtime.

I noticed two people in the family room. They introduced themself, and it puzzled me why two men were in my house at such late hour. They wasted no time and quickly started talking about their mission.

"We are from the church your wife and son have joined, and we would like to talk to you about joining as well!"

What kind of church and what religion?

"We are Christians. We call ourselves born-again Christians."

I had never known that definition of a Christian.

"You will love it, for it gives you a new perspective in life, a foundation to build your relationship with God and people alike and bring you inner peace."

I appreciate the offer, but I am a Catholic, and that is good enough for me. There is no interest in changing that. Now please leave me to my news and my Heineken and go home. I am tired from a long day's work and want to have this time to myself. Thank you, and good night.

There came a rebuttal. "You should not drink alcoholic beverages, and you need to respect the decision of your wife's choice, and then there is your son in his formative years. That is all-important to them."

We will have a talk about this among us. Your five cents are not needed and not wanted. Please leave.

The arguments kept on coming. They had answers for everything. That lasted five minutes when I finally had enough. Understanding that they would never leave freely, I excused myself to the bathroom.

I undressed, took a long hot shower then I grabbed the bathrobe, and left for the bedroom next door.

By locking the door had caused alarm in my wife's head as she tried to open it in protest and now pounding her fist against the wooden door. I did not open until she could assure me that these people had left. Only then did I open it and expect a fight to break out.

I will call the police to get them removed and gave her a short scolding-type answers and commanded her not ever allow people in the house without my knowledge and prior consent. It is a violation of my privacy and darn right trespassing.

Words of trespassing, police, and violation of privacy resonated with her. The discussions ended with that.

The following day, the same scenario again. I became angry at my wife allowing them inside again. I learned that they pushed their way in and would not leave.

I was now confronting them and gave them a choice!

You can leave through the door, or I will throw you out the window!" With this, they left!

My wife made attempts to lure me into this church and even asked me to donate ten percent of my salary to the church.

I was not successful in getting her out of patronizing this group of people.

I had asked her to find a job and contribute to the family finances. The son is attending school. Giving her too much idle time.

It crossed my mind if there was any other motive?

She had withdrawn from engaging romantically and spent every free minute with these people.

We grew apart; this church drove a wedge between us and the marriage. My suspicion grew about an illegal cult group that had nothing to do with religion. I tried to learn about them by asking around.

The more I learned, it became clear that this was a group of unsavory characters looking to lure unsuspecting people into the group to exploit them financially and even beyond that. My alarm bell went off.

Every effort to reason with my wife had fallen on deaf ears.

****

Work continued with new challenges. The part-owner of the hotel was an insurance company who sponsored for a major tennis tournament.

It was played on the sports arenas concrete floor.

The hotel housed the players and tournament organizers, while the food and beverage department received the service orders to the players' lounge and other food service areas.

The challenge was the US tennis team against the Australian Tennis team.

Pitches as a final season play-off, it attracted television coverage and spectators filling the arena.

The insurance company's senior meeting and travel planner had the oversight of all services. As an experienced man. He met with me on all details and impressed that in the past years, not all services had met his satisfaction.

On time set up and delivering the complete order was his most significant concern.

We had been warned and much to prove to him.

I devoted all my time delivering a perfect performance.

The wife of one of the Australian players took an interest in shopping at the civic center's high-end stores.

Her breakfast started way past the regular service hour! The room service operator did not recognize her VIP status; thus, I got her call transferred to my office.

I pulled the strings and made the kitchen produce her order for delivery to her room. Happy and satisfied, she called back with a smile and a big thank you. From that day on, I kept an eye on her service requirements, champagne, snacks, lunch, or cocktails. She shied away from paparazzo and spent time in the centers or hotel confines.

She recognized this personal attention at the end with a personally delivered thank-you card and a signed tennis racket from her husband.

These Aussies had been friendly? Despite their accent being hard to understand, they had grit, loved to have fun, drank good wine and beer, and joked around. It's easy to like these kinds of people.

* * * * * * *

I received coaching from marketing on strategies and methods to make sales calls, press the flesh, and ask the customer for their business. It had scared me to no end. I am an introvert and was dominated by my parents, mostly my father.

Maya made appointments, and the schedule had been kept with the customary German punctuality. That required of me to be there five minutes early.

Mustering up all my courage, I put on my best suit and ventured out into the world of Hartford companies.

The first appointment surprised me with the easy and casual way one I was received and was given the opportunity to speak on services, products, and commitment to make their event successful. So far, so good until I came to an association of legal professionals.

The meeting planner raked over hot coals on an incident that had to do with the presidential suite. In learning the details, she articulates that the hotel had vacated the Senior Vice President suite accommodations in favor of a hotel-designated VIP.

The association will never ever patronize this hotel again.

I left the office and took a deep breath. It did little to shake this experience. I found comfort in knowing that a simple solution could be found, and I will be delegate it to the front office plus sales and marketing.

On to the next stop! A veteran from business executive levels headed up the Chamber of Commerce. His secretary, a noble-looking woman with great posture and displaying authority received me graciously! She was the actual organizer who booked, planned, and executed civic and social functions?

She welcomed me warmly, offered coffee, and started to talk about her needs.

"Work with me on space, dates, and cost. This organization is interwoven into all business branches in this city. Then there are fundraisers, or parties the chamber pays for that may recognize the accomplishment of private persons or in business, charities, and culture like the symphony or theater. For these, I need your help to keep the cost to the minimum yet still put on a classy product."

"I see that your résumé shows considerable experience, and since you started as the Executive Chef here, I have followed the PR events for the restaurant and enjoyed your food. The GM was kind enough to share your résumé with me for this meeting."

We shook hands on that and, from this meeting developed a cohesive business relationship. The catering department received her endorsement from chamber members. Business picked up in leaps and bounds.

"Press the flesh. Ask for the business. Sales calls are now a newly acquired skill. Thank you, Mr. Marketing."

* * * * * * *

I found a different route to go home. Among the small stores, I noticed a massage service in this new neighborhood. "Get a massage, stress relief, and relaxation" had been on a neon sign. It sounded good and would make me feel good after a stressful day.

I entered and asked if I needed an appointment. "No," this Asian woman told me. "We have time available. Half hour or full hour and followed up with a better deal! $50 is the price, okay?"

Okay.

I was ushered into a dark-lit room with a massage table and soft music.

"Please undress and cover yourself with this towel facedown," she said, pointing to an opening for the face to breathe.

Within minutes, the door opened. A girl's high-pitched voice was now telling me that she would give the massage. "You like Swedish or deep tissue?"

Explain, please!

"Swedish is soft, and deep tissue is better going into the muscles. Let us do the deep tissue."

Now she oiled me up and started to knead the muscle structure of the shoulder, back arms, upper leg muscles, and lower leg muscles. Then she climbed onto the table and continued barefoot by placing one foot on my buttocks while the other foot took on the duty to continue the massaging.

Just like my Filipino pantry cook at the hotel, only more intense.

Turning around, a pretty Asian girl, small and with so much strength! *Excellent*, I thought.

With a big smiling face, she asked, "Everything okay?" A nod and she continued with her task. Shoulder muscles one more time, arms, and now the fingers got the attention. The stomach in a circular motion, making ever wider circles to the pelvic area, touching the hairline, and paying meticulous attention to it while she watched my face for a reaction.

The reaction came from another muscle, freestanding now, which amazed her with a big smile.

She went on to the lower leg muscles, then the feet and toes, before returning to the thighs!

Added oil was applied and massaged up and down. She had to get into the inner leg parts. Going down to the ankles at times, she equally maximized the upward motion to the crotch and testis.

"Oh, your number one, so significant, you can do! My boy was in full attention now and pulsating.

"Do you want this massaged too?" Surprised, I said yes, and she went to work with exceptional skill on getting this boy his full attention.

"We make a happy ending, okay?" And so, she did!

She earned a big tip, hugged me, and I left happy with a new experience.

* * * * * * *

Doris from the chamber called Maya and let me know while doing my rounds in the kitchen. "It is important. Call her quickly."

How can I help you? I opened the call.

"We have to meet, and can you come to my office, for my time today is limited. 10:30, okay?"

I braced for something big without knowing what this urgency was all about.

"We have an event sprung on me just now at the civic center arena."

That is odd. Why the arena?

"The other space is booked with an exhibit, and the party is quite large. We can set up tables on the concrete floor and somehow lose sight of the bleacher area, and then there is this high ceiling. These elements need a creative solution and should not cost too much. Can you think of this, and we can meet later tonight over a drink at the hotel? The F&B can be substantial, for this is paid for by some company interested in promoting a new product."

I gave her my word, left, walked toward a city park, sat on the bench, and let my imagination wander. She had mentioned the name, looking to promote this new product. In there lies the solution! But what could it be?

Weighing the space, I added up potential solutions. Soften the concrete floor with AstroTurf. The center's operations manager could contribute this for the rent he now receives in a place that otherwise was idle.

Maya was always a great sounding-off person, taking part in my thinking process and pointing out potential pitfalls. Her support to me was more than being a secretary. We bonded on so many opportunities and projects she should have been a manager.

92

There was still empty space on both ends that needed help. I let this sit, and once I could meet with artists, creative juice would come to the surface. I was counting on this! Can I find an artistic bunch of people to create something, an art exhibit or whatever, to block the view of the spectators' area and the cold floor?

Now what can I do with this ceiling? That was a tall order! *Tall* being the best word, it spawned a crazy idea! What about balloons? This company wanting to promote this new product and would welcome advertising space, just funding the cost of balloons that may be available on a rental basis.

On the walk back, my mind was now in overdrive. I made notes on my pad. Hoping these ideas fall on fertile ground, I felt assured and prepared to meet with Doris that evening.

We took a table in a quiet restaurant section and told John the manager to keep us undisturbed. Notepad and pen in hand, I told her the crazy ideas which had come to mind! I wanted her to be prepared and soften the shock of being simply over the top.

The cold concrete floor found acceptance, and the civic center would be able to give the artificial grass. The need for artists getting involved she hailed as a great idea. She had a connection to an art school and the artist community in a village outside Hartford. These people forever seek exposure and opportunities to sell their paintings and sculptures. It is doable and a creative idea.

Now the coup de grace! Balloons, to envision it, she had to close her eyes and find equal enthusiasm. "We will lower the ceiling this way," she started talking, "and the colors will brighten the large arena, and this company needs to spend money on advertising for this new product, so we are now not only providing the idea, but also advertising space. What a great move for them and a solution where everyone benefits!"

I had her going full speed! This company may also be interested in large banners in front of the spectator's bleachers and blocking the view of the empty space. Another opportunity featuring their product with colorful graphics and shrink the space of this huge arena.

"With these ideas coming together, we will have solved this problem and not have spent a nickel of our funds, brilliant!"

Diligently work lies ahead and as it came to the event, it turned out a spectacular party attracting the attention of the media.

Party guests in awe, and all contributors getting their money's worth, and the company officials could not be more pleased. . I did not believe that this would ever be out staged nor forgotten.

* * * * * * *

On the home front, nothing had changed. Our son was again in Germany during his summer vacation and spending quality time with the Grandparents, Uncles, nephews, and close friends he had since developed., It provide ample free time to my wife for her newfound church activity. Communications between us was now reduced to family finances, the honey-do list, food, and small talk.

The hotel's picnic is now scheduled, giving the management a chance to mingle, be on their level, play a ball game, and drink a beer together. The human resources office had planned activities for kids, mothers, and younger females while the male population hung around the beer kegs after the game was either won or lost.

My wife chose not to attend.

Catered by food and beverage, I felt the need to give them a hand and shares the burden. All food and beverage employees, whether appointed to work for this party or being off and a guest, pitched in to clean up rapidly not punish the few on duty. Even room service operator girls and cashier girls pitched in. Everybody had fun,

Time to leave; a cashier had just lost her ride home, so she asked me which direction I was going and if it were convenient if I could give her a ride home.

No problem, this is on my way home. Let us go!

She was giggling and happy, had a beer or two but was not drunk, just feeling the effects of the alcohol. We passed a gas station and a major highway intersection with the usual fast-food places and motels. "Can we go there?" She pointed to a motel. By now, she had her hand on my leg with clear intentions.

I said, yes, but it is wrong, you know.

"Do not worry. I will not tell it ever to anybody. I know it can hurt us both. The opportunity is so ideal that it would be a shame to miss it!"

I paid cash for the room, entered, and with lightning speed, she got undressed.

94

Working on my belt followed and dropping the shorts, she did not waste time making herself available.

A few extra pounds on her buttocks did not hurt. She was horny and had to have sex right now. Sex was fast and furious. She wanted it hard and from all sides. A maniac?

* * * * * * *

The civic center event was planning another event on the arena floor. This time the center's management is hosting this concert labeled as a charity affair. A social setting for a classical concert was the purpose.

The hotel will supply white tablecloths, food, and beverage services on individual sales. Round tables will be placed on the arena floor to accommodate eight persons each.

Small plates as sophisticated food for snacks was the idea we received for our direction. These combination plates with cheese, cured meats, pâté, bite-size seafood items hot and cold, fruit, bread, crackers, and pickles. Yes, that was the idea.

The center will handle the ticket sales to individuals and small groups of company employees, large families with that kind of interest up to six hundred. The Boston Pops Orchestra will be performing classical pieces with a mix of musicals, while Dame Joan Sutherland will be the center showcase with heavy opera areas.

It became a sellout event fundraiser!

The event got underway, Arthur Fiedler doing his magic with the orchestra, and Dame Joan Sutherland blasted her voice into this great hollow space. Acoustically not ideal, but the event turned out a huge success.

Each time Arthur Fiedler left the stage after each piece and applause acknowledged, he walked behind the stage. A bottle of Wild Turkey whiskey was awaiting him for a sip, or gulp as his refreshment. He liked his refreshment, took a shot after each musical number, and returned to the podium to conduct another piece of fine music.

Towards the end of the performance the bottle had been empty. His steps took a wider aisle and slower than before while he held himself up on the guardrail at the conductor's platform.

The orchestra must have known his routine and played without the conductor's lead.

‎* * * * * *

When my son returned from Germany, I had to pick him up alone at the airport. By now he had developed an excellent command of the German language. He was proud of himself, and being the darling of all the relatives, he savored the favoritism he received there.

He told stories of playing in the river and throwing tree branches and rocks to build a dam and back up enough water to swim. There was no other place for kids to swim unless Oma or an uncle took him to the lake. By now, he knew the area as I do and took full advantage of the goods at the butcher shop—liver sausage and heavy smoke belly bacon cut into fine slivers and eaten raw. Fresh raw milk from my cousin's farm was his favorite. He drank a liter on the way walking to Oma's house.

As a ten-year-old teenager, he often spent time inside the production area of the butchery that housed the sausage-making machines and the smoke cabinets. At times he received an apron to aid with simple duties. The slaughter of the animals did not faze him negatively. He understood that food was produced in this facility, and everything tasted fantastic. A Fleischkäse from the oven with a dish of potato salad and mustard from a tubelike devise became the norm for him.

This kid had learned to the point where my older brother, now running the shop had contemplated if he could become the beneficiary to inherit this business one day. His wife had not been able to give him a child.

In his luggage, he smuggled the vacuum-packed smoked bacon. Oma was no longer allowed to wash his used socks as they became the catalyst to throw off the scent of a dog from the agriculture inspector. A dog with its ultrasensitive smell would tip off the agriculture guys and prompting a search of the luggage. It seemed to work for him, and he never had to go through an inspection, which made him proud.

Home again, he noticed the chill in the air! Asking me what had happened, I took him on a long walk and started talking about the sequence of events.

It all started with the miscarriage. Martin did not know about this. "You mean I could have had a little brother or sister?"

"Unfortunately, Mother Nature decided against it, not your mother's fault," I impressed on him.

I let it sink in and continued how it started with this religion. Oh yes, what a farce. He had seen through this himself and pulled back from attending church. Relieved to find support and a change in directions, we continued comparing notes. He also had noticed a change in her. Answers got short, snipping on him. Constant criticism could not be blamed for his coming into the difficult years.

He volunteered that she had often gone off, leaving him alone to his schoolwork. Never any explanation!

Winter was approaching now. The first snow decorated the landscape, the trees hung full of the wet stuff. The trees at the end of the property at home had threatened to break. A warm day following saved it from that. The long-term weather prognosis had predicted an extreme winter, bitter cold and snow. Unusual temperature changes creating ice, freezing rain, sleet, and heavy downpours of rain, only to turn into a sheet of ice overnight. This stuff played havoc with my sinuses. Migraine headaches and a constant runny nose bothered me continuously.

Our boss, the GM, sent out invitations to management and office staff to a Christmas party at his residence in Glastonbury. The catering department was honored to serve this event and prepare the food his wife had chosen. The chef did his utmost to integrate her housewife food items into the professional list, transported all items to the house and then changed his cloth in his car to party attire. Beer, wine, and hard alcohol were left to me. I made sure that we had the good stuff for our consumption.

A nicely decorated house with a Christmas tree, garlands, shimmering lametta, glass ornaments, and mantelpieces set the holiday mood.

The service staff does the setup, and the Maître d' received close supervision from his wife.

Be careful, be careful not to break or damage the furniture. Do not make a mess in the kitchen and the floor must be kept clean and dry. Those form of bossing the hotel employees left a bitter taste to those who had to endure. They took it in stride.

It was not the first outside catered function, and the party got to full swing. Formal by the GM's stature and personality, but hotel people knew how to loosen up a stuffy atmosphere.

After a stiff drink, good jokes and a loose tongue contributed to a fun party.

Suddenly, the front door was open, not ajar but wide open. It was promptly shut again by the person standing the closest to the door. Cold frigid air came in. "What is the matter? Who opened it? Did someone leave without saying good night?"

No, it was him, the General Manager doing it, hinting to ending the party. The door was now left open while everyone took a refill and moved away from the draft.

Every guest knew the purpose, and it became a game. How long could we stretch out this party? Watching him became a sport now. What would be his next move? We wanted to force him to make a formal announcement, not a hint with a two-by-four!

And so, he did, for he had run out of options.

His head was red as a light bulb, and he showed frustration. Now everyone obliged thanked him for a frat party, showered him and his wife with compliments on the tasteful house, and all was okay again.

****

Winter did come vigorously.

A sold-out hotel, not a single vacant room, busy with banquets, and a whole crew on duty set the stage. The lead singer of the band playing in the lounge was a stunning tall, slender body and blonde hair with the voice that captivated the audience. The bar was filled to standing room only with customers in a party mood.

It started to snow in the afternoon, light, fluffy flakes dancing in the air and then got heavier in volume and wetter snow as temperatures had been rising slowly. Now a wind got into the game as this storm developed into a fully-fledged blizzard by 8:00 p.m.

Snow is drifting and blocking the lower areas of the streets and accumulated in droves.

Snowplows could no longer keep up with this monster storm. Television broadcasted the weather update and issued warnings to the population to stay off the road. Say at home, it too dangerous. First responders will not come to the rescue any longer. Then the order to close the Interstate and all city roads,

The management team met with the resident manager taking the lead and made plans for accommodations for the in-house guest, local customers, and our employees. We need every available space converted to sleeping dormitories.

Let us do it in a way mot to create a panic situation.

The front office took inventory of cots, sleeping mattresses, blowup mattresses, heavy-duty blankets, bathroom towels, wash cloth, pillows, hygiene products, stuff to brush the teeth and whatever came to mind.

Meeting rooms and every available space, including the pub, pool area, lounge chairs were assigned a specific group of people.

Bedding got distributed, and signs at the door assigned the rooms by the plan. So far, so good. We were ahead of the game.

Guests attending banquet functions and those having a fun time in the bar did not capture the full scope of this emergency.

The front-desk staff received instructions on handling this and, if needed, getting help with an irate guest. Management was right there to take over.

The banquet maître d' held off with the announced until the end of the function to explain the situation and the game plan to get sleep, makeshift beds, washing supplies, and towels. Only toothbrushes had been missing from the supply list. We could offer baking soda for brushing with the index finger and salt for a saline solution to rinse and gurgle.

The nightcap hour was proclaimed in an effort to keep the bar customers in the lounge. Happy hour snacks came from the kitchen, cleaning out every scrap of food and turned into a seasoned snack food. Many of the customer made it their dinner.

The restaurant patrons got the same message. The bar people, oblivious, just kept drinking.

The band got the news and was asked if they would be kind enough to extend the hours with live music, and they agreed. We fed them a complete dinner to sustain the musicians and singer. A separate board room was set aside for them with cots and supplies.

Every employee was in the spirit to help and in high gear. It looked like they catered a party and took part in it. The kitchen prepared a satisfying meal for the employees and served it in the cafeteria. This room was later converted to an employee dormitory.

Even the pool with a limited amount of lounge chairs got overnight guests of special status.

Thanks to the resident manager taking the lead, it worked like clockwork. None or almost none (there is always one in a crowd) of the guests had any negative comments. They saw how a hotel crew came together and pulled all strings to help them to weather the storm.

The band did a hell of a job and finally settled in a good night's rest. We kept the music going with records, and once the people thinned out, finding their assigned domain for the night, the bar was finally closed.

The Chef, restaurant manager, and banquet maître d' had plans to get settled. The feeding of the masses was at hand the next day. We appointed the pub to serve a breakfast buffet and limited special-request egg orders. The banquet rooms housing the front office and housekeeping staff needed a wake-up call and clear out the bedding to a storeroom in a neat fashion, for it was going to be needed tomorrow night. That room, being spared from becoming a dormitory, was opened first.

A second breakfast buffet, more on the Continental line of food with enhanced items like yogurt, cut fresh fruit, and bread, were handled by banquets. The bar also was used for an enhanced Continental buffet by the bar staff.

The restaurant set up a full-service breakfast buffet and opened shortly after the pub.

All employees got their food from the employee cafeteria. The chef saw that this was equal to the guest's food. Easels with paper pads notified the guest what, when, and where there was food.

Hotel guests got a charge to their folio while the others could not be held to a payment.

Lunch was easier. We could funnel people to the civic center restaurant's fast-food places and concessions. A welcome break for the staff! Dinner demand followed this pattern. The center catered to the captive audience with pleasure. A windfall business that was otherwise meant to be closed.

The lodging arrangement for the night was also more manageable. Locals walked home or received a pickup from a friend or relative with a four-wheel-drive vehicle.

By now, I had been on my feet to the point of losing my feelings. My back was aching, and no place to sleep. I finally took a banquet tablecloth from the party and made myself a nest in my office.

Where was the Filipino girl from the pantry to walk on my back? She had been scheduled for the morning shift.

The crew who had lived in the downtown area walked to work and received a hero's welcome.

I had a front-seat view from my office overlooking the main street and saw the efforts of snowblowers clearing at least one lane in each direction. Engineering hand-shoveled an exit lane from the garage to the road. Now the guest with a vehicle could make their way out of the building and hopefully find a passable street to get home. The highways still had been closed, as per news reports. These reporters had a story not to be wasted. They cruised and reported into the station on street openings and driving conditions.

By night, which left us with hotel guests either depending on Interstate driving or flying out of Bradley Airport. It returned to a civilized order in the hotel. Rooms came open for us to get a good rest as all this settled in on the third day to go home finally.

I had to shovel an entryway to the house, then took a hot bath, and sleep for twenty-four hours. When I awakened, I was confused and had lost track of time.

When my wife told me the time, I was shocked.

Ravaging hunger set in, and I ate too fast. A bellyache resulting from it had to be cured with a good shot of cognac. Fortunately, I still had a bottle of the fifty-year-old cognac saved from the Escoffier dinner.

The hotel hired a sales manager from the competition. Her name looked English, yet she had a distinct German accent which she tried to disguise.

Are you of German descent?

"How did you find out?"

My accent is still solid, but I can hear some variations in words we Germans have difficulties getting right.

"You are very observant!"

Welcome to the team. Please contact me if you need help with catering or food ideas when selling a group.

"Thank you. That is assuring, and I usually mess up on this."

I carried on our little get-acquainted talk by reciting my skills, earlier jobs, and knowledge of wines and other beverages.

Let us work as a team. Maya, my secretary, is efficient, cooperative, and my right hand. She runs the show in my department. When you have a chance, I will take you to the kitchen and introduce you to the Chef, Sous Chef, and banquet Chef. We are off to a good start!

I took her with me to sales calls at times when she could sell rooms or conventions with huge presentations and breakout meetings. It was a productive way, appreciated by the clients as it saved them time, and details while received all the personal attention.

With time, she talked about herself, her past, having been married for the third time, two boys from her first marriage, and the nature of her current husband. She warmed up to me and gradually showed small gestures of affection.

Then one day at the time to go home, she had waited in the garage for me, made it look like she was just ahead of me, said something complimentary, and pressed her body against me, which followed with a long kiss on the mouth.

A deep breath followed this surprise as she continued to advance toward sex. Not here. We are not alone, others are coming, and it will be a scandal.

"Okay," she agreed, "but what about making a date for sex in a hotel across the street? It would be discreet, and we could be on sales calls to camouflage being absent from the office."

It is out of my comfort zone, cheating on family, both of us, and work.

"It will be all right. I just have to have sex with you. It drives me crazy thinking of it."

What do these women see in me? On my way home, I tried to find an answer to it!

* * * * * * *

Breakfast had still been the staple of the operation making out traveling guest happy,

New menu items bad bee added and offered by word of mouth.

On the hot side we replaced the eggs Benedict, a poor seller, and a huge time waster. Creative omelets, poached eggs in a zesty tomato concasse and fresh herbs, a French toast from yesterday's croissants soaked in sweetened eggs and milk mix flavored with vanilla and cinnamon, yogurt dishes garnished with berries, slivered toasted almonds, and a fruit plate of seasonal and tropical fruits artfully arranged to embellish the various color.

In contrast, apple pancakes, walnut crepes, or *Blinis*, which we call from the Russian heritage with a custard filling, added considerable excitement. We quickly learned to sell this via suggestions to the female customer first and later on display at the entrance. The men followed as they always do!

It had been a big production that called for a constant checkup. I started to eat my breakfast in the restaurant daily. Servers had to hide the identity of the order at first. Sometimes I could entice Maya to join me, and then I took the salespeople to breakfast to see if they noticed the difference. The resident manager made sure he got these coffee beans sent to his suite. He was a fan and gave us full support. The following introduction had to be the director of marketing and general manager.

The resident manager suggested hosting an executive committee meeting in the restaurant on a quiet day. Great, this now covers the front desk that we wanted to sell breakfast to the guests at the time they check into the hotel.

The menu had been preplanned, and all-new menu items got into the limelight. The coffee smelled inside the room as soon as one approached the front door. Oven-fresh, hot cinnamon buns contributed to this feast of the senses and noticed.

The meeting now had a new schedule. The resident manager counted on it, for the actual agenda items had been hashed over and on paper just for meeting sakes.

"How did you guys make all this happen?" The General Manager looked with amazement. It was a cohesive effort spanning the scope of the executive office, pointing to the resident and the controller. Jim did the legwork and documented the cost and revenue impact and, of course, the service and kitchen.

I looked back at this action as it had been dear to my heart, knowing it would not be easy. It required open minds and the right partners to pull it off. It is still one of the crown jewels in my list of accomplishments.

"What's next?" Jim inquired. He knew me too well by now that something had been brewing in my head.

The desired effect of getting hotel guests into the restaurant became a reality. Still, there had been days when this was not kicking in full force.

It had to be introduced and sold as hotel guests made it up the elevator to the room.

Bellhops liked to talk. It enhanced the tip.

I needed to sell them; sell the salesman, and the sale comes naturally was my logic.

I asked the front office manager, an attractive woman and new in the job at the hotel, if she could gather these bell staff members at a convenient time and day. She did not take part in this famous executive committee meeting; she had not been on the staff then. I invited her to join me the following day for breakfast so we could plan this meeting with all the details.

She said, "You need to get their attention, motivation aside from money and some form of recognition. Knowing that they usually beg for food from the pub right behind the front desk, their stomach is the motivator. For the recognition factor, some way to track the productivity had to be part of it."

We are hosting them for breakfast once! This way, the stomach gets to experience the food, and it stays with them in the brain. "What about the evening, guys? They are the most important ones."

"We have a rotation of the shifts. First up when we open is the best time. Catch them when they work mornings"—one by one- not to shorten the checkout service.

****

The time came when our trusted general manager announced his transfer to San Diego. My eyes lit up. "My favorite city," I blasted aloud.

He received a newly constructed hotel on the beach and was getting to the point when a General Manager must start his planning.

A sales director was to join him, and the engineer followed a week later. He was excited to get this project. A proper handover has always been necessary.

****

The dinner menu planning came to fulfillment, items selected, tested, and tested by a committee of a cross-section of hourly and management employees.

The wine list now must meet up to the expectations. Methodically, the selection process between the chef, F&B controller, restaurant manager, and me, this committee now had to taste these wines. Wine merchants made suggestions and offered to print the list.

There were great wines not easy to pronounce; then there were the usual ones found on all wine lists. Very selective wines that could wet the whistle of a wine connoisseur had become a feature on the list..

The food had been selected to be everyday items that could not be left out and new creative food standing for today's cuisine. Wines had to follow this lead, be comparable with the new dishes, and be priced attractively.

This seemed an easy and enjoyable task, but these wine salesmen pushing their superior products forever and trying to gain the majority of the selection just got on my nerves at times.

The hotel would print the menu: I made the announcement. We did not need to be in one of their back pockets.

There was, however, one of them who had been the owner of a new company. He was soft selling his ware. Let the wine sell itself with tasting; through this, he won us over with a third of the choice. The others bad-mouthed him. Why not? He was a new competition with a different sales approach. Finally, being done, implementation day arrived; training took place on service procedures.

The kitchen produced one of each new dish for the chef's introduction to get into ingredients and preparation methods. Servers needed to take notes on miniature menu formats as a cheat sheet.

Being done with the food, we let them get a fork and devour these dishes.

To reiterate the information received today, a promise to feature one of these dishes daily as a taste panel as a standard training tool. I am serious! Before the service, the restaurant manager would go over service procedures, make corrections to the previous evening's service, and then taste this dish once more. This action had to be done until all service staff could recite the details of each entrée, appetizer, and dessert. After that, it would be continued to introduce daily specials. A test would eventually be administered.

Now for the wine sales. So far, a poor showing with the former list.

The plan has components; I told the Chef, restaurant manager, bar manager, and the food, and beverage controller.

The service staff had to become intimately knowledgeable about our wines. Not the kind of knowledge needed from a sommelier. Get comfortable pronouncing the wine, describing the taste, flavor, and aroma, and deciding which menu item it was best to pair. (I had to elaborate on this term.) Then the need to handle the bottle's opening, pour it properly, and not allowing drips.

"Here is how we are going to do this. I will take the lead on this. Servers will come in a half-hour earlier.

"One wine type will be introduced, pronounced, and repeated loudly until they have it right. A brief description will follow and once the bottle is open, a taste portion is poured to the servers.

"Now we have some wines being dead inventory from the old list. The bar manager will play a role in selling these. He rolled his eyes, not knowing what came next.

Ordinary jug wine was the choice of the so-called house wine. Chablis, Burgundy from a bulk producer poured automatically to any patron in the bar without a word. Cheap and profitable for the sales price was five times the cost. Beverage cost! It had to be 18 percent.

Gary, the new bar manager, had little knowledge about wines and did not drink any wine at all, for he was a liquor guy. Beers, yes, and any kind of cocktail. He could recite them, stating the ingredients.

I had to open his mind to a new concept. He likes white wines from the Moselle, Rhine, and Alsace, France. The fruity character was easy to drink and pleasant on the palate. While he received training behind doors, he learned about wines, got to taste them, and formed a relationship along with basic knowledge about a whole new world for him.

"The concept is simple. The wine by the glass, this quality product we so proudly pour and make for a high beverage cost, will get competition. Remember a choice of one is not a choice! Times are changing. People travel, learn about their goods in foreign countries, and taste them. Those are facts!

"These wines left as dead inventory will be offered in a limited selection in the bar as wine by the glass.

"The pricing is set as one-fifth of the bottle price. Yes, this is a higher cost, but look at the higher sales price, equal to a cocktail.

It will bring in more revenue plus offset your labor cost, supplies, glassware, heat light, and power and your salary! It will wash with all the volume.

The servers and bartenders will need to learn the grape type after which these wines are named after. Merlot, Cabernet Sauvignon, Pinot

Noir, Beaujolais. I know it is not easy. Those are all reds. The whites are Chardonnay, Sauvignon Blanc, Pinot Grigio, Riesling, and more! Do it the same as we do with the restaurant servers. They get the hang of it! Display these wines on the back bar.

Everybody knows Fleishman's vodka and gin and the sort of these; they should be under the bar. No need to advertise the low end of alcohol. Show the name brands and premium brands, something we need to work on in earnest!" I got a strange look; now, I was in his territory. I left it at this, scheduled the introduction, and conducted the first training session with a talk about the reasons, time changes, and what it would do to the tips.

* * * * * * *

Mr. Murry had arrived with fanfare. He came from the flagship hotel, the Boston Sheraton, which he announced at his first staff meeting.

I recognized him from my failed interview drama, but he did not show any recognition toward me. Simply fine by me! I did not need or want his attention. It would be a question of time now. Nasty storm clouds had been forming now.

I went about my work, avoided him whenever possible, and kept my mouth shut at staff and executive committee meetings.

One day, I was called to his office, and now he wanted to know how I managed to run two significant positions in this hotel. "You should have an assistant! This is too much for you. I will give you my secretary as an assistant catering manager."

She is the gossip girl, Maya pointed out. Neither of us liked the idea! What were we going to do?

I told Maya that for now, we had to put on a good face and leave it up to me. She was not cut out for this, the hours, the stress, dealing with meeting planners and social hostesses, the bride, and the mother of a wedding.

She was pushed out of her job; he wanted someone new. Now she was being promoted to her level of incompetence.

If anyone is qualified, it is you, I told Maya. Now that the position is established, there might be a chance in it for you! She smiled!

I like Maya; she is such a great person, loyal, and has a good heart raised up from an Italian family.

Katja was excited about her promotion. I was wrong, and she did ask for a change in her work, a career past a secretary's job.0

The GM's secretary acquires the inside knowledge of a hotel's functioning in the most profound and confidential areas. Secretaries do indeed go that route of sales associate and are thriving in that position.

On Monday, she reported to work. I had a training plan for her guidance. We handled her with kid's gloves. She might as well see the less pleasant side of the job as she may expect to get a comfortable office job. The service end of the work is never visible to those in a nine-to-five position, and behind the scenes can be a bit rough at times.

I started with a tour! You need to know where we work behind the scenes, learn all the terminology, what this stuff is called, and how the housemen function. Then on to the kitchen! You want to have the Chef on your side. Therefore, communication with the banquet crew is foremost. Again, there is a language of its own, and you must learn to use it. This makes communication correct and efficient.

Last but not least, to the beverage section. The bar manager sets up the banquet bars. These bars can be hosted, cash, or a combination of both. Bar sales generate a respectable profit. Various beverage brands are used depending on the price and profile of the customer.

By now, I had her head spinning! "There is much to learn," she whispered.

Oh yes, Katja, much to learn, but you have resources in me, Maya, the department heads, and any leading worker like the banquet chef, sous chef, storeroom clerk, and food and beverage controller, Jim. Getting overwhelmed is the wrong approach. Let us take it one step at a time.

You must know that we have to go out and find new business all the time. "How do we do this?" To start, we need to know who is hosting local banquets. Service clubs, companies, associations, sports organizations, the civic center staff, the chamber of commerce, municipalities, funeral directors, wedding planners, florists, churches, ethnic organizations, Jewish and Orthodox Jewish organizations.

"Okay, I understand! Now tell me how we will go about this in specific terms."

You will become a detective and investigate many of these potential customers. Everyone has a leader. That is whom we need to talk to. He is the decision-maker.

"Can you be more specific?"

The first step will be for you to go to the other hotels on weekends and write down discretely the names of parties listed on the function tablet in the lobby.

"Weekends?" she almost yelled.

Yes, that is when they have the parties we are looking to steal.

Do it with a recording device? Here I have one that I use. "You are doing this too?"

Yes, I have been doing it, but now it falls in your lap. You are supposed to be an assistant, aiding with the workload. The information we get from this is valuable. It gives the date of the party and the kind of event, be it a cocktail party or dinner or a festive celebration with music and dance or just a meeting.

"Meeting? That too?"

Meetings are held to pass information to groups of people that are likely to plan an event.

Loyalty, price, personal preference, location, and parking play a role. Once you have the information of the person leading a group, get the address. Depending on the level of desire, Maya will make an appointment for you or both to make a personal sales call. You must pick up the phone within three rings or less when a call comes in. Your line must stay open, and the second line as well. No personal calls unless there is an emergency.

You know the office procedures and filing process. I would like you to do this yourself. Help out Maya when you have quiet time. She is a busy gal and now has two to handle.

I have a little project to get you started.

You are familiar with the function books that show all rooms we have, and, in it, sales and catering note tentative and confirmed bookings.

Undetermined simply means the sales folks have a lead, hoping to book this group. They then block space to cover the maximum use by the group. They ensure the meeting space is available when the group books. Then they release the rest of the banquet space to us.

This is always a subject of heated debate. How tentative is tentative, what is the revenue potential for rooms and how little from food and beverage, and the rental money is what we argue repeatedly.

You will see when this comes to the surface. Go ahead and do an inventory of the space. Record each room that is vacant each day of this year or what is left. Also, record the booked rooms, if definite or tentative, from sales or catering. We tally the rooms booked by the status and by whom.

"From this number, we can apply an occupancy factor to it. It will be an eye-opener!"

"How do you do this?"

Simple mathematics! Are you good at math?

"Well, I would not know how to go about it!"

Let me walk you through this exercise.

We know a few data that are a given: the number of days left in the year, the number of rooms vacant showing in the book for these days, who booked it, so we categorize them, us, and divide the number of vacant days by the remaining days of the year. It is that simple!"

"Oh, yes, I understand now. I do not believe this had ever been done,"

Maya confirmed and said, "What a great idea. This just came into my mind recently when I overheard sales bragging about how busy we are and almost nothing left to book! It will show them."

Keep in mind, besides food, beverage, and service, the salespeople sell time. This space, this guest room from this time to this time! Time is the most perishable item. Let that sink in!

Maya now expressed amazement. "That is so very true."

You can use this to support your arguments whenever a dispute arises. Maya should be my assistant catering manager. She thinks ahead like a manager, mature, sharp, and, by comparison, much more attractive. The most precious things come in small packages. Maya is a petite person. All that chocolate she consumed did not stick to her ribs. Energetic and always on the go, burning off any excess calories.

She will make a great wife to a lucky guy. I hope she is choosy and does not fall head over heels into blind love. Sometimes I feel as If I was her uncle!

Katja did an excellent job with that assignment; she was systematic and thorough. She recorded all information on a large piece of paper, which was straightforward to read. This activity caused considerable interest from the sales staff. Not realizing the effects, it can have and becoming a revelation, the curiosity factor was in high gear.

"What are you going to do with that?"

We make copies for the executive committee but do not distribute them just yet, then I present it at the next meeting and hand out the information. There will be discussion following.

Departments like security, engineering, and the resident manager had little to do with it. Interest was generated, and the front office familiar with occupancy rates took a hard look at it.

The director of sales had been there to represent the department. Immediately she voiced a protest. It was mud in her face and in direct line of her responsibility! She had realized that this was exposing space that needed to be booked, and all the tentative had never materialized and never erased.

The GM calmed her down, asked her to keep the book up to date, and formulated an action plan for her sales staff to go out and call on accounts. Cozy times in the office just got a fresh wind.

Maya wanted to know the reaction, then put on a smirk smile. "It serves them right, about time to get them off their butts!"

The learning curve for Katja was long and hard, primarily when covering a wedding or group function in the evening and on weekends. She now realized the dedication it took to make the wheels go around. She got to like the little treats from the kitchen that were received from banquet foods, beverages, and sometimes a tip from the generous host, and the ceremony and order of action, a wedding, was led by the bandleader!

* * * * * * *

About two years back, a phone call from a man identifying himself as a regional director for a major hotel company asked to see me.

Mr. Charles Baker had somehow received information about me and showed a strong interest in recruiting me for his company. He detailed how this company runs, the quality of employee treatment, near future expansions, and with-it opportunities for advancements. I agreed, and we set a date when he would be in the area for dinner at the hotel.

I had no idea how and who gave him the information. He knew a great deal; however, he never gave it all to show his knowledge or source.

I felt flattered being asked. All my job searches had been the other way around. His efforts and persuasions came across to me seriously and made me think about it.

The timing did not fit at that moment with my family life. Second, the wife and these religious influences resulted in neglect of the child. I committed to staying put and had no reason at that time to look elsewhere.

I told Mr. Baker that this element was essential to me, and I would like to wait at least another year. He understood, thanked me for time and dinner, and wanted to ensure that I was okay with him looking in on me whenever he visited his hotel in Springfield, Massachusetts.

We left it at that! He did indeed show up twice that year and one more time the following year. He stayed connected with letters and information he sent to the hotel in plain envelopes.

Winter was approaching, and the busy fall season was winding down. The General Manager settled into a pattern of embarrassment for the beverage department.

This became clear to me when the beverage manager described the incident from the previous night and other times before. He was pale and shaking and had difficulty getting to the point.

This time took the cake, and he did not know how to deal with it if this continued.

What had happened the evening before, at about 8:30 p.m., the GM came to the bar and started drinking gin martinis. One after another, pouring it down like water. Not too long, after about five or six drinks, he fell off the barstool intoxicated and had alcohol poisoning.

Security came to lend aid in dragging his body to the service elevator and down to the loading dock. The front desk had called a taxi to meet them there, packed him in the car, gave the taxi money and address, and sent him home.

Gary signed the bar tab! By accounting procedures, any signed check had to be substantiated with a reason for the complimentary service, like customer entertainment or something trustworthy that the bean counters could defend. In this case, Gary was at a loss. He gave me the check to handle.

"What are you going to do with it? I am not signing it, and we are going to white out your name. It is going to the controller to handle and to confront the GM." The hotel controller had a dual reporting line to the corporate office.

He was in the most vital position and could not be fired.

This man has a severe alcohol problem. At lunch, he often ate outside the hotel in a bar or restaurant, or should I say he drank his lunch! Knowing what had happened by now was common knowledge on all levels.

In the morning, he started to show up by 11:00 a.m. and needed a quart-size pitcher of orange juice to rehydrate, After that he performed one hour of work. Bracing any personal contact during that time, all managers found ways to stay away from him, ignored the beeper calls, or called back to the secretary to explain why he was unavailable right now. Down the dishwashers giggling when he came to the kitchen confirmed their knowledge by all of his problem.

After lunch and with a couple of drinks under his belt, he acted more civilized! Nobody of management rank except the controller had the leverage to confront the man.

He would ruthlessly yield his power.

The marketing director had checked on him at his earlier hotel and received detrimental information. The reason for his transfer was a demotion. The dirt came out as they succeeded in getting him out of their hotel.

A flashback from my interview at the Sheraton Boston Hotel reminded me of when he had shown up to interview me by 11 AM. All the excuses the secretary had to invent had been excuses and covering for him. I also remembered seeing the orange juice jug on his desk.

That raised a flag with me. Now he wanted to be nice to me and relieve me of the duties as catering director. It was too much to handle both jobs for anyone, and so he hired a man for the job.

Maya warned me that he was not an honest man. By her female intuition, there was a different agenda behind it.

I called Mr. Baker to inform him that the time was ripe now.

My vacation time had accumulated to three weeks and had to be taken or lose it. My son and even my wife supported a trip to Florida. A getaway would do us all good.

Mr. Charles Baker invited me to stop in Washington and come by the Headquarters building. It was an opportune time since he had all the regional directors there for the monthly meeting; this was a procedure; they preferred to interview candidates by involving all the regional directors.

Skilled interviewers get the candidate to talk, which was the case with them. Nervous at first sitting in an empty office while these directors occupied a small meeting room! Six men, one by one, spent twenty to thirty minutes going over my résumé, experience, outlook on life, and management styles; all had their own style of conducting the interview.

That being behind, we traveled to Florida, rented an RV, and cruised from campground to campground. The warm ocean water in December did the body well and awakened the desire to return to Florida at one time.

Maya called me at home with urgency in her voice. "You will not believe what this GM did." Her voice was shaking, and I could hear her crying. "He replaced your job with this catering guy he had hired a few weeks earlier."

This hit me like a ton of bricks!

"What are you going to do?"

First, I have to face the devil. It will not be pleasant, but I must keep calm and hold my nerves.

Then he has to pay me severance for the years I served in that company. Third, I had an interview with Murray Hotels, the corporate F&B director. Mr. Baker has been promoted since, and I expect an offer letter any day! I am not so concerned for me as I am for you!

I will be in tomorrow morning to face this monster at eleven a.m. If you have time before, let us chat downstairs in the restaurant.

Chapter 9

"I wish I could do something for you. This company which I am joining has expansion plans with opportunities to grow your career. The training with Murry is the best and foremost from what I hear and can tell so far.

The post office held the offer letter for my return from vacation. I signed it and mailed it back already. It is moving fast. They are asking me to start with training even while I am still here.

The hotel in Springfield will provide me with preliminary training so that I can commute there, and I am already on the payroll. All of the information I had received was coming through with lightning speed.

"Once I am settled in this company, I will look for positions for you! Keep up the faith and bite the time." We hugged, and tears in our eyes proved our closeness in this job. Ww have grown together in this position and our close working relationship.

Now, I must face this idiot!

I just barged into the office. There is no appointment needed to express myself while he was gulping down the orange juice. Before he could speak, I started my opening salvo.

I can't argue with the decision to fire me, for that's the power you have, but I certainly disapprove of your cowardly style.

"We had to do something: fish or cut bait."

You have just unhooked your most productive fish. Now eat the herring that is left!

With that, I turned to walk out. He called behind to assure me that I would get severance pay. I was gone and never looked back.

* * * * * * *

The hotel in Springfield had already been expecting me. We want you to gain an insight into the F&B department. The General Manager greeted me and introduced the Food and Beverage Director my mentor and guide for this training program. After a quick tour of the hotel, I received a ring binder with the so-called "tasks.

"The tasks are self-explanatory: read it, pick a cross-section, and physically perform the duty as designated. Do this at your pace and announce your assignment to the department manager when you enter their territory. Schedule the time and the assignment with the guidance of the person assigned to assist where needed.

With that, I scheduled my tasks and time and spent two weeks at the hotel.

After Springfield I was sent to a hotel on the outskirts of Boston. A different type of business clientele and a super busy hotel located in the high-tech growth are of Boston suburbia.

I started to do tasks in the storeroom and met with the person in charge.

A tiny woman aided by strong boys and a reputation for efficiency was her trademark. Her handwriting was kept to tiny lettering and obviously made a statement with it to the corporation and the co-workers.

She earned the title and reputation of being the most organized storekeeper in the corporation. Storekeeper. Her inventory turnover had been the highest by a landslide.

* * * * * * *

During my time in the Boston area, I called on my former company and asked to speak to the president. To my amazement, I reached him on the phone and was able to state my grievance to him in the way I was released from the position in Hartford.

Mr. Hogan was graceful, wanted to learn all the details, and asked questions about the hotel, the GM, and his relationship with the other managers. He then asked me if I had received the severance pay.

I had not as of now!

"How many years had you worked in total for the corporation, meaning all three properties?"

Twelve years, as I recall.

"We will check it and send you a check for one week's pay per year of service. I am sorry for this unfortunate event. It is not justifiable, but if you ever want to return, we will be glad to have you coming back."

116

I do have a job as I am calling from the Murray in Newton. I will give this company a try!

"Good, you are in good hands with this company, but keep us in mind. Sorry again, and good fortune. Bye!"

That was impressive when they delivered the check the next day by messenger. There was a solid base in this company, judging from this call. They must know all about this guy in Hartford. The handwriting must be on the wall, and he was not handling the pressure well by seeking shelter in alcohol.

* * * * * * *

Training had now shifted to a schooling venue at headquarters. A test kitchen served as the facility to train all newly hired chefs, food, and beverage managers, and second-line managers to get intimately familiar with the procedures and systematic management of a food production facility. Recipe from a huge file had been assigned to everyone. Every participant received a different recipe and must bring it to completion! Those without actual culinary training had a bit of a nervous reaction. The recipes had to be followed. Once in motion, we learned that the recipe was so complete that basic culinary skills did need to play a role in producing the food item.

Standard procedures include sanitary standards, "the clean as you go" program, and methods to store delicate food including keeping leafy products fresh. With it came the treatment to prolonging the shelf life of berries and other highly perishable items.

Amazement and praise came as an expression from all participants, and a solemn commitment to adhere to this system resulted from this one-week training course.

The second week, all members of the food class plus added newly hired managers from disciplines did not need the food course were assembled and housed in an outlying motel.

The subject of teaching was directed to management skills and the culture of the company from its very first beginning. It included how to manage employees, the handling of grievances, wage reviews and training methods. The importance of providing the employees a cohesive and fair working climate, exercise care and compassion and give them the right working tools.

'The proper care to the employees will guarantee the proper treatment of our hotel customers."

Nothing had been left out from this week's seminar. Painstakingly, every detail of the hotel operation came under scrutiny by professional trainers. They amazed me; I had never experienced that level of training.

How do people learn? What makes them want to know? Fundamental questions are now answered. It was a revelation! The seminar was intense and demanded the full attention.

Observers stationed in the back took notes and compared behavioral patterns and body language. They kept records of it. They do they take this seriously!

On the last day, a festive dinner kicked off the evening. The wine with the meal appealed to the group. We looked forward to a closing ceremony; the mood reflected the atmosphere of a party at tables. The students who had taken advantage of free wine had shown a noticeable effect by their boisterous behavior.

Again, observers stationed in strategic places made notations of all action.

A count of one/two separated the students into two groups. Those with an even number gather in room A. The others go to room B."

The room had round tables for facial contact. Male and females mixed were now receiving the ground rules to play a game.

"Eagles and Starling as the name! You are playing against the other room in A. We will present you with a problem you must solve as a group! The messages will be carried and relayed by these two people. The groups that bring a resolution solving the problem will be declared the winner."

Eyes wide open. The people with a glass of wine too many now sobered up as best they could. Something serious had to be proven. Serious stuff! I thought this could make or break employment.

Now the subject matter came to the surface with few words to explain. It centered around a fight which can ignite rapidly into a war.

Opening statements from both teams had been exchanged.

I was part of team B.

Team A sent a message of an imminent attack to which we needed to respond.

A specific time limit was allowed to discuss the strategy and to find agreement with the group for a suitable reply.

Responding to an aggressive message with the same tone and content was concerning to me and most of us in room B. We pulled together and made everybody participating in the debate and settled on the posture, that by inflaming the situation was not in the best interest seeking a solution.

Let us just ask a question to the motive of the aggression from A The premise of: "Every action will be answered with a reaction."

Why provoke the other side and escalate? No. we will seek a clear response.

I noticed that more observers had shown up to see the process by which this group was dealing with the attack.

The message from room B was sent to room A.

We could hear the calls for a stronger challenge from the room next door.

It gave us time to discuss our strategy and how we can fend off a second attack, only to provoke us. We had since bonded and formed an alliance and now we are thinking in Unisom. We had a plan and had seen through the scheme.

Our message is now torn apart with aggressive wording and carried by a few male students. The others at the table withdrew from the action while the aggressors are now calling for a challenge and stage open warfare. Let's see who the stronger group is. Loud voices gave us the advantage of listening to their strategy.

Are you cowards or what? We challenge you to an open fight and testing the strength Come on and meet us like soldiers!

The message was delivered to room B and read aloud.

It is not an answer to our question. No reason was provided for their attacking motion. We have no obligation to respond in a direct way to them.

We must find another way and offer to negotiate. If we fight, we will destroy our unit and get nowhere. When we can negotiate and come with a voice of reason, we expose the lack of cause for a fight and stand taller.

Coming to a fight without a weapon, is to win the battle. An attack is unlikely, for a fighter is also primarily a coward.

It will reflect our determination to build bridges for a better future and find peace and prosperity in it.

The message was delivered and is now being discussed in room A

Disarmed by the challenge to negotiate, they finally realized that the game was to seek solutions.

Team B had passively challenged us, and they were setting a trap. It was time to wave the olive branch and work toward a mutually beneficial solution.

The game was over, and Team B took the trophy.

To my knowledge, nobody got fired, for, in the end, it was resolved.

Notes of this found their way into each personal file; I was confident.

****

During the training, I received a call from Mr. Baker asking me to join him at a new hotel. Training had been in full swing, and tonight they needed participants to eat in the restaurant to supply physical training for the kitchen and service.

I was impressed at the commitment and expenses this company put forth to give all new employees this hands-on experience.

He explained how this training was organized with professionals in all areas of food, service bar, stores, and cleaning. Nothing was left to chance. Two weeks of intensive theoretical and practical hands-on training gave these employees the skills, confidence, and knowledge to perform the job from the first day of operations.

A task force assembled from sister hotels chosen for the exceptional performance in the home hotel received the honor of being the trainer of the new hires in a mentorship role.

It was to safeguard and one-on-one training, which is highly effective. Then as the new employees got better, the task force pulled back.

There would be a critique session after each training like the one tonight! Employees and task force voiced the issues, placement of serving utensils, kitchen procedures, feedback from guests taking part in this meal, and whatever needs tweaking.

What do you think of the company now?"

"Very impressed. I am lost for words.

"I did not promise you too much. Are you sold and ready to go to an operation? I have another reason and a proposal for you."

"The company is growing in leaps and bounds." He named locations with hotels in various degrees of completion.

"The regions are getting too large for the directors to keep oversight. What about a regional director's position?"

I was lost for words momentarily and then said, But I have not yet worked in any of the hotels!

I said it in a tone of protest.

"You are an experienced manager. A good manager manages himself first. Further, I have seen what you carried out in Connecticut. My F&B director at the Springfield property tracked you. You will do fine! I have confidence in you."

"The General Manager from the Parker House in New York will start a new regional team, and I want to nominate you for the job. He has the final say on acceptance, but no worry. He needs a good foodie to back him. He is strictly marketing oriented. You will be working here at the headquarters. That gives you resources among the other regionals and me and also uses these trainers. They are a phenomenal resource and know all the properties and staff."

How can I say no to that? I had been thrown into jobs without prior preparations for all my life. I will take it.

Chapter 10

We moved again, sold our house and apartment property, and looked around the Washington area for an affordable house. Inside, the Beltway was simply unaffordable. Then certain areas also had expensive homes for traditional buildings and small lots. We loved our large backyard and wanted to get something with space around the house! The realtor then took us to Springfield, Virginia, about a 45-minute drive to work. "Okay, that is manageable. Owning two cars will also help shuttle the kid to middle school and transport for shopping.

Will it not motivate the wife to look for a job, and finally contribute to the family budget?

The house we settled on was backing up to a lake and park. Used as a recreation area we would see an occasional jogger or person walking the dog past our fenced backyard.

The living room faced the backyard with a huge window looking at giant oak trees. All the rooms were spacious except the kitchen. The adjacent dining area with a table to seat eight persons comfortable provide ample space to entertain diner guests. Two bedrooms upstairs of equal size made the selection to choose one as the master bedroom difficult. The larger bathroom became the deciding factor in the end. The basement floor contained a utility room with a small workshop for tools, the furnace, air conditioner, electric panel and the water meter connected to the local utility company.

Next to it came a bedroom-den which Martin quickly claimed as his private space.

Teenagers are in need for privacy. His mother objected, but he persevered and won.

The front entrance led into the formal living room. Its elegant appointment made for an impressive entry to the house.

The women of the house went to work to place all the souvenirs on mantles, shelves, credenzas, and selected corners. The oriental carpets from India found prominent places to show off their beauty.

It kept her busy while I settled into my new job at the headquarters.

She did an excellent job and proved to be a great homemaker. Now it was ours, and we felt at home again.

Silently I had hoped that this religious sect would now find an end. Removed from their hub in Connecticut and living in a new area with a foolproof economy fed by the government, she would find work and get occupied productive.

Our son was now entering middle school and was bussed to school .

Always the concern of the parents when a child changes schools and starts new with making friends. He embraced the dynamics and took a liking towards the teachers. Friends were made quickly as he settled in without a hiccup.

My work had now a new challenge. The team was new in the position, but veterans in the company had the advantage. Traveling as a team to all five New York, New Jersey, and Connecticut hotels also included Barbados as the place in the sun.

The regional Vice President, our team leader invited us to dinner to make the acquaintance and then laid out a preliminary travel agenda.

Everybody had a chance to shake hands, share some personal stories and size each other up.

Each hotel received a brief review with priorities pointed out to each one of the team.

Then came Barbados to be reviewed. It sounded just so exotic.

An expansion project was planned and already under construction. Not much more was revealed, just that this property enjoyed a special attraction to the owner of the company. He will be spending his vacation time at the location.

The first go around will be as a team. A one-day visit to feel the pulse, as he was calling it.

We will fly into LaGuardia and travel by cars. One for the Vice President, the rest will be shared. He had plans in New York settling a move to the outskirts of Washington DC.

We arrived at the hotel, where the General Manager had been anxiously waiting for our arrival.

With key in hand, we settled into the room and went straight to the boardroom for the first assembly of management.

Introduce yourself individually and tell us who you are and what you have done at this hotel.

The VP had asked for that, and it surprised them. After we made our introduction and also included a short synopsis of the professional history.

A tour followed with the ending location of each individuals working territory.

The Food & Beverage manager wanted to take me to his office, but I asked him for a tour of the restaurant, bars, banquets and of course the kitchen.

The purpose was to get acquainted and test competency. What better way than seeing the place in operation, read the body language, make eye contact, and see how the employees are reacting to the F&B manager cruising past them.

He quizzed me on company policies, procedures and was looking for soft spots in my experience.

Shooting from the hip when reciting my company experience, I was not allowing him the leverage to undermine my position. That kind of experience had given me a foundation from which I will build up my experience with this company.

Can you match that?

The question surprised him for which he did not have a spontaneous answer.

My conversation turned to questions of how he was conducting business, the imminent issue, sales, and salesmanship, and how you solve problems.

The policies and procedures referred to the SOPs; they all had that down pat. There is no need to hammer on it. They know this better than I.

I inquired about the kitchen, the Chef, food creativity, and bar operation and asked to see the menu, wine list, and bar menu.

Tell me what sells the best and why. Who is your customer? How many are coming in from the occupied guest rooms? What is your average check, and how much of that is wine? What is your banquet occupancy?

How long is a barstool occupied, and do you have any promotions in the marketing efforts to attract new markets?

These questions left him speechless. Except for total sales, check average, food cost, and bar cost, the sales-oriented questions never found an answer.

With this, I took back the baton.

From now on, you will be dancing to my music, but I will be there to show you how.

Item by item, the unanswered questions received a thorough explanation, their effectiveness or potential, and from there, he realized that there was a new broom in the closet and new breeze is blowing.

* * * * * * *

Identical scenario repeated itself about the same way in every hotel. Managers called ahead giving their counterparts in the other hotels a heads-up from a friendly colleague. In the end, the effect stayed the same. As time was kept short, I left it as "food for thoughts" with a promise to visit soon with quality time to go deeper into the subjects.

We met as a team over cocktails after each hotel visit to exchange impressions.

I was kind but hinted at a bit of the flavor of my discussion and forthcoming opportunities. I got a smile from marketing and a big nod from the VP.

Then off to dinner in the dining room. By now, the guys were sweating blood; nervous movements and overbearing service gave away the weakness.

The food came out good as only safe menu items got ordered. No need to stage an embarrassment; we needed to work with them. They were the implementors of ideas and policies, and we needed a workable relationship.

Chapter 11

Off we go for a visit to Barbados!

The flight from National airport in Washington took us to the connecting flight to JFK and a direct flight to Bridgetown, Barbados.

Three and one-half hours got us there. We arrived in business suits and ties which we quickly took off.

Tropical humid air enveloped our bodies. The AC in the taxi was worthless. Better to open the windows, the driver recommended to us. We took two vehicles for the five of us. The extra person was the trainer Maggie assigned to the region.

We were informed beforehand that this hotel had a service problem in the bars and dining room. Maggie's mission was to find the underlying cause of the problem and from there, we would correct it.

We welcomed her with open arms, a lovely woman in her thirties with blond hair, a sporty body, and a good sense of humor.

The marketing director wasted no time cozying up to her; no such luck; she was all business!

Arriving sweaty and hot, the German General manager came to greet us.

We went to the room and immediately changed into tropical cotton attire. Loose fitting shirts with a spec of décor. Linen long pants, and loafers.

"Great, this is how we dress here. Now you fit right in."

The tour of the *Castle*, as it was referred to, was built by a pirate who plundered shipwrecks that he had lured to the reef.

The deep waters and the reef is the rough part of the island. The beach had to be climbed down steep stairs to the sand.

There a stately Bashan woman ruled with an iron fist. Officially, she was running the hamburger shed and Bank's beer. She exercised her role over everything that took place at the beach as if this were her own. It was necessity to try her hamburger with hot pepper sauce and the local beer.

We missed lunch due to a late arrival time at the airport, so a burger was welcome. The woman cooked it well done, and I breathed with relief. It could have spelled disaster if it had been medium or raw meat. The pepper sauce was in place of ketchup as it would be at a fast-food eatery. This sauce hit the spot, eyes tearing, and called for a refill on the beer.

I was used to hot Indian food and was able to tolerate it. The sauce had a good flavor, but the burn affected my colleague's mouth.

I lectured that beer, or any other liquid does not relieve the burn; it comes from the oils of the chili peppers. Use salt, rub your tongue against it, spit it out, and wash down the salt. These team members did not know about my Indian experience.

The rest of the day went with the usual getting to know the managers and staff on all levels. I made it a point to stay low-key to give a gentle impression.

I found it valuable as a first impression.

The Barbadian people expected an arrogant and superior attitude as it had been under the British rule before independence. Now they are free and no longer in the service of the British Masters.

The Chef, of German roots, had been in the Caribbean for years. He joined from a neighboring island and was used to getting his food shipped frozen and vacuum packed.

I quickly learned from the Chef that the specification were not adhered to, and inferior quality was often mixed in with the order. It needs to be corrected. Will you help me with it?

Fresh papaya, guava, mangoes, bananas of all sizes and flavors, sour oranges, and green limes grew across the bay in Saint Lucia.

The island of Barbados had poor soil and suitable for sugar cane only.

We asked Giovanni about this service problem.

"It is only with the servers; they look unhappy. We see it on their faces, a sad or angry expression. I cannot tell you, but nothing makes them happy, nor can any money motivate them."

We learned this at headquarters.

The restaurant manager did not volunteer any solution; however, I had that gut feeling that something must be the reason. It was the only area with this noticeable problem. Housekeepers with the hard job of tending to rooms in various buildings and spread out all over, never displayed this attitude.

I told Giovanni that the corporate trainer was on this team visit and that this issue was her reason for the visit. We had to produce something. Giovanni later reasoned that this was an island-wide problem. No matter where one goes, the server's male and female only took such a pasture. Bartenders, cooks, and even dishwashers all had this happy-go-lucky personality. Shaking my head, I was lost for an idea.

Later that evening, at dinner, we discussed the day's events. Maggie was dining with us, and the guys still talked about the burger and hot pepper sauce. The service staff did a respectable job technically, promptly, and attentive, but with sour faces.

Giovanni apologized and told everybody what he had tried so far. It was not for the lack of effort, and he could not be blamed for it.

Who has the best service on the island? the VP announced. The GM gave his opinion of being the best resort in Barbados. Are they smiling? "No, they were only better for the service style being very upscale and formal."

Are there any places that have smiling service staff?

The F&B director mentioned a beach restaurant on the opposite side of the island.

Are they smiling because they like the job?

"The staff there consists of students attending the university from other islands."

Can we hire the same type to solve our problem?

"It is difficult as we would have to transport them from the university dormitory to the Castle and back. The restaurant is within walking distance of the school. We looked into that already, but it was too costly and would not get enough of them."

We must think about what made them take such an attitude. Nobody will talk about it and keep total silence, a shame!

The conversation now stirred toward the earlier announcement that the company had approved an expansion of rooms with a new building plus a specialty restaurant.

My thought at once envisioned a compounding of the problem. There had to be an answer!

Building supplies are shipped in from Miami, and the list of furnishings, equipment, and other stores is now prepared. The construction would begin within two months. A project manager from the company would be the person in charge.

Maggie looked at me with a big question mark on her face.

"We need to talk tomorrow morning. Let us sleep on it. We can get more information from the staff. this issue is going to fall in my lap and yours as well!"

We hashed over options where the answer could be coming from at breakfast. The executive housekeeper with the happy-go-lucky maid crew did not volunteer any wisdom. Bartenders, we noticed, showed a better attitude but had adopted the same philosophy at times from the servers.

An infectious disease? None of them gave us an idea. The front-office people, as a last resort, were just déjà vu.

Frustrated to no end, I thought it seemed hopeless, and to accept this as status quo, it not an option. The corporation's owner liked to spend his holiday season with the family.

Right here in Barbados.

* * * * * * *

That afternoon, the Chef and I had an appointment with a food vendor. He supplied most products, imported the wares from Florida, and was one of three we could choose. The Chef complained when he received excess fatty meat and dented cans. Sometimes the flour was alive and had to be rejected, and there were other minor issues. We took a taxi to his distribution building farther inland.

On the way to him, we noticed harvesting sugar cane was going on. I told the driver, "Harvest time, happy time; what is being cut?"

"Sugarcane! We get the workers from Saint Lucia and other small islands."

Why is Barbados importing labor when it has a 25 percent unemployment rate?

"We do not cut sugar cane, which means we do not cut sugarcane anymore!"

Bewildered, I just shook my head.

* * * * * * *

The purveyor of goods was American. He told us the story of how he got into this business. He had no experience in it.

All the concerns of the Chef quickly received assurance to be corrected. He had planned a trip to Florida next week and assured us this would be on the agenda. He replied that he relies on the suppliers from Florida. The correction had to be made there.

The same taxi driver took us back. He needed to wait. There was no other way to get another taxi. The statement he had made about sugarcane harvesting did not leave my mind. However, he resolved it in his mind.

I tried to engage the Chef in this, but he was not interested in the issue. He had his kitchen, and the cooks are happy go lucky characters all the way to the dishwashers and night kitchen cleaners.

* * * * * * *

Maggie was getting ready to play tennis at the hotel with the GM. "Do you play tennis?" she was asking me.

No, but I do have a racket from John Alexander.

She knew that name, the Aussie, instantly. I told her the cut version of how I received this racket. "Come on and put on shorts and sneakers. The GM is still tied up with the RVP. That can take a while. I will give you a quick lesson."

This was now my introduction to tennis. I learned various basic skills, and a drill that lasted twenty minutes was just enough, and I was relieved by the arrival of the GM.

I was more for being a spectator. Both had been playing for some time and had a good command of the game. It was pleasant to watch since I had an idea now and could notice when mistakes had been made. The counting now also made sense. Technically and with strength, the GM dominated Maggie. Despite his superior power shots, she managed to outplay him. Laughter and handshake sealed the results.

After that match, we sat down for a rum punch and chatted. I told them what we had done at the purveyor's place and its result. I also mentioned the word I had with the taxi driver, still humming in my mind.

"We don't cut sugarcane." Stiff and resolute was his tone.

At this moment, a light went off in my brain.

Do you suppose this has something to do with the time when white plantation owners owned the sugarcane fields and the black population had been enslaved?

At these times, these plantation owners were the masters; they used enslaved people to service the white family. Can you see what resemblance it has to the job as a server?

I could see by Maggie's smile that she caught on to where I was going, and the GM affirmed this time before independence.

"Yes, that must be it!" Happy that we have a beginning, Maggie was delighted and fired up to search for a final solution. How do we finally solve the service function, or would it always be the same? Ideas were now perking up faster than I could describe them. We must give them status. For a servant was the lowest position, always at the master's service, and I was sure that the female help was exploited for the benefit of the Master.

Maggie agreed. "What do you suggest? I can see it in your eyes. There is more!"

First, they need to be reclassified by the human resource department and given a different title. I am thinking of service keepers, a takeoff from housekeeper, or service specialists. Something of a superior class! Then the pay as primary generated from tips, must be also seen as demeaning. They are the only job classification that is subjected to it.

I told her the story of the pot washer in India receiving the promotion to soup cook.

She knew of the caste system and had never paid attention to it. My detailed activity and the sweeper's social status, also referred to as the untouchables, created a strong emotional reaction.

She got up from the chair and hugged me when I finished the story.

"You have a good heart. Thank you for telling me that. Now I get the deep meaning of what this job title means to them. It is less the function but how others see them. The tipping is another obstacle. Respectful professionals do not beg for tips. You are so right!"

"We must bring this to the RVP and GM tonight at dinner."

Okay but let us present it as our idea and solution. This way, we start with two votes, just in case. She smiled and agreed.

"We need to sell them first and after the employees."

Selling the brass was easy, so simple a solution; why did I not think of it?

You are too close to the forest to see the trees. It's a proverb also used in Germany, which the GM then repeated in German.

Maggie and I started to put a plan together and checked with the controller and regional controller. At first, cautiously reserved about a pay scale change, the regional controller said, at least give it a chance and explore the monetary impact.

Revenue would come to the house, and the payout had to be accounted for. The cost estimate would not be that far apart. An increase would have to be budgeted in next year's schedule. Still, time to do that, was it?

With that hurdle passed, the only other challenge would now be the server's themselves individually and collectively.

"What do you think the best way to get the word to them?

We do need to have them buy into this. The question was presented to Maggie; she had been thinking in the same direction. "Will it be received with suspicion, or can it receive their embrace? It can be an unforced error or an ace, using the tennis terminology."

"You are learning fast! This game got the bug into you."

With a teacher like you, how can it not influence me?

Smiling at the compliment, she promised more lessons.

The restaurant manager, whom we suspected to know much more about this sour-faced servers, had to be the first to sound off. We would draw the same conclusion about him. It would be the confirmation of going in the right way.

The restaurant manager was surprised to receive an invitation to join the F&B director and the Suits from the US (nickname) to attend an important meeting. This level of management only took part in the F&B meeting.

We started by reiterating this nagging issue and the fact it had to find its own solution. Then I started with the story and the taxi driver's dialogue as I watched his eyes looking bored. Taking notice of this, I appealed to him to be patient as I worked my way to the point.

This preface was essential to set the stage. Not everybody had the wits and speed to follow a rapid presentation. I needed to go slow!

He perked up once I got to the slave time in the country's history. This spawned a personal experience with his parents and him during his childhood. Most certainly did it resonate with his grandparents having lived that life as slaves. It was time to get to the point since I had his undivided attention.

Ms. Maggie and I had analyzed this scenario and concluded that the job title was the culprit of the sad faces, for it was too close to the work of a slave. Even sugarcane is no longer a worthy job to pass over the slave times. Deep wounds are being opened with the demeaning job title.

"We propose changing this title to project a higher rank and noble duty. It will change the social status overall, give face to the individual, and sublabel it as a restaurant specialist of services.

The title we are thinking of for now is a suggestion, and we welcome better ideas from you and the crew. Is restaurant keeper an option? The bartender can become barkeeper, doing away with bartender or barman/barmaid and alluding a managerial authority over his domain?

We are planning a salaried pay system: yes, a guaranteed salaried income, doing away with tips.

Excellent service comes with skills, good organization, and personal pride.

Professional skilled restaurant keepers do not rely on a gratuity.

Thanks to your excellent work and leadership, they know the job well as they already are performing on a level of sophistication far exceeding our expectations. You have trained them well. Thank you for that.

The salary amount will have to be worked up by the controller and put into the budget. It will parallel other professional trades within this property.

The regional VP and GM enthusiastically supported this solution. It has the regional support and will be presented to the senior VP level upon the return to the home office.

We did not have to wait for his answer. It was written all over his face with the biggest smile flashing his impeccable white teeth.

The presentation to the service employees was left to him. They had heard that something was being changes and eager to learn these details.

An important meeting was taking place, and with nothing else shown in advance, the tension could be felt in anticipation of the news.

We proposed changing the status, work title, and pay structure! At the same time, we had asked to assume minor duties.

Helping the hostess in seating and starting self-cashiering so we can assign the cashier to the front desk. Keeping supplies orderly, supporting an inventory, and managing these chores themselves. I announced the new addition. "A specialty restaurant will be set up, and we are seeking ideas on the food concept. Anyone's input, if adopted, will be rewarded!

Just like the reaction from the restaurant manager, the answers were written on their faces with big smiles from ear to ear!

"When can we start? How soon?" Eager to embark on this new journey, Giovanni explained this would have to be approved at corporate. Numbers and budget adjustments were made to set it up in stone so no one could ever reverse it after us!

With that promise, we released them from the meeting. Chatter and joyful expressions followed among them, leaving to go home and for the first time they can actually disclose their job function in the restaurant to their family. We just hit the jackpot!

Maggie and I had now a question for the restaurant manager.

"Charles, you have been here for a long time."

"Yes, madam, I started from the bottom up as a busboy for about seven years."

"You have seen many management changes."

"Yes, madam!"

"Was this issue ever on the table for a discussion?"

"About two years ago, it came up as a complaint, and we had been asked to tell how we feel and if we could change it. I was the head waiter then and took on the role of speaking to all restaurant employees. At that time, they voiced their dissatisfaction with a demeaning position.

Would monetary rewards for positive guest feedback make any difference? They declined this. It is the job itself that is the problem. I tell my family that I work at the hotel but never explain what I do in particular. That satisfies them, and I do not get the nagging from Mom!"

"Thank you, Charles, for your openness. It was discussed, but nobody listened to the underlying social effect."

"That is right, madam, but we had a very autocratic general manager then. It would not have made it out the door. After that, it became taboo to even think about it. Shameful we carried the burden. It was a good-paying job, but not an honorable one. Even friends from school or family did not learn what the work entailed in the hotel, and those unfamiliar with hotel work never suspected anything. For that reason, we do not have relatives from any of us working here or in the hotel."

"I understand," she acknowledged his reasoning. "Now may I have a question for you, please!"

"Go ahead."

"How did you figure this out to such a detail?"

"You must ask this man!"

"Please, sir, I am puzzled and must know. Curiosity kills the cat so that I will be the cat!" He smiled.

I started my story from my experience in India. "They have a caste system, as you may know.

"It is social structure to control the masses, low educated but easily influenced public to prevent uprisings. Condemned to work the dirtiest jobs in the lowest caste, the 'Untouchables' or Sweepers, and are kept hungry. With this method, they control the masses.

When one is born into this caste, he is cursed to stay on that level, as do their children."

Impatient to wait for my point, I motioned him to be patient.

It was like having a personal assistant. Then I touched on the reaction within the ranks of the cooks and how we handled this. Then came the details on my pot washer, how diligent he had been to finish his work, never complained, and made every free minute count learn something from aiding me personally. The illustration and effect of my visit to his house, meeting his family, and how it had been seen gave him "face." When the opportunity arrived to fill a cook's position, we promoted him to be the soup cook.

He understood that this experience embedded the strong feeling for this social injustice and how it related to this situation, helping to bring a happy solution. He asked for a hug and gladly gave him one, and so did Maggie.

"Will you be engaged with the opening of this addition?"

"Yes," she assured me!

"Can we lay the groundwork sometime soon? It has to be built, and that process goes much slower than in the US."

Who knows what and whom we will deal with in management? The GM has been here years, and I heard him hinting at a transfer. The same with Giovanni!"

****

I thought we deserved a rum punch. The regular bartender had returned to the tiki bar while the assistant kept the place going. Smiling from ear to ear, he offered his special punch to try. "Banana daiquiri, which is my specialty! Very ripe bananas are one of the secrets. They have the most flavors, and in the blend, we use extraordinary rum. The manager does not know this, but I have a following here and must keep it going," he explained and felt he had to justify it in front of me.

He made a friend and unshakable supporter for a superior product. You can charge a little more and still maintain your following.

He had almost overlooked my position in food and beverage. I smiled, assured him his secret was safe with me, and who could argue about the best banana daiquiri on the island? "Somebody needs to hold this trophy! If a contest is ever held to find the best rum drinks and select the winning barkeeper, I want you to win it.

"Keeper, I like it already," he announced. "But sadly, we do not have an organization to bring this about. It would be fun and newsworthy, thinking like a marketing brain."

"The stately Castle, with all the shady history, could be the hosting property. This could be organized if the F&B director who knows managers in other places. Do it in a small intimate group, the future proliferates as it happens once.

Rum companies would eagerly contribute to the product and offer price money and publicity. You gave a superior product here. Why not boast about it? Besides, the Castle's reputation and the company's name will benefit immensely.

"You just planted a seed and, besides, made a lifelong friend. They will love you and roll out the red carpet on your next visit."

That will be a while, if we do the budget review here or at the latest during advanced construction status.

"I would like to see that!

Hinting at a visit together, we switched to the training needs in the hotel. Not all were in perfect shape. Assistant management levels and locally staffed department heads had management skills to learn. "Working as a team in a remote location can always improve, and I will probe into this tomorrow."

It looks like you are setting up a visit! Nice thinking.

"So far, I have spent all my precious time with your issue, but worth every minute and full enjoyment. You are smart and fun to work with."

A second drink sealed a close working relationship that proved being successful and lasting!

Back at the home office, while drafting my report, Charles came by my cubicle and mentioned that he had heard something from Barbados. Would I have time to brief him even before the report was completed? Yes, of course, and eager to do so.

He is intimately familiar with this issue. This problem had been nagging every regional director since the hotel joined the family, and it is the owner's favorite place to take a family vacation. The solution is going to be an essential step.

Amazed at this solution, he also took great interest in how I came to this conclusion. "

Remember the experience in India. I never told you how I broke the caste system.

He, of course, was familiar with the country's social structure and the caste system. He had hired Indian F&B directors into hotels. One was at the hotel near the office tower and was used for housing visitors and relocation personnel. I had met this Indian man my brief stay during relocating to the area.

I looked at him with a reserved level of trust, spoke words, and closed the conversations with the Indian equivalent of *okay*, as *hatcha*. That caught his attention for a second.

Continuing with the abridged version of the story, Charles quickly added it up. He realized how much this experience led me to the solution. "Great job, I am proud of you, and of course, I will push for the change in human resources and finance. The senior VP is an easy sell."

With the team visits completed, the relationship with the team members received a large boost. I was no longer the guy from the outside of the company.

The regional VP held a group meeting and sighted the most critical deficiencies in the operation. We will gain his support by setting the date and visiting the General Manager to state the issues and directions.

De-briefing the GM must be done before we leave the property!

My priority hotel was in New Jersey.

The shuttle flight to LaGuardia, then a rental car, a map, and first directions from the rental agent to hook up with the interstate system, I arrived by mid-morning at the hotel. Breakfast service had been completed with only two tables left to serve.

I met with the GM in the restaurant for coffee and a Danish pastry. The GM was a tall, brown-skinned man with a strong baritone voice. He had a few questions at the start, gave me an overview of the F&B director and Executive Chef, and sent me on my way to meet with the department managers.

The F&B director assembled his team on a round table in a banquet meeting room, introduced each by name and position, and then turned it over to me.

My introduction had opened with a statement that I was indeed an outside hire in the company.

The first managers saw me as a disadvantage for my lack of company experience.

A brief background description included my nationality, my Chef's experience, and places I had worked.

Mr. Baker recruited me into the company and proposed the regional position.

"I look forward to a mutually respectful and cooperative working relationship. I am not an auditor. I prefer to find a creative solution and make the department efficient and successful. It will become our success.

I had the full attention of all. "What I want and insist from you is that you are open, honest, and a participant in our goals and aims. Any directions from the headquarters need to be understood, and I will do my best to sell them to you.

That means you must buy into it to the fullest and implement it once understood and agreed upon. I am not in any position to invoke changes. I have six properties and will not live here, and you do, so it is on you! Does anyone have a question?

Okay, let us leave it at this. I will catch up with you on my tour.

At the F&B office, I met the secretaries of the GM. Catering, and F&B shared one person, then marketing and sales and the receptionist reported to the sales and Marketing team.

It was not a large property, nestled in the New Jersey countryside. Corporations and manufacturing spread in and around town supplied the base business for the hotel. The restaurant and bar attracted locals. Good restaurants had not yet set foot in the area.

I asked the director to give me a detailed rundown of his key employees. He did so with great detail.

They all had known that the company was embarking on explosive expansions with new hotels. Everybody had smelled a promotion in that. It was no secret that the Regional Directors played a significant role in placing talent into new hotels.

Kissing up had to be expected. I hated that and voiced my distaste openly. I just wanted to clarify that performance, career, and growth potential were the determining factors in my book.

The employees in the restaurant! How would you rate them? Evasively, he said that they were doing fine.

What about the kitchen?

"I leave that up to the Chef!"

How much time do you spend in the kitchen?

"I make my tour, do health inspections, look up the production charts, check the walk-in refrigerator, but otherwise, I hate to get in the Chef's way."

Is your background restaurant manager?

"That is correct. It is my turf."

Then everything should be perfect with the service!

How are we doing in catering?

"You see the numbers compared to the previous year. We are ahead. That is all that matters!"

Is it? I asked with a strong annunciation!

"Why? Are you implying that we do not do well?"

No, that is not my real question.

Are the guys making outside calls? Are we reading the competition's reader boards? What about weddings? Do they interact with the sources that deal with weddings exclusively, and who does weddings most and why?

A barrage of questions had him on the defense. Since this department reports to you, serves food and beverage, and produces a respectable profit. Don't you wonder if these folks maximize their time and efforts?

He was stunned and silent.

Now, let us look at the menu and beverage lists.

Here is the menu, a standard menu seen in all hotels as the menus had strong guidance from the corporate menu department and recipe cards.

Okay, that shows nothing regional; I mean, a specialty from the New Jersey shores?

"No, the company would not allow it!"

The wine list was boring. We work with a wine merchant, and his advice guides us. Who puts this together? Us! Who else? "The restaurant manager!"

"What about the catering guy and the Chef?"

"No, I do not want them to mess in it!"

Are you a wine connoisseur? Do you drink wine yourself?

"No, I prefer vodka or beer."

So, it is safe to presume that your wine knowledge is limited, and the reliance on the merchant is the only way to put a list together?

Who prints the list? This is the best. It does not cost the department a penny! The list confirms all you have just said. Thank you for being honest. He looked puzzled!

Not everyone is a wine specialist. I do not blame yourself for this list. It is a widespread problem when a wine merchant gets his foot too deep into the operation.

"How should we go about it since we do not have anybody with substantial wine knowledge?"

To start with, have three or more merchants propose wines without knowing what is now being sold on the list.

Take a piece of paper and describe what type of wine, price range, quality standard, region, a foreign country you wish to have. Include the director of catering in this process and also the Chef. Chefs often are wine drinkers and have excellent knowledge. Why not tap this well?

It gives you a start to work with. Do not worry about the cost of printing. You run the show now, not the merchant.

"Also, do not worry for now if inventory is on hand and this wine is left off the list. You have not sold it by now. I have a plan for it, but later.

Follow the guideline and do your homework!

The leftover wine inventory becomes wine by the glass, in the restaurant and the bar. If the wine bottle has not sold entirely, recork it and sell it the next day. The price formula is one-fourth of the selling price rounded down. You yield five drinks out of a bottle using a standard wineglass.

"Wine bottles must be displayed in a prominent place at the bar and visible to the customer. When a glass of wine is ordered, the bartender or sever will automatically offer this wine as a choice.

The so-called house wine has just become cooking wine. The jug of wine goes away.

Print your wine list at an offset printer on a quality stock paper. The cost is minimal, but it will communicate to the wine drinker that the list is fresh, agreed?

"Do you want to have dinner here or go out? We could check out the popular freestanding restaurants."

I need to make a call, freshen up, and make my notes for the report. Let us stay in the house and see what the kitchen offers. Tell the server and manager not to show what I have; the server should not know my position. I will be just a customer being entertained and get the catering director to join us if he is free.

****

"Gary, the director of catering, had a ballroom for about 350 guests catering a dinner on rounds of eight. Small meeting rooms served the business community with meeting space and cocktail parties. The occasional wedding or social function was so rare that all weekends had been empty.

"I talked to him about the space and the usual disputes with the marketing department. No, we never have any issues. There is no conflict since we do not have a convention hall. The groups are usually during the week. That means you service the sales group function. "Yes, one can say that."

"Have you ever done an inventory of the occupied space and recorded the vacant rooms, what day of the week, what time slots, and by whom, meaning catering or sales?

"No, I am not clear what you mean by that." Hotel rooms measure occupancy factors. Banquet space is, in a way, a room that gets business when occupied. When vacant, it draws down the occupancy, as does a vacant hotel room. You and the front desk are selling time! Once the time is gone, it never comes back. It is lost for good!

"Now I get it," he acknowledged.

"Do this exercise. Draw a diagram with all banquet space listed by time sales period breakfast, lunch, meeting, party/dinner, and do this for one year. You can then color-code the sales function one way and catering functions in another way for easy identification. Then calculate the total space available for sale when all rooms are empty; that equals zero. Now add up all the time slots for the year and divide it by the total available time for each room, and as a total, it will give you a percentage of room occupancy. Now you will see a number in the 30 percent or more or less! Follow me?

I am sure the sales and marketing director may be interested in it. A lesson learned; it will shed light on the need to drum up business since the space is available. Rental fees can be looked at and adjusted down on less attractive days or times of the year or increased during high demands. Spend time with the sales folks, go through with a fine-tooth comb, and then form an action plan. Have you ever gone on a sales call all by yourself?

"No! I do not know how to do this!"

Now came the time to let him know that I inherited an ailing catering department right out of the kitchen into management and how I turned the sales around. I hesitated and was being nervous the first day on the road. Quickly and to my surprise, it is easy and, in most cases, pleasant to call on potential clients. They find it honorable when someone takes the time to visit, like to chat and learn about yourself and of them, which forms the basis of commerce!

You must lay the groundwork. Take someone with you who has experience first, then bring the Chef or F&B director for high-profile potential and go for it. Know that they host meetings, food functions, cocktail parties, awards, dinners. Have the secretary make an appointment and come prepared. Get the sale!"

We spent the rest of this dinner discussing firsthand experiences with short stories, family, sports, hobbies, and food. The dinner, a standard menu with steaks, chops, fish, and chicken, had been guided by corporate and backed up by the recipe file. It was well prepared and served hot, and there was nothing to complain about.

The server was an attractive young woman. I was sure she was selected for that table and may even switch stations previously assigned. The restaurant manager had carefully supervised her. I paid her a compliment for the excellent service and efficiency and for giving us the space when the talking was about business. There was hardly any business in the bar, but the few customers looked like hotel guests.

It was time to go to bed, but a strange feeling kept me awake until 11:00.

The morning came fast, coffee with the GM. He was an early riser. I took the opportunity to plant a seed with him on a breakfast plan to get the businessman into the restaurant. I briefed him on the wine list discussion and catering plan in a condensed version.

"I am so happy to hear this. For the longest time, it had been a thorn in my side to get this wine list done right, and these shark salesmen were out of the business writing it for the hotel. Now, this function space occupancy sounded interesting."

"Like a guest room and looking at it from this perspective, one gets a whole new outlook on all these square feet that cost energy, cleaning, maintenance, and taxes. These department operators often forget that cost. All they worry about is food cost, beverage cost, labor cost, utensils, and supplies; all other stuff falls into the engineering lab.

Tell him I want to see this and take part in the strategy session. There is a whole new world to be booked. Tell me, where did Charles Brown find you? I am so glad to see fresh blood in the company!"

I liked this man. Down to earth, easy to talk to, open-minded, and sharp as a butcher's knife!

I appointed this day's schedule to the kitchen. An area that could and often will occupy a good half a day. The chef, an early riser, was waiting for us by 7:00 a.m. He offered freshly baked goods delivered from the bakery, hot coffee, the usual weak brew. If I wanted eggs, it only took a couple of minutes. "Thank you. I know this very intimately, for I have spent the better of my twenty years in the kitchen." He accepted this without another follow-up question.

"Then let me show you around."

"We have a product delivery just now. I would want to take a look at this. Please come along."

The refrigerated truck had just pulled up; the driver with the invoice in hand gave it to the storekeeper to check off the items. The chef pushed up close, opened the lettuce cartons, and looked at the cut of two heads. "God, this is fresh; then the potatoes did not show any sprouting, broccoli, bananas green-tipped as ordered, apples eighty counts. Oranges with the Sunkist label and lemons also, specs got the scrutiny as he proved his knowledge of the USDA standards guide."

Looks like a good supplier, I mentioned to the chef.

"Yes, he is reliable, but checking keeps them honest."

The driver smiled, collected the signature from the storekeeper, and off he went; ten more stops. It tells me something when delivery of produce arrives as the first or second stop. This account is precious to them.

"I never thought about it that way," the F&B guy said.

"Oh yes," the Chef agreed. "They know who pays the bills on time, and word gets back quickly, when the staff does not receive some scrutiny."

Back to the kitchen, looking over the line now cooking omelets and eggs in any style ordered. The process was calm and orderly, with no screaming, or loud talks, just announcing the orders by the lead breakfast cook, then a reminder to the servers for pickup!

The walk-ins all looked clean. There was no odor, shelves were organized and labeled, and bins with salad dressing. The pantry person was already at work to soak the lettuce and other greens to prepare the crisping bins. Ready to cook vegetables, onions, and peppers in shallow rays prepared by a team last night, production schedules on clipboards, function sheets for a luncheon, two cocktail parties with hot and cold hors d'oeuvres, steaks lightly oiled, all seemed by the book. This Chef knew how to use the company's system for his success and efficiency.

I told myself to make a note on him; he would soon outgrow this hotel and be ready to take on an opening.

I asked him if this was an excellent time to talk in a quiet place. "Good time is never, but to make time is now." Kiddingly, he smiled, and I knew, and he knew we were talking the same language.

In the back of the restaurant, he sat to start a conversation about the dinner business. Not about the dinner food. I assured him we were not getting the hotel guest into the restaurant. I knew it was a stigma. All hotels were fighting this unless you had a freestanding restaurant.

I have a theory, actually a proven theory! It has been bothering me that a lousy dinner house with a dirty kitchen gets all the business from us," he hollered. "What do we need to do?"

I know many hotels have tried umpteen things but got nowhere!

"Then tell us what you did. I know you now well enough that you are holding good cards."

I started to go into every detail of the experience in Hartford. The coffee, the freshly baked goods, cinnamon aroma, vanilla, the captain's table, single-seated guests, and on and on. Every little detail was now explained as these two men listened with alert minds. "But today, I hear that my successor tore it all apart to save money, all-mighty food cost!

The result was enormous.

Not my problem, but it hurts anyway. Speaking about food cost, it is the devil in disguise!

If you had a chance to sell a chicken dinner at 28 percent cost instead of a lobster dinner at 38 percent cost, what would you sell?"

"Is this a trap?" the F&B man asked.

No, it's mathematic?

"Please explain!"

The chicken dinner gives the cost or better than the target cost, right? The lobster dinner, in contrast, brings a higher cost but also a higher price and, therefore, more revenue. We measure not only the cost of the product but also labor and higher than the cost of food. Then you need soap to wash the dishes, tables, floor, and everything else, replace glassware, dishes, linen, and much more. And last, as the GM pointed out this morning, heat, light, and power, building and machinery maintenance. So, while carrying a higher product cost, the lobster dinner is the more valuable sale!"

"Now, that is an eye-opener for me," both men confessed.

I have another one since I am on a roll!

Anticipation captured my attention.

When you as the Chef create a menu item, you and this man here set a target sales price, correct? "Yes." Then you go about assembling the food items, meat or fish, starch veggies, sauce, and garnish and weigh all items to keep track of cost within a margin of error. Right? "Yes.

That is the way to do it. Is it really the only way?" Question marks on the faces. This was really fun now.

Let us do it the opposite way. Start with an idea, a recipe of high popularity. As the Chef, you go ahead to create the best and most attractive and tasty item with no regard to food cost. Then you take this item to the customer. Let us call it market, offer it for sale to the highest bidder, make this your menu price, then measure the cost and record it. If it has a high appeal, it will sell for a great price and may even fetch a surprisingly low cost per unit. If it does not sell or has soft appeal, create something else.

It is how manufacturing works in principle! "Interesting thought, but we cannot take it to the market." The F&B said,

"Yes, we can the Chef chimed in. We can produce it as a special and see how well received and then price it from that experience!"

He glowed, and I smiled. This Chef is on the ball!

When I watched this Chef in action, I noticed how he made the system work for him. The consistency of the food, presentation, taste, and part control speak for themselves.

* * * * * * *

The other New Jersey hotel, much closer to the monster city of New York, had a unique market niche that they discovered as a lucrative windfall. The pool was sold out as a membership for city customers on weekends. It made sense when one was cooped up in a small apartment in the city and in a workplace; the urge to escape this concrete jungle was imminently desirable.

This hotel offered the right package.

The extra revenue was also enjoyed by the food and beverage department. Poolside beverage service, creatively made and served as if on an island with palm trees and sandy beaches. The lobby restaurant filled to the last seat. Yes, business is good.

The F&B director proudly elaborated on this. I met them and found him tired and absent-minded. Whom I met briefly to say hello, he seemed absent-minded.

The young Chef had his place in good order. There is room for improvement, but overall, he had his place in shape.

The catering department had a busy calendar, catered to meetings, room rental, small parties with cocktails, lunch, and evening get-togethers. Dinners and social functions are noticeably absent.

We had a similar discussion on banquet occupancy.

This became the challenge to which I put the director to the test. Other revenue areas can also be analyzed for maximum profit.

The imagination of the Catering Director had its limitation. The mechanical approach to running a profit center would be the Achilles' heel.

I invited the F&B director out to dinner to allow for private time and learn more about each other.

After the second drink, Paul started to relax, and his tired look is now given a full explanation.

"This is not a complaint against the GM. But he is always here; hell will be paid if he does not find the person when something is wrong.

"Food and Beverage are a diverse department. If someone wants to find something, just keep looking until something turns up, and my area is his target.

He made it a point to either scold you that moment or, in the case you are not there, indeed, the first thing the following morning. I do not know if he ever spends time at home. He does not take a day off on evenings, weekends, and all times a day. For this reason, all managers are here to be available, for then at least I can correct it on the spot, and the next day, I do not get the spanking before breakfast.

"I can understand this! There is no easy solution, but you must take time off, get your rest, and take your chances. You walk around like a zombie, being present yet not really effective!"

"This is something the RVP has to tackle. For the time being, you need to form a coalition, find out about this man's family life, and then bring it to the RVP at his visit next week. There has to be something very wrong with this man! At the close of my visit the GM was unavailable for debriefing. He will have to read my report in place.

Chapter 12

The following hotel on my tour took me to Manhattan, the heart of New York City. A high-rise building right abutting the next building with a covered entrance.

The doorman in a colorful uniform and a whistled in hand, controlling the traffic, and greeting the guests while opening the door and waving the bellman to duty.

The Bellman took it from there, gathered the suitcases from the trunk, and escorted the arrivals to the front desk for check-in. Then up the elevator to the room, where he quickly checked the room, lights, and all, the bathroom mirrors.

The much-anticipated gratuity into the palm of the hand was much appreciated. The amount was checked once outside the room.

I had to endure the same routine; it allowed me to disguise questions about the working climate as small talk. These guys liked to talk!

He was positive about the hotel room area and his domain but also hinted that they could not recommend the restaurant. "You wanted to ensure the guests get a first-class meal and service."

The best place is the bar. If I got to see these people at checkout, I could kiss a tip goodbye! Do you get my meaning?

VIP: wow, this is a first, a bottle of wine, fruit, and chocolate as a welcome presentation compliment of the Director of Food and Beverage!

Kissing up already or simple standard operation for this high-end hotel?

Arriving late in the afternoon, we did agree to meet in the morning. At the restaurant's entrance, the way into the room I crossed the bar with a substantial population having a stiff happy hour drink. The last call drink as time was progressing toward 7:30 p.m.

Now I was sitting in the middle of a sparsely seated restaurant. From ceiling speakers came music, or shall I call it elevator music the kind one hears in every public building!

I noticed a young couple and they looked familiar. Oh yes, also company employees from the home office. They waved me over and invited me to join them for dinner. I gladly accepted, for I detest sitting alone at a table in the middle of any restaurant.

I much preferred patronizing the bar if food service was available. In this instance, I had table companions, a chance to get to know one another and carry on an intelligent conversation.

Their department, or as it was often referred to the discipline, had been human resources. Personnel issues at a union hotel are never-ending. They had come for a fact-finding of the hotel's problems, too many to tell right now, but the food department had its own problems. "There is something not right in the kitchen! Good to have you here; you can probe into it from your angle?"

"Glad to do so. I suspect more issues will surface once the digging starts."

We received the menu from the captain, who was in charge of the table by his-announcement.

My way is usually to read the entire menu first I gave a warning for the table companions. It was not the regular company menu; they must have received an exemption or taken it upon themselves to depart from the standard fare.

Now my mind went directly to the kitchen. Was it based on recipes or ad hoc from the Chef's experience and skills? I ordered veal, something I liked and reserved room for a dessert.

It was featured prominently as strawberries with zabaglione. Spelled the Italian way, the style of food pointed classic French cuisine. I had been trained on French classics in Zurich.

Looking forward to a tender cutlet in a cream sauce with mushrooms, actually a standard dish with gnocchi. It struck my fancy.

Then the dessert to crown the evening meal. Juices accumulated in my mouth, and I had high hopes for an amiable prepared dish.

My table friends placed the kind of food order to what they knew. The food came out promptly and hot. They ate with satisfaction, but while it looked good, the taste was not there. It lacked flavor concentration, a sign of a poor finish. I did not say anything but made a mental note.

My facial expression had given away my reaction as the HR couple inquired if mine was okay.

"Yes, it is okay, but that is just okay, not excellent. This is an expensive cut of meat, and it deserves better attention." I lost them on my kitchen lingo as I tried to walk them through the preparation process.

I volunteered my culinary training, mentioned places I had worked, and wanting not to become or sound like a bragger; I cut it short.

Now the anticipation for the dessert is one of my all-time favorites.

It is made with a fluffy egg sauce, whipped over hot water with sugar and fortified wine.

The head waiter announced that the kitchen had run out of it!

I was disappointed, but it prompted me to start a barrage of questions.

Does this happen often?

"Sometimes, when we have many orders," he said, trying to disguise his lying. He then flagged the head waiter to take care of this situation. He said he would check with the sous chef and come back with the same answer.

Let me do this. Do you have a can of Sterno someplace nearby?

"Yes, catering and the kitchen have that."

Now, can you organize a small stainless-steel bowl, one to whip things like cream?

"I will try!"

My table companions had been wondering where this was going!

I am sure you have eggs; got to have them for breakfast, I said with sarcasm. While you are in the kitchen, also bring a whip. Then place an order of sliced strawberries that should be available.

By now, this head waiter got nervous and flagged the restaurant manager.

Until now, the staff did not know my position or name, a privilege only available on the first visit!

The manager took over, wanting to know what exactly I had in mind with all this cooking stuff. You are out of strawberry zabaglione, so I thought I will make my own.

"The chef must not have the ingredients," he protested with his best authority.

Ingredients are as follows. Wine, I have here to use mine from the bottle. Sugar is in this jar. Eggs you must have! All that is missing are the tools, a stainless-steel bowl, a whisk, and a heat source, and I was told that there is Sterno. The rest is elbow grease and skill. At that point, I gave him my business card!

He must have had a minor stroke, for he turned white, lost blood from his face, and had to take a deep breath to compose himself. After apologizing to no end, I waved him closer and asked him if anyone knew how to make it. "I suppose the Sous Chef must know." You see, this was handled by the lead cook so far, and he had overstepped his boundaries. Being told by the waiter, this was a regular occurrence. Then the Chef had to train cooks in this procedure or take it off the menu. Not your fault. You tried your best to cover a deficiency. The Chef has to answer for this in the end.

Union, you know, each person doing a job! "Thank you." Relieved, he told me he would speak to the sous chef to see if he would do it.

About eight minutes later, the waiter served their version of strawberry zabaglione as I ate scrambled, sugared eggs sitting on top of strawberries, trying not to reject it!

"This does not look like you had described earlier," my tablemates commented.

They do not know how to make it. It is that simple. None of the crew's fault. This is on the Chef's tab. It will be added to my schedule!

* * * * * * *

Breakfast was uneventful. Coffee was an upgrade from the standard brands and showed that this hotel ran independently of corporate SOPs.

Women customers occupied the room and ordered items with yogurt and berries found great acceptance. French croissants, fluffy crispy, crusty French rolls, and Hero marmalade in portioned packages. Honey, bagels offered with cream cheese Schmier, a New York expression for spread, and optional smoked salmon. Cold cuts of smoked ham and cheese made an exciting menu choice.

Cosmopolitan New York City caters to the entire world. Indeed, different languages are spoken in the lobby, at the bar last night, and now at breakfast confirmed this.

I took notice of the service efficiency too. It was a different place now. Prompt, friendly service from a primarily female staff created a warm and cozy atmosphere. The hostess pointed me out as the corporate guy after being served. Still, it made no noticeable difference to this seasoned server, for they have high-profile executives and Broadway performers in here all the time.

By about 9:00 a.m., the Food and Beverage Director had joined me for coffee. He had eaten at home, so he said he had to fight the masses of commuters on the subway and make his way on foot from the nearest station.

It must be a daily hustle. Do you not get tired of it? I confessed that at one time, I was offered an Executive Chef's position via a recruiter to come to New York City. I turned him down!

"But why?" He wanted to know.

Because I grew up in a pristine German countryside village, and this would have killed me, simple as that.

"I grew up in the city and would not want to live elsewhere. So much excitement, activities, and the models, what a feast," he bragged! "I cannot see myself living anyplace else."

A young, charismatic man from an old hotel family welcomed me. We went to his office and looked in on the General Manager. He had just recently taken over from my RVP.

He requested to be briefed before departure on what I saw as the current concerns. "The hotel was not visited when going around as a team. For that reason, this is a recovery mission, seeking the issues from your side. It will be discussed before I leave if I see any during this visit."

I mentioned dinner and breakfast impressions. That was really all I had seen so far.

On to the F&B office. His secretary was chosen for her impeccable appearance. The comments he had made about models stuck in my mind. Skills would have to be proven in due time.

I asked him for a breakfast menu, complimented him on it, and asked him where his coffee came from. "A New York roaster. Here one can get everything. That is what is so nice about NYC."

Agreed. What influence does the corporate menu department exercise over the menu choices?

"None whatsoever! We do not give anything to corporate for approval, kind of work on our own."

How was the previous regional director handling this?

"We seldom got to see him. Once a year for budget review, and that is about it."

I begin to understand, but get ready, I will be much more involved. We all have a boss to report to, you understand!

"I suppose, but we want to keep what we have. All in the framework of the SOPs!"

"I will use your breakfast menu as a blueprint to impress changes on the hotels in my region. It will get the backing of the VP of Food and Beverage. His sign-off is needed, and the corporate test kitchen will produce the recipes and guidelines, quality specs, and recommendations for corporate purchasing. They will visit you soon to set up the process for them to get involved.

"I heard horrible stuff about them." I do not know of negative information, but I am also new. Purchasing is complex since they rely on purveyors to deliver the goods. "Can we exercise influence on which they choose?"

I suggest hearing them out and not pre-judging it. They handle sixty hotels now, have qualified buyers, and control procedures.

I instantly smelled a rat!

Now my dinner experience! I took it slow and aim and touched on the good and failures, injecting the reaction of my table partners.

This is what happens to the average customer off the street. Do you get hotel guests patronizing the restaurant?

"Basically, the first-night stays!"

What do you attribute this to?

"I do not know, but we have so many first-class restaurants in this city. They are preferred over hotel restaurants."

Unfortunately, this is the way in all hotels. We need to find a way to get them sold to come here, but first, you and the Chef need to fix the product. Incidents like the one with the dessert cannot be the norm. Further, the classic French menu better gets to be classic French food. It has ways to go before it meets the standard.

Long faced, he referred to the Chef.

Talk to me about him.

"He is of German descent, has a bunch of trophies in his office, and talks big. I am not a culinary-trained man, so I can hardly dispute his claims."

Okay, but how are his management skills? You know, does he train, teach his cooks to get better behind the range?

"I have never seen him behind the range. He does not get dirty, not that involved."

How about the kitchen organization, and product handling?

The company has specific procedures to handle and preserve delicate food, berries, leafy products, fresh fish, expensive meats, and recipe cards.

Are they in use?

"None of the above!"

Did you attend the corporate food training class and the management seminar?

"Only the management seminar for a week. The food class was closed due to a hotel opening, and these folks had to be there to open up the property."

Has he ever gone through this?

"No, never, but I do not really know."

How is the Sous Chef?

"He is from Jamaica, has a hardworking ethic, and is used as the workhorse by the Chef. He does not get any training either, just gets thrown into the job here, sink or swim."

That points most problems to the Executive Chef!

We tour, and then we can meet with the Chef. Tell him we will see him in the kitchen and make himself available.

The tour started in the catering area office on the lobby floor. A sharp-looking woman was managing this department.

She answered all questions with knowledge and confidence. "Oh, we do not have a problem with space. We own the room. We cater to high-end social businesses, weddings every weekend, fashion shows, corporate thank-you parties, and award celebrations."

"Socialites must show off the latest hairstyles, makeup, and perfume. Tomorrow, Coco Chanel will do a kickoff reception to introduce a new line of fragrances, Eau de toilettes, for women and men. The first French perfume company is breaking into the men's market. It is promised to be grand. Jennifer Garner will start as the spokesperson.

The entire world of models and agencies will attend. Everyone wants to get their picture in the fashion magazines."

I suppose this is an event you will supervise, Henry. As I looked him in the eyes, he smiled.

Then there was a quick and substantial response from the DOC Elizabeth. "He just needs to stay out of the way. We will handle this internally. We do not need obstacles!"

He blushed as it obviously had to do with chasing models for personal attention.

Thank you for your time. I can see this department is in good hands. We will chat another time! Good success tomorrow.

The tour of the kitchen started in the lowest areas of the building. Receiving is found in an awkward place, then there was a fish butcher. He was the only one authorized by the union for this job, then the chicken butcher, the same story there. Well, at least they had the separation of highly perishable and bacteria-rich food. Flashbacks from the operation in New Delhi brought a laugh. To whet it, I told him the story. "You must tell me more about this place. I am sure that there are stories!"

First this, now the meats. Pork and beef were in one unit. I spoke to the butcher. A knowledgeable man knew his specs and started to show that the primal loin part was too fatty. It had a spec that called for this measurement, and that fat thickness and the ends had to be squared and not angled. All contributed to waste and loss. This stuff was worthless and had to be discarded. A look at a worrying face confirmed my suspicion.

"There is our fireman!"

What exactly is his function?

"He will start the ovens in the kitchen and bakery and heat up the ranges. Then at the end of his shift, he goes home, and another man comes to turn all that cooking equipment off. Union protection since the days of coal-fired stoves and ovens. We cannot lay him off. The union will go on strike. You do not want to meet the shop steward or his boss. Mafia controlled, they specialize in fabricating custom-fit shoes, cement shoes!"

Thanks for the warning. The whole picture started to appear. The union had gotten too strong over the years, nibbled away on hotel controls, and written it into the contacts and labeled, past practice!

Have you tried to talk sense to these union managers?"

"Yes but got nowhere!"

This is now stuck in my brain. Every problem has its solution! The issue was that these guys did not personally own this hotel, for if their own money were at stake, the approach to such problems would be different. I knew, telling this to myself. I made a mental note to explore it further.

Now to the bakery, which had the nicest space I had seen so far. The baker produces all the breakfast bread, lunch and dinner rolls, banquet orders, pies, and other items about rising dough requiring baking. " His day, or shall I say, his night starts at two a.m., and he works until eight a.m., Henry explained." "It is six hours because he does not get to take any breaks. Therefore, the hour union meal break is taken off the total work hours, and they also have four fifteen-minute breaks by the contract."

Okay, I understand.

"He works alone, and when the dough is ready for baking or baked goods ready to come out of the oven, he has to do the duty."

I do not have a problem with it for as long as it has been documented and given to the union as an exception. When and if a second person is working with him, this exception seizes to exist.

Has that been done?

"No, it was not done!"

How long has this been in force?

"It is now three months."

You have a job to do. Document the reasons, the problem it had created, and the solution was collectively worked out on a test basis. You are now ready to make it firm as an exception-only status. Add this in plain language that this is only in force for the duration of the one-baker class.

And that it cannot be integrated into any future contract. Verbally, you will emphasize that this was not something the hotel was ever bound to consent to. But in the interest of fairness and work conditions, this was worked out to preserve harmony in the workplace.

"What you do not tell him is that the Pastry Chef started at seven a.m. due to his public transport schedule, and he wanted to have the bakery space to himself. The baker working his total eight hours had, in fact, created a conflict and handicapped his productivity.

If you do this right, by all means, engage the GM in it. It may give you an opening to start a dialogue with the union outside of contract negotiations. This tough-guy profile they project is a front for a normal human being.

"Do you have anything in mind?"

I briefly touched on the service issue in Barbados. "Nothing specific, but once planted in my brain, I tend to think of it until a light goes on with a potential solution. I made him see that every problem, no matter how difficult, in reality, has a solution.

I would think if you can find small little issues where a hotel's long-standing and outdated policy is in effect and, in reality, makes the workers do it just because but not for any good reason,

You can propose to give this to the worker and not give up anything. In exchange, you ask from the union to disband stubborn rules of no value to the workers but costly to the business.

Scratch my back, and I scratch yours!

Suspiciously and reluctantly, he agreed to look into it. You must do more than look into it. You do not take your car to the mechanic for him to look at only. He needs to fix it! I will come up for a visit when I have a bright idea.

The Chef was waiting as it had taken longer; he looked angry. My apologies, for this place has so much history. Let us sit down someplace quiet.

The conversation quickly got on to the dinner last night. He did not have any apologies but defended the action of being out, was his right to exercise. That was a stiff position he took.

I let him talk, thinking of handing him the rope. An undertone of a threat was in the air.

He went on to talk significant about his experience and accomplishments, pointing to the trophies, naming hotels in the city, and being able to work in any of the premier hotels anytime he wished. Going further, he ventured into skills he had. He said the kitchen management had never been better, and he personally trained all the cooks in classic French cuisine. That was huge!

Now I had the floor. Where in Germany did you do your apprenticeship?

"Never worked in Europe. Was born here, I hardly speak the language."

Then where did you start your culinary training; you know, the first job?

He hesitated at first but knew he had to produce something. He named a place that was no longer in existence a large restaurant and banquet/wedding hall in the Bronx.

Was the Chef there a French Chef? He rolled his eyes and showed his annoyance, then he made up a name and lied about it, his eyes moving to the side.

I changed the subject and told him things about me and our shared aim.

"This restaurant does not get its fair share of the hundreds of guests in the rooms. We are actually bad-mouthed by the bellman. They would fear the loss of tips if the guest had an unpleasant experience, like I had, as you may know. He wanted to defend the dessert, but I cut him off. This is not the biggest problem we have.

The menu is not classic French cuisine and not classy overall. It is pretentious!

I was trained by Chefs of enormous stature in this field, and I know well what it takes to get to this level. We will never reach that plateau. So why produce that if it is not in your comfort zone.

Mix it with the up-and-coming new trendy food and do this exceptionally well? To dramatize it, I said! You are better off preparing the best hamburger in town and doing these consistently than something fancy half-assed! Do you get my point!

By now, I had considerable anger built up and had lost my appetite to go on with this phony Chef.

I have to go now. We will continue some other time.

Leaving the kitchen, I asked Henry at what time he came to work every day. Ten a.m. was his routine, and when would he leave? 4:00 p.m. sharp? He had to catch the Long Island train. That is six hours, and today he came in early, but we did not get with him until close to 11:00 a.m. That was the reason for his mood.

We went out for lunch to a little café with great crusty bread sandwiches and a beer. Now was the time to reflect on the past events.

Henry said that this had never happened before here. "It was straight but honest, and anyone that cannot handle this has a problem with honesty."

Good, Henry, I am glad you see it that way. Now I want to go to one of the restaurants you lose your hotel guests to."

There are many, something French.

Okay, La Grenouille on such and such street. It was within walking distance.

"Do they serve other stuff than frog legs?" I joked "I sure hope so."

****

The restaurant had been hailed as one of the best and most prestigious in the French food category. The bellman also spoke highly of it as, by chance, the same man who checked me in recognized me and asked where I was headed. With his assurance, I walked the streets of New York once again. The last time had been at my landing by sea voyage when I first immigrated.

New York has changed immensely. Gone were the low-level five-story buildings and had been replaced with skyscrapers, modern street markings, and new shops with super fancy show windows that made one think, *Can I even afford to set foot into this place?* The streets and avenues crossed one another.

A hostess greeted and seated me while she had a good look at my business suit. "Is it from Brooks Brothers or custom-made?" Nothing was remarked, of course, for her facial expression spoke volumes.

My table backed against a service station: waiters chatting in French, with noise mixed in with glassware, under-liner dishes made ready for good service, silverware to be replaced in between courses, and the glassware ringing when touching one another on the tray lined up, prepared for the trip to the table.

I reflected on the fact that a single customer would always get a lousy table no matter in a hotel or freestanding restaurant. Things are just never changing! Then the server in the classic server's uniform in black with a bowtie offered the menu to me and explained that this menu was prix fixe and would be served with four courses at $65. Beverages were extra. "One can choose from a few items in each course category, and here is the wine list."

"Do you serve wine by the glass?"

"Oui, monsieur. We do have a house wine."

"Can you tell me what label it is?"

"It is a French table wine, red, rose, or white!"

I noticed sweetbreads as the hot appetizer, and veal caught my eye. "I will take the white wine svpl."

"I will be a minute for the food selection." As usual, the entire menu choice received my scrutiny.

I was looking to refresh the selections of a genuinely French restaurant compared to the hotel's choices!

"My selection settled on the Ris de veau in a vodka sauce and dill, a soup to start with perhaps the consommé, the main course Jarret de veau au jus, and pommes dauphinoise with the legume du jour. Dessert I will do later!"

"Very well, I'll get this on order."

The kitchen sounds traveled to this station, all in French kitchen terminology, en command, the term *Bien cuit*, and other loud-sounding words without reference to any sentences. This got me thinking of the time in Zurich.

The soup tasted delicious. A concentrated clear broth with finely diced vegetables. Then the sweet bread, a gland harvested from a milk-feeding calf, soft and tender with flaky texture, all delicious, embellished with the sauce that had fine threads of fresh dill.

The main course was a cut from the hind shank, half of the leg as a generous part had been browned at first for roasting flavor, then finished in the braising method with a mirepoix and deglazed with wine and stock to soft cook this muscle meat.

the enticing aroma came from the various herbs and wine in the jus. "Absolutely delicious." These cooks and the chef were indeed skilled in their craft and mastered the fine cuisine of France.

"Dessert?" was the question from the server.

"Crème Brulé svpl. espresso?"

"Sorry, we don't have this kind of coffee. We are French, you know. Café press, perhaps?"

"Yes, avec crème!"

A delicious experience, great food, expertly prepared, a bit noisy behind since the servers openly discussed in French the various attributes and lesser ones, the anticipation of the extra tips from each of their tables, mine included. I thought that this was the only negative aspect of otherwise having experienced a perfect meal.

Now the bill. I handed the server my Visa card, and he disappeared.

Shortly after that, a French woman in her late fifties, I guessed, quickly said directly, "We do not accept Visa! Do you have an American Express card?"

"No, I do not have one with me, and I do not carry enough cash, for this is New York," implying the street security situation.

"What are we going to do?" she growled.

"Why will you not accept Visa? It is a card that is more popular and accepted worldwide. There was no choice like offering to leave behind my watch, driver's license, green card, and visa card; all received a flat no. "I will pay my bill. Just give me a way to get either cash from a bank or ATM."

"No, nothing. You will stay here until this bill is paid."

"I will leave without paying now, come back tomorrow, and settle. You cannot hold me as a prisoner. Do you want me to wash dishes and work off this debt?" I added with more sarcasm.

"We will call the police!"

"Go ahead. The officer will at least listen to my predicament and your uncompromising statements!"

I finally pulled my business card and explained my mission with the hotel at Central Park, the position I had with this hotel company, and that I would try to get the hotel to pay on my behalf. At the same time, they could post this charge to my room's account.

She had to process this and consulted my server, who actively spoke to her in French, obviously to salvage his tip, if at all possible, despite the gratuity included in the $65 price tag. When at last, a light came on in her brain, she took my card and placed a phone call to the hotel front desk. This took about ten minutes, a long time to wait; this situation has created a spectacle in this restaurant and drawn the attention of surrounding tables.

"Agreed. The hotel will send a check, and you are free to go." No apology, no good night, and I were unsure if a tip was added. Glad to be out of here. This entire experience of a great meal just had been ruined by this arrogant woman!

I went to the front desk to apologize and thanked them for bailing me out of jail, as it seemed. We were secured, and he was a company man. The night manager had handled it and knew from the reservation and registration plus the imprint of the credit card that this was a no-brainer.

He asked me about the food, which I described with high praise. "Yes, I have eaten there, and I wish we could produce such quality, and then we could actually get people in there.

The question comes up daily: the guest just checked in and did not want to venture into town for dinner. A hotel's safety is much more preferred, but when we get negative comments, it is hard to send them in there."

"I am in full agreement. I had my own dilemma on the first night."

"I heard about this dessert issue. Was that you? How funny!"

We chatted a bit longer and compared people we knew from past employment. "This is a small world, once inside a hotel job and getting around." He knew people in San Diego. He had been a front-desk clerk, just starting out, and wanted to go surfing in Huntington Beach. Others came to the surface in a roundabout way. Nice man. Very personable and friendly, the right man for this position.

Chapter 13

The last stop was in Southern Connecticut. The hotel did not have the familiar look of a company hotel. It looked stark, and cold from the outside. Too much raw concrete, or was it painted in that tone?

First impressions, I thought!

The General Manager was out of town. The Food and Beverage director took me on a tour of the

facility, restaurant, bar, and banquet rooms in progress to get set up with meeting tables, cloth, and water jugs on each table.

Then the back of the house eventually reached the kitchen! Hello to the Chef and Sous Chef, both on duty early in the day. "Busy day ahead, not so much, but he was covering to free up time for me and be available for talks" Nice, thank you" I motioned to the Sous Chef and received a smile back.

"No problem, sir!"

It was too late for breakfast and early to check in the room. "A full house last night," he mentioned.

"Nice, typical business travelers, we have large corporations here, and most traffic comes from them. On weekends we clear out."

This means the meeting space is used for meetings, luncheons, cocktail parties, and an occasional dinner. The restaurant should be a busy breakfast place, and on the nights when meeting participants are on a free night, how do you capture them for dinner? I asked.

"Some mostly go for cheap fast food to make the per diem last. Our prices are high and no coffee shop as an alternative."

I know New England is cold and wet for six months, but the summer has some warm days into fall.

I see you have this terrace. For what is it used?

"Mainly outdoor cocktail parties before dinner or heavy hors d'oeuvres to make it a meal."

Have you ever thought about setting up a grill station with a Weber gas grill on nights when you lose them to the town? They have to share cabs, walking is too far, and here you offer the all-American favorite food, priced affordably, but keep them in-house. You have a chance to sell a beer or soft drink as well.

"Hmm, never thought about this. What do you think of this idea, Chef?"

"Great, can be done. Just let me buy the grill. It has to have some power to generate the heat."

I took a look at the menu. "This does not look like the standard company menu. Is this your creation, Chef?

"Yes," he said proudly. I have been around the block and want to feature specialties of mine. A Chef needs to have this freedom."

I understand. I have been a Chef for years.

A company, and especially this company, has developed a sophisticated system with recipe cards at its core, a control chart to manage measured quantities, forecast for restaurant volume to aid the Chef and kitchen in managing a complex process. We have this system to prevent costly mistakes, minimize waste, and manage food production to get a good product on the plate.

"I know all this, and I went to these classes at headquarters, but I never got comfortable with all this paperwork and control procedure. I am more hands-on! It makes me feel like a clerk, not the Chef."

The F&B director, Robert, just rolled his eyes. This man was a handful and too much for him.

The short time in this position put him at the disadvantage, I knew what to expect during the upcoming kitchen inspection.

The following inspection took a different tone I am concentrating on the system only in part, giving the Chef relief, for he was expecting a grilling, but it never came.

My focus was now on sanitation. I took it thoroughly, item by item, scrutinized the mops, all showing the wear and never receiving thorough bleaching. I checked the sanitizing procedures in every area and found the same neglect. The overall impression at first was that there was much room for improvement. All the Temperatures are off, and basic rules are ignored.

I thanked the Chef for his time and left without another word.

Robert took a deep breath in his office and said, "This was an eye-opener. I knew he was sloppy and pointed out much of this when I first took the job. He bullied me." What do you young punks know of this business? Go through what I have done, and then talk to me.

A tactic of intimidation, but we had to harness this man, or his career would be short-lived.

"Any Chef change is difficult. The good ones have a position they will not leave, and finding one is tricky."

Do not concern yourself with it. Concern yourself with the way the department is operated.

I illustrated how the Chef in southern New Jersey ran the kitchen by the book: the system ran it for him. He was not flamboyant, just a former food production manager who was given the helm to continue what he had been doing, just on a broader scope.

The company has these kinds of people; they are created by vigorous training.

I looked at the number 2 in that hotel; he would make a great Chef for a place like this once it was set up with all the tools. Still not strong enough to take over a place as we have here now. That will require a team of corporate trainers to turn this ship around."

You were thrown into this job, with little support from the GM and no support from my predecessor or the regional?

"I am afraid that is all true!"

We take a break. I can check-in. You want to catch up on calls and papers. Let's meet for lunch at one p.m."

I had to catch up on a ton of notes from this morning. Too much is wrong here. It cannot go on for long, or we will face some kind of health disaster, a time bomb is in my hands. It requires meticulous documentation to the smallest detail. It will cost the Chef the job, but he is practicing this bully type of intimidation and still cannot organize a kitchen. We cannot tolerate this.

I had called the director of catering to join us for lunch.

Shelly came to the table smiling, expressing confidence and calm! An attractive woman in her late twenties had made the switch unexpected from sales to catering. These transfers usually go the other way. She could not realize her ambitions by just selling rooms and small groups.

"We have almost no competition within a fifty-mile distance.

The location is in the heart of the industrial park, which drives the hotel's income."

She asked for ideas to fill the vacant Sundays.

"Those are the toughest days in this area"

I must confess to being caught off guard right now. I will keep my ears open, and if I find a solution for it, gladly, I will pass on the information.

Her diligent effort to improve sales run into a dead end. "What can I do you do in this situation?"

I would take a good look at your rates. Supply and demand are the regulators of the rate. Rentals, drink prices, menu prices, AV setups, and whatever make money with can yield an incremental revenue boost. Be cautious with getting too aggressive and attempt to disguise it as a package if possible."

"Tell me more, please."

I listed the ideas I had discussed in other hotels and examined the beverage sales, bar pricing policy, and wine sales.

You will find ample opportunities to enhance the revenue for your department.

Weddings are an open purse. The bride wants the most beautiful wedding, which I have difficulty seeing as rational.

I am too logical and practical.

'Did your wife not have the most?"

I will tell you later about my wedding.

You can engage a wedding planner to pick their brain. They are much closer to the family and can sniff out what can be added for added value and revenue.

"You have great ideas. I want to spend more time with you and learn."

Here is another idea. Do you have these civic functions, the fundraisers, the chamber of commerce, you know, when the event sells tickets to companies and individuals?

"Yes, mostly on weekend for fundraisers or midweek for the corporate chamber type."

We received the food orders and soft beverages. Nicely and efficiently served by a young man. He was unobtrusive, quietly placing the food in front of each and then seemingly disappearing. He was within reach, just not visible but stayed within distance.

Now, I have to tell you a story. "Oh, good, I like stories." She smiled contagiously. This woman is a charmer and so easy to communicate with. She keeps an open mind.

Hartford Connecticut, the sister city in the north and state capital, has a civic center. The Whalers hockey team made it their home.

I received my chance to hang up my Chef's apron and change it for a business suit. I will give you the short version, okay?

We needed to move out a good amount of wine. It had been at risk of spoiling, and for this, we developed this idea.

We structured the menu for these events to sell wines à la carte. A small wine list, glasses pre-set, and a discount on the price you get. The key to creating the time to sell is the starter food.

Combining the appetizer of a cold variety with the dinner salad on a dinner plate and preset the plates gave the servers about twenty minutes to transact the wine sales and service.

Tables were hosted by a company that pressured the boss to spring for the wine, and on tables with mixed people, the one with the taste for a glass of wine equally could not just buy himself a bottle. He had to offer it.

That was often shared when somebody else bought the second round.

Servers poured the wine to the rim. While it is technically incorrect, it served the purpose that whatever number of bottles was ordered did not fill all glasses. One or two glasses did not get their fair share. They came back for more, more sales! A rapid cork extractor had been mounted on a banquet table, and all bottles left the area open, ready to pour.

Then came the food, served from trays and Escoffier dishes with covers, and the cash-out took place after dessert during the speeches or just before.

"Brilliant idea; there is a ton of money to be made.

"Now you have to tell me what the problem was at that hotel!"

Okay, but the short version, no pauses and time wasters.

The short version was about the food arriving cold at the tables.

Going on with the details, I was finally arrived at the conclusion. I got applause from both table partners.

We left the room, and I told Robert, "Hang on to her. She will get stolen otherwise. Treat her special, she is. We will have a suitable opportunity when the time comes. She is outgrowing this facility.

Robert, you have your work cut out. I would recommend scheduling a slow kitchen day to perform a spring cleaning. Get bleach, a grease cutter, rubber gloves, and eye protection. Then tell the Chef, Sous Chef, and a bunch of cooks from the top-ranking down to come in old cloth or give old cooks' pants and jackets and tear this kitchen apart. After that first cleanup, it will be to the kitchen crew to keep it clean.

"Clean as you go will be the slogan after that."

"I will be in touch.

On the flight back, I was able to fully relax. I fell asleep for a quick power nap. Then my thoughts focused on the week, realizing that this kind of business trip was physically and mentally exhausting.

For a moment, I was confused, thinking I was going to another hotel.

No, it was Friday. The weekends is mine at home, or was it?

Should I go in for a couple of hours on Saturday to get a head start or skip it and leave it to next week? There were no trips on my schedule for the next two weeks. I will have enough time to get all this done.

My son gave me a great welcome when I entered the home, and he announced that we were building a boat. A boat? I do not have any idea how this is done!

"Oh, do not worry. I can tell you tomorrow."

The wife had a home-cooked meal ready, Swiss items, and what a difference after a week of restaurant food; there is nothing better than a home-cooked meal, no matter how good the restaurant!

After a solid night's rest, Bircher Muesli for breakfast and Gevalia coffee it made me feel that is life worth living!

Sonny, as we nicknamed him, demanded the attention.

He verbally described the steps to build the boat.

"We need wood, glue, nails, a saw, and then we do it." The process was so clear to him; I wondered where he got the idea? His description and words did not seem all that clear or easy.

I started to get the supplies from a hardware shop and needed the tools, for I was not a handyman since anything past an electric wall plate was a challenge to me.

"It has to hold both of us and must be that long," as he marked it off in the grass. "Then we need this thing to steer in the back."

What about Mami?

"Oh no, she is afraid. She will not get in it."

"My thinking of the back is a square piece of wood that matches the height of the sideboards." So far, so good,

The boy helped me as we progressed, but when he noticed that the front did not reach a sharp point, he started to rebel and became emotional.

"This is not a boat. It will not be good enough."

I am sorry, but I am not a boat builder or a carpenter. It takes special skills, and I do not know how this is done. I had to exercise authority to get him calmed down.

The boat was built as-is, and waterproofing was yet another challenge. What can we use? "The hardware store has this white stuff in a large tube. We get some now."

I used the salesman on the floor in the paint department to recommend the best suitable material. He gave me two tubes and a gun and a quick instruction.

He could read the novice approach, so he did his duty to help me. It took another trip to the store for two more tubes since the boards had significant gaps that needed to be filled.

Once done, Sonny wanted to go into the water.

Wait, this has to dry first, one or two days, and then it should be watertight.

"But then it will be Monday," he protested!

We will take it in the water next weekend.

"Can we do it after school? You are not traveling next week!"

He made it a point to keep track of my schedule.

Yes, we will do that.

I hoped it would work; I looked it over every evening when he was in bed, added paint, and double-sealed all seams. I finally felt satisfies and assured. A huge rock fell off my shoulder.

Finally, the launch!

A ceremony with a make-believe champagne bottle and a name had to be part of it.

I had been curious where he was getting these ideas. His mother finally disclosed that a TV movie of a father, a ship captain, had built a dinghy for his son and did a launch and all that went with it.

The boat worked, and he had bought plastic oars and started to row on the lake while he pretended to be the captain. "Papa, you are the motor, and I am in charge!"

A mountain of papers welcomed me to the office and needed processing.

Writing my reports would be the toughest of all. I did not have the support of a Maya. It depressed me to think just how I would maneuver this.

I shared the secretary with another regional director. He is a Southern veteran and acted like a bully to assure his priority status,

"He is the new kid;" I overheard him saying." Besides, he is the outsider", something he had not yet accepted.

Then there was the issue with my English writing, clear sentence structures and constantly slipping into my mother language plus spelling errors.

The aid of laptops or desktop computers was slowly making an appearance at the secretaries stations. Priority was given by seniority.

* * * * * * *

The RVP called a meeting with all directors to get the feedback before he embarked on his solo trip to the hotels. He could not wait for the detailed report, but it would be grand if the information would be ready in time for his arrival in New York by midweek.

I saw it as my opening to muscle these reports on the front burner by using his deadline.

At the briefing everybody had ten minutes to cover the most pressing issues.

I did my best to condense and cram it in this period, skipping on details and outlining the core problems only.

Then the VP of food and beverage crossed my path on the way back to my office space.

He had the urgent desire to hear me in person! His time was generous. He wanted the details and analytical thinking. When a solution came into the reporting dialogue, he paid meticulous attention to it, took notes, and promised support where his involvement was needed.

With a smile, he added, "I knew you could handle this job and brings new ideas into the company. Thank you. Good job."

Now came the moment I feared to tackle.

The enormous pile of reports, memos, and less critical general informational papers needed my attention.

The department had been growing, and with each added position, the need to produce paperwork had increased. CC to everybody to justify the job. Every director had this issue and hated it as I did. Was there a solution? We had to bring this up at the next regional meeting.

These paper pushers must be streamlined and funneled to only the pertinent recipient. If a hotel from the region is involved, then only to this director, skipping all others.

I called my secretary to inform her of my time restraint. I pointed out the need to rewrite the languages, and if she felt to alter the wording to make the point better, she should go ahead and do it.

She assured me, that my handwriting was better than that of Donald and she can read between the lines. Since the language is more or less the same, She had done y this job for years and adjusted to numerous new children. It was her term for the people she serviced.

"Now this pile. What is in it, then how much had to be answered ASAP?" She must have an idea since she would receive it and then distribute it to the two offices.

"Oh yes, this pile is growing weekly. Donald hates it too and spends up to half the morning reading it and settling whatever needs a quick reply.

We can make three piles. I will help you prioritizing it.

One pile will be reading only. It's the lowest priority and you can take it on a trip and read on the plane or hotel room.

A pile for the time-sensitive stuff, and you will see that there is precious little Give it a half-hour to handle. And so, the mountain just got dismantled. To just one more small pile for signature only."

"Thank you, Tina. Now have a look at my handwriting."

"No problem. You should see the handwriting of my second child," as she liked to refer to us.

Tina, in her fifty-five years, had spent years in this company. She had earned seniority like no other but preferred to stay in the trenches. "There is more action, and that is fun to me."

Writing the reports flowed easily from my pencil,

Thanks to the detailed notes; it was a re-written with complete sentences. Maya could have just taken my notes and written the reports for me. My disciplined habit from the days of catering in Hartford came in handy and saved time and headaches. I will be writing these reports, hopefully, more positive ones in the future.

The seniority of Tina rewarded her with receiving a computer with Word processing, easy corrections, and spell-check, and even pointed out the structural errors for corrections. She was fast and correct, the mark of a professional secretary.

"I can still do shorthand if you prefer to dictate." I was not trained to speak the words. I had to see it on paper and be able to rewrite it. For that, I used pencils.

Finished with all of them, Tina commented that she had no problems with my writing and then said that she had not seen a report with such honesty and a direct approach to the issues. It would be interesting how the veterans would react. I was sure that Charles would distribute it to all F&B regionals. He liked this style; it must be the German way!

The reaction was prompt. My regional teammates reading the issues also faced problems in these hotels. They remarked about the speedy completion of the reports, themselves still laboring with the same mountain of paperwork and complaining about it.

I referred my colleagues to the Tina system, a process needed to receive a patent or copyright, I said kiddingly.

By now, it was lunchtime at the company's cafeteria. On my way down, I bumped into Charles and, shortly after that, the CEO and owner of the corporation. The son of the corporation's founder had taken this company from family restaurants to a hotel chain. Indeed a great man, if not an outright genius!

Charles stopped to greet him and introduce me. He gave me a warm welcome and wished me great success.

He turned to Charles and said, "Now, promise me one thing. For every German, you must hire one American." This was meant as a tease and in good spirit

Both men laughed about it, he went toward the elevators. But before he disappeared, he said, "A word to remind you.

"Your foremost duty to the company is to carry forward the spirit in the people program."

Charles elaborated on this during lunch, gave me advice on the content of the reports, and asked me to tone down and soften the approach.

"I am all for it to call it as it is, but I learned a lesson from my first report that had ruffled the feathers of a general manager. He took issue and caused a wave of problems for me as I lost his support on the property."

Was it in Springfield?

"How did you guess?"

Just looking at this man told me all I need to know.

"You are very perceptive," he added.

When one works with people like I did in catering, many characters cross the path, and lessons are learned. It will be a strong trait.

Lunch was simple and fast, but I wanted his guidance now.

I am currently looking at my schedule, what is my best approach to accomplish these topics? Keep me in the loop on all developments. First reactions on the property will guide you in the right direction. Follow your instinct.

"It is always good to use to work through the General Manager. Follow the protocol. Do not deviate from it. In the case of Southern Connecticut, this man did not give me the time of day; he had made himself unavailable. If he is not available, then say your regrets in the report."

"What are you planning next?"

First I will follow-up with a phone call to the F&Bs, then measure the progress, if any are accomplishing. It will be different in all hotels.

Then there is much to be learned about the addition in Barbados, the restaurant concept, menu, product sourcing, a Chef change, and then making an action plan for each subject matter by hotel.

After I to go out in the field again. Issues must be taken to a conclusion. I have a handle on the characters I am working with and will learn more in the following days.

Budgeting is in the not-too-distant future. Here is another soft spot to dig in my heels. It will be new to me, meaning to be on the other side of the table.

"Good. You are on the right track. You will do well."

Thanks for the confidence in me.

It was a time to bond with all the support departments, I T, folks who computerized the SOPs, and recipe cards, then the first responders to a hotel getting ready to breathe life into it.

A new man by the position of corporate executive chef was introduced by a VP of Systems and support.

His name is Toni, another German, but Charles had filled the American quota first with support staffing in the Beverage section.

I approached Rob on the wine by the glass initiative. He jumped on it and wanted to go chain wide.

I suggested to him that he should prepare a presentation for the regional directors' meeting and then read the temperature. Differences of opinion had to be expected; all of my colleagues came out of a hotel or restaurant operation.

"Do not take this as a rebuke. These ideas sometimes have to gain their support. Try to bring it as a question, lead them to the answer, and then when this perks up from one or more, I will jump on the bandwagon. "Great talking to you; we will get along fine."

The menu department has been run by a single woman, Genevieve. She had free rain, efficient, and all by the book was her approach. When

I made my introduction to start the conversation for the Barbados specialty restaurant, she looked lost, did not know how to handle it, and brushed it off.

Thinking that she may want to consult with her superior, I backed off and left it as a question!

A young man introduced himself as the department's recruiter in the hallway. We chatted a bit and exchanged our backgrounds.

"So, you are the new director!" his mission was to find new talents, go to colleges, and canvass the best potentials from the graduating ranks for entry-level assistant managers.

"Yes, we have something in common! I wish to give you a lead to an outstanding candidate, ready to jump ship."

"Great, can I have his name?"

"It is her, small but feisty. We worked together in Hartford, where she is still in the same position. She was my right-hand support.

She may have been promoted by now, and if not she will be a prime candidate. She will make you proud.

"I will drop off her name and address. You would want to approach her cautiously, for this hotel's work climate is explosive. She keeps me abreast.

"I am going to the college in Springfield, close to this address, and I will call her at home."

Do this in the evening. I will give her a heads-up.

The VP in charge of all these support technicians asks me about the Connecticut hotel and the Chef.

The first order I left them was to clean up the kitchen and have it spic and span. Only from that basis can I work a plan forward; for that, I have ideas in my head.

For my next visit, I want to get a menu revision from the menu department for implementation. This will give the F&B director the control. I will back him since the GM can in not be bothered with F&B issues.

Can we go ahead with the menu change?

"Yes, by all means, it will be the test for him to comply, especially with an invitation to spend a few days at a kitchen run by the book.

"Either he joins or may even quit. Preempting a termination! I think the latter, so we need to look at potential candidates soon."

"Touching on the other initiatives, I included the beverage department, restaurant services, the catering initiatives, and personalities."

"Oh yes, glad to get to this. I am looking for a suitable Catering person to lead this area from here. This is long overdue.

"Now for the last but not least.. Can you lead me to Maggie's office?"

Hi. "Right there. What a surprise! So glad to see you again! How is your tennis?"

Nothing happening, no time, no partner, all work, and no play.

"We have to work on that the first chance we have."

A few properties can benefit from your expertise in training.

"Oh, good, where and what in particular?"

"The property in Northern New Jersey has issues with the GM. Every department is suffering due to his overzealous conduct and then terrorizing them about every little thing he can dig up on his time on property, which is all the time.

I explained how everyone in management looked tired, lacked sleep, and just being there but not managing.

"The RVP will be there this week on Wednesday and addresses this issue. Not sure what the outcome will be but expect dramatic actions.

"Sometime after that, we must put these people back on track. That is where I can make a solid contribution."

What better way to rebuild a team that by stunning women with charisma, smarts, and skills to teach the basics in management and form a team together again.

"I am so flattered by this. Gladly will work up a proposal for the RVP to review.

Now we had a bit of time to talk about personal stuff. "How is your son?"

I gave her the scenario of building the boat and how he had seen it in his head but could not explain it thoroughly. "He has imagination. Let him grow on with this. It will be the foundation of his future!"

She wanted to get something off her chest.

It seemed as if she talked about the relationship with this man who organized tennis tournaments for the ATP.

"He is never home. It left only time for the break-in December to spend time together! I cannot travel with him and hold my job that I adore. I also like my freedom, and there seems no happy medium. I know he loves what he is doing, traveling the world, rubbing elbows with the world's best tennis stars. It is all exciting, and I understand this."

"I am sorry to throw this at you. I suppose I need someone to listen, cry on his shoulder, and get it off my chest! Everybody needs that at times."

Glad to be of service, and I could not wish for a nicer person to dry her tears on my shoulder. Any time. I mean it.

"Stop it. You make me laugh!" We hugged and went back to the grind.

* * * * * * *

On the home front, my wife received an urgent call from Switzerland; a cousin let her know of her mother's failing health. Not knowing the cause, she knew that for time she had problems but was, in general, a difficult person to obey doctor's orders. "Be prepared," she had said, "and look into a flight."

By Friday, it had been the end; she had passed away and now needed to get a funeral and estate to be settled. The funeral home practically handled most arrangements. "We can organize the funeral preparation and notify the Austrian relatives, set a time and date for the final service. Can you be here by Tuesday?"

"I looked into the flight, and the best direct flight is from Dulles Airport on Sunday evening. I will arrive in Zurich on Monday morning. Can you get me there, please?"

"Of course, I will take you to the airport and pick you up when you return. I just need the carrier and flight number and times."

That being done, the home arrangements had to be organized. Our son had to go to school, and for that reason, I altered my schedule.

Superiors received a call to advise of the schedule change. "I will still come to work once he is on his way to school.

The school received my contact information. I will have to leave early to be home in time for his coming home from school.

All this arranged, the wife took off en route to Zurich!

She hoped getting everything settled within a week. Only the closest family members were in attendance, and a funeral was without fanfare.

Mother had been living alone in an apartment with minimal possessions. Sign here, sign there, and the death certificate will be recorded with the AHV, the Swiss pension agency. Releasing the apartment and vacating the personal possessions only took half a day. She rented a car and drove to Germany to hopefully unload whatever stuff had sentimental value: pictures and things from her youth.

All this happened like clockwork.

My parents granted her wish to take her belongings to the attic.

Her stay was short; her flight returned her on Sunday morning to Dulles Airport, Washington DC.

* * * * * * *

She never took a job despite promises. If one could not get a job in this economy, I did not know why. Simply not making the effort. I started to look into her daily activity and found printed material about the same religious order she had joined in Hartford.

Bad news, a fight was going to be inevitable. I let it go for now. The boy seemed to have rejected it. He made no mention of these people. She must have kept them away from home and did it secretly. Fear that the kid would tell on her. He had taken to me now bonding with every free moment and always having something lined up for spending our free time together.

My travel schedule had to be copied for his time tracking. Additionally, he wanted to have a contact phone number whenever and wherever my traveled took me, including Barbados.

Something was up! How can I find out more?

During this week, taking care of my son, was guided by the arrival of the school bus.

I recognized a woman in the neighborhood from work. *Is she with this IT group?*

We were going to work at the same hour, and she came to my cubicle to propose carpooling. "We are three women that share the driving duties. It would be nice of you could join us." I thought of it, and the savings would be large. These women wanted to have a man to drive on rainy days and winter. I agreed.

We set the time for pick up at my door since I was the last one on the trip. "One of us is the menu girl, you know her, she is farther away but parks her car at my house right around the corner. Glenda, the third one, lives in this neighborhood, and we work together in the IT group.

"Now we have you Treb, Ginny, Glenda, and Tracy. Here is a list of home numbers. Let me have yours and do tell your wife. No scenes with the rolling pin please" She giggled!

No, this will not be that case!

My rationale for joining had a second plan. Driving solo tended to have me leave the house before the son went to school and without breakfast, and always in a hurry to get to work.

That timing will change. In the evening, I must return home on their schedule, which will make me leave at a regular time also.

A sense of normalcy is achieved.

"Tracy will keep the rotation, and when you travel, it will reset without you for that time. Of course, one phone call to me is enough whenever anything surfaced out of the ordinary. Tracy is the captain of the group."

Carpooling had been encouraged with posters around the building. Parking was always at a premium. The company was growing, and staff additions further put pressure to relieve the situation. Word spread quickly on the floor. "Three young women in your carpool! How are you going to handle this?"

Croissants," I replied. "Feed them, and they stay quiet, I said jokingly!

Now off to the races on a Tuesday shuttle flight; I started at the Jersey hotels again. In the South, the task would be easy, with a check up on them and a progress report.

The Chef continued his fine work, corrected minor items, and was fine example. I asked him a favor. Would you be willing to host the Connecticut Chef to demonstrate how the kitchen runs like a model operation?

"Yes, I would gladly do so. Is he open-minded?"

That much I cannot guarantee. It will depend on the progress he needs to complete by this week. Nothing is written in stone at this moment! I will make it a condition.

Catering followed through on all suggestions. The numbers will show by the end of the month, in small amounts. It will accumulate with time. Thank you for your efforts.

The restaurant manager was nervous. He had started to apologize when the F&B director cut him short.

"We have not implemented the wine-by-the-glass program for reasons that we fear to suffer much spoilage, do not have the means to refill the opened bottles with gas to preserve the wine.

Is that your best excuse? Does the GM back you on this?

"He is not in the loop at this moment."

"I realize I cannot force you to do it unless the corporation will issue a directive chain-wide. Let me, however, give you a fair warning. The new beverage director has been briefed and will support it enthusiastically. He is preparing a presentation for all regionals at the next meeting. The VP is for it.

It just needs to be structured with an SOP. So here is a heads-up. "I will wait for the SOP. I don't want to stick my neck out!"

After that, I took a tour and did what is better known as *the people's program.*

Shaking hands, acknowledging the excellent work, and inquiring about well-being and fair treatment became essential part of a hotel visit for the director.

They look up to me. I must be a good example. Employees are introverts and speak only when asked to speak or asked for an answer. Others on the opposite side gladly shook my hand, chatted freely, asked me questions, and were highly informative. This is a way to take the temperature of an operation.

I made a mental note for the GM debriefing.

I drove to my problem child in Northern New Jersey. I would stay overnight this time and have a look at the rooftop restaurant.

The RVP had been here, the resident manager is in charge. The action taken by the RVP had been swift and decisive.

I quickly learned that the GM is forced to take a one-month vacation and is ordered to take two solid days off weekly thereafter. Any violation had to be reported by the controller.

"We have not gotten around to implementing what had been discussed. This GM situation just consumed us. Bravo to the regional's decisive actions" You should take a day off now.

"No, no, I am already energized by today's action. Go on. We lost time the last visit. He was a different man now."

We have to get into this visit down and dirty and catch up on lost time!"

We started with the tour. I took the time to start the people's program; therefore it took much longer.

The hourly employees showed relief, not knowing the details, but word travels fast.

The coffee shop looked tired and dated: a counter with a soda fountain like a drugstore, then the tables beaten up, and waitresses in old-fashioned uniforms distinctly projected a dislike to wearing it.

The expectation was that I could snap my fingers and wish it away. I would include it in my report, but this was a significant expenditure that needed sign-off from above, the red tape like in the government. You could understand that only the company owner would get it done with the snap of a finger. "Yes, of course, I just gave it a shot!"

The kitchen I had seen in good shape remained this way. No real issues, but after I shook hands with the cooks and dishwashers, I had to be the boss after all and find something.

Just like the health inspector, I canvassed all critical areas. Yes, there was one. Now on to my second spot to find slime for sure. The ice machine did not disappoint me but caused long faces on the Chef, DOC, Restaurant manager, and F&B director. "You know your spots," he remarked.

You just learned something, follow through form this day on!

The catering director took my proposal on wine sales whenever the occasion presented itself. Weekday demand from the corporate market left little or no space open.

There are opportunities to massage the rates, add value to meeting rooms, and have coffee breaks.

Doing away with the well-brands and reworking your bar program. With the short distance to New York City, the rates could reflect the prices in the city, not as high, but an adjustment would not be an issue.

Make sure you show the added value and service. The customer always wants to look good in front of his audience. Remember that, always. It is a doctrine.

"I thought we had this department so tight no more could be squeezed from it. Now you have opened our minds."

Take a trip to the city and roam around a hotel. You will be amazed at what you see and learn. I do that and pretend I am a manager, walk into the back of the house, and ask questions.

I took a break to write my notes in even more detail. I wanted to get the secretary to the point as Maggie was, just write the reports by taking my notes and getting her into my mind and be thinking alike.

We meet for cocktails upstairs and then have dinner if you are still okay?

I need a stiff one!

By 6:30, we met up in the lounge at a cocktail table. I would have preferred the bar, for there is always where straight talk took place. Just not in front of their boss.

He chose a table designated for an attractive cocktail server." Suzy"

I ordered a Negroni cocktail served up.

While Suzy was unfamiliar with it, the bartender had mixed the perfect cocktail with gin, sweet vermouth, Campari, and a lemon twist. I always liked to get an aperitif-style drink.

He had bourbon on the rocks, and specified Jack Daniels.

We talked on the lighter side, personal stories, and that sort of small talk, but in this conversation, I mentioned how I introduced this wine by the glass and wine sales by the bottle in the Hartford Hotel.

He noticed this and wanted to know how it turned out and the details. "Are we allowed to do this?"

Can anyone take it as a negative-selling wine, add it to the dinner tab, and create a new bar clientele?

"I suppose it is worth the try."

I was pleased with how quickly he took the bait. *No worry*, I thought. He bought in already.

He noticed my lack of enthusiasm about the menu. The food came out well prepared, it had just lacked charisma. The menu had the corporate signature but failed to point to any signature item.

A Steak house by concept, yet I asked him. *Where is the beef?*

Modest volume despite a full house and a great view of Manhattan's skyline.

Dinner as a steak house theme was really off the mark.

"What can we do without corporate involvement?"

Let us analyze it from a culinary perspective. You have good meat. The trim can be improved. All this stuff at the bottom of the sirloin steak is too chewy to consume, and it gets left behind. A prudent customer sees this as being part of the steak but inedible'

You give a starch, baked potato with all the trimmings and the potato must be a sixty count?

"Yes, it is!" Eyes rolling, he told me he just got confirmation of my knowledge to food specifications.

"The salad is excellent and crisp with the basics in place. I would say that you could offer to mix the dressing in a large bowl with the lettuce and then dish it out tableside.

Give a little extra attention and all the sauce will be clinging to the leaves.

Vegetables had to be ordered separately. This concept of vegetables à la carte is outdated and does not supply a balanced meal.

Yes, never mind that Americans do not eat vegetables. How can they if they never get any, and if it's ordered extra, it comes straight out of the water, no seasoning, no special prep to enhance the flavor. The Chef and cooks need to learn the preparation of vegetables, and this stuff has color to garnish the plate. It is delicious and contrasts with the potato and meat if prepared with love.

Does this make sense? You do not need corporate approval. Stay with the menu, cut off the grizzle, and serve a generous part of compatible vegetables.

Add different weights of the sirloin steaks, the same meat at a larger price. It will make the Carnivores happy.

Then I was itching to tell the Hartford story. Always the Hartford example, I see now just how much I had carried out at that hotel.

The restaurant was dying, with no flair, no business. The hotel guest went across the street for an inferior meal. I searched for a solution and ran into walls with no restrictions from the company or GM; the customers did not bite.

Then one day, I realized that the menu was like any in the city's freestanding restaurants. Better presentation and better preparations did not get the recognition they deserved. I had no salesmen inside the hotel, the bellman!

I rewrote the menu, leaving from the everyday items available everywhere. I relied on my international repertoire and mixed a selection from every corner of the world known to me, always featuring the most popular items.

Intensive training of the cooks and servers had to learn the ingredients, and cooking methods, and choose words to generate a mouthwatering description. It was a huge effort getting everything ready to introduce this menu.

I staged a publicity stunt since the marketing guy did not want to distribute any advertising money to it. I made the food section with the menu and descriptions of items, great exposure of publicity. The food critics noted this and checked out the restaurant in due time.

Meanwhile, I coerced the assistant engineer to fabricate a steamer, a rimmed dish the size of an eight-inch bamboo steamer. It was easy to tap into a steam pipe.

Now the bamboo basket got filled with standard vegetables, bite-size, cut in the bias: carrots, zucchini, cauliflower, peapods, Bok choy, Napa cabbage, and red bell peppers; for an array of colors.

One basket per table is presented and served by the server. The rest came back, and since it had not been touched, it was reusable.

The menu featured food from Spain, Italy, and Greece; the Balkans with appetizers, Central Europe food like Swiss and German, Wiener Schnitzel from Austria, Northern seafood again as an appetizer like Graved Lachs, Asian food appetizers, and main courses, chicken pakora appetizer, chicken curry, Japanese noodle dish, Indonesian satay with peanut sauce, Polynesian dishes from the South Seas with coconut milk and flakes, tropical fruit garnish, and when available, we garnished with edible flowers.

Paul's jaw dropped, then remarked that I took a big gamble. I had a free hand, but I had convinced the GM that I could solve problems. "What was that?" he wanted to know.

That is going to be told on another rainy day! It just so happened that it had started to rain that evening! But you see, I had done my homework and researched the hotel guest's profile. People from all walks of life and more from other countries came to do business with these conglomerate insurance companies: Aetna, the Hartford and Connecticut General. I had a clientele that knew all these dishes on the menu. The trick was to deliver a consistent, genuine product. It was a calculated risk, and it paid off.

Now I had to find a way to get the servers comfortable with a new wine list, equally diversified and hard to pronounce. This challenge was attacked by introducing one wine only at a training session. They had to pronounce it, repeat it individually, and then receive a short description of what a guest could expect with the first sip. Fruity, dry, oaky, and all the simple nuances a wine would get as a description! Then they tasted the wine; their mouth was watering, searching for the described flavors and qualities.

We also added a one dollar per bottle bonus and a contest for the most sold bottles receiving a nice bottle of wine to take home.

I was right with my prediction. This was the only wine being sold this night and the following night. They had been intimidated by the name and product itself and had never tasted any such fine wines before; it was a revelation.

Then came the second bottle, and so forth! It caught on. They made money, and the house-made sales and profit.

Paul looked at me with amazement. "How did you get away without any local New England food?"

"We had it but featured primary seafood items, lobster, scrod, clams, shrimp, but because these items had to be fresh and live in the case of a lobster, we presented it as "today we have just come in" item, then the preparation description. We also took the prices up. A low-priced restaurant is seen as mediocre, not worth the try, and certainly not the place to entertain clients. This way, we bought short and wanted to be sure that we ran out."

"Run out?" Yes, we called it **86,** a code internally used to communicate to the servers.

Yes, that was the lure to come in again the next day and further communicate the freshness effect. Sometimes the customer wants to be fooled.

"I can learn much from you. My mind is open now. I want to have a success story."

It is in your hands. Commit to a plan, take advice, seek input, and sell it to the staff. They are your salesmen. Speaking of a salesperson, I almost forgot how I sold the bellhops on the menu by invitation and served them a meal on the day off.

Bring your wife, mistress, or girlfriend. Make it a special evening, I told them. These guys talk and have a captive audience on the way to the room. Once sold, the restaurant got filled. What a powerful sales force! But wait on this until your product is top-notch.

Dessert was offered on a tray featuring a selection of cakes. No, thank you. I pass! "You have to try this!" The chocolate cake is divine."

I am stuffed, thank you.

Let me tell you what would sell me.

After a heavy dinner with significant portions, of red meat you feel stuffed. Only a real dessert can tempt me now.

It needs components to become a taste teaser: something soft, a custard, simple pudding, or mousse, add fruit, berries colorful and acidic, and something crispy and crunchy and a dab of unsweetened whipped cream.

Components can be bought. You won't need a bakery or pastry cook it could just be a unique cookie, add a flavor from a liqueur in one of the items If this is composed and creatively arranged, it will cost less than this cake from a bakery, which charges sixteen dollars. But never mind the cost.

The most expensive dessert is the one not getting sold! "

"How do you figure that out?"

If you take this cake at sixteen dollars. In the beginning, with all pieces still on the tray, your cost is 100 percent. That is what you paid. Every slice sold reduces the cost by the sales price. Now take a four-dollar price for dessert. With four pieces, you have reached zero food cost. For now, the cake is paid.

Add more sales and now you are making a profit. When the last piece is sold, bingo, there is a profit of twenty-four dollars assuming ten portions!"

"Interesting calculation!"

Just another angle, but of course, you will not sell out tonight. It is simply too slow.

On the other concept, you have components. Pudding is simple enough; then you have strawberries for breakfast. They are here, and if not used, find another buyer in the morning, the crunchy stuff. Make it easy. Buy the crème-filled cigar wafers, whipped cream, topping, and Triple Sec. All of these components are here, still usable the next day, and therefore, the calculation is based on an item cost of purchase or production in the kitchen.

"That was an informative evening. I wish you could spend another day."

Me too. However, I have a tough nut to crack at the NYC hotel, the one at Central Park.

"What is going on there?"

Union, old bad habits will choke us if not faced off! I will have to tell you another time. I am going in with a hunch and a plan, which is all I will say for now. You take a good day off. Take your wife to dinner and try to see it through my eyes.

"I have a new perspective."

"The RVP has sent out a bulletin to his team announcing the action at this hotel. Nobody is allowed to contact the General Manager until his return. After that, there will never be any mention to this day. He has to gain face again, reestablish his position, and then earn the respect of his managers. As the RVP, he will communicate with the GM and coach him on wellness. All written reports come to me, and I will disburse them as proper.

He is like a wounded animal; at that stage, they are vulnerable yet also dangerous to themselves. Strictly confidential and to be shredded or burned after reading!"

He is a no-nonsense man, I had to admit, yet he showed compassion and the desire to turn a bad situation around for the benefit of the individual and the company. A lesson learned and a good night's rest was in order.

* * * * * * *

The trip to the city had started early to mitigate the traffic and to be able to secure a parking spot. The park house in this block had served me before, and the parking valets would take the vehicle there and back within a reasonable time. Cost is something one cannot weigh; it is what it is. Getting access is more important. The trip was a nonissue; arriving as planned had paid off. The doorman just started his shift and promptly took care of this process, all for a twenty in the palm of his hand. Then the hotel porters arrived to take my baggage.

"Is it going to have to be stored in our secure room?"

I am not sure yet if I get room to stay over.

"Oh no, do you want me to check on it? I can do something for you!"

He was fishing for a tip, a very handsome tip if he could coerce the front desk to walk someone and place me. No, I have to play by the rules. I work for the company.

I handed him my card, and as he glanced at it, a tip was for the storage. "I will get you a tag stub to claim whenever a decision comes about."

I noticed the catering director crossing the lobby to the adjacent banquet room. She waved me over to get a look.

A very ornate room with fancy crown molding, sophisticated wallpaper, and a massive chandelier in the center illuminated with soft candle-shaped lights. It looked like a social function was getting ready.

"Here is one of these socialites' events, a children's hospital fundraiser. This room is sold out. Too bad that the larger ballroom is already booked for a corporate group. It is a crazy day with all that is going on."

I will not be in your way. We do not need to meet. My schedule is in a different direction. Is the banquet Chef able to handle all this business? I am sure it will be sophisticated food.

"The food is simple. The aim is to keep the price tag low and maximize the net for the charity. But Willy is a super guy. No matter how crazy it gets, he keeps his cool, he is incredibly talented, committed to his craft, and works independently of the main kitchen, thank God. He is a lifesaver!"

I made a notation of his name in my notebook. "Do not steal him away from me, please. We are a team," she pleaded.

No worry. One does not fix what is not broken!

I went to the restaurant for breakfast, and again the difference in the atmosphere created by the happy faces and the manager personally doing the seating at the start was so noticeable compared to the dinner shift. I quickly glanced at the reservation book to see if any evening booking had so far been recorded.

Since she had minutes, we talked about the dinner reservation recording procedure.

Is the front desk taking it? How about the PBX personal? And does it get tallied up at the end of the night?

She had all the answers since she had been a p.m. server and often covered the door. While we chatted, she kept an eye on the entrance and motioned the closest server to fill in for her for the moment of her not covering the door. I will not keep you long. Just one more question. How is the communication between a.m. and p.m.?

"We get along, having worked for him for some time. I know the way he operates."

Do you keep a shift log from a.m. to p.m. and vice versa to communicate information pertinent to the meal period?

"Not really, I should say. I do leave him notes since we take reservations as the only location. There are many special requests and VIP notifications from above."

Who takes over in the between time?"

"The bartender does. He is conscientious, a service partner of mine while working the night shift.

You are getting busy, but if there is time later is uncertain, for my mission is unpredictable today. But I have enjoyed this chat and hope for more. Thank you.

This room had small tables and none near the kitchen entrance; thanks, at least we do not have this problem. I took my time to eat, knowing the arrival time of the Chef and F&B director. Only Henry and the General Manager Frank knew about my visit.

I was reading the *New York Times* available in one of these handles, two wooden sticks clamping the paper in the centerfolds for easy handling. Very European, the *Wall Street* and *New York Post* got active users from single customers.

My table was close to the door. I noticed that she had used the name to greet every guest. She knew names and used them freely in a formal way. "Mr. Jones, we have a great morning for you today." "We always enjoy your way of getting me to a good start." These could not be regulars that came in four times a week

She had the gift of remembering names, which makes her very personal. I need to clone her; She was the epitome of attention to detail.

The data I received from the F&B office confirmed the huge draw she got from the in-house guests. "We have a jewel in her" was my opening statement even before I could say good morning to Henry.

"Yes, she is good. Treat her special. She has a future in the company."

"She is now in my book and starting to develop a backup."

She is doing this already. She does not want to leave the room naked (her expression of no door covering) if she ever misses a day for illness or weather. The day off is already getting a similar treat!"

How does the restaurant manager treat her? I felt the need to tie up this conversation on the way up.

"Okay, there are no real problems, but he is jealous of her popularity, and she gets a good share of tips, much more than him, and deservingly so!"

The admin arrived at the executive office and waved us into the GM's office. He received a heads-up on my mission; he opened up, expressed concerns, and cautioned me to be careful. I proceeded to outline the plan in detail, actually more than I had planned at first, but he demanded to know and had little knowledge of how a kitchen worked.

I explained procurement, the product flow, meat trim, and part control systems.

"But how are you going to be able to prove anything?"

With luck and a poker face that may not be necessary, but push comes to shove, it can be calculated from yield records, my training from the first profession as a butcher in Germany, and also cutting all the meats while I was Executive Chef. An audit trail will surface that the product had been consumed.

"You lost me," both confessed.

No worry, I have it in hand, nothing is forgotten in this territory. I feel quite at home in it. Speak the lingo and know the character of the players.

Then off into the arena torero. The bull was waiting but not knowing that we were coming, I hope. "No, it had been kept tight." Good. The element of surprise is always a warrior's first weapon.

The Chef sat in his office with coffee. It looked as if he had just arrived at work; by now, it was 10:30 a.m.

Good morning, Chef. Would you have time to spend with us?

"It is a hectic day!" Henry interjected.

The banquet Chef has it under control, and most of it is in the evening, implying it is past his work time.

The first and most important high-profile event is over by now. This is the in-between time. It should not take hours, I said. With uninterrupted time, we will be all right.

His face said it all—guilt. *What are these coons up to now? I do not trust this Kraut bastard*, all that was written on his face!

I started. "This situation in the butcher shop with the union demanding that these people keep the position, weather there is work for them or not, is really against the law of economics.

"Yes," he agreed, "but what can we do?"

We can be extra nice to them!

"How so? What do you mean? Explain, please!"

What if we tell them they do not have to come to work? They will get the paycheck sent to their home address. That way, they are avoiding the hassle of commuting and save the cost of it on top!

He needed to think this over before answering.

"But why would the hotel want to do this? There is a benefit to it for the hotel. Let me name it.

The facility has to be kept by engineering, constant machinery breakdown, and this stuff is not getting younger. Then we have to keep the lights on; extra energy for cooling and freezers, cleaning products, and employee meals are what come to mind off the top of my head.

"Well, yes, there is constant machinery breakdown. The freezer is about to crash, and so is the buffalo chopper. I was going to ask for that to get replaced. A total failure would cause a lot of spoilage on a weekend when the shop is unattended."

So, do you think we can sell it to them?

"You must know, I cannot speak for them."

"But what about the union?"

Why would they object? The men stay on the payroll, accumulate benefits, and deduct the union fee. Nothing changes but for them to stay home.

"Okay, now who is going to do the work?"

None of the company's hotels have butcher shops.

Those older hotels started with a shop, abandoned it, and turned it into storage. Never have enough of that, right? The meat we buy, and use can be bought in portions and manageable quantities, and we won't need a jobber to pick up the waste!

Naming the jobber provoked a reaction in his eyes that did not get lost on me. Now I knew that I was on the right track. This jobber played a significant role in what I suspected to be a ring to apprehend the meats and fish delivered but never reaching the kitchen, for the orders had all been overstated.

"But this inferior quality. We will not get the aging and specialty cuts. Can they be on order as such?"

Explain specialty cuts. "We do have requests in the evening to cut certain-size steaks, sometimes eighteen ounces and even twenty-four ounces, like the steak houses do. We must keep pace with them, or they steal all the business!"

That can be handled by the Sous Chef, who does it now, I guess! Get one or two strip loins one by one, and trim them for these particular cuts. The quality you are getting now is only USDA choice, yield grade 4, really nothing special.

"You know your meats."

My first profession was a butcher, but more than what butchers do here. In Germany, we also make sausages, ham, salami, dry-cured beef, and ham, all starting with killing the animals and slaughtering, you know?

"I have never been to Germany and do not relate to it." Should you go there and research your roots?

"Corporate procurement is preparing to assume the entire purchasing function. You will have that monkey off your back!

"No problem doing this. I have done it for a long time, It's second nature, you know. It gets to be a routine like tying the shoelaces."

We look at the purchasing power of these area hotels that can yield much better prices. Quality control comes with it, and computer records are up-and-coming.

He was running out of reasons to stem the tide. It is not multiple choice. You and I are midgets to try and talk them out of it.

Imagine there will be eighty hotels, and everyone does their buying: what a diversified product and quality specs we will have. Today's Chefs, yes we still call them Chefs, are production managers working with the company's system that is getting computerized as we speak. I carpool with these women, so I know firsthand where they stand.

By now, he had started to sweat. His comfort zone was being dismantled.

Now, while we are on the subject of system, can you tell me the product flow as it happens right now!

"I do not understand product flow!"

I know that the kitchen food preparation is neither run on the company's system. There is no production planning, no commissary, no forecasting from the restaurant, and much more! You understand what I am talking about?

"Yes, I remember when the hotel integrated into this company. I was supposed to take part in this training at this Mickey Mouse kitchen in Washington. I got out of it, claiming not to have a competent backup, so the GM denied my attendance."

That is what I thought.

Now, let me explain what I mean by product flow.

Let us take the beef. The primal cut of the strip loin comes to the hotel, either with the rump attached or not, by selecting the order. It hangs in at walk-in, preferred with a steady temperature of 35 °F and an 80 percent humidity, right?

The butcher gets around to it after good aging (really a decomposing process in a controlled fashion to break down the muscle fibers).

He will test the tenderness by pressing his index finger into the lean cut at the front. Satisfied, he starts the deboning and trimming excess fat; then, he trims off all the tough cartilage at the bottom right above the bone line and the skin to cut left from the bones on the inside.

He has another trim to remove the dried-up front cut, and bingo, he now has a loin ready for cutting steaks.

Mignon and Chateau Bryant. Do you get this with the tenderloin in? Yes. Then this brings the first cut to peel out the tender, packed in tons of fat. He peels the fat and trims down to the silver skin.

So far, so good.

"Yes, go on!"

"The trimmed fat gets put aside for a jobber to pick up, and so goes the Cartledge. Unless the Chef wants it for beef stock. Does the butcher weigh this primal at the beginning, keep track of the amount was cut away? "I am not sure."

Don't you want to know the yield?

"It is always the same; doing it once in a while is good enough!"

Continuing his job, he now cuts New York strip steaks as listed on the menu or for a special request of a different weight, or a ten-ounce for banquets. Ten to twelve cuts are realized or yielded depending on the weight or yielded weight.

There is this word again. The predetermined quantity or whatever amounts he had cut, and I suppose he does not keep track of the count. He just sends it to the kitchen.

There it ends up on the grill as the orders are coming in. By the end of the day, the grill cook takes it back to the butcher shop, so the butcher knows what he needs to cut the next day. Am I on track? "Exactly!

The same procedure goes on with the chicken butcher, the fish butcher, and the pork. Just not that amount of trimming with pork and fish, but the chicken must be deboned. I do not think you buy half a pig.

"No, I am not crazy!"

Let me summarize this, for we did not come here to explain the function of meat handling. But old Henry just learned something. These office cats need to roll their sleeves and get into the trenches with you. Agreed?

"I say this all the time, but to get the fingernails dirty is already too much drama."

He was teasing and loosening, just as I wished!

"You see, Chef, the problem with your system is not only these guys hanging around there and not enough work. Idle hands get into trouble. Do you know the proverb?

The heart of the problem lies in the fact that there is no control. You do not know the number of steaks that got cut and ended up on the grill station and the count that comes back to the butcher shop after service.

However, we have a count on the steaks sold. The dupes with the orders are now turned into Henry. He must do something to pass his time,

I said light-headedly, keeping the tension at bay.

"You rely on the integrity of the butcher safeguarding this noble cut of meat. Any animal has only two sides, so a bull's yield is maximal twenty-four to twenty-six steaks.

Don't you think this deserves a little more care and security? What if the grill cooks take a steak a couple of times a week when he returns the unsold steaks? It is on the way to his locker. What a great opportunity!

"I know he does not do it," he protested.

"How do you know? Tell me. It is only by your trust in his honesty. An opportunity has turned many persons into pickpockets, thieves, and burglars. We lock our houses and cars, secure the money in the bank, and take the jewelry to the safe. Need I say more? "I suppose so."

We have done an audit on this meat situation. We now know that not all the meat that enters the shops below is getting sold. A yield calculation of the total quantity we buy does not match the selling records. Yes, this man has been busy lately.

Now the final blow! His head was now starting to glow. *Good, this is working.*

Since we know, substantial amounts of meats are leaving the back door. I mean a whole lot! He started to say something, but I preempted his word.

We figure about 59 percent of the meat we are paying for never makes it to the kitchen, neither gets cut nor unpacked and ends up on a truck owned by the jobber. He has a perfect disguise to get hold of this stuff, refrigeration on the truck for the fat, and room for the property going south.

He is a union guy; we know this. He also goes around the little joints, greasy spoon cafeterias, roach coaches, individually owned fast-food joints, and even renowned restaurants bragging about their aged meat. We cannot rule out the occasional steak disappearing from the returns, for we have no system of control.

We are capable of delivering hard proof.

Now, all this stuff can be orchestrated below, but not without the person determining the quantities to purchase. The calculation to set up this value is simple. We know the yield; the rest is a matter of computing the numbers.

By now, the sweat was running down his face.

"Do you still want to defend it here or wish to call a lawyer, for we are ready to press charges, lock you up in jail, and mark you as a felon for life? You will never work anyplace else!

"I do not want to call a lawyer. What I want to know is what will happen with a confession."

"We will not press charges; you will lose your job. The company's pension is the 401(k)is yours, except for the unvested part. You will have to sign a release not to use defamatory language against the hotel and the company, and lastly, you will fire these guys down there for the same reason, including the storekeeper. This confrontation took place in front of the controller and Henry.

If you wish to have the shop steward present, for he secretly is you, we know this too.

He can come right now. I handed him the phone, but he turned it away.

Henry was sweating too, but for a different reason. He called the controller. He had been waiting for it, prepared the confession paper for signature, paid the time worked this week to the minute, and released the document with copies to the Chef, my file, the GM, corporate HR, RVP, and corporate F&B VP.

All documents had an original signature. This was overkill; however, I wanted to impress him that we were dead serious.

Then off to the dungeons. He was composed when we arrived and explained it in a short version, for these coons knew the gig too well. Then he stated the termination he was executing as his last function being the Executive Chef and also a union member, an assistant shop steward.

Security had been on standby to see that only the personal stuff was taken, then escorted to the back door and locked behind. The same procedure for the ex-Chef, taking his memorabilia and the trophies and being escorted out the front door! "Give us the name of the fund you want to transfer your 401(k) to; unless you wish to keep it as is, nothing will happen to it, just personal preference! Good luck: you will need it.

One last question in front of the doorman. "What about references?"

We will verify your time and employment position, nothing less, nothing more, okay.

I need a drink, never mind the time of day!

Back at the GM's office. "How did it go?"

He is out and with it the whole barrage downstairs. It was not that hard. I just had to go slow, point by point, coming to the climax. He gave us enough signals by turning up like a light bulb and sweating profusely. Confirmation to the end that we are tracking right.

"Great job. The union will have a cow. We will need to talk about strategy on this subject." Let us have lunch. I could kill for a great glass of wine!

The first sip is always the best! Food orders took little time; the person in charge knew where to seat us at a quiet table, and nobody seated nearby. She is such a detailed-oriented girl, easy on the eyes as well. I could not hold back a compliment about her to the table companions, nodding with agreement.

You have your work cut out, and for God's sake, milk it for all its worth!

The GM had tuned in at once. You just created incredible leverage for us, got rid of five bloodsuckers, and I chimed in one more to go, the fireman!"

"Right!" The F&B wanted to know how to go ahead with him. "We do not have a wish list?"

"You mean he will quit?"

Not in a million years. He is living in another world. The union will do the work for you.

Smiles from the GM, but he let me continue. "Now you have to use this leverage smartly. Be the nice guy, more smiles.

The GM was now reading my mind while the F&B guy needed to be taken to the water to drink.

The union had just received a blow right into their guts. They are smart enough that we could have taken this all the way to publicity about union theft. The media would embellish the story to dramatize it, something the union could not afford in a time when memberships are shrinking, and big corporations are taking them on to Deunionize thousands of workers. A weak position! They had their time for too long!

A predator seeks the weakest prey, nothing different from human nature.

Call for a meeting, place a recorder on the table, but do not turn it on. It is just a prop that may be needed.

Have the controller there in a formal boardroom setting. You know the shop steward will be accompanied by his boss, the president, or whatever title they grab. Offer coffee, Danish, candies, and the work, make them feel comfortable.

In a low-key fashion, the hotel is looking for a way forward! We do not want to bust the union, but what happened has happened for the worst reasons. To recruit an executive manager underhanded is the worst of all, besides the thousands or millions of product pilfering.

We do not want to know the time it all started. It makes us vomit, discussing it. The union turned a blind eye to it or may have even enjoyed our dry-aged steaks? The noise of protest! We do not know, and now that it is over, we close the books on it, take a hard lesson, and implement controls.

The company has it all worked out. A procurement company will take over the purchasing, and we do not expect any interruptions, Will we? Oh yes, it will be hands-off!

The next thing is to ask them to establish a friendlier version of hotel-union relations. The first gesture is your first move! Do you want to offer a concession to us? Thinking, no answer. "Let me give you a hint.

We still are and have been paying for a position protected by you in food and beverage. Oh yes, the fireman! Do the right thing, will you? Take care of him! He will have to come off the payroll, but you put him on a pension. He is the age and has been for a long time.

"Okay, agreed"

Now, we still hold a bunch of IOUs in our hands. Think about reparations towards the hotel and the past practice items you are intimately involved with.

The noble thing is 'it's better to give than to receive.' It will make you feel good. We are glad to accept but hate to be beggars. Get back to us when you have had the time to review.

"One last point! Nature has it in your organization to get even, in that case with the man that exposed this crime. We did not prosecute this action for reasons we need to run a business, nor are we vindictive by nature. We are seeking a friendly working relationship. We all have a living to make, so your vendetta better not be directed using a contract from a sister branch against him or his family.

A word of caution, he is well-connected. His son is a Navy SEAL and is particularly good at the trigger aside from the legal profession he is now pursuing. He has the full transcript on a device like this (pointing to the recording device). The confession and release documents are in his safe with an upgraded life insurance policy."

With this stroke, the hotel took over the employees' care and policies. Future contract negotiations should be a conference of reasonable minds for the better of the employees and employer.

I did not stay overnight. I drove to Connecticut, hoping I would not get walked to another hotel.

I was arriving after 10:00 p.m. a time when the hotel released the unused reservations that had so far not show up. I went to the bar for red wine, now available as a Cabernet Sauvignon. The count was four; therefore, giving a comp to the regional director was safe. The bartender was complimentary about how fast the wine was selling. "I guess the chef will inherit the jug of wine for cooking," he joked.

"Better satisfaction, never just one glass, more revenue, and a 20 percent-plus tip. I love it. Most guests had never had a choice of this quality, totally delighted, dragged in their travel companion, and even ended up in the restaurant.

I had overslept; total relaxation and adrenaline draining out of my veins had caught up with me.

I skipped breakfast, hoping for a Danish offering and, of course, the coffee.

The F&B director enthusiastically reported on all that had been carried out. "The kitchen is deep clean, although hard work had turned the entire operation around! The cooks are happy, motivated, and eager to meet with you. Yes, they have asked for a meeting, can we? Of course, it is like the people, all part of the job."

Then he went on to the wine by the glass. I never imagined it to be so easy; it sold itself.

Good products usually do! I kept my comments low-key, still showing fatigue from the day before. Then he started to tell me about catering. "But wait, that is her show. She deserves the credit."

"A noble gesture," I mentioned, "low-key."

"Are you okay. You do not seem to be yourself?"

The Catering director came to the office at once and started to tell us all she had done. "Thank you so much for your ideas. I will make my bonus now." Her infectious bubbly personality perked me up, and I smiled, hugged her, and promised to do some more brainstorming.

"I tell you what I had gone through! You know the hotel in New York, the only Union Hotel in the company and that in NYC!"

By giving the short version, I could see how he quickly followed me and, at times, jumped ahead of the dialogue. "You did a fantastic job. How did you pull it off?"

I had my butcher experience to draw on, used it to establish a solid professional base and not give him an inch to escape.

Further, I can put on a poker face to short-circuit it without having to show documentation, a big bluff. Then the experience from Minneapolis when I had a similar situation, not to this scale, but in principle the same, so I had to clean house.

You know how satisfying it is when someone gets fired, loses the job and livelihood, and now has to go home and confess to the little woman, and yet he thanks you!

"Very gratifying! Are you a monster?"

No, I am a nice guy, just never cross me, and then the devil in me awakens!

The Chef gladly accepted the compliments, was fired up, and asked me how he could catch up on what he so blatantly ignored during food training.

With the hotel's permission and yours, I can set up for you to spend a week with the Chef in Southern NJ. You come prepared. I thought of it on my follow-up visit. He is glad to teach you the system and show you its benefits, consistent product quality, cost, no waste factors, happy customers, happy bosses, and a happy wife, for you can now take two days off. But challenging and persistent work comes first. The rewards after that are constant.

With this, let us take a hard look at the menu. Take off all the intensive items that have quality fluctuations. You have the sales counts for high-cost items that do not sell. Then suggest to the menu department and back anything that is not a recipe at this time with a recipe in the company's format and do a test with weight and measurements.

Now is the GM here? "Yes?"

Then I would like to meet him and report on progress.

He was friendly upfront but just a facade. In his heart, he hated the company that came out in the way he spoke in all negative terms. I kept the meeting short, just a courtesy call, and planned my return trip home hours early.

Chapter 14

At home again, my son gravitated toward me, wanted to know where I was, and had to show it on the map. By now, he had become familiar, for it had become a routine.

So far. Did you drive the car?

I had to fly. I showed him NY, then drive to this place, then to this place, then to here, and lastly to here, then back to the airport. All this engaged him with great interest. I showed this location on a different map with details of the airport.

"Then what did you have to do there? Did you cook?"

I laughed. "No, honey, I am a manager, and now the job is different. I have to inspect the kitchen to see if it is clean, then I have to go and meet with every employee and shake hands.

"That is a lot of hands!"

The innocence of a child is just fantastic. The imagination produced at that age as I took a quick flashback had gotten me to become a culinary-trained cook with the ultimate goal to be a Chef.

I told him that the cooks were stealing meat in this hotel here. "Did you put them in jail?"

"No, but the punishment is far worse than jail."

"What did you do?"

I made sure that they lost the job. If someone goes to jail, he gets food from the jail, and the government must buy this food. After losing the job, he was now without a paycheck and had to tell his wife that she better get a job so they could eat, and it will be hard to find another job.

"Yes," he said. That is real punishment."

Nobody wants a thief!

"I know what you mean," he said as he pointed to his mother.

"Let us have dinner. Mami cooked a fine meal. Her cooking skills are exceptional, inherited from her mother, and never disappointed any of us."

I decided to let them know that I would have to go to the office, hoping to return by 2:00 p.m.

She was disappointed but understanding once she heard the details of the NY action.

* * * * * * *

I need to write up something. I do not believe the secretary can summarize the entire conversation as I showed her the tape. Besides, I want to put this into the bank's safe deposit box along with the termination papers, confession, and release.

"Is there a danger?" One can never know." I am scared!"

Any attempts to harm us will trigger the FBI. I am taking precautions to pre-empt any reprisals.

Precaution that is all! Keep the child at home and don't go out alone.

"Should we go to Europe?"

Maybe a good idea as soon as school gets out!

On my desk, the office received an upgrade with the personal additions. The cubicles had to be shrunk, and I finally had an office with an inside window and door for privacy. A note from Charles had asked me to put time aside to meet with him and the RVP jointly to save time.

By now, the news had spread, as I could tell from the few who worked Saturday on a regular schedule. I had to excuse myself from not getting dragged into storytelling but getting my report completed. It would be another high-priority document. I left a note for the regional director to give me a priority and allow the secretary to write up this report.

I had not been abusing this since the first report; there should be no complaints. Fortunately, the secretary could take short notes in complete sentences, saving me precious time. After that, a look at the priority items and take care of signatures.

I knew the boss would call me to his office to report. I allowed extra time for this. I set aside the ones requiring a visit to an office.

Maggie had been in as well, came over when she had found out that I was here, hugged me, and wanted to know all about it. "We have to table this now as I am pressed for time. I have an appointment with my son."

"Good, have fun, but Monday, we need to plan out the training, and there is also a request of some urgency from the Barbados folks."

I love to do this. Meeting with you is a treat. I should be charged for it!

"You are, but payment can be done with trade." She winked her eye and threw a kiss.

* * * * * * *

Off to the most important appointment of the day. The boy had plans as expected. Hopefully not another boat or construction project! It was a surprise, he announced. "First, we go to the store to buy the tool, then we go to the park, and only then will I tell you the surprise. Mami will come also. She has to do a job."

He bought a soccer ball at the store, but I was not allowed to see it, and a whistle for the mother. All were hidden in a large paper bag. At the park, it was ceremoniously unpacked.

"Now you have to teach me to play soccer. Mami will be the referee. Here is your whistle. You need to use it when Papa fouls me, and then I get a free kick, okay?"

That will be fun. Let us go. It has been a long time since I played as a youngster his age, but one never loses the basic skills, just a little rusty. Basic ball handling and shooting got much of the practice. Dribbling is a skill he can practice independently and with other kids.

Then penalty kicks from an eleven-meter distance had been too far. His leg muscles would need to grow with playing the game, so we set it at six meters with me in the goal. That was fun. I made an honest effort, letting the corner shots inside the net. This was a good exercise for me too, and he and even the wife worked up a little sweat.

"I can join a team once I get better. We will do more of it every night on the neighborhood street, the backyard, or coming to the park."

If you can get some boys together, you can play a game and learn the rules. That will be great fun and good practice." I showed him moves he could practice on his own to learn ball control and use the backyard. A

206

makeshift goal would get built. "I can do this myself. Let us get the wood!"

Monday was my turn to drive the carpool. I asked my wife to bake up the frozen croissants for my carpool companions, always hungry, always starving for the sake of staying slim or, in one case, getting slim. Glenda was on a diet but complained that they do not work but, at the same time, have a sugar addiction.

I made my round to collect them and then returned home under the pretense that something was forgotten. My wife had been waiting for us and delivered the small pizza box to the passenger side. "Oh, pizza? Thank you. Goodbye."

"Have a safe ride!"

Open the box; it is for all of us. "Oh, my goodness, did you make this yourself?"

No, I have a wife for that. She got up early to give you a treat. Doubling up on it, I said, Now that is what I am married for!

"You chauvinist! That was not called for." They were laughing. The conversation got to full speed.

All in good fun. It was not meant that way, but she is a good cook and a great mother. So far, she has raised our son solo. Only now do I get to spend quality time with him; he loves every minute!

* * * * * * *

These women did not hear of the nuclear bomb that hit the NY Hotel.

Weekends were given, regular office hours on a steady pace unless a trip to a hotel opening broke the routine.

First on the agenda was the report to Tina. "Highest priority and watch out. It is a hot one. Do not burn your fingers on it. Joke!

Immediately the RVP and VP of food and beverage meeting began in Charles's office behind closed doors. His secretary of Asian descent had wide-open eyes, not knowing yet what was happening. She looked through the window. She tried to read the body language, but little was revealed. She must have expected fireworks.

I spoke calmly and was going through the report systematically, words spoken, going through the event from the start systematically, just as asked. I delivered it with every detail, reaction, and body expression to deliver the authentic flavor of this activity. They listened without interruption intensely like a child hears a new story for the first time.

I explained how I had built up my credibility from my earlier profession and hotel experiences.

When I arrived at the point when I let the cat out of the bag, it had to have a build-up to deliver the shock effect.

He lost his breath, sweating like a pig. It took him a moment to realize that he had lost his game. He was caught in the net of information presented with carefully selected words.

The controller ended the storekeeper with the dual reporting to accounting. The rest was easy, he confessed, papers read for signature, releases, and commitment for non-defaming conduct as I handed copies to them, the assurance of his 401(k) transfer if desired, and the promise not to engage in legal actions in return for a quiet departure.

Then I told him that until he left the hotel, he was still on the job, and there was something he had to do to these butchers, namely, to deliver the termination. He had been party to this and heard the exact reasons for the cause and pink slips issued at this very moment.

The GM, F&B, and Controller plan the follow-up with the union. Since they had been implicated in this action, their protest carried no weight and led them to volunteer to end the fireman. This man is now gone and will receive his Union pension.

Future relations would take on a different tone. A frequent meeting between the management and union would be conducted on a mutually beneficial basis, with the union making offerings to improve the climate and paying up on the IOUs, which are now in the hands of management. Let us examine past practices that tended to sneak into labor negotiations and tighten the rope on management. A long list is known to the union. That was what we were talking about paying back the IOUs.

The last advice then emphasized staying on top of this upper-hand leverage and never letting them get on top. Keeping this out of the assistant DA's hands and so not creating newsworthy material has long-lasting value. Never forget, as the Quebec license plate says.

"There you have it, no prisoners, no legal stuff, no union action, and five men off the payroll. Corporate procurement needs to hurry to take over the reins.

Charles touched on the staffing needs. "Do we need to find a Chef to replace him?"

"I think not. Here are my thoughts, but not yet been shared with the hotel!

"Promote the banquet Chef to Executive Chef. His assistant can take over from him. He has a good crew, is well trained, and works independently in the banquet kitchen. As the leading man, he will not abandon the banquets; on the contrary. He will bring the two kitchens together for joint production efforts. Recruit a strong food production manager and a commissary cook. Then back them up with corporate staff going into this operation to set up the system and train the cooks.

"With that, we will be okay. Pay this banquet Chef well. He has been underpaid for a long time. A bonus at the year's end would not be a mistake either.

One more item: corporate training could do some good. Train the trainer, yes, teaching them how training is done effectively. They need to know how people learn.

"Deep breath. Bravo, this is a home run that won the ball game."

How about a penalty kick to be more on my turf of sports?"

Charles laughed, which was carried out with a big pat on my back.

By now, the Asian secretary Tammy had received my report, read through it, and about halfway through, looked up at me as I came out of the door, asking me, "This is what you just talked about?"

Yes. "Then I will read it first since he knows about it."

"Yes, all this and more!"

"More, you must tell me, please!"

"Let us do it at lunch?"

Oh yes, great, thank you. My treat.

I was in a conference and pressed for time. All the guys had heard something or another; it was front-page news at the corporate gossip wave. Everybody wanted to know, but I told Tina to send them away.

Maggie came over to confirm that she received word and training inquiry from her VP of HR. "We need to make this a priority," she was informed. "We can do this in one session in New Jersey. Both need the same seminar, and having a few more make it more productive, better interactions, and saves time and cost."

She had come to tell me this plan. No date set, but soon. "Let us have a little time to rework the structure there. I am all for it."

"Good, but I want you there with me, for support, you understand. You are the star in the company that shines the brightest. Your authority will keep them alert and participative. Be ready for a visit by the CEO! The RVP has to report this upstream, the senior VP hotels, ten straight to the CEO!"

"I would love to hear the details, the strategy. This is big. I want to know." This came as an order.

Do you have time for lunch? You know, a bit longer than normal. Can you get an excuse to leave the building? Tammy wants to know too, and this way, I can treat you, good-looking women, to lunch while I tell the story. She had already secured the time; he was going on a morning trip.

Meet me in the lobby at eleven-thirty. I drive you to a little café al fresco. Near the office, this place received its share of corporate people.

They were nodding and waving hands; lunch was in progress as I went through the gory details in an abbreviated fashion but not skipping in on strategy and built-up tension.

"Sounds like a movie script," Maggie commented.

"Yes, it does. The confidentiality agreement can assign no rights. In twenty years. Certainly not now! Part of the deal!"

Maggie displayed the usual affection: touching, smiling, and projecting her appreciation had not gone unnoticed. Comment with a jealous undertone was given when we arrived at the F&B office. I found this interesting and wrote it off as women's feuding, or Tammy did not like Maggie.

The rest of the day had been occupied with the other hotel's reports and follow-ups.

Chapter 15

Barbados calling! What is going on there?" The construction folks presented blueprints of the restaurant and said that the building pace was ahead of schedule. Completion will be realized in three months. We need to shift into third gear since everybody has been on a six-month completion date.

I must now engage all my carpool companions, the menu department. The kitchen trainers speak to their boss, the corporate Chef to pick his brains on concept and menu planning, corporate recruiting for cooks, a Sous Chef from a prominent local restaurant, and the procurement lady who buys supplies and equipment.

Oh yes, not to forget the food and beverage, buying team. Did I forget anyone? Yes, my favorite trainer in HR."

I quickly visited the VP of systems to walk through this list item by item. "Let us add the beverage guy and the service trainers. They can be valuable to it, and he has never been there. These assignments are out of the country, with him having years of experience and influence over the support staff. This way, they can check on control procedures, tidy up what needs to, and set up the new operation. Now that this service problem is solved, it makes the job easier."

"What about the menu? It should have a Caribbean flavor. For a specialty restaurant, it must be unique."

"Do not go too crazy, stick to the system; whatever is new requires recipes for the file. Ginny can incorporate items from the menu file and add Caribbean flair to it. On your next trip, which should be soon lay the groundwork, get a list of typical local products, spices, fruits, and veggies, and go to the best restaurants and apprehend menus. Are you good at this?"

A greased palm at the door gets one anything. It will be on the travel expense list.

"Okay, just get the RVP to sign off on it."

This is like a race car. Jump in it on the run and do not look back.

I had thought of these men having a comfortable job. It is hard work, mental work, and always in the limelight. I must get used to it and love it too!

* * * * * * *

"Maggie told me she received a date for next Tuesday to conduct the training. Both hotels were notified and confirmed to attend with four persons in Northern New Jersey. We start at 10:00 a.m. giving these people time to get out of the city. The hotel will set up a meeting room with the material asked. The rest is on you and me.

Just tell me exactly what my role is going to be. Primary to be there. You can sit in the back or be in front of me. You will be needed when a dispute or misunderstanding arises, and they always do. As the trainer, I do not have the leverage to settle this. Clarify the position of the department. It puts me in a negotiating position to get them to solve their problem. Now, this can and will work if the participants show reason, but just one hard head will set this in jeopardy and fall apart, then all the effort is in vain.

"Besides, you see how it is conducted. Learn it, and in the future, you can use it on the moment's notice or fill in for me."

"I cannot split myself in half, and there are many hotels between the two regions."

I will plan on being there. It would be the week of the regional meeting on Thursday. As long as I can make it, I will be okay."

Tuesday morning, the early shuttle to La Guardia, by now a familiar place and route to negotiate without the map. With my early arrival, I had time for breakfast and quickly got an update from the F&B director. He affirmed that the GM was a different man now, and it had become an absolute pleasure to be here. The team building would help the department heads and assistants to form a cohesive hotel team that was the expectation.

Maggie joined as she had stayed overnight! "Are we all ready to face the music?"

At the meeting room, the early ones were already securing the seat next to the best-liked person; the others were filing in until the very last one with one minute to spare.

Maggie opened up the meeting, introducing herself and me and reiterating the purpose and goal of this session. "It will turn out as good as your participation will be. Do not hold back. Nothing goes into any report. It will stay with all of you. Understood?"

Twelve people showed up and got a number assigned by counting to 4 going around the table—four groups with diverse disciplines, which was ideal. Now we see gaps between departments and characters.

Then the seminar kicked in full gear, questions presented, answers returned and agreed on, and if not, a debate over pros and cons, hopefully, to come to a consensus quickly.

I had heard both sides of the argument and formed my own opinion on a neutral basis keeping the benefit to the business in focus. When it took a specific time over the allowed period without reaching an agreement, that was my signal when I got introduced into the game.

The egos drove these arguments to a standstill; therefore, it was easy to deflate this hothead and bring it back to why we were hired.

At one particular time, it was very heated. No one was willing to budge, so I stood in front of the group, legs apart like a gunslinger, and said, "Now we have what is called a stalemate. Normally these standoffs are settled with a gun until only one man's left standing; then, there cannot be any more standoffs!"

That broke the stalemate, and both opponents gave in a bit for the solution.

You see how humor can solve problems; this was a teaching moment!

In the afternoon, we entered a phase of them getting tired and edgy. Another age-old dispute surfaced between two department heads. Again, a hard line in the sand was drawn; nobody was ready to give an inch. A matter of principle, one had said.

This was a bit of a giveaway, and he had no fundamental reason to take this hard line. Both departments reported to other regional's, but my being there had to play the role. Common sense told me which way it had to go to move forward. The principles stayed the same; it had to be for the hotel's good and, foremost, the guests, who were the real bosses.

Again, I took my position but in a relaxed posture. I said, "We are forgetting for whom we are working!"

"The company," one called out. "The hotel" came from someone else.

"All correct.

Now I have a quiz for you. What is the fastest way to decide between three opposing parties?"

Pause, silence, so quiet one could hear a penny fall. Does anyone have an answer?

You kill two of them!

Laughter and agreement and the hotheads got a deflation for a mutually beneficial arrangement. "Let us not forget the person for whom we are working. You mentioned the hotel, and the company, all good answers. The best answer is the hotel's guest. Let us never forget this. Any decision made must have the welfare and service to the hotel guest in its foreground."

"Very good," remarked Maggie. "I must remember this and incorporate it into my script."

The seminar was completed, and we all had a toast with a new wine the food and beverage department wanted to introduce.

The wine was a Chardonnay from Kendall Jackson. Great, tasted fresh, just a bit of oak keeping the fruit alive. The F&B man announced that this wine was available by the glass now in bars and restaurants, especially for the city people. Wonderful idea. He looked at me, thinking I wanted to add to it, but I waved him off. Let him have the credit! This was his moment of glory.

Maggie asked to talk about Barbados. "Shall we go to the bar or restaurant?"

"No, privacy will be disrupted right after the seminar." Everybody was seeking her attention for brownie points; "Do you mind if we go to my room?"

"Okay, let us go!"

* * * * * * *

We talked about a strategy for that project. The cast of characters was different. International senior management, German, Italian, Spanish, and local Bajan; other island staff in assistant jobs; veterans like the executive housekeeper; and the chief engineer and Chef.

"Was he still there?" She had questioned if he could survive.

214

Yes, he was still plugging away, but with a changed attitude. We turned up the heat under his tail, and he got the message. There were still ways to go until we were there, but he was no longer fighting it!

She touched my shoulder and poured a glass of wine. At my request, the bar manager placed a chilled bottle of this new Chardonnay in her room.

"You know, it always amazes me how you try to salvage one's career. Of course, that was a brave move in the case of NY. No one would have tackled this, not even the RVP."

"It is my passion to see people grow." I then told her the story from Montreal.

She now snuggled up to me on the small sofa, ready for storytelling. "I like to listen to your stories. They all have happy endings." "Okay, here it goes!

I was the Chef Saucier in this mega hotel, the biggest and best at the time. My station was staffed with four cooks, including myself. One German, a young boy of nineteen years, and two Swiss cooks with good experience. The cooking line station at the front section, where the Chef announced and food passed to the servers, you know what I mean.

"Oh yes. My father has hotels, and the kitchen has always been my favorite place. You get treats, but the action is fascinating."

Two cooks worked in the back line, for we had double stove setups, and one cook worked with me out front. We called the German boy Seppli and Alfonse, Foni, worked the back while Peter, the other Swiss cook, worked with me. We put out on average eight hundred dinners all cooked à la minute and had to remember every order by heart, for the dupes stayed with the Sous Chef."

I felt comfortable using kitchen language; she knew it from her teenage years.

This was the preset, and now on with the story as she looked me in the eye, smiling that warm, cozy, comfortable smile to melt any heart.

When I left the job for India. "India?" "Yes!

But another time, I went to the Chef and recommended Foni to be awarded the Chef saucier position. He was too shy to go and ask for it, typical European. He was going to wait if it got offered.

No, you have to be proactive here in the Americas.

"I found out later that he got the assignment, did a great job, and ended up Sous Chef when one of them made Executive Chef at a sister hotel. From there, he received an invitation from the Swiss pavilion organizer to go to Tokyo and run the food operation during the World's Fair.

"That was coming to a successful conclusion; the Dorchester Hotel in London made him an offer. During their tenure there, he made television appearances, wrote a book, and finally got so famous that a bunch of investors who had bought a church hired him to partner in this project, a converted church to become a four-star restaurant. More books, cooking for royalty, traveling to other hotels as a guest Chef with all the excitement and publicity.

By now, he has become a desired commodity.

"I attended his wedding in Switzerland at an old castle, and in typical Foni creativity, he staged a spectacular day for his beloved wife from his hometown. What a guy I can call a true friend. End of story!"

Maggie was touched by this story and showed her affection to me.

The activity heated up. A kiss was my reward and more of them. It was a perfect ending to a successful day.

* * * * * * *

Back at the office, I set up a meeting with Ginny and Willi to brainstorm menu ideas I could take with me to Barbados next week. Willi had experience and contributed great ideas, but Ginny kept putting on the brakes. Her repertoire was limited to the company file. I could not blame her. "What the farmer does not know, he will not eat," I said in German to Willi. She looked at us as if we had cursed her, but I said, You should come to Barbados and do the menu there while you can enjoy the local food.

"That would be nice, but I am afraid to travel out of the country and need to get a passport. I don't think the boss will approve! There are Caribbean restaurants here in the city!"

Let us check it out. Willi and I will take you out to dinner then.

The restaurant was a disappointment, already Americanized, with watered-down spices and only abbreviated Caribbean dishes on the menu.

Willi and I talked about the genuine flavors of the Caribbean. "But you will be serving Americans," she protested.

216

"That is correct. The more reason we have to show the genuine cuisine, for when we lose them to the local joints, it will not be adapted to the American taste, so they take it there. Now they will get it here.

If it is too hot, it will have to be marked, and there are other dishes available, or they can have sauce on the side, plain and boring!

Willi fully agreed with me. I have suggestions to look over, add, or delete, but I do not want to go there empty-handed. Their contribution is important. They are the ones producing it, and for that reason, I want them to buy in on it.

Chapter 16

On my flight to the island, I remembered the tennis lesson from Maggie and silently hoped she may be there. She had mentioned it in her room in New Jersey, and then I forgot to ask her about the travel schedule.

Off the plane, I got the familiar aromas of burning sugarcane fields harvesting for the good Appleton rum. Humid and warm trade winds, a pleasant climate year-round. Never snow or ice and bitter cold, how I longed for an environment like this. Florida would be my best shot!

The hotel had sent a car to pick me up, no taxi hustle, nice; they must want me on their good side! Had news traveled to the island of what happened in New York, I remembered that the director of Marketing was working with a team in New York to sell the US market. The news must have been conveyed!

The restaurant was farther ahead in the finishing phase than I expected. Management was out in full force to greet me, and accommodate me with a VIP presentation, very island style, and then we took a tour of the new building. Freestanding was a great idea to build an image with nice tropical touches, tasteful decoration, and fully air-conditioned. "Someone did his/her homework," I said.

"She is the architect who put this all together."

Nice. I am pleased and impressed. Now tell me that you did not forget the kitchen! I was joking. She laughed and mentioned that she was familiar with those properties when the kitchen became an afterthought.

"You must know that I am a passionate hobby cook, always looking for new stuff, and I hope you will share some of your secrets."

How can I resist such a charming request, please know, there are no secrets in cooking. We can copy everything.

"Do not tell me the chicken guy!"

No, I know Joe's stone crab in Miami Beach with the sauce for the stone crabs. I laughed aloud to everybody's curiosity, then told her I had copied this recipe.

"How did you do it?"

Taste, I pointed to my tongue and a little help from a coffee lady.

"How so?"

"She worked for a food conglomerate that sold everything, continental coffee, but coffee was the starting point, and they never changed the name. This company formulated a special mayonnaise for Joe Stone crab. I got to taste the mayo, and indeed it was distinctly different. This was the tough part to decipher. I found out that they mixed the mayo with yogurt and a small amount of honey. The flavors had been easy. Then the restaurant added dry English mustard, lemon juice, and finished.

"Now I see it. Yes, the taste has a little sweetness to enhance the sweet flavor of the crabs, then the bite from the mustard and creamy texture with no dominance of vinegar, which mayonnaise only would bring to the recipe. "Simple. Now I have it too!" Make it your own. That is what all Chefs do!

"You are a genius."

Let us not go that far, please.

She proudly showed me the kitchen, explaining the reason for the location of various equipment, bench space, spice cabinet, condiments, and wine and oil bottles. "The traffic will flow this way so as not to interfere with the food pickup area.

We place the dish area right here. It does not call for a colossal flight washer. A single tray washer can handle the forty seated guests." I smiled with gratitude, then said that she had cooked half the meal already. Taking a second, she said, "I think you approve of the layout, making the Chef's life productive."

Correct, we understand each other.

"Have you finalized the menu?"

I explained the protocol I must adhere to with the menu department. The new corporate Chef and I laid the groundwork. "I would like to see it. I have been here and found great eateries, but the best food is at the local shacks. We can go to a couple and graze through the food offerings."

I like that!

When she looked over the menu, she liked items but had reservations. "Explain, please, so I understand."

"You spread this food all over the Caribbeans and ignore the best the island offers. You will see my point after we have tasted the cuisine."

We set the time; she had a car to use and would do the chauffeuring.

Now it was time to look up the Chef, feel his pulse, and have a chat.

He was in great spirits, so happy to see a landsman, and spoke German. He must be homesick.

Have you gotten any leads for a restaurant Chef?

"No, so far, only the usual cooks, but nobody of caliber."

You know this town. Where would you look, I mean, if we can steal a guy?

"Difficult because of the tenure in these places, part of the inventory by now."

Here is an idea; not sure what will come of it, but would you join us, meaning the architect, to canvass places where she is raving about the food. She likes to cook, so I have reasonable confidence in her.

"Oh, I know her. She is a great woman and put together a first-class kitchen. I asked her to add a steam facility, thinking of another cooking method. We will need to decide the final product once the menu takes shape." I gave him a draft copy, just ideas, nothing in stone yet. Verstehst Du?

"Yes, I am game, at six p.m., okay? Meet us in the lobby. I will inform her of the addition. "We get along great. I like her a bit too much."

Oh, be careful; your bachelor status is at stake!

We grazed our way through the town, ate an appetizer, a soup, and main dishes in a restaurant, then returned to the simple places and found more great food I had never known or tasted.

This is all inspiring food and could be given a lift with better meat or fish, shellfish and fruits, sauces, dips, mild, hot, fiery, and sweet ones—what a contrast of flavors, just what I had envisioned.

A young girl ran one place. "Are you the owner?

"No, I am covering for my mom. She is usually here, taught me how to cook, and told me many times that a good cook always has a job and food. I am called Priscilla!"

I glanced at the Chef to see if he noticed it. He was too preoccupied with the architect and missed the cue.

I gave the girl a business card and asked the Chef if he had one on him, and by dumb luck, he did.

Give it to her.

"For what?"

I will tell you later.

I asked the girl to look me up while I was on the island. Can you make it there?

"The Castle? Oh yes, my brother can get me there on his motorcycle."

Tomorrow, good. Go to the lobby; they will find me.

Her eyes lit up like the planet Venus. She gave me her name, Priscilla, very flowering and befitting this beautiful young girl. You are of age to work legally?

"Yes, I am twenty-one as of last week."

"Happy belated birthday, Priscilla." And with that, I joined the waiting grazing companions.

I was up and on my feet by 6:00 a.m. The front-desk employees pulling the red-eye shift looked at me funny. They also did not know me at this point, so I introduced myself.

I want to do something with this table. It was a historical dinner table during Sam Lords' tenure. I ran the idea by them. Independent thinkers, with no prejudice, was the opinion I was looking for.

"What a great idea, and it can be made into a dramatic show."

It turned out that both were actually in drama school; she hoped an acting career was in her future. Their enthusiasm was contagious." I know the right man who could play the Captain Lord's part. We act as wenches, serving the beverages."

At that point, the Tom Jones party came to mind with long dresses and low-cut blouses with pitchers of wine and beer. She had as much in her head to start writing a script. "When can we start it? "

I need to present it to management, get approval, and then obtain proper drinking containers, menu, service staff, and organization to get the hot food to a staging area.

"I help you in any way I can," she belted out with enthusiasm.

I hope I can use your enthusiasm to infect the players that have to approve and the ones that have to produce it. It never hurts to let the idea grow among the hotel staff.

"Great, I work day shifts and nights. That gives me ample opportunities. I will do my best!"

You are a charmer, a pretty charmer, I added.

Smiles were returned and a sweet, "Thank you, sir!"

Breakfast al fresco at the restaurant, blackbirds, cruising among the tables picking crumbs and left-behind food from leaving guests, and sometimes dipping the beaks into the loose sugar bowl. It is all part of the atmosphere, the soft breeze and fragrance of blooming flowers everywhere.

Paradise, I thought. These people living here would not even see it as tourists did. They all wanted to come to the US; once there, then they realized what was left behind.

Giovanni joined me, Bona sera. "How was your soiree?"

I talked about the impression, particularly the food, and not remembering all the names. The Chef knew most items and talked about the array of flavors and aromas, textures, and spiciness.

"Do you think we can make something out of it?"

I believe so if corporate signs off on it.

I laid the groundwork and reason that this restaurant menu was not precisely corporate either. They carried weight at corporate, a vast department just coming into its prime with all the projects in the pipeline! This architect, Stephanie, knew her food. She was passionate, and that was a plus.

I had firm hopes to create something unique.

At his office, we reviewed the action plan, and staffing for service potential restaurant manager or captain, whatever the title. I saw a fine service guy or woman with classic service training being hands-on and involved physically on the floor.

We agreed on this, him coming from this angle to his position. Servers, we could pick the best from here, the restaurant. "Both shifts had examples that would respond to the upgraded service. I will be fully engaged into this process."

Cooks, lead cooks, or sous chefs, we had not been successful in attracting anyone. HR was making efforts to get the word out. So far, no candidates, and I did not see a cook from the existing crew being the right man.

What about a woman, a girl, I should say?

"Why? Do you know anybody?"

I met a girl at one place with excellent food. She had been trained by her mother in cooking skills to do the job as well as her mother. The girl has also been preached to become an excellent cook, for any great cook will always have work and food. Basic survival skills left over from the colonial days.

"That sounds interesting. Can we talk to her?"

Yes, today is her date of destiny. She has my card and will be driven here by her brother this morning, say mid-morning.

Guessing from her facial expression when she received my card and invitation to come here to talk about the possibility, she will be early if not here already and killing time at the gate.

Let us stroll to the entrance gate to ensure the security guard does not hold her back.

A big smile with impeccable white teeth greeted us, and yes, the security guard had questioned her reason for coming to the Castle.

She showed the man my card, but to no avail. He did not know this man, and I would have to dispatch my helper to verify this name with the front office.

He is doing his job, I explained and apologized for the delay to her.

"Not a problem, sir. I do understand this."

"Come along," I introduced Mr. Giovanni, the Food and Beverage director. All the employees called him that way; their surname was unpronounceable. They were used to the English tongue that could not even pronounce my name with the umlaut sound! Try to get Stracciatella out of their mouth.

She felt so important having the honor to meet such high-up management. Being a former English colony bred respect into the blood of the Barbados population!

I enjoyed her enthusiasm, her uuhs and sounds of amazement, so beautiful, and that kitchen, a dream for a cook as simple as I was.

We want to serve high-quality food, this being a specialty restaurant. The customers will be paying a high price and expecting perfection from service and, of course, what gets on the plate. It will be there for generations to come.

We would also adopt items from your mom's place. We will credit your mom for creating these dishes featured her

It will and bring her guests from the hotel to her restaurant. We get our guests from the USA and Europe and from South America too. It helps to get this kind of exposure.

We had gone around the town and tasted the food of establishments, sophisticated and straightforward like your mom's restaurant. We liked your food the best, and since she has been training you to be as good as her, that speaks volumes to me.

She listened intently to my speech. Never cut into it but sat there taking in every single word. She would repeat it to her mom when she gets home; I was sure of that. She was a girl with discipline and obedience raised by a strict but very loving mother. Her conduct throughout this interview was witness to this.

Now we have to consult our boss.

"There is one higher?"

Yes, the general manager.

"That sounds very big!"

We laughed at her innocence. Yes, and then we must decide what we will offer you. We will have a job for you, that is certain. That is if you want to work here.

"I would love it; it will make my mother so proud of me!"

How can we get in touch with you?

"We have a pay phone next to the house. We use this as our phone communication, and any ring to it will get answered by one of us. I have sisters and little brothers. They all help.

One more thing, do not concern yourself taking me away as my mother's stand-in. She is already training my younger sister. Here is my number from the phone booth." She had it written out neatly with her full name, address, phone number, and nickname.

Thank you for your time, Priscilla, a nice name and befitting a beautiful girl.

"You are very kind, sir!"

With that, she disappeared. I thought she was flying, but at least skipping to the front gate. "You will see me again," she said in her local dialect, and the guard was happy about it and apologized to her.

"I can see her doing the bulk of the cooking in there. She will need help managing and dealing with the servers and learning control procedures, but not for long. I see her as a take-charge person, ambitious and eager to prove her worth and beyond to us and her mom. She is a quick learner, getting to finish in the top tier of her high school class. Her personality speaks volumes.

I do not want her to be introduced to the main kitchen cooks or cooking style that would derail her. The Chef has to adhere to this, no exception! And for God's sake, he will keep his hands off her! A pretty girl like her is easy prey for that. She will get a direct pipeline to report to you, Giovanni. Do you agree?

"Certainly, you are correct. I will see to this!"

Now we need a senior cook who can assist until she feels confident to run the show. Think about that, skills are secondary, management skills is what we need. The organization is paramount and above integrity.

"We get the Chef in on that.

The service I leave in your capable hands. We will get corporate support from the kitchen side and service. I must ensure these people come with the right frame of mind. We do not need an autocrat to dictate SOPs.

"When the menu is final, and I am thinking of involving Priscilla in building it, she will have ownership in it, and you will have to pay her as a casual labor by check or cash for this time.

She has to write recipes for all the non-corporate items. I am confident she will master that, being a stellar student at her mother's school of hard knocks.

It will bond her even more to the product and give her status within the ranks of cooks.

"You have it planned already to the smallest detail."

Got to, for they are sticklers in Washington about deviation from the norm. But with the homework done precisely, there cannot be any arguments. We also have a corporate Chef now with considerable credentials. We should be successful with luck and push from Mr. Baker. All I have to try is that the company's owner will be here during the holidays and put this to the test.

Occasionally one has to call in the markers.

"You mean the NY story?"

You are right on that!

For budgeting, put her in on a Sous Chef pay grade. The offer should state the wage at the upper pay tier of a skilled cook. It will amaze her, and once she takes over, the sous chef's salary will kick in. I do not want to take advantage of her.

She is humble by upbringing, and I will not abuse it. She will also serve as an ambassador among the locals, that this hotel is paying a fair wage and gives good treatment.

With this in the clear, I noticed Maggie exiting a taxi at the front door. "What a surprise," she yelled and hugged me. "I had no idea that you were here."

"I got here yesterday on account that the construction is nearing completion. Thanks to a dynamic architect, the restaurant is way ahead of the rooms.

"Any other excitement? I am already expecting this from you!"

Giovanni and I made a discovery, the first Executive Chef in the company, give it a couple of years.

Giovanni responded, "You are optimistic. I have seen the type before in other jobs, and they all materialize."

Really! Do tell me, later, story time!

"I like that, look forward to it, and now I have to go to work. Is the GM in?"

"Yes, go ahead; he does not have appointments."

Okay, that is a surprise, I thought to myself with a grin. Tennis lesson tonight and with benefits.

"I want to get a hamburger down below."

Let me come with you. I must show my face, or she thinks I forgot her!

"That sensitive?"

"Not that, but she is all alone all day and appreciates the chat and attention."

As usual, the women running the shack also run the beach. The burger was well done, and the sweet potato fries with the hot sauce burned a hole in the stomach. One Banks beer or two will set the day right.

So far, we have struck gold. Now we need to convince the boss. But he does not involve himself in food and beverage. You take good care of it. Why should he?

Let us talk about budgeting.

Your numbers run incredibly low on the expense and supply cost side. Do you have enough flatware, dishes, glassware, janitorial supplies, cookware, and good knives?

"All in good shape with a safety backup."

Go ahead with bringing up the cost to cover your butt for next year.

"I do not understand!"

It works like this. You are on a bonus program. You are in good shape to make the max bonus plus.

The profit over and above the max bonus line will reflect the budget expectations. The company will be looking forever to show better numbers to satisfy Wall Street, meaning the shareholders.

They are owners and greedy. You leave money on the table like a gambler walking away with the most chips, but when he returns, the dealer has taken them to the house account. The same is here. Your budget number being way under, let's say in China, glasses and flatware will be booked at the low number for next year's budget. If you experience a higher loss factor, you will be short on funds, then be forced to plunder other categories, and so goes the snowball effect.

"I do understand now."

"Then let me stack up on inventory and bring it to budget levels.

Do not go crazy to be noticeable.

Buy stuff you need for the new restaurant. At the start, there is always more breakage and inventory losses. Until the employees have a set of four, they will take merchandise little by little, which will not be noticeable. They do that over time so as not to draw attention to it. Just a matter of fact! Good advice.

I do not know if the budget is done here or in New York as the sales will dominate the discussions, and the rest is based on history. Put a little in that you can give. Like the health inspector must find a deficiency. He will look until he finds it, so let him discover a little harmless mistake, and he goes happy." He laughed!

By 5:00 p.m., Maggie was looking for me. "Tennis lesson?"

Yes, I love it; I even bought a new racket and balls.

A Tennis outfit, also tennis shoes. "You are getting serious about the game."

Got to look the part. "It is a method to intimidate your opponent! That is if you are up for a match. Are you?"

No, not at all; just wanted to feel right and to belong.

The lesson picked up from the last fundamental stuff. "This time, we will work on the forehand, backhand, and footwork. This is your strike zone. Your instructions are excellent and beneficial. These details allow me to practice on a wall at home with no partner.

This was a good drill!

Cocktails after a shower? Good, I'll see you there. The managers are there, so we can pick their brains.

The first impressions had been good. Usually, the tensions were noticeable at the front door. You feel the same way, which is so true. If they only knew. I would change the subject matter, skip the team building, or do the short version. "Do you require the F&B director tomorrow?"

I am spending the day with the Chef and the new female star. "Do not forget; you promised me story time and remember the happy ending!"

How wonderful a memory! A wink with the eye, and off she went.

It must be a nightly ritual, but tonight was the General Manager's reception labeled "Meet the Managers," a must-attend and a welcome speech with a drink and tropical snacks.

The brain-picking was short-lived. They made it to the exit once the formalities had been concluded. The idea was to mingle, yet I did understand that the cliché questions were always the same. "Where are you from?" "How long have you been here?"

This stuff gets old quickly.

A quick dinner and then this story for tonight. On the way to my room, I inquired about how life was at home. "Same old, parents are in California, no siblings, no friends at work other than you."

"You are my salvation, she said, giggling. And the boyfriend is in China, Shanghai, big tournament to the finish line. So, I bury myself with work, and take on extra assignments!"

Sitting on the bed, she snuggled up to me as I began telling her about last evening, grazing up all food places until we stumbled on this last place.

The shop was operated by a young girl, covering for her mom, she explained, almost apologetic. The food stood out from all the others in freshness, seasoning, temperature, and presentation, and one can see a professional is at work.

I told her about the architect and how she knew all these places. I told the Chef. He was equally impressed, never knew this place existed, a bit off the usual the tourist track yet easy to find.

"A woman, this Architect?

Yes. And good-looking at that. A flare of jealousy but only a blimp, then on with the story.

She loves to cook, and as a result, we are getting the best designed and equipped kitchen.

After only tasting the food and taking small bites, the girl made a comment:

"You sure eat funny. Why is that?"

I showed her my card and explained the purpose. She caught on quickly.

I told her about the restaurant, gave her my business card, and asked her if she had an interest in joining an international hotel company.

It is the Castle as it is known locally. She had no idea that the owner is that corporation.' Bright-eyed, she nodded. "Yes, that would be more than I had ever dreamed of."

I asked her to come by the next day, which was this morning. Her brother will bring her on his motorbike. I thought she would show up by ten. She was early, and with that, the hiring process began. We showed her, so I verified it. We showed her the restaurant, and she was so impressed could not find words to say how much.

I watched her body language and facial expressions and tried to read what I could get from them all along. Besides the verbal talk when she described her family life in meticulous detail.

Are you not going to be missed by Mom? No, Mom is training the younger sister now and coming along fast.

Mom told her that when one is an excellent cook, one will always have a job. And food too! Remnants from the colonial days!

Then we asked her if Mom would share her recipes beforehand so we can write up the company format and have documentation CYA, you know! All too well, so strict, and so rigid!

We will put credits on the menu in a prominent way for the hotel guest to see. Hopefully, they will look her up as a result. It certainly could not hurt. It was more information as she could absorb.

She asked intelligent questions, wanted to know about job security, and when we said how long the executive housekeeper and engineer had been here, it put her at ease.

She gave us a paper she had prepared with her full name, address, telephone number, and her mother's full name, where she had gone to high school, all prepared in neat handwriting. I do not have work experience because I only worked for my mother.

Almost apologetic and so humble and plain.

I told Giovanni that she was special and would have to be protected from predators. She is coming tomorrow morning to help us put the menu to paper. She will be paid, of course, but I would bet she will not be expecting it, may even try to turn it down.

"How are you going to place her?"

"I was thinking and told the guys also that at first, she should do the cooking, applying her skills, and be paid like a senior cook, be guided by a food production manager to handle service and paperwork, the management stuff.

I will bet that if she is guided correctly, her management skills will be natural, and she will take over even as a cook. But when she is ready, she gets the title of Restaurant Chef on the pay grade of a Sous Chef.

That is a beautiful story, and the ink has not even dried."

A big kiss sealed the story with tears in her eyes, and then what came naturally must come for the happy ending.

She stayed the night, asked for seconds, and fell asleep in my arm. At 4:00 a.m., she sneaked back into her room on the same floor, not causing noise to wake another guest.

She joined Giovanni and me at the breakfast table, bright-eyed and bushy-tailed, one could say, plus her happy demeanor and flirting personality always charmed the male gender. Was this from her father or mother? My bet was on the father!

Giovanni inquired about the seminar's time needs. He did not see the need for it, nor relish sitting down and being locked up in a meeting room. He was one of the managers who needed to run and stay in contact with those who produced commerce. Then look for ways to become more efficient and make life easier if this could be combined with efficiency as these two are always connected.

Egos had been standing in the way, as it usually is. I also did not see the need; however, there had been a time when this was an obvious problem, and the RVP determined to do something about it.

"I think we will wrap it by noon," was her reply. "Scheduling conflicts had it moved back, and now you boys kissed and made up."

"Not that intimate" was Giovanni's response, "but yes, we found a way to coexist and solve our problems in private and reach a consensus."

"Thank you for this insight. I shall probe it gently."

"Old wounds are healed and remain that way; I know how delicate these subjects can be, but as women, I bring added armor to keep this in check."

Well-spoken, I added with a grin, knowing all too well about this weapon she carried.

"How is your schedule in F&B?"

We have this super girl coming in to take part with the menu choices for two reasons. We want to adopt her mother's food items and learn about ingredients, which will come from the family's recipe treasures through her participation.

"Go on!"

"The second effect of this participation is to show her the process this takes in a large corporation and to give her ownership of the menu. What better statement to a guest for her to say, "I wrote this menu!"

"Bravo, you will empower her as she takes ownership of the quality of the food."

Exactly, this is what I envision.

"Noble objective," Giovanni added. "Are you both signed on to this commitment?"

"Of course," we both replied in unison.

We have the afternoon off unless the GM has other ideas. We both leave on the same flight. "There is time to debrief him in the morning." Right here is okay by me." I will let him know Giovanni committed!"

"Do you want to meet at the beach below?"

"Yes, fantastic. I need salt water and salty air in my lungs to disinfect all of it, so we do not bring home any tropical bugs. Funny, this is rational."

Anything can be rational, all in choosing the words!

"I have to remember this." A good laugh, and off we went.

✳ ✳ ✳ ✳ ✳ ✳ ✳

Priscilla was early as I expected, all wound up and ready to talk about her mother's reaction. I offered breakfast to her. "Thank you. We eat different, simpler food, rice, beans, plantains, whatever the land provides. Eggs are costly unless one keeps chicken, but the mongoose likes the chicken meat too much, and with the snakes declining, there is a shortage of food. The good thing now is that the mice and rats are getting hunted by the mongoose."

"We are waiting for the Chef and will use this back table to do our work." Then I faced her into the corporate procedure to save time and the need to explain at a later time, for the need to understand is essential.

She was a brilliant girl, she would grab this fast, and then we could concentrate on building a menu. I left my proposal in the folder, I did not want to influence creativity with ideas that may come into play, but first, I hoped this young, fresh mind had much to offer.

We set up the categories: appetizers cold, then hot, then salads, followed by the main dishes we called entrées. It is from the French term.

"Is it because they have the best food?"

Look at what your family does." This is a matter of opinion. The Italians have great food, so do the Asian counties, and so does the Caribbean Basin.

A big smile and pride glowed from her eyes. Getting included with the fabulous foods of the universe was huge!

Four items were chosen for the appetizers list, six for the entrées, and two for desserts with components that would make it in combination with other things.

I must explain to Mom to do something like it. I explained to her what I envisioned as a proper dessert and the function of a dessert. "I understand that it gives energy from the sweetener, supplies acid from the fruit, and simple comfort from the crunch part. "You see how we already are learning from each other!

The rest of the food selection had been chosen from the high-cost natural products.

Now comes descriptive wording on preparation steps. "The American customer would otherwise occupy the server too long with endless questions. It saves time for the server.

They must tend to wine service and know the choice on the wine list.

"I want to learn about it."

"I have a book I know by heart. I will gift this to you. I made a note to the file, VIP, do not forget. She saw my notation and smiled with great satisfaction.

Jointly we described the food and made it sound delicious for the guest.

"You make this sound so good I am getting hungry."

Now we are done. The biggest hurdle will be the people in the menu department. I have a bit of an advantage. The corporate Chef, you'll like him, a fellow landsman." That means countryman in German.

We took her into our confidence and planted the seeds for a typical local menu.

"You mean the seed is an idea, and she will grow to it?"

You are terrific, right on. Recipes will have to be written primarily for your Mom's food.

I have them here, worked it up, and double-checked it. We have people that specialize in it, and the new chef will also help; besides, she is in the carpool I belong to drive to work.

Now I understand the advantage. You will have her undivided attention during the drive! I love this thinking. One day you may work in this building.

"Not sure I can grow that high."

"But I would love to visit one time later, much later. We have to prove something right here first." Talking like an employee/manager, she could make it big in life. Hopefully, she would avoid the pitfalls and circumvent the sharks.

The Chef will buy us three a hamburger at the beach, and then I'll introduce you to our special lady trainer. I believe we will find her there.

Maggie was getting an order going as we arrived.

Great, Maggie, it is my distinct pleasure to introduce to you our staff for the new restaurant.

She blushed with her chocolate skin and said formally, "Pleased to meet you, madam," with a bit of motion as if she had just met the queen of England.

"You are so pretty. Also, my pleasure. I have heard all the great things about you. Join us for lunch. There is a table big enough for everyone. Please come along."

The Chef organized the food and carried the beer to the table, condiments, and napkins in the dispenser.

"This is such a beautiful spot here. I never knew it existed on this island!"

I started to tell the story of how this hotel was founded. "It was a man's castle first, and he was a pirate and made money by plundering shipwrecks that he had lured to this beach by making fires at night to mislead the merchant ships to a wrong location. Thinking it was the harbor, they crashed on the reef outside the beach. Ships are guided by lights in two colors, white and red. The sailors say it's 'red-right-return.

The red light has to be on his right side, the starboard side as it is called in seaman's language, to return in a deep channel to the harbor's safety.

"You know all these sailors' jargons," Maggie commented. "You surprise me every time we meet."

You do the same. I could not hold this back with a smirk!

"At one time, when the old pirate died, the Castle got sold by the estate and converted into a hotel. Someone private tried to make a go of it but failed; not enough rooms, not big enough to carry the upkeep and taxes, power, plus it needed to be renovated. A company bought it for a low price, pumped money into renovating the Castle, built a wing of guest rooms, the restaurant, and the central kitchen, and ran it as a resort destination. Advertising in the US travel magazines helped him do a successful business.

As he grew older and had no children to take over in their father's footsteps, he was looking for a buyer, which is how this corporation bought this place. Again, the company put more investments, adding more rooms. That is why we have so many individual buildings and now more rooms and this new restaurant.

The happy ending will be written at a later date!

Only Maggie understood this double meaning.

As Pricilla got ready to go home, I asked her to stop at the front office and pick up an envelope waiting for her. They can also place a call for your ride if your brother is available. Otherwise, we will prepay a taxi for your ride.

"Thanks. You all are so kind to me. I love you all." A hand kiss, and she was on her way back.

I told the Chef that the envelope with a written job offer as a senior cook, the cash pay for the time she devoted to this work today, and an estimated starting date.

Giovanni had budgeted her preopening pay under the construction budget. "You need to call her in from time to time before and explain employment policies, introduce her to HR, all department heads, the GM, and the kitchen crew.

She needs to be fully employed once the kitchen is up and running. Training, practicing the menu items, test cooking, and staging a practice meal are all part of the pre-opening activity.

Corporate staff and I will guide and organize much of it. It would be best if you appointed your most trusted cook to managing the production, buying procedures, paperwork, and control procedures by the book.

It has to be structured as we work with expensive products We need to prove to the company that all is following SOP and create a model operation. You have your work cut out between now and the opening.

The brass will be here and the owner of the company. He has a soft spot for this place!

Cool heads prevail. Just do not waste any time. Go and triple-check all of the steps.

I am available by phone or fax, and if something dramatic threatens this success, I will fly down and take the bull by the horns, which would not be the first!

Once this girl is ready to lead, she will be promoted to the title of a restaurant Chef, pay grade Sous Chef, and run the show with your oversight. Then she will be given an assistant to groom for her time off. I have a hunch already who that could be!"

"Who?" he asked.

"Just cool it, all in good time!

"This completes this project, had to be delivered in a most sincere tone, and yes, a witness is always good to have present.

"You have carried out a great deal. Was there any preplanning?"

Only a menu outlines thinking to adopt a cross-section of great Caribbean dishes. Never in my dreams would I have expected the entire task to be completed, including the Chef producing it. She is a fireball, poised, humble, and very sharp. She must have graduated top of her class.

A total package plus easy on the eye. Watch over her! Yes, easy.

Giovanni has an order to keep the Chef on a short leash!"

We ended up using more than half of her mother's dishes. The rest we filled in with the high-end-cost products, seafood, lobster, filet mignon, and sirloin steak. Her mother's food items were low-cost, but you would not know. The skill applied to the food turned it into this perceived and much-enjoyed premium product. She could clean up if she had a better location.

I always judged a cook by what he started with. I see these characters on TV taking the most expensive ingredients to build their fancy food dish. Anyone could get this done, but the one who started with a chicken leg and then delivered the first-class plate, I pulled my hats off to him.

Here you can see what cooking skills and imagination can provide. This was her training; I have respect for her mom and her. Too bad we did not get to meet her mother, but she will be invited the next time for the training and test meal.

I will send the hotel limo to pick her up and take her home the next day, let her enjoy her daughter's success, and experience the Castle's hospitality as a VIP.

"Great, you have your heart in the right place."

Now another idea! "More stories:" yes, of a sort, as everything does turn into a tale, short or long.

The first night I had a dream about this place, woke up, and could not go back to sleep. Since it had been about five in the morning, I looked at the dream's location.

Vividly remembering all the details, I went to the lobby and looked around. The lobby had been the subject matter, and this ghost of the original owner, the pirate lord, was serving guests dinner.

Two lovely young girls from the night shift at the desk watched with great interest. Their night audit work was completed, and copies made; they had time to chat and now followed me intensely. "Are you looking for something lost or misplaced?" one asked.

No, I did not lose anything, but I am looking at the space if it is feasible!

"What do you mean by feasible?"

"I had a nightmare, not a scary one, a dream of an idea that makes sense. We should use this lobby for something.

This beautiful table was once a dinner table to host guests by the original owner, the Captain!

"Yes, I have this idea too that this table should be used as a pirate's dinner."

Set, by invitation only, evening tropical attire in white, the ceiling fan restored to function as the cooling. Servers in white jackets and smiling, girls in long skirts and low-cut blouses pouring wine and beer to the guest and keep filling the glasses.

The Captain Lord shows up in his pirate's captain uniform during the meal. The wooden leg, pounding on the floor to draw their attention to him. Then he greets his guests, inquiries about the meal, and goes on with a yes, you guessed it, a story" from his seafaring life.

Fifteen to twenty minutes will pass to give the service and kitchen time to produce the dessert, flaming bananas in brown sugar, lime juice, scotch bonnet peppers, and rum, is carried into the room on a wooden plank while in flames.

Then the girl said she had been thinking of this many times but never dared to bring it forward. During this very night, it would not let go away. It just came perking up repeatedly! It had been the exact contents of my dream!

At once she noticed my enthusiasm and went ahead to tell me that she was still in school, a drama school. She wanted to make a career as an actress. She also knew a person who would be perfect for the pirate's role, someone in the family, an uncle, or even a father or older brother and her work partner, and she would gladly play the part of the wench.

What do you say to this story?

"Fascinating, cooperation between two unknown persons connected by a ghost! A real ghost could be the one connecting you. They work during the night, and how else can this come about, circumstances? No, there is a power behind not understood by the brain unless highly spiritually connected! Do you believe in this?"

I cannot believe it fully, but powers are over us whom we do not control. I am too much of a realist. I have to see, feel, smell, taste, then believe, really believe.

Back to the idea, I think it would be a fantastic promotion and booked out for months once publicity hits the news waves, and this is what they eat up. A unique feature that no competitor can replicate.

The question is now, how and to whom do I tell it? Timing will be crucial. Perhaps wait until the construction is finished and the opening behind.

But if we can pull it off, it would be the big bang to perform it for the dignitaries attending the opening.

In that case, the idea must be accepted to develop and be produced.

Produced, we need a producer.

I am sure this girl can fill that position also. Then I would leave it to food and beverage to staff it and the food is easy.

* * * * * * *

We sat in the sun and forgot the power the sun had in the Southern Hemisphere. No burns yet, but the need for a lotion with aloe would do good. Going back to the hotel, I went to the lobby and bought the cream from the gift shop; this girl may be working the day shift with luck. "And if not, we can ask her to stay on after her night shift to meet if you and I are successful in selling Giovanni and the GM with the idea."

"You and me?"

Please, I will need your support.

"Of course, just kidding. It will be a lively dinner conversation. I am told that the Chef is pulling extra registers."

She had already been in the shower, carefully toweling her body in her room.

"Will you do my back gently, please? Now we see the effects of sun exposure. It is good that you have tanned skin by nature and are not subject to severe burns. Same with me."

"Now, do you want to shower too? You should. This way, we help each other apply the aloe lotion."

Good idea. And so, we were both naked as God created us. Her body was more attractive than mine.

Perhaps when the lotion had time to work, it would be better! During the lotion application on her back and legs, her upper thigh had been on fire, so she volunteered to open them up to access the inner side of the skin. Gradually and gently applying the green stuff and massaging it, my hands' motion reached the innermost part.

The natural reaction took hold, and he was waving at her. A soft sound spoke volumes; the sun had had its way with us as the desire for sex was mounting.

We would take the time to do foreplay only, with no penetration, tease all erogenous zones, and play with all areas to arouse the body. "You do it to me, and I do my part, but short of an orgasm. Just close enough to want it so bad, tease to no end until we go to dinner. Then after we pick up from where we left off, you will get me to the high point.

You are still working on your climax, the contractions of my vagina will put you over the top, and you will come inside. No worry, I am on the pill."

My boy responded and retracted to cool off and up, again and again, in total exhilaration. The chase was the best part of the hunt.

Her body had a profound effect on me; it was challenging to bring it to a pause.

She went into the shower while I went to my room to get dressed. No need to arrive together, false feelings, no need to spread rumors; this was our sweet secret.

The GM was very hospitable. Something made him happy. The corporate contingent was leaving, or he heard the progress made in food and beverage, plus the result of the seminar pleased him.

Maggie had arrived before me. Reasonable, less suspicious; we had a special cocktail the bar manager wanted to try out on us. "Guinea pigs," I joked.

"No, he is outstanding. I remember him telling me all about Falernum. He knows his product."

I took this opening to float the idea of staging a drinking contest with hotels and any bar taking part.

The idea resonated with the barkeeper, food for thought."

Maggie at once reacted with jubilant enthusiasm. "You are full of ideas."

"Not mine; it is his. We only casually talked about it when he explained the secret to the best rum punch. Let him have the credit. He will take ownership and work to bring it alive." The GM joined in with his form of jubilation.

I had never seen this cold-blooded German so worked up. I earned brownie points with him right at this moment.

I would create a wine-based cocktail for those hard-core hard liquor drinkers as an introduction to wines from Italia. This time he was daring, left from the traditional daiquiri, or blended drink bit, and used wine as a base. The drinks arrived with a description of the ingredients and preparation; garnish chosen.

As he preferred to call him a tease, I thought that Signori Giovanni introduced the cork-finished wine by the glass. Another jab that was noticeable but meant as a tease. They respected each other!

The drink combined with a touch of mango nectar, combined with the slightest of lime and the zest from the rind floating, a light white rum, and topped with stirred-up Bardolino Chianti and half shot of the most delicate rum now just making his debut on the island, stirred not shaken and served in a wineglass.

"Refreshing, a perfect aperitif," I mentioned and earned his approval, "The perfect transition from cocktail to dinner wine, red, of course." Once found, every layer of the flavor came to the surface, a true revelation. "Do you think he can win this contest?"

"Hands down," said Giovanni.

He overheard this. "Are you talking about this?" He pointed at me. "You do not waste any time, do you?"

Smiling, he walked back to his domain.

Dinner food came as a surprise. I would never have thought that the Chef could produce this type of dinner, creative, skillfully prepared local fish with tropical ingredients, which I had never tasted. A starchy kind of soufflé, crunchy at the top and soft light through, plus deep-fried plantains sliced lengthwise made for a dramatic presentation.

Then a mousse of mango whipped up from egg yolk, egg whites, and whipped cream with almond brittle flakes made from sliced almonds and caramel sugar crushed once cooled supplied just the amount of bite to force one to chew it while prolonging the delicate mango flavor. That is the idea of a dessert.

He was listening and wanted to prove himself. The cooks peeked into the restaurant to the nearby table to see our pleasure in this meal.

We asked all of the cooks to come to the table when we gave them a standing ovation. The expression on their faces would forever stay in my memory.

During the meal, Maggie supplied the transition from the drinking contest to the pirate's dinner! "Go ahead and tell the story. You are the best storyteller I know."

I started with the dream or nightmare as I first thought of it. I described the details of my search in the lobby with curious onlookers from the front desk, then the dialogue with the girls and the revelation of the simultaneous thinking process.

The audience started to take an interest in it. Then as the story transitioned into a real opportunity to recreate such an event as a promotion, signature performance with the unique stage being set only this Castle with its history could produce, the lights went on, and I had the full attention of both.

The final blow came when the production of staging such a theatrical performance combined with a memorable dining experience could be carried out with contacts of the two-night shift girls from the desk and themselves in it too.

The only part that fell on the hotel was to tip off the media for publicity and the coordination of setting the table and servers delivering the goods plus the wench serving the beverages. Relief on Giovanni's face, he at once signed on to it.

The GM, who was a bystander collecting the praise and glory from the guest, was a shoo-in. Now the pièce de resistance! "Can we plan to make this the centerpiece for the grand opening?"

Relief came from both as if they had just discovered the solution for the opening. We had been searching for a spectacular event like this, on a larger scale, but this would be very intimate, kept to the dignitaries from the company and press, and deliver a big bang. The rest must be happy with the gala buffet and drinks. The locals went for that. Media coverage would deal a blow to the competition.

The dinner party broke off while Giovanni pulled me aside to connect loose ends. That being cleared up, he was about to break away as I mentioned that the girl with the story would be waiting for the two of us to hear the good news.

Now the timing at our talk was wide open, and nothing committed, just an exploratory move, but could you imagine the reaction we got from her?

An entry into acting on a small stage, but stage performing in front of an audience. "Wonderful, it is what you have expected? I knew I could count on you."

"You are a bit the actor yourself. Good night, *bona sera!*" The girl must have jumped for joy and glided to get home.

"Does your brain ever take a break?"

I am a thinker, the thinker man, I was told once. But what a fun night so far.

The best is yet to come. We pick up where we left off.

The warm-up progressed rapidly. In no time did both of us reach the brink of explosion, but a little more tease she commanded, and then there came the point of no return.

This intimacy delivers fireworks, stars, and the best climax in my life.

We were out of breath, and our bodies stayed together, savoring the aftermath of this highest height, breathing in between passionate kisses, and feeling the sweaty skin rubbing against each other.

By 8:00 a.m., the sun had awakened us, and the adjacent rooms had been to breakfast. We both packed the luggage, ready for pickup by the bellman. We skipped breakfast but ate a couple of pasties from the executive office, coffee, and juice. That was good enough after such an elaborate meal last night.

Briefing the GM only took an hour since he had been party to all conversations and been briefed by Giovanni on the specialty restaurant development.

The girl from the front desk showed up at the secretary's desk and asked for me. I had heard her and motioned her to join. Timid in front of the GM, I assured her the groundwork had been laid.

All we wanted for her was to go through the actors' and producers' roles. She perked up like a sun reaching the flower, started to explain her situation, the person she had in mind, and yes, the teacher could be the producer. I could even get credit for it. Now I had not been able to present this to all these people. I wanted to wait until I got a positive signal from the hotel. Now I would get busy committing them.

"When do you anticipate having the premiere?"

"We plan to do the first one for the grand opening in about four to six weeks.

"It will be company dignitaries, even the owner. That is not set in stone, but we need to plan; get all props, costumes, serving tools, and develop a menu."

The GM had by now taken the lead, then asked me, "Do you have any idea about the food? It is natural to serve food from a specialty restaurant. It is the closest to the lobby, and the food will be a feature to promote it.

Beverages, we use what you have; there are enough selections. Banks Beer is good, rum, of course, and Giovani will have an excellent Italian wine to offer. It will be poured from pitchers by the wenches in long skirts and low-cut blouses.

I can ask the costume department to make the captain's uniform. They are good at it and always amend something to make another costume from it.

We will, of course, pay all of your actresses and actor a proper fee. That solves our problems. Please give me a budget for the production cost.

"Yes, I will get this to you. Thank you all for such great news. Thank you, a little money helps pay the bills. She jumped outside and never reached the ground for a mile."

The taxi waiting, we said our goodbyes, feeling good about all the accomplishments beyond expectation.

* * * * * * *

The flight was three and a half hours to JFK, then a change over to the shuttle for the last leg to National Airport. Neither of us wanted to talk shop, so the conversation went to tennis.

"I am going to be in NYC for a tournament. My boyfriend will be working it, and I have access to tickets. What are your plans for that day? She said it would be a Friday."

Nothing firm. I do have unfinished business at the NY hotel; I have not been back since I dropped that bomb. I had to let time go to settle the dust. It is high time to check on the restructuring, how the boys get along, and whether the progress can be reported.

Then there was this new construction promising to see the contours of inner space, and my boss encouraged me to visit. I will schedule it accordingly and combine it with the Connecticut hotel.

The new hotel under construction will be a sensational hotel with innovations, no details revealed."

The visit to Connecticut was also a follow-up and, as expected, supplied an excellent opportunity to write down all the niceties carried out to that day.

The turnaround in the kitchen was remarkable. The weeks of training in a sister hotel supplied a revelation for the Chef as he took it all in and finally understood that this system did supply more than just a blueprint to run a successful food production.

The creativity of a great Chef is not constrained. "Get used to the paperwork.

This admin staff is often the stumbling block for a Chef to accept, and then there is always a younger man on the team to appoint to this duty while affording him a future promotion to production manager."

On to the city and the uneasy task of finding the truth and results. God, I hope all this action had not been in vain.

My suspicion had been with the F&B director. His weakness for the pretty babes could be an opportunity to set a trap!

The usual professional welcome from the doorkeeper and bellman, then the front desk, having gotten to know me from this restaurant fiasco, greeted me and assigned me a room. "We have checkouts from the convention and missed capturing the tennis tournament at Madison Square Garden, so we are not crazy busy.

I will see a couple of matches. Maggie is there now and has a ticket for me. Her boyfriend is on the staff running the show. Yes, the top players are all in a heated battle.

Tonight's the semifinals. That is promising to be an entertaining match with the characters involved. As a tennis fan, she rattled off names, Bjorn something, Ivan Lendl, sounds German."

"No, he is Czech."

"Jimmy Connors, I remember him from Hartford, and last but not least, the NY bad boy McEnroe."

"Yes, I have seen him arguing with the official at his prime. I wish I could go!"

"Not in my power to get a ticket. I'm at the mercy of Maggie's boyfriend as it is, but front-row seats.

I will go stand by, and somebody will hack a ticket. Worth the money. This is going to be the battle of all battles!"

Maggie left a message on the phone in my room to come at 6:00 p.m. "A ticket will be at the will-call ticket counter." She would be there, sitting right next to me. The boyfriend did not need to get suspicious. He already fought, tensions were high, and he had ego problems with the players. Just play it cool.

With the ground rules found, I should be on my best behavior.

"Let us then face reality here at the hotel. The GM gave me an overview while waiting for the foodie. "He is doing his controlling in the storeroom, has been busy, and dropped weight."

Good to hear he turned the corner too. He got the subliminal message from the action. It could have gone sour with dire consequences. I know all too well all hell would be loose now.

"You took a calculated gamble, did your homework, settled on the strategy, and completed it with the grand finale. I am not a gambler or a hunter.

It did make me appreciate the thrill of winning a gamble, and as for the hunter, his thrill is in the chase more so than in the kill. Both have their satisfaction in the end."

"Well-illustrated, I have to remember this! Here he is. You boys do what you do best. Have a good day."

On the way down, I received a quick overview pointing in the right direction. The appointment of the banquet chef was the correct way. The Sous Chef gave him a hard time and resented it openly until I sat him down and leveled the playing field. Support him. He received this promotion for his accomplishments and for proving great organization skills.

"But banquets are easier than running the main kitchen."

Different but not a bigger job. Let's realize that there is only one restaurant and room service this kitchen has to service. The Chef was hands-off and useless. He took all banquet production out of here because it was unreliable to count on these guys. That is a reflection on you, and a bad one at that. You have a choice. Do it or find something that suits you better!"

"Are you suggesting I should quit?"

No, not at all, but you must work hand in hand, be a reliable assistant, and bury your crutches now. The hotel and I want to see you succeed, learn, and become successful in your way, and opportunities will knock at the door, understood?

It took him a day to digest this straight talk, and he returned and was a changed man. He would get a nice raise with his next review for loyalty and improvements he carried out.

The Chef had taken the lead instantly. He was a natural leader and made positive changes by getting the proper cooks into their element, so they all were in their most vital skills position now, and it showed in the quality, attitude, and food presentation.

"Are you staying over; want to have dinner here? The food is better than La Grenouille, and we take Visa."

I have a ticket to the US Open at the Garden, front row!

"How did you pull this off?"

Connections with high-ranking personnel!

Not showing the connection, we carried on the inspection and met with the Chef and Sous Chef, still apologizing for the dessert the last time. "*Forget about it* as they say in NYC."

He laughed, water under the Brooklyn Bridge.

The former butcher facility had been converted into a repair shop by engineering. "Glad you are making good use of it!" The chief was like a kid in the candy store when he got the word. Now F&B got excellent service from its technicians. The rest went to storage for various departments.

Corporate purchasing had made a speedy transition. Now we have delivery dates and not a daily drop of stuff with all these drivers snooping around. The staffing is scheduled and streamlined. Great improvement! Food cost is no longer a problem; still ways to go but on the right track. I am so pleased with your leadership and accomplishment so far. Let us go to the restaurant then, look up catering. Is she in?

"Yes, a light day; she should have time and express wanting to talk with you."

Jennifer greeted us at the door and offered us a table. Thank you. I want to have a look at the bar quickly.

The bartender, a veteran with seniority, was not yet on duty.

Most products stayed unlocked on the shelves since the restaurant got locked overnight! Do you see an opportunity here? Knowing that the bar was not his forte, I wanted to test and lead him to the answer.

"Looking at these bottles, there is a hierarchy."

"You mean brands?" yes, and more. What is your price structure? Do you have tiers?

"Yes, we have the house brands. They are in the cabinet below."

"Then all call brands as a higher-price tier."

I know you do great with cork-finished premium wine by the glass.

"Thank you. This is going great, and what a revelation. No longer do we have wine-collecting dust down there. Works like a charm. Anything and everything sells. The guests are so surprised and happy."

"Customers come in from the street, become regular, and bring friends in with them. I hope the bars and hotels do not catch on."

Wishful thinking, this concept is catching on fire. Competition always spies on others. Got to keep up.

"I should do more of this. We all learn from each other!"

Back to the bar. You do not see the potential here, so let me walk you through it.

Create three or even four tiers in the pricing. You do this by changing your display. Call brands are these, I pointed them out. They stay on the back bar. These shelves need to be enlarged, a pet project for your newfound friend, then these bottles are prominently displayed.

The third tier is fewer bottles in stock, which go on the top. The term *top shelves* get a new distinction.

Do a reasonable spread and shop competition to stay in line with competitors.

You will have to watch how sales shift. If the premium or top shelf takes off, I suspect it will expand this product line. Again, homework falls into your lap.

This profit center has not yet produced its fullest potential looking at the numbers. The cost is a bit high also.

In time, you may want to do away with the house brands, advertise premium brands, then start up from the higher category and lose them down selling price. The cost falls in line, more dollars, more money, more cash flow to pay all bills.

Massage this gently. Do it gradually. No traumatic moves, so the customer will not notice a bit. Just make sure the bartenders are in on it. Do you have a key for these cabinets?

"Yes, I can get it from the safe."

While you do this, I'll go to the room and get a gadget. Meet back here!

"The cabinet is now open. Let me see this choice. The low end of the product line needs to be upgraded! It would help if you wrapped the label not to be embarrassed with this stuff.

"The bartenders are asking for it," he said, half apologetic.

I pulled a bottle of gin and vodka, removed the pourer, and smelled it. Gin has a distinct aroma, but the vodka is almost neutral. Then I took out my tall slim measuring glass and a glass hydrometer and filled the measuring glass until the hydrometer started to float.

Now read this line I asked him!. What do you get?

"Is this a proof measuring device?"

Yes, it is, and you are getting what?

"I see thirty on the line."

Okay, the liquid returned to the vodka bottle, rinsed, and now we do the gin. The reading was twenty-eight. What is this telling you?

A blank look, this boy is naive.

This stuff has been watered down by the bartender. I will tell you the scam.

The bar business does cash transactions, especially the walk-in traffic. You mentioned there is a following of regulars. The bartender gets to know these friendly guys, buys them a drink on the house he is not authorized to do, and then keeps counting cash sales. These get rung up as zero. The register makes the same sound if with money or zero money.

At the end of the night, he counts his zero rings and multiplies them by the price of the drink. I guarantee they can do this in their head, with practice, you understand. The cash is removed from the drawer, and now he has joined the hotel as a partner!"

"Partner?"

Yes, a partner in profit! Now you understand it.

"Tell me how he keeps count."

"One does it by memory, others use matchsticks they throw in a glass hidden below, others shift coins from one pocket to another. They are very inventive. This is where your beverage cost goes. Take the calculator and find out the amount it takes in added revenue to make the beverage cost what it should be. It is a guideline with variables, but you get the idea.

"You know every trick."

Learned it in the trenches. School of hard knocks! "Should I act on this diluting?"

No but replace these bottles. Is there a switch od staff from last night?

"Yes, the regular bartender is off."

"Good, remove the diluted bottles, mark the line of the liquids with a magic marker, date it, and keep it in your office. On the replacement requisition, mark it as breakage, for you have to have an empty one for a full to keep the par straight.

"Explain this a bit, so I went through the entire control procedure the storekeeper must follow guidelines.

I never knew that!"

Life is full of surprises when the regional comes to town!

You just received a black mark. Learn it, read the SOPs, and follow up on it, then test it if there is any collusion, for it is partly based on the staff's honesty.

Making a count of the par on an irregularly while in operation at a quiet time will put the fear of God into these cats. There is a par list. Get a copy and count the full and empty bottles; it's a quick procedure that keeps them honest.

Inspect what you expect! "Lesson learned."

Now I need you to give me a strategy on this watered-down stuff.

Here is what needs to happen. Remember, the union is still alive. We need to catch this guy red-handed. This is why nothing is done right now, and it is good that we found out about them not being here.

The next time you pull this is at the end of the night shift. Yes, it will be a late night. Pick a busy night for regulars off the street, a Friday or Saturday.

Get a room with your wife so you can rest before and be fresh. This way, you avoid this late-night subway ride.

Arrange for a witness, the night auditor, or a neutral person, then pull all gin, vodka, tequila, light rum, anything, and everything light in color or white.

Have the night auditor record the proof measurement of each bottle while you measure and assign a number with a marker and line left of the liquid, then move on to the next while the one measured is returned to the place from where it was taken.

Very calm, organized with a poker face, do not give away the element of surprise, and remember! Now walk away but return with the night auditor and security.

Here comes the bomb as you reveal the action, reason, and result, computing the difference of the proof amounts to xx much. Have a prepared scale by proof. All should be eighty proofs, an easy calculation. But you are not yet revealing the amount!

Then you accuse him of stealing. You are a thief! We have the police underway, a bluff, to arrest you, for the hotel will press charges! You will get a rumble or two making an excuse or blame on someone else.

With this, you reveal that all had been measured in the morning, replaced the diluted once with an unopened one, and the other guys will be facing the same judge!

"He will break unless he is a criminal. He will see himself unemployed with a tarnished record and look for another profession to make his living and then he will confess. All in writing, of course, witnessed by the auditor and security, you send him home.

Now the union, a déjà vu from the time before, the strategy is another deal not to press charges. All bartenders are released from the hotel's employment and releases signed not to pursue a legal defense and to badmouth, putting the lid on them and the union ones more.

Then the friendly follow-up meeting with the GM and acceptance of more concessions. You just loaded up on the chips to cash in. This will be your feather in the hat. Leave me out of it, okay?

"Great deal, and a million thanks for this lesson."

"Now, let this pretty lady take us to lunch at her restaurant." She smiled and understood the compliment; my companion took a minute to catch on. Jenny expressed her delight with the changes coming out of the kitchen; finally, we were proud of our jewel. Food is improved with creative garnishes, very New Yorkish, just what I have always envisioned. Kudos to the entire kitchen.

Let us discuss what we can and need to do for these women. She is the heart of the restaurant! We need to give her something before she gets stolen!

"I have her fill in on the restaurant manager's night off. She at once made a difference in the attentiveness of the servers. The captain is giving her a hard time claiming her lack of experience in fine dining, but she stands her ground."

Do you see an answer in this?

"Yes! Just how do we handle the restaurant manager?"

"I have nothing large on him, and he also sneaked into the union."

Not a surprise to me; he is the shady kind. Is he not responsible for the bar when on duty? It's right in front of his nose?

"Yes, he is technically responsible for the bar."

How much does he involve himself with the bar?

"He keeps an eye on it, and at closing, he has to cash out the cashier and bartender in the back of the front office.

Nobody else gets involved with that, like the night auditor.

"No, he was told once to keep his nose out of it by the restaurant manager." Yes, of course.

I smell a rat already. This place is a beehive, and one can easily get stung! Now how are we going to do this?

It has to change, and once we get him out, you make Jenny the restaurant manager for all meal periods and do not be stingy with the salary increase. A bonus on top.

It must be a sting operation. Searching my brain, it came to me.

He saw me light up and asked, "What? You have an idea?"

Do I ever! We add him to the bartender list!" Question marks on his face. I continued,

When you pull the caper with the bartender and get this all going, keep him there as an observer. He will catch on quickly and get uncomfortable, even wanting to leave under a pretense, but you insist him to remain. Anyways, he has to wait to cash him out.

Then when all is done, he should be in an uncomfortable position, fidgeting, making erratic hand movements, working his hair despite the ton of spray or grease he adds to it, sweating. Make him see the entire process, and at the close of it, do an audit of his bank with the night auditor.

I strongly suspect it will be over by a large amount, for this is Friday, or better yet, Saturday and Sunday are his days off. We will accumulate his payoff from the bartenders, another partner in profit if this pans out the procedure all over, confession, witness, security, the works. Have the Union fire him? More chips to cash in for the future!"

"What a stroke!"

Do not screw it up. You have now learned and saw all critical steps, the element of surprise, and the tension building for the kill.

I told your boss it is like a hunter going in the woods. He enjoys the chase better than the kill. For somebody always gets hurt.

With this, we came to the GM's office for the debriefing with big smiles.

What are your cats up to now?" Henry chimed in, saying we have set up a hunt, not a wild goose chase but a hunt with victims.

As he explained the way we got on the track of it and then the strategy to follow with the result equal to the kitchen, he smiled and said it was high time to catch this crook. He had to be the instigator and supplied cover for manipulating the money.

"You will put Jenny in charge of the service and make her the manager."

That is the plan, and she has an assistant trained to take over the a.m. shift and another in the pipeline from supervisor. She is worth her weight in gold, but we cannot afford that kind of pay, but we can show generosity.

Reward those who have earned and deserve it. That is the spirit.

With this in motion, I will say goodbye. You have the ball now. Run with it to a touchdown. I will keep his feet to the fire to pull it off. No worry. We will not let this opportunity go."

****

On the way to the elevator, I was stopped by the catering director. "Yes, I know you have requested to speak with me. I have the time now, Elizabeth. Where to?"

"Mi casa," she said with a smile. "You have never been to the catering office. Allow me to introduce you to my domain."

Organized as expected, sample place settings, wedding pictures, props, and fancy decoration made this an ideal place to sell social parties. "It is my bread and butter. What can I do for you?

"It is a personal favor if you do not mind. I have a cousin in this business who works at a competitor's hotel, the Helm. It is a place of torture, what this Helm woman does to her managers. He wants out before he ends up with ulcers in the hospital.

"Do you have any openings for him?"

We have a hotel under construction, very much advanced at this stage. I will present him to our people. Can I get his résumé?

"Already there."

You are prepared, good. I see he has substantial experience.

"Yes, we both trained at the Waldorf in its heydays under a master catering man. I shall never forget the training he provided, so we are the same chip of the rock."

How did he ever get involved with her? She has a horrible reputation.

"That is a long story; no time for it now, and he can tell you this in person. We can arrange for a meeting on your next visit."

Good, what about you? Are you still happy with this assignment, or are you getting itchy feet?

"I am okay, but why are you asking?"

There is another mega hotel built near the city's heart. It will be a while, but I would like to nominate you for this hotel. Bigger, much bigger than this, but in principle, the business is the same: more staff and assistants, but good leadership is paramount.

"I would like to think this over. I am so close to my client base here I hate to give it up." They follow a good leader "I suppose so. But give me time."

We have time, and it is going to be your decision to make, yours only, no pressure, I promise.

She gave me a hug and a kiss on the cheek, and I went to my room to watch tennis matches, all were reruns.

Chapter 17

I walked to Madison Square Garden. A need to walk straight up. Good posture and long strides lubricate the spine and prevent back pain like preventive medicine. So many people complain of back pain. I was a bit early, found this will-call ticket window, and with the ticket in hand, the ushers led me to the seat.

Maggie greeted me with a handshake and an eye, signaling him to be close. "He will stop by once the next match is underway, supplying a little break.

This is the first match this evening, and it will be a slaughter. Watch Ivan Lendl. He is a strong, tall, muscular player and has vicious shots to upset his opponent, John McEnroe."

Her boyfriend did stop by to say hello. I thanked him for the ticket and kind words, and he went off.

Memories from Hartford came to mind I was then not t that close and more from a distance and in the back of the scene. I tried to think if I had seen him there, or was it someone else? This man was everywhere, directed the workers in every direction, and seemed in perpetual motion. This must be his job. Not easy to handle that kind of personnel, the officials from ATP, and players with egos larger than life.

Ivan won the toss and opted to serve first. The sound from the racket meets the ball that close up was something to get used to. He did have a powerful serve. There was a clock measuring playtime and the scoreboard. The serve speed was also measured; how can anybody get his racket on a high-speed serve?

He served a kickball, Johnny returned with a recovery shot, and Ivan took advantage by coming forward, taking the ball in the air to get it to the opposite side. No chance for JM. 15–love was the score announced, the second serve ready to fly off the racket, this time down the T, another difficult serve with higher speed, not visible from my side. JM must have expected it by taking a more central position but moved back from the baseline and returned to Ivan. This play went on until Lendl won the match point.

During a break, Maggie's boyfriend stopped by, and the dialog turned again into another fight,

She told him she would return to Washington tonight with the last shuttle; she needed to prepare for a seminar and would be on the road next week. He left angry and stormed away as we heard him mumble, "Have it your way!" Obvious tension had been them would not go away.

"Do you mind if we leave now? I need real food in my stomach. This food from street vendors and chunk snacks is not nutritious. I need a decent meal. Are you staying over at the hotel?"

Yes.

"A favor, can I bunk in with you? I do not have a hotel and do not want to hurry back."

Your wish is my command, and I will buy you dinner at the hotel. I must experience the new cuisine. It is the job, you know. She smiled again and pressed her head on my shoulder while we walked arm in arm to the hotel.

We sat and talked calmly about her relationship with this man. "He is a good man. It is his and my job that keeps us apart. Neither wants to give. He loves this travel gypsy life, I guess, for now. I cannot imagine this can last forever, and then what? "

"He is educated in business management but does not have any corporate business experience. Leaving this well-paid job would mean working his way up from the near bottom."

"In my case, to give up my job, good pay, travel, and working with people like yourself is unimaginable. I would become a groupie on the tennis circuit. You are permanently traveling and living in hotel rooms and do not need a house or flat to live in except for three weeks in December. Even then, tournaments want him to organize and offer premium pay and bonuses, and he goes for it. His rationale is to accumulate savings, invest them, and buy a small hotel once he has enough funds."

"So that is our dilemma, what did you call it at the seminar, a stalemate. I tried to hook him up with my father to manage his casinos. The management of the hotel operation had to be given to local people. The government financed them and took a stake in them to assure compliance.

But casinos had been my father's exclusive and sole property.

He did not show any interest. I have to be my own man, not a kept *lackey* living of the shirt tale of your father."

Dinner was surprisingly great, with nice touches as described and no management except the maître d' I observed him hanging around the door.

He seldom visited the tables or checking up on delays from the kitchen, I started talking to Maggie about him.

Do you think he is doing his job? Just watch him. Where does he spend his time, and where are his eyes fixed on?

She observed him and said, "He must be in charge of the bar. He shows more interest in watching the bartender than the restaurant."

I saw the same when I ate here on my first visit, but with my back to the entrance, I did not get a constant look at him. Something strange struck me then and never left my guts.

You are observant, I said to her. "Trademark of a woman to keep an eye on her man! Ha, ha."

"I know you better than thinking that there is not something cooking with your remark."

Two points for you. Yes, there is, but later. I cannot let the kitty out of the bag just yet. She has to turn into a tigress first.

"I got it now, but you will tell me upstairs."

Yes, if I get enough time. I stopped as she smiled.

"I give you time, and there is time afterward, too. I am staying, remember?

It will be a sweet ending to a frustrating visit here. Just do not let your frustrations out on me!

"Oh no, it will be warm, fuzzy, and compassionate. You are my favorite person."

I gave her the key to go ahead, and then I conveyed my compliments to the Sous Chef and cooks with a quick look into the kitchen. "Thank you, Chef, much appreciated," I said good night to the bartender, who offered me a nightcap.

Thanks, another time. Good night, Mr. Maître D'. A smile on his face confirmed the much-improved quality in a cautionary tone. Then a quick look into the banquet room as they finished a company dinner party with guests lingering and talking.

The guestroom door was ajar. Maggie was in the shower, and I quickly undressed to catch her before she finished.

Rubbing soap all over her met with no resistance, stimulated the nipples to rock-hard toys the size of a blackberry, then the back scrub was given and reciprocated, and the tender area was without soap to start the foreplay.

Since I knew this body by now so well and all the sensitive areas, I left no stone unturned, got her to moaning before the shower ended.

Aa quick towel, and half wet onto the sheets to make passionate love to her. The more one does it together, the better it gets.

The wordless communication flows and brings out all the emotion; This is no longer just sex. This is actual lovemaking, loving each other. What a wonderful, warm, compassionate woman! I was rapidly falling in love with her.

"Now, I want to hear all about this Maître d'."

Do you know what the Maître d' is? The *D* is short for *de*, followed by the area of responsibility. Like they all are, Chef de cuisine, even Chef de service. The best description for Maître d'hôtel would be the General Manager labeling them as the master of the hotel!

"Is this going to be a story?"

"Yes, but an unfinished ending like Schubert's Symphony. "You know this music?"

Yes, I love classical music, opera, musicals, operettas.

"You amaze me every time!"

"No, on with the story. We do not have all night."

The night was young, hinting at an encore. I continued with the tour and ended at the bar when an idea flashed in my mind. I'm not sure exactly what, but it made me stop and look at the bottles. Then it came to me that I had overlooked this area so far and needed to ask questions. First, the price structure, selection, price, and brand quality tiers, then looking at the well brands below in the cabinet.

Strange that the least expensive alcohol is locked up while the high-end brands are left out on the bar top.

No real reason, he explained since the restaurant gets locked overnight. They are secure. That is an answer but not a rationale about locking the cheap stuff in a cabinet in addition.

It must be precious, locking up the house but leaving the gold jewelry out while the custom jewelry is put into the safe.

"I see your point!"

I pulled out a bottle of gin and vodka, took off the pouring spout, and then smelled it.

Vodka does not have a strong aroma unless it is flavored vodka. Not in this case, but a strong alcohol smell comes forth. The gin, of course, has an aroma from the Guinevere berries, so when I smelled it, a little aroma came up, the same as the alcohol with the vodka. When he left to get the keys to unlock, I came up here and fetched this.

"What is it?"

"A scale to measure the alcohol contents of alcoholic beverage. See, the sale goes to one hundred and this one to two hundred. That is alcohol by percentage and proof on the opposite side. The proof is always double the alcohol.

"Interesting!"

I placed this scale into this container and poured the alcohol in it until the scale floats. There is the reading of alcohol in percentage and proof. Both bottles showed lower readings, one 40 and the other almost 50 proof. These two bottles then got taken away and replaced.

We did not want to create an alert. These bartenders are stealing, selling drinks for cash, pocketing the money, and diluting the liquor not to raise suspicion. The consumption of liquor can easily be reconciled and controlled to see the excess consumption and money shortage, a simple audit function."

"You lost me on that."

You need to know yields, shot size, mixed drinks, and it gets sticky anyway. Now back to the story!

After this, I sat him down and walked him through every detail he had to follow. He just never knew, that and worked on blind trust!

This is going to be his show, understand? I am not coming back, and it is his job to begin with.

He now has to be here on a Saturday night, bring his wife and stay over. Before closing is the sting going down.

"You sound like the FBI now."

Yes, it pays to watch the program.

He will keep the bartender from cashing out with the Maître d' and pull every bottle with clear alcohol and all those with light-colored alcohol like tequila, light rum.

For that, he needs a witness, so the night auditor on duty will be aiding in a bar count, nothing specific, and be on standby. He will record the proof of every bottle, type of liquor, and brand; The bottle gets a line marker showing the fill level and a number. These guys like to have multiple bottles open to the halfway mark on a busy night.

I received another tip when the bartender bragged about the wine sales and how this repeatedly brings locals off the street with their friends.

They do not only come for the wine!

With this exercise completed and done without any explanation, the bartender will be on the brink of explosion for curiosity. Tension is running high, and of course, the bartender heard the proof numbers but had to disguise his awareness and played cool.

Now the blow when the action is revealed, and for what purpose, the bartender will play dumb or push it up to other bartender, but few excuses carry weight.

He runs out of reasons, lets his head hang, and asks for forgiveness, this being the first time, and he was put up to it by the other guy and on he goes to soften the blow.

At this time, security makes the appearance all perfectly timed and on cue.

Maggie was squeezing my arm with anticipation for the finale. Now the open accusation that all bartenders were involved in stealing. We have tested the stock several times and with every bartender.

He can confess, and we will show leniency, for it is not our objective to involve the law, but, if need be, we are prepared to call the police officers right now.

As he will be pulling a phone in the attempt to place the call, here comes the admission.

Papers ready for a written confession and signed document not to use legal defense and use defamatory language about the hotel. All signed and notarized by the auditor.

We are prepared to press criminal charges since we are talking thousands of dollars and have enough proof of it.

More papers to protect the hotel. The job is lost. You are fired for what will be known as an unfortunate mistake with consequences.

"What about the union?"

Life is kinder when one tells the truth.

"Good night, what a wonderful story."

But wait, there is chapter two. The Maître d' has the bar's responsibility, and he is next.

He checked out the guys and cashed out the proceeds of the bartender. With my suspicious mind, I recalled his interest in bar activities while neglecting the service. He has to be in on it.

The bank count, which should have been $200 to be able to make change for the cashier and bartender, revealed $3,000 over in cash.

Where is this money coming from? It cannot be by supplying change. There was no answer but a quick confession and the paperwork he had known by now terminated him on the spot, the paycheck will be ready for pickup at the front office and have a good life.

Revealing this gameplan to the GM, later on, he looked at me with amazement. "Do you bring a new broom every time you come here?"

No, this was coincidental, but my instinct led me to it. I have a good nose smelling rats.

It will go down next weekend!

The replacement of this position will be the opportunity for Jenny taking over as restaurant manager and also the bar. She has an assistant ready to take her place tomorrow, plus supervisors in the pipeline to fill in the gaps. While the outcome is still pending, the happy ending is already written.

"What a wonderful story. You must write a book." Yes, okay with my English. I need help.

A big kiss and benefits on top of it. After catching her breath, she once more reinforced her belief that this was book material. "These are wonderful stories."

There is no time at this juncture, and time is the essence to writing a book. "At least write down notes and keep them in the office. Once you find time, the urge to write may be there, which helps refresh the memory. At your rate, you accumulate a couple of new stories weekly, sometimes daily."

I love you for your confidence in me. Now let's get some sleep. We have to get back early and straight to the office."

"How do I sneak out?"

Do not sneak. It makes you a suspect. Act as if you had a room booked. Join a group of people and walk out. I will be out front getting a cab lined up, then goodbye, and we go. The morning crew does not know what happens at night. In the cover of darkness, the goblins come out.

"Stop this. Go to sleep." She cuddled up and was out in a minute.

* * * * * * *

Briefing the VP of F&B on the upcoming action came as a surprise. This time, the action and results were pending. He expressed reservations about whether this guy could handle it. My assurances are founded on the fact that he had seen the kitchen action when I took the lead.

time he had explicit details on the steps to take and how to bring it to the blow. If he failed, he had watered it down and makes himself a suspect, if not an accomplice. It was a logical assumption. Keep your fingers crossed.

"I like you're thinking."

Following this information I reported the good news on the progress in the kitchen, the positive effect of corporate purchasing, and the plans to replace the Maître d'. The food production system was being worked out but with great difficulties and still unfinished.

To turn around the ship, they needed help. A couple of corporate trainers and a task force Chef or food production manager for a week or less would do him good.

Agreeing to it, he would approve it at the earliest date the schedule allowed. "You did good work for the hotel and softened the tight grip of the union.

"I love the way this is going down. The best part is how you structured it so that the union has the burden to save face and avoid bad publicity."

"You will receive a raise every six months to catch you up to midlevel in the pay grade."

I was surprised and pleased. I could only say, Thank you so much. This is the best company to work for in the hospitality industry.

"As promised, remember way back in Hartford."

Yes, Hartford's my turning point in my professional life. I hope the seed from Hartford does not destroy the family life.

"You do not have to talk about it now, but if you ever feel the need, I will gladly be a good listener."

The RVP's briefing on the upcoming actions required a more detailed description, particularly how they had orchestrated this theft and how the controls had been ignored.

'That happened under my nose," he said with guilt.

Your F&B director and restaurant managers had the responsibility, and from what I have learned, the previous F&B guy had been let go under the suspicion of improprieties?

"Yes, that is true. However, we never got to the bottom of it. Regional support was as good as zero."

Do not blame yourself. The good news will come next weekend, and the changeover brings new blood to the scene.

Jenny will be the new restaurant manager, her assistant to take over the a.m. shift, and she has supervisors in the pipeline in a classic Jenny style."

"I love this and what you did in the kitchen." We will send help and bring the kitchen on the company's system.

Catering is in good hands, and she is happy there. I see her as a candidate for the mega hotel, and she has a cousin at the Helm who needs to get out before Ms. Helm kills him. I mean, cause ulcers with her constant badgering.

"You are a terrific strategist. How did you learn this?"

School of hard knocks, I said and wished him a wonderful day.

With the reports written, I left early to make it home as a surprise. My son was home alone doing homework. When he saw me, he jumped at me and cried, "Mami left me alone."

"She went to the store food shopping and promised to be back shortly."

"It is now to hours, no word, no call."

"Maybe she is having car trouble."

"But why not let me know? I am so worried."

Be calm. It is nothing to worry about.

She came home with one brown bag of groceries and was turning red in the face seeing me home early.

I had pulled my car into the garage to be out of sight. The early homecoming had a colossal effect, and the unpleasant surprise, a "*Gotch ya,*" now confirmed by her red face. To make things worse, the kid asked her, "Is this all you had to buy, and it took you two and a half hours? Why did you not call me if you had problems? I was worried to death!"

She was speechless, thought hard to produce an answer, but could not deliver, then breaking out crying, she ran to the bedroom and cried for a long time.

Once composed again, she asked me not to press her now. She would tell me when our son was in bed. He must have overheard this since he made every effort to keep his door ajar and tried to listen.

Now came a confession.

"First came the solicitation to join this group. This group she was following had revealed themselves as a cult with rituals. At first it was harmless; after that, alcohol was mixed with spiritual yoga, which was practiced in a secluded location and usually at night. I went once when the boy had a sleepover at the neighbors but left when I could see where this would end up".

"Other members attending encouraged me to take part at another time and described the outcome. They were trying to make members into sex slave. I stopped going, yet they kept coming here when school was in session, knowing I would be alone. I fought them and remembered how you had thrown them out of the house in Connecticut."

"I had planned to tell you all this, and you can go there to scare them and keep me alone. One of the men knocked at the door late one night, trying to seduce me. He had me pinned down and was ready to rape me. I threatened to call my son and wake him to call the police."

"All this is heavy stuff; as I suspected from day one, there was something wrong with these people. You do not believe the number of women blindly following and going along with whatever they commanded."

What are you going to do? "I am scared"

You do one thing. Do not show your panic. They will be back quickly and are afraid they will lose you now and tell on them. A criminal investigation can be the outcome if it continues we will take my car into the service and leave it there for the week.

I was going to travel but I will change my schedule, thinking we could take in a symphony concert or an opera, whatever is offered.

You tell one of these disciples that I was traveling again and be gone for two weeks to Barbados, out of the country. That will make them bold and show up in force to get you back into the ranks with special status or something. I will be here and stay out of sight. I must tell Sonny to choose indoor projects.

When they come, you will greet them, let them come inside, and I will come out from the shadow with a recorder as the conversation progresses.

I will tell them that your confession, show this recorder, and whatever is said will be added to it.

I have already tipped off the agent in charge of the areas law enforcement of the activity. I am ready to press charges for multiple violations, like attempted rape, disturbance of the peace, infiltration of the family life, seductive behavior under pressure, and actual sex rituals going on weekly with other women.

I have the address and have done research on all names already.

That will be my speech. If they do not run away by then, I will call the police, seek a restraining order, and see where it takes it.

They are cowards. My poker face will not give away the bluff. They will run, and that will be the end of it.

You will then go to the courthouse and file a restraining order against all the names and the organization's name, plus the women that know your address. It will be a basis for calling the police if they come within three hundred feet and then get arrested.

Just one call, no questions asked. I suspect they all have criminal records and pending warrants for their arrest! You understand this?

After that, no more! Instead, you will get yourself a morning job, anything to be productive, any job. Be a cashier in a grocery store or work as a sales job in a department store, anything to keep you occupied.

I will not repeat this; the next time, you will be on your own. I hope I made myself clear!

Nodding her head, she promised.

I called early Monday to get days off for a family emergency. "The secretary, Andrea, will convey it to Mr. Baker. Then off to the mechanic, just a service, but do not hurry. I will not be able to pick it up for days.

"No problem, the car will be waiting for you almost as new, smiling and kidding." The man had a sense of humor, and by now, he had found out how I responded to his comments.

Within two days, this confrontation went down by the script. She played the victim's role, pleaded to be left alone, and as these three men started to apply pressure and threats, I entered the scene.

Voice recorder in hand to be visible, my role kicked in with all the force and bluff I could muster up.

The resistance and counterattacks did roll off my skin. I stood firm and produced the name of the agent in charge.

The standard title used for an FBI agent responsible for the area was well understood and prompted a facial reaction.

I knew I had made headways and would now deliver the final knockout punch. Pulling up a printout from a computer folded in half so it could not be read, I described it as a rap sheet on two of the men.

The FBI will easily obtain the third, and they will be pleased to get a lead on all of you. A warrant is still open to be served and executed. I spoke this word so slowly it sounded like the spelling E-X-E-C-U-T-E-D.

Now they retreat with an empty promise to leave the wife alone and stay away from her. Not good enough. I wanted absolute proof of it to let this go without punishment.

What am I saying, stupid?

I told myself; that criminals needed to get locked up, for they were a threat to the population, ruthless predators exploiting the weak.

"What will you have to offer?" The three men were now talking among themselves, whispering but audible enough to make out the gist of the talk.

The one with the lesser rap sheet wanted to go to the police and turn himself in and hope to convince them that he had lived a clean life since his last legal encounter. The third man joined him, obviously a minor infraction, and then the lead guy who had led the charge wanted nothing to do with it, flatly refused, and played hardball.

"Come on. You will get the lightest sentence turning yourself in. The longer it takes them to find you, the harder they will press for the maximum penalty. Now they have you in their hand, and running is not a good choice. You know the proverb, *You can run, but you can't hide.*

I let it sink in and did after minutes, and pressing for an answer, he finally conceded.

Heads bowed; they made their way out the door!

I took a deep breath, poured a fresh cup of this exceptional coffee from Sumatra added milk, and took a big gulp with a deep breath, releasing the tension.

"How did you pull this off? I mean, where did you learn this?"

I started in Buffalo, then Minneapolis with guys getting the ax, then most recently in New York where I got the fat cats and the union to become my latest victims.

The next one is going down from a remote location in New York!

Yes, the hotel manager will have to conduct this himself.

"Can he do it? Why not you again?"

I suspect he is highly motivated; more I cannot tell. But I will tell you about every detail from the past capers.

Relaxed and with a long-awaited overture for sex from her, we sat relaxed after a light lunch of Bircher Muesli as I started to tell her about every detail in an organized fashion so she could follow. She is intelligent, just not knowledgeable of corporate life. Too much time had elapsed since she had been gainfully employed. Finally, at the conclusion, she nodded, giving a complete understanding of my situation and the tension I so often took home with me into a sleepless night.

The relationship flourished again. We did make it to a play called *Amadeus*, the life story of Mozart, at the National Theater.

The excellent stage setting, acting and costumed in the time of Mozart's life, and his music interwoven with the various speaking parts was food for the soul. It revealed that he was made into a knotty boy by the royal females using him as the toy to entertain their friends on selected soirees. The meager pay kept Mozart and his wife hungry and dependent on these tête-à-tête relations. After that, the boudoir play had become obligatory to be chosen for future performances.

A delightful play we thoroughly enjoyed and realized that classical music was part of our passion. Once hooked on it, we now needed music CDs.

We do not get enough of it. One more day was spent with the boy looking for a stereo disk player, new speakers, and an amplifier.

At the music shop, it looked as if this music had died and was no longer reproduced past the old tapes.

So much choice of pop music, shallow stuff turning more primitive as time went on; at least it had melodic quality with a lyric that could be understood and told a love story.

The store clerk took us to the back row; yes, this was what we were looking for. The choice had been sufficient for us as we searched for the familiar music dear to us. Five good disks, symphonic recordings with music from Mozart, Beethoven, Dvorak, Schuman's unfinished symphony, piano concertos, and Van Cliburn dominated the choice.

Lighter pieces with operettas from Lehar, Strauss, Kalman, delightful happy music to lift the spirit.

Now I had to prepare for the next assignment.

Barbados specialty restaurant and the grand opening of the new wing with fifty rooms.

"I would like to see what all is involved if you don't mind. I know nothing about the work you do on your travels."

As I opened the file folder filled with documents, reports, and notations, I went ahead to sort the paperwork in sequence to have a starting point and the current status.

Then the notes of unfinished business, which were large. The bulk of the groundwork was set up in the draft format; it needed to be refined and chronologically arranged as the activity should flow.

She followed with great interest, drawing from her waitress time in Zurich. Sometimes a question to explain terminology in English; she knew it in German.

I went over the service procedures, jotting down ideas about how we could refine them and prove superior service. The conduct of the servers was the foremost tool.

Providing efficient service, being knowledgeable beyond any customer's expectations, the knowledge of wines, and reciting with confidence the wine's origin, were offered on the back of the winemaker's name and personal notes. Then most importantly, what this wine would best suit with food is called pairing.

Giovanni will have work done on this subject, especially with the Italian wines. He tended to neglect the French and German and ignored the Chileans and Argentinean choices.

We must have these even as you believe them not worthy of this European offering. Let the customer decide. We get our fair share of guests from the South American continent. I was explaining to her as if I was speaking to Giovanni. It's a subject she knew well enough.

This being in the notes for the *"To Do"* list, now another look at the menu.

With a smile on my face, I envisioned Priscilla in action, working to prepare the food as she had done at her mother's place.

"Why the grin, something I did or said?"

I will have to tell this most delightful episode but let me finish this first. I changed the words used to describe the food, too many repetitive words used, and alternatives found and entered.

I will fax this ahead, so it gets there before the printer gets to do his craft.

The menu had been accepted at the home front. It took arm twisting but enthusiasm from the VP F&B, the corporate Chef, and my secretary, Andrea, the boss's secretary had a profound effect. Using her charm toward the boss and influencing the menu department resulted in a sign off approval.

What is your problem, Ginny? The recipes are here and approved and will be adopted into the system. It will enrich the company's repertoire!

"Now to the beverage area!

It did not need preparation with this guy. He already has his signature drink, the aperitif choices, and after-dinner selection with the addition of Appleton's finest aged rum challenging the great cognac brands.

Indeed, making inroads with the sales if presented as an exclusive offering to the Castle! The company was willing to print an exclusive label making it known that the Castle would be the first to pour it to consumers.

I noted the need for an oversized snifter and a warmer with a candle to present this bottle at the table and the portion size to be 2.5 ounces minimum on the free pour.

Additionally, we will gladly supply a taster to win over the skeptics.

All registers pulled; this has to become the signature product to put the finishing touch on the evening. Exclusive to the restaurant further entices guests to patronize this place, bring your friends, and entertain customers. The price is equal to a XO cognac. Now for the final touch, we will add an incentive to it.

Once the bottle gets to the level with three to five drinks left of this liquid gold, the buyer of the last shot receives this ornate bottle as his memorabilia. It is estimated that it will fetch a collector's value of one hundred dollars with an auctioneer. Bottles are numbered, showing limited production. Appleton had thought of everything.

We secured sufficient supply to guarantee availability. The company added bottles as a gift to be given to selected dignitaries and one bottle for me.

I shall treasure this and only share it with true friends."

By now, my wife was so taken by the detailed work. She was at a loss for words.

"I had no clue of your work. Now I understand the time it takes. So sorry for nagging on you. I have a new appreciation of you."

You must tell our son about these things on his level of understanding. Mothers have this ability, while fathers can get frustrated. But wait, there is more!

I then opened the Pirates folder with the menu, table setup, beverage list, and service procedures all very much defined.

I only wanted to visit all details once more to see if anything had been left to chance or forgotten; a new idea spawned from it.

As I leafed through the papers, I explained the event in great detail, leading into how the idea came to life, the dream, the same vision in the front-office girls who had that very same thought that night, as if she was searching for a receiver.

When finally found one within her spiritual power and then how it all came together.

The sequence of the evening will be staged as an exclusive event only available at the Castle and turned into a theatrical production to re-enact the time of the pirate's life.

It will be spawning the romance of that time in the female audience and disgust in the males. It should become a sellout for a month in advance.

"Even if not yet sold out, the reservation will state so at the beginning, creating the allure to book at a later time or putting him on a waiting list that could serve to fill the table or have a backup for cancellations.

It is a game, a marketing tool creating the brand.

Every product gets its notoriety form clever marketing.

I lost her on this strategy.

I made a highlighted note to follow up on this with the front office or executive secretary, whomever they had chosen as the designated reservation taker.

The GM will have two seats in his pocket to accommodate a VIP or corporate dignitary. The marketing folks in New York must also follow this path.

I will brief the GM first. He needs to get the troupes together, and I would expect that marketing will be on the island already. They never miss a good party.

I am ready for the next assignment. Will you take me to the airport? It will be at least ten to fourteen days.

Leaving the car there made me nervous.

"I am sorry. I have to take the kid to school early. He must take part in an event, and Mama must be there by his special instructions."

Okay, but I will take your car this time and leave it at the airport parking. My car is now serviced and will not give you any trouble.

Leave the car out and visible into the evening; when it gets dark, lock it in the garage, double lock all entrances, and keep the phone nearby all day and night. Bring the boy upstairs to be extra cautious. Besides, it will serve as a deterrent should these crooks have changed their minds or are free on bond.

Should anything happen, here are the agent's phone and hotel numbers. I will put them on the alert should a call come from Virginia.

I will also ask the corporate security man to be on the alert. I will let him know if there is an intrusion, and he is living in this neighborhood and has been briefed. He will identify himself with a corporate business card. Okay, we are all set now. Then off to a good night's sleep and early rise.

* * * * * * *

The taxi drive to the Castle from the airport along with the sugarcane fields that had been harvested, had the remaining stalks burned to enrich the poor soil. The land looked desolate, a desert until new sugarcane grew here again.

The summer rains would do the preparation, breathe life into the landscape, and with it, hope for the next harvest. Since the local population did not cut the sugarcane, the rum distilleries supplied well-paying jobs processing the product and shared the wealth derived from in the way they support social services.

Large international liquor conglomerates tried to muscle their way in, but to no avail. It was all local, with no foreign investment in these companies, grown organically and capturing market share with superior products.

Local refineries in financial difficulties received no-interest loans from the government, and competitors supplied collateral. It was homegrown controlled, and they were sticking together while being friendly competition. Keep our product excellent and exclusive!

New distilling method was shared and protected.

The driver had been telling me this, proudly reciting the island's unique position in these tropical waters!

I told him about my mission with the Castle.

He had guessed from my attire that I had to be an executive for the Castle. He also knew that something was going on as he had had more rides in the last few days.

"Tell me more about it, so I can talk up the place. It is my favorite resort, especially since my cousin is now working there."

"She had been tight-lipped, must keep it a secret to preserve the element of surprise. She is a fast learner, picked up this phrase from me, thinking."

I talked with him about a grand opening with a lavish celebration topped off with a dinner party and cocktails.

Steel bands sounding off the Caribbean tunes, dancers in traditional Bajan costumes, and fireworks at the beach to entertain prominent guests will be part of the celebration.

And there is one particular event, which was kept secret and would be exclusive for the best clients and dignitaries.

"I believe the prime minister will come," he added. "And I am dying to find out what this special event is. I will pressure my cousin for the information."

Good luck, I said. "She plays a major role in it and will not disclose the details. This girl is committed.

"Yes, I know her too well, and I must tell you that whoever found her and orchestrated her hiring will not be disappointed. The family and relatives in a grand circle are so proud of her. She is a princess! And worthy of it! Do you know this person?"

Humbly speaking, it is me. Believe me when I say that at my first look at her, I saw her potential, and everything she did after that further reinforced my belief in her.

I look forward to seeing her again, working with her on all details, and I assure you that this girl gets first-rate treatment from the hotel and company.

"Thank you, sir. This is most assuring."

I had arrived at the gate to Paradise.

* * * * * * *

The front desk was busy checking hotel vacationers from the same flight. I was asked to come to the manager's office, given the sign-in form and a key.

"We have a little bungalow for you this time, a small token of appreciation for all you have done for us. Priscilla is my niece. She loves you to death as a professional person and holds you in the highest regard."

I had tears in my eyes as I listened to her. "It's okay. Emotions are human quality. Where and who would we be without it?"

She hugged me, wiped the teardrop from my cheek, then said, "You have your heart in the right place. It makes you that much more a noble man."

Composed again, I noticed the future captain's wench in action, checking in and waving me there while busy tending to the guests signing in." Will we get together after my shift? About eight pm?"

Yes, of course, and I almost said. *"It is a date,"* but I held my tongue, not implying any strange thoughts.

The bungalow was set up as a little freestanding building and found off to the side of the large rooms buildings. Privacy is OK. I like that. There will be enough turmoil and masses of people to look after. Then the work takes hold of my time, meetings with every manager to the last man on the totem pole.

Priscilla receives quality time to hear her update on the preparation for test meals.

I want to invite your Mom to the test meal as my guest! I hate to eat alone, and I would be honored to have her witness the food, hear her critique from the originator of the recipes, and to make her acquaintance. We will send the company car to pick her up and take her home.

"She will be tough on me, but good, that is the purpose of the test. Critic is not a criticism!"

Another company term she picked up just by being alert.

"Happy to tell her. She will make a new dress for the occasion!"

Not necessary, no formal attire on the contrary. We dress low-key, not giving away rank and privilege to the servers. I will be recognized. However, the manager will be told to serve me last, to ignore my function in this, certainly no special treatment. I want to see how a customer gets the service. The same for the food, promise?

"Promise, sir!"

The Chef was amply prepared to deliver the goods for the primary banquet and the preceding cocktail party.

Snacks will be kept light to absorb the alcohol and still preserve the appetite for the fine meal planned.

Good, this is in the bag, and so is the wine!

"Yes, boss, all done. Giovanni took care of that. He also did extensive training with the designated servers on the art of fine dining, as he now calls it. The same for the wines, highly organized, taking a page out of your book from, I think, Hartford?"

"Yes! Spelling, pronouncing, tasting notes, pairing options, and actual tasting, turning these kids are alcoholics! Just kidding, but they have developed a taste for wine!"

That is not just training but succeeding on all fronts. I am so glad to hear all that. I will be jobless; don't you think so?

"That will be my greatest joy if we did it all so well that you can enjoy the party. I know all too well that we foodies always become the slaves for the event. If it goes well, a thank you, but for every little bit going wrong, here it comes down the pipe, excuse my language."

I look at all your preparation to the smallest details that usually get overlooked. "You take credit for that, will you?"

I have the final menu here ready to go to print.

"Great, all approved! How did that go down in the end?"

Better than expected. I had help from every corner of the building. The brass loved it, even the VP of Logistics, but the girl who carpools with me took convincing. The good part was that the two other women in the carpool and I had her undivided attention; those two are the ones in the recipe recording. When they received the recipes, they quickly mentioned how nice they had been written, and such a formal presentation made them feel important.

The reading made them so hungry. All requirements are met, and what else is there? How can we go wrong with food like this?

I added then that her daughter will be the restaurant's Chef. That took it over the top for her sign-on. I do not know what more can be done.

Everybody was on her tail to sign off. It needs her signature. See, here it is, and even the boss's secretary, Andrea, hammered her, peer pressure to no end. It pays to be good to these girls. I bring them gifts from travel.

You must have chips in strategic places to cash in!

"I heard from the marketing guy that you had laid the groundwork for more of these chips as IOUs with the NY union."

Word gets around. Even I have not received confirmation on this. This went down Saturday like a movie script, according to him.

"The Pirates dinner will be coordinated with food from the specialty restaurant.

The engineer had special-made carrier trays and one tray is lined with copper for the flambé. It will be a smash: I cannot wait to see their faces! For the rest, you need to talk to Giovanni."

Has anybody been assigned with booking the reservation? "The GM's secretary."

"The the theatrics are in good hands with the cute front-desk girls!"

The meeting with Giovanni only took fifteen minutes. All the details were secured and will be rehearsed in two days and the final dress rehearsal with the costumes. The director/producer takes control of the script and timing, lights, and whatever details we laymen would not dream of. Leave this to the professional.

Wage payments budgeted, approved, and payroll is all organized."

I have one small item. It will not take any of your time.

I explained the need to create demand and exclusivity, he almost finished my sentence.

"Yes, this is a loose end now. I am not sold on her, being the GMs secretary. She will not be here on weekends and coverage is demanding seven days attention.

Reservations is a better solution. We have good people there and daily coverage. Calls are answered promptly. I will bring it to the GM for his approval.

"She has a personal relation to it since her employees initiated the idea and there is also a personal connection to Priscillas family."

Makes good sense!

* * * * * * *

Satisfied with every detail being in good hands, I put on my shorts and bathing suit to catch the sea breeze and salt water ahead of schedule. A Banks beer is always a welcome refreshment and never stays with only one.

Wise man had told me that it is challenging to stay on just one foot; two are better for stability.

I took that to heart!

The beach was modestly busy; carryovers from last week, people often booked two- or three-weeks' vacation to get their rest, bring the kids to play, and enjoy the leisure life.

A woman took a hard look at me and spoke to me. "Are you from corporate for the grand opening?" She took a cue from seeing being solo. I affirmed. Then the second question, "Are you here by yourself?"

Yes, I came to work, food, and beverage. Work here never ends.

"I know. I have the same situation, tired, overworked, and no days off. I needed an escape. That is why I am here."

New York, by your accent?

"Yes, and you? From Sweden?"

No, not that far north but Europe." I let her guess.

"Then Austria?" Getting hot.

She liked the tease. I noticed from her wicked smile. I gave up so soon. I began to enjoy this game.

"You like games?"

I learned beginner tennis right on these courts from a colleague. "Him or her?" Very curious, she had to know for whatever reason.

An attractive her.

"So, I thought."

You have me figured out quickly.

"Being in the business and contact with people, one develops a sixth sense, I guess! Now you are German!"

You knew this from the beginning! "I just wanted to stretch out this conversation"

Can I buy you a beer?

"Thank you. Normally not my usual beverage, but a gentleman cannot be refused."

Beer in hand, I sat next to her. "What game is this over there?"

I do not know, but I will find out for you. The women in charge will know.

I had two oversized ping-pong paddles and a tennis ball a minute later. It is a way to compensate for the wind. The regular ping-pongs are too light, and the wind blows them away.

"I like ping-pong. Do you have time?"

A little, but I still have more appointments later on.

"Do you ever stop? You know the business, work never ends. One has to stop to rest and then start up again. "When is your appointment?"

"The end of office hours, meeting with the GM and F&B director. He likes his toddy after work, and I get his full attention over cocktails.

"Wish you luck. Now I have a curious question. Why is the head of the hotel called the manager and the FB guy labeled director?"

It is by the nature of the job function. The general being the highest rank in any situation, he manages the finances, budgets, people, and sales. Altogether, he does not get too deep into any area.

The Food and Beverage director has distinctive departments with department heads, managers, and someone to head up a smaller section like room service and purchasing. He sets the direction for the department and delegates.

Therefore, he is directing the activity, like a director that runs a movie. There the GM is the producer. I never understood that title. When the director is done and delivers the final product, it is up to the producer to set up distribution and produce the payback and profits. You see, it is all in the wording.

* * * * * * *

Ladies get first to serve.

These larger paddles and a tennis ball took us time to find comfort. The net is higher, but the table looked the size of a standard ping pong table.

We took minutes to practice and get a feel for the game, the serve, spin, and whatever shots one dared to show. It took me minutes and shots to get topspin down, now thinking of Ivan and how he managed to get it, then a slice. Yes, it works the same.

It all seemed so much easier than with a tennis racket.

She tried her best but only produced straight shots that ended in the net.

"How do you manage to clear the net all the time?" I thought to give her pointers She has the ambition to challenge me to a game, I want a worthwhile opponent. As my mind wandered, she was catching on and became competitive and playful. The topspin she mastered with a short practice, and suddenly the exchange got more interesting.

"Now how about a match, you know, the count to 21 wins by two!"

Game on.

Her opening salvo was a straight ball easy enough to return; I chose a gentle return, giving her the confidence and enjoyment of the game.

With the rotation of service, the game was now more intense. She kept up, won a point, lost a point, sometimes letting her catch up if her count dropped too far.

My game was steady and in my control. I allowed her to gain and, at times, give her the upper hand, and then I increased my efforts to catch up and set her behind in the count. My confidence grew with a variety of drop balls, a slice, topspin, and side spin; all of these tricks had her so confused.

She fell behind and looked discouraged. Then the count came into the teen numbers, and I allowed her to score points on obvious errors I had created. Then back to rotating until we reached 20-20 each.

She is a quick learner and copied a topspin twice, which scored her the win, 22-20.

Overconfidence, yes and getting careless. Never underestimate a losing party when the back is against the wall.

Sun Tzu came to mind! She had caught me off guard.

You won. Congratulations. The ceremonial handshake was not enough. It had to be sealed with a hug and a kiss on the cheek, but close to the mouth. I thought for a moment if I had my head a little more toward her, she would have capitalized on it.

Revenge tomorrow. I must clean up and get ready for my next meeting.

"You are on."

Perhaps bit later if you don't mind hanging here on the beach.

"I love it here, will never leave!"

* * * * * * *

I took up the subject of the Pirates dinner. I met the GM and F&B for cocktails at the corner bar. He was up to date on the progress, except for the marketing strategy. Yet another cocktail special to taste, but no recipe released.

To manage, it must be handled as an exclusive at the point of first contact, booking the rooms or groups, and that should be the front-office manager.

"You prefer her over my secretary?"

Is that what you had planned?

"Yes, thinking to keep control in the executive office."

Not a wrong thinking, however, the merits of a sale without being transferred, put on hold, receiving a voice recorder during her break, and then there are the after-office hours, weekends, and calls interrupting the sale. All these adversities can make or break it.

"I did not think that deep. I agree, settled! Thank you for your insight. You are a thinker, man! Anything else?"

A personal favor.

"Go ahead."

I wish to invite the girl, our special Priscilla's mother, tomorrow for the test meals. She has given us so much and personally wrote out the recipes with her daughter as the cook. I want to honor her by seeing where her darling daughter works, showing her a professional kitchen, experiencing the restaurant service and beverages, plus of course, her food, prepared by her Girl. To top off this recognition, can we send the hotel car to pick her up and return her?

"What a wonderful idea! Please do it."

"You know this guy here Giovanni dragged me to this place, and we both met her. What a wonderful woman. She is in high regard in this town, well-known especially since her daughter hit the jackpot with this job."

Yes, this is how they value this post. The affection for this Castle, as they refer to it at all times, runs very deep. You know Sam Lord had an excellent reputation. Nobody knew what he was doing at the beach plundering shipwrecks. They know he was kind to his household, paid them well, and showered them with stolen goods and jewelry from plundering the shipwrecks. He must have kept mistresses, never married. That showed their gentle side to him. No matter how long ago, everyone earned a share of the estate upon his death.

Priscilla's great-grandmother was on that list, and this is how her Grandmother got into the business, actually started as a street vendor.

"You are indeed a storyteller, Maggie told me. How did you get this information?"

The taxi driver on the way from the airport. These guys are full of information. Just get him talking. To make it credible, he added that he is related to Priscilla, her cousin.

One more benefit of having her mother here she will be my guest, and I will get her unbiased appraisal of the food.

The meeting with Annie from the front desk took place outside the Bungalow on the cooling-off evening. I offered her a glass of wine, which she gladly accepted, then went ahead to bring me up to date.

I had already received an update but listened to in case there were any deviations. She ventured into the publicity and activities the school had worked up with the cast.

"We expect the newspaper to attend, take pictures, and have a feature in the travel and food section the following weekend. Now we are targeting the Television media and are pulling strings with the help of the school. The schools want this show on tape. It will serve them with publicity and their reputation."

"Strong interest has been created but needs authorization from the head of the company. This will be a local production, and they are affiliated with ABC, which could take notice since this is a popular vacation destination for the New York market. A little bit of luck goes a long way."

"The event will be labeled the very first theatrical production of the school, headlines, the list of actors in the play, director, producer, stage manager, scriptwriter, author of the book that will be you, and lights, cameraman, editor, the whole array of people as if this were a great motion picture. It is a bit blown out of proportion. These people think big and plan to get NYC exposure. A future stage production for a Broadway show can be created from it and so forth. I was assigned to research the character of the pirate and learned exciting factors adding to the storyline. I will therefore be mentioned in the credits as well as an assistant book author."

She sipped vigorously on the wine, received a refill, and took another large sip.

"Now, for the pirate's background I must tell you these historic details."

"He started as an Irish boy who left home for parental abuse and the lack of food. Curious by nature and daring got him into trouble with the village elders, who demanded to place him in a monastery until he had outgrown his teen years.

He got wind of it one night, overhearing the parents debating which monastery he should attend. One of them took in children like him who needed structure, discipline, and to teach them a craft.

Not suitable to serve the Catholic church, it was the only revenue source for the monastery.

The parents produced the money and counted on the monks to structure the boy and teach him with skills of a trade. He would quickly find work or freelance once he left the monastery and be self-sufficient.

He will also be bound to pay back school money to the monastery for the following five years.

The monastery supplied modest food and clothing by producing work tools for the craft they taught the kids.

Children had been accepted but kept apart in separate convents. Once a week, hot water was supplied to do a sponge bath. Baking soda, also called bicarbonate, had been the oral hygiene method, haircuts once a month, and regular soap to wash the hair. After the washing and drying, some kind of powder was sprinkled on the scalp to prevent lice and fleas.

Locked into this building, while watchful eyes kept on them in control, was an adjustment. In time the kids accepted this life and realized, that they are better cared for than at home.

No more beatings, at least two meals, porridge, vegetables for lunch, and sometimes eggs or cheese. Once a month, a small amount of meat from a rabbit stew or chewy lamb muscle meat oven baked until eatable. Certainly, much better than at home. This food is nutritious, as showed on the large bodies of the monks.

Sammy, as he was referred to, showed promising progress, took on extra duties in the kitchen washing, cleaning, scrubbing burned pots, degreasing the wooden tables, and moving the ashes out of the stove.

Polishing silver and flatware used exclusively by the monks and cleaning the chimney at designated intervals. For this, he received an extra part of meat to be consumed out of sight by the schoolmaster and learned the skill of preparing simple food by watching and offering help.

The monk in charge of the kitchen liked Sammy. He was a great helper, never complained about too much work or being hot in here, worked tirelessly, and made himself available at all hours.

One day, he asks the cook, 'Why do the monks use only silver to place the cooked food on and then use silver as a knife, spoon, and fork to eat it with. Is this not expensive while otherwise living such a simple life.

It is to protect the health and kill bacteria in the food. You see, we all have bacteria on and in our bodies. We do not have a doctor here and would not like it if one would demand us to disrobe and show all our private parts.

We are Christians, have our rules for purity, and follow these by heart. The best cure is always prevention. This is why I thoroughly cook all fish, fowl, game birds, pork, rabbits, and whatever we get as donations from the farmers and hunters. The same goes for eggs, fish, and shellfish,. All food is served piping hot.

You are very observant. All this is for prevention. Your cleaning duties keep us safe.

How so?

When cleaning the preparation surfaces, cutting boards, knives, cooking utensils, strainers, pots, and pans, I always make sure that the water you use to rinse is boiling and that kills any bacteria. Then the items like worktables and surfaces that cannot be immersed into boiling water, you are using vinegar, is that not, right?

Yes, it smells horrible, but not long.

Now, some more procedures! Sugar is a preservative used on fruit and berries. Salt, we use to preserve codfish and meats, primarily the pork. Then you see me putting food into a glass with a spring top to seal. This is a conservation method and will stay good for a long time. Fruit is cooked with an equal amount of sugar until thickened, then put into these glasses and sealed with wax and a lid are called marmalade.

I will let you taste this soon since I have to cook a bunch of elderberries.

Is that all?

No, there is yet more. Smoking meat after the salt is called curing is also a method. It keeps the mildew off the sausages. The same can be done with fatty fish like this salmon I will cook for dinner but also need to be spending time in a salt-water solution. We call it brined. Then the Swedes use this fish and cover it with sugar and salt. Yes, both. Then they add pepper. See here; I have expensive spice from large trees in a tropical climate, like South America and Asia.

Wow, you know so much. Where did you all learn this?

Just like you are learning now, from an elder monk. You see, in a lifetime, we do learn something every day. We must pass this knowledge on to others, younger men like you or women, and so it carries forward from generation to generation. Each generation learns more from it, expanding the knowledge, and so we move forward in life called progress! Sometimes we make a mistake that turns out to be a discovery of something we never knew.

Tell me an example, please!

This cheese, for instance, was placed in a cave where the air stays cool in the summer. The mountain covering the cave and deep inside the earth is incredible. This monk of ours did that. He wanted to pick it up for eating. He found white stuff all over it. It was what today we call mildew.

Curious to see the cheese under it, he scraped this white stuff off and found the cheese okay. He washed the cheese, cut it open, and now he was in shock. Blue veins had formed running through the white marble-looking cheese. He would throw it out, but throwing away food is a deadly sin.

It's just not done. Someone can eat it; if not us, animals will eat it.

His brain was working fast to find a way to cover his mistake, for the headmaster will take away the job which he loved so much. He hid the cheese in the kitchen under a cooking pot but went outside with crumbs to give it to the chicken. 'If they eat it, live for days, and not look sick, I will try it too. If the chicken gets sick or dies, I will cook it in vinegar sauce, which will be safe to eat. What then?

The chicken loved it. It was cheese and protein, and they fought over it, so it must taste good and safe. The chicken flourished.

There is nothing wrong with them, and now he has the assurance to try this cheese himself. And oh, so delicious, creamy soft, and the flavor so different but pleasant. With this, the Stilton cheese was born.

The French monastery had the same experience, so word traveled quickly by messenger to start production, make it an exclusive for the sanctuary, and sell it to the noblemen. A patent was being written, but the recipe left out critical steps.

One cannot be sure of the safekeeping of the recipe. Now one more thing that came from this cheese mistake.

The monk had noticed that the mildew he had scraped off and put aside was left there overnight. In the morning, he saw a change in the looks and texture. It had liquefied. Not knowing what to do with it, he washed it down the bucket and threw it out with the trimmed vegetable peels to rot.

'It will help the garden soil. Scared of it and thinking it may have been a mistake, he kept an eye on it, still seeing changes with the stuff. Then a pig got hold of it, ate it, and we thought the pig would die. It had already been suffering from an unknown illness, showed watery eyes, running slimy stuff from his nose, and would have to be killed in the next few days before it passed away from this illness.

In three days, the pig showed improvements in his health. The nose stopped running. He ate again and recovered entirely from this mystery illness in five days.

He must tell his superior, for there has been a miracle from God. He must know this.

Meticulously describing every smallest detail and bringing a piece of the cheese as proof of his story, the headmaster took this information and engaged the medical monk. One of them took on to study medicine. This monk wanted to see this substance and look closely at it with great interest, but the pig had eaten it. The cook started a repeat process with fresh cheese and again placed it into the cave.

They waited six months to see if God would come about with another miracle.

Now you see how humans learn daily, and you must never stop learning; you are a very bright young man. It gives me the joy to see your progress every day.

Annie went on with the Sammy story despite her stage of intoxication.

"This boy had now learned multiple trades. Carpentry, masonry, blacksmith, the art of creating a watertight roof, window, and glasswork, plus the cooking skills! He was now on a level to fill in for the aging cook.

"In his mind he developed a plan to escape. Doing all this work, having proven himself over the three years there, he wanted to go out into the world, get on a ship, and sign up as a tradesman to work the ship.

"During a religious holiday, the monks spent the day in the chapel praying.

This is my ticket to make it out of here. Sammy cooked the main meal for lunch, kept it special for the holiday and extra plentiful, for he knew not all would be consumed.

Sammy had sewn a bag from burlap and packed provisions from leftovers and durable meats, cheese, and whatever he could take without being noticed by the old cook. A water canister, more food from the cured sausages, hard cheese, and root vegetables.

Baking soda to keep himself clean, for so much, had he learned from this old man. It was a treasure chest of information he would now put to good use for himself. Never mind paying back school money. He had worked hard from the lessons received and was grateful for the excellent nourishment.

I know the old cook will not hold it against me. He knew me all too well. Live well, and God be with you.

"He made it to the ocean shore, waited for a schooner to drop anchor, and waited for the dinghy to come ashore.

Surely the captain will be the first on shore. He greeted him with, "Ahoy, Master, I am looking for work. Do you have anything to offer? Here are my trade skills. I can be of good use to you.' He had dug up seaman's terms from a book in the monk's library, studied it, and put it back.

"One of the sailors had passed away from old age and too much rum, plus he liked to fancy the shorefront promiscuous girls. He may have gotten something nasty from them!

"'Go on board. The yeoman will sign you up. The pay is food, a bottle of rum every other day, and all the fresh air you can breathe.'

"Sammy's first job and a hammock as his bed were good enough.

He needs to catch all the rats that made it on board from the last port when the ship had docked quayside. 'They climb on board over the mooring lines, and then we have them as blind passengers.

The once we missed must be caught quickly. They multiply every couple of months. Time is critical. Go down to the lowest level, set traps, and when you see one, kill it, but not completely.

Make them cry. The others will hear the crying. They jump ship and swim to the harbor. They can make it to shore. Get busy, lad! We are safe from them while we are anchoring.

When we take on provisions and ammunition or cargo, will we have to go to the pier again!'

Sammy knew what to get from the galley. The cook took shore leave, and Sammy got morsels of meat for bait. In no time did he catch two of them, one still alive and screaming. She had seen the other one getting caught with the head in the trap for the kill and tried to escape her temptation, but too late.

One leg did not clear the spring-loaded metal, so she was in pain. He let her scream and took her to different parts of the ship levels above where they had stored provisions. He could see how a bunch of them had made an escape to the whole leading out to the water. To be assured that all had left, he went around all areas while this one was still alive. She had stopped screaming, so he rattled the trap to cause a movement of the trapped leg, and the screaming started all over again. All clear, he released her into the ocean water, where she drowned.

"'Good job, lad. You will do us good! Ever handled a firearm?' '

No, never, but I learn fast.

"Must know how to shoot to kill! We often face the threat of pirates at sea robbing our cargo, killing the crew, and taking the ship. We practice at sea when the old man returns with fresh bullets."

Where are we sailing to?

"To the warm waters, getting too cold and stormy in these waters, will be good. I need fresh supply of rum soon. We will be under sail as soon as the master returns. We are set otherwise, good with food for weeks on out."

Working the ship's chores gained him a quick reputation and respect for his way. He took on almost any job, whether tending the sails, repairs or climbing up the mast to be on the lookout.

They met a ship they knew near the Florida coastline but got away the last time. They sailed so close to it that they could climb on board with guns hidden and then staged a holdup, putting the gun at the captain's head. Treasure chests got transferred, and the action only took a couple of hours.

"The getaway with the wind from the north gave us the full sail for the power and speed, all well planned and rehearsed. Give us your worth, and we will let you live another day. You see, the element of surprise under the disguise of the flag you had set earlier."

Now I know your business. It is not cargo. It's pirating!

They made it to the southern Caribbean and had planned the heading for Venezuela. On to the island coming up. We need to resupply rum and food.

The port of Barbados came into sight, and lights showed the town and harbor. Headed that way in the dark of the night, the lights now showed a red color. 'It must be the entrance, red starboard,' the helmsman yelled, lowering the sails to reduce the speed, and taking aim. Getting closer, the ship suddenly started shaking noises from the Kiel. Loud scratching noises told him that something was wrong. 'Get the captain out of bed fast. Hurry, he commanded.

But it was too late; the ship had come to a screeching halt and turned into the Easterly wind. Water pouring from a large gash said it all. A reef has claimed its price.

Rowing ashore to see the bay, the ship was now sitting on top of corals firmly propped up but permanently anchored, the hard coral grinding deeper to hold this majestic schooner prisoner. They set up camp and got to thinking what we will do next.

The wood from the schooner served as building material. The galley was undisturbed. It became the kitchen in the house. Once sheltered, the blame game set in; verbal exchanges and name-calling escalated to fistfights and gunshots. Sammy took rescue behind palm trees until the fighting ended. The only one left standing was the captain's with his lower leg injury and bleeding heavily.

Sammy took a piece of his shirt to tie the upper part of the leg to stop the bleeding and then dragged him on a blanket to rest.

"You have to fix this, my son. Give me two bottles of rum, the first one I will drink, the second one you use to sterilize the wound, then take a cloth and soak it with rum, set it on fire, then burn the wound black.

First, give me that stick to bite. It will be brutally painful, but it will be the only way for me to survive.' And so, the captain ended up with a wooden leg.

He died years after, left all to Sammy, and recommended him what he can make out of this place.

"Build yourself a castle" You have all the skills, rename yourself with a lordship's name, and become an honorable citizen. There is money and treasures to trade. You need to be good to your servants and the townspeople. They will respect you and never question your heritage."

End of story.

She cried over the ending, hugged me tightly, and made overtures for a softer touch. Emotions running high, I returned her kisses, then cautioned her of the consequences. If this comes to the surface, it could handicap her acting career. Sobering up by now, she realized the mistake, thanked me for listening, and left to go home.

* * * * * * *

The day to stage training meals had arrived Everybody was a bit nervous about serving and cooking the first meal with watchful eyes on them.

They had been told that after the dinner would be a critique session that gave them more reason to be nervous. However, once the actual service started, the training took over the nerves, and it came as a natural. The good drill session had paid off. Aside from minuscule errors that the non-pro would not see, it came off without a hook.

Mama was shocked as this huge American car rolling up and a man asking her to come in and take a seat. "I shall have the pleasure to take you to Lord's Castle."

She caught on, her daughter playing the big shot now, paying for such an elaborate drive. "I shall have a word with her not to disband her humble heritage."

I greeted her at the gate, introduced myself, and escorted her to the restaurant. Her little darling waited for her arrival and was eager to show off her domain. Priscilla explained the function of every machine; the range and cooking utensils; the professional knives for different use, she bragged; then the food products neatly packed into bins, trays, and fish and seafood iced down with shaved ice.

Mama was overwhelmed and oh so proud of her princess. She expressed her pride and satisfaction with her body language.

Remember we came to see you and had dinner there not long ago.

"Oh yes, how I could forget such a handsome man visiting an old woman.

Thank you for giving us the pleasure of hosting you?"

"Does he always talk that formal?" She looked at me.

In this business, it becomes the language, for every guest becomes an honored guest until he has paid the bill, I added as a joke. The humor was not lost with her and had been passed on to Priscilla.

Appetizers were served with the right speed and discretion; they just appeared unless one was waiting for them. Clearing took place in the same quiet way, and then the main course, which had to be selected beforehand, arrived with the aroma of the food giving away the hidden service. It filled the room, and uuhs could be heard from nearby tables.

She ate at a steady pace, took small bites, chewed it, and gave the impression that she was looking for specific flavors and textures. Then an approving nod and on with the next morsel. The plate was cleaned to the last crumb; she started to describe her experience with this meal.

"Priscilla had always been a natural at cooking. Starting as an eight-year-old, not tall enough to reach the counter, I had to set up a workstation to her height to meet her demand to help me and not as a temporary fad. No, it turned into a passion at her young age, and she still has it."

"It was perfect. I could not do better. She does better than me! She now works with superior raw products and all this modern equipment."

"If you do not know already, she is in seventh heaven, thinks the world of you, and refers to you as her messiah, for you took her into her confidence and never wavered on her ability. She would get on her knees and ask you to marry her if you were not married. I am not kidding."

Are you not getting carried away? "I mean it with dramatization to express her most profound gratitude."

I understand and am deeply moved." Holding back my tears!

The dessert I had chosen for her blew her away with colors, textures, acidic qualities, aromas, and flavors. Once reaching the tongue and roof of the mouth, she ate it like the red wine drinkers move the flavor around in the mouth to get the most flavor out of it. Mesmerized, she was ready to leave, but I begged her to stay for the critique. "Criticizing this, there?"

I cut her off. It is not criticizing. It is a critique that covers the great and lesser great, if any. It is a self-critique like a paper critique. If he liked it, he would write great articles about the restaurant. When one has to look at their performance, they are hard on themselves, and at that point, management takes the opportunity to apply praise and thank you's.

"I get it now! Now I am curious about my little darling's conduct and comments."

As predicted, the F&B director opened up the dialogue encouraging each to rate their service performance. Comments about service speed; then a beverage order got mixed up, condiments were late, just little odds. "What have you heard about the food?"

"Everyone reported rave reviews with one exception. The guest found it too hot, spicy hot, but he finished the plate."

I interjected that this would be the most common remark to expect regardless of any described detail to the guest. "They think they can handle hot food, like in the USA.

Hot food from Mexico, Thailand, India, or the Southwest is toned down to a mildly desirable level. The benchmark comes from there.

You mentioned that this guest finished the plate. However, when authentic food is served, and the spice level reaches the point of being too hot at first bite, there is no reason to compromise this recipe. It would distort it and give a bad experience.

Their taste buds will be adjusting to it. The mouth delivers more saliva, and the authentic flavors are now taking the place and are supplying true enjoyment.

What you can offer at that moment is salt or a lime wedge to suck on. This gives relief. The salt rubs the oil off the tongue and gum, and the lime juice further cuts the oil of the hot chili to make its way to the stomach.

Mama smiled, and the daughter started to clap her hands. When the round reached Priscilla, she was super critical of the temperature of the food.

"I want to see the steam rising from it. I need to work on the timing." No other comment from her. Tough on herself! I looked at Mama.

She nodded, got up, and spoke. "This, my dear darling daughter, will come with experience. The more you serve, the better the timing. Do not lose any sleep over it. Your food was so much better than mine."

Everybody got on to their feet for a standing ovation. She ran to our table, kissed her Mama with a big hug, then turned toward me and held back, but I sensed that she needed a bit of encouragement as she fell into my arms like a toddler, hugged, kissed me, and apologized all at the same.

"I cannot help it. I must express my emotions to you. It is therapeutic to me!"

And to me too!

We laughed aloud, and the whole crew joined in on it.

There was not a single person with dry eyes in this room.

The next day turned out to be my lightest day. It was clear, for me to stay out of the way.

Every department had its work cut out, that was clear, and in seeing all these employees at work, it was undeniable that the flow had been planned and organized to the last detail.

* * * * * * *

I took the notepad to the beach and parked under a palm tree. This free time would get me a head start in documenting the activities and bring it up to date. The reading material surfaced a memo with a scheduled team meeting. Then the regional directors' meeting, the bar operations, and the Executive Chef filled up my calendar.

Besides, I had just been away from home for two weeks; a break was in order.

Deep in my thoughts, I noticed Stephanie standing in front of me, paddles in hand and throwing a ball in my lap. "Ready for the encore?"

No, I am sorry, I just noticed this pile of work, and it had been neglected for a week. Urgency will have to be the priority over playing the game.

"You work fast. I had been watching you, very concentrated, intense, and organized. Very observant!"

"Aren't you having the grand opening?"

Yes, this comes at me tomorrow. For today I have everything delegated; It's best for me to stay out of their way.

"Well-spoken," she remarked.

With the early morning light comes *Showtime,*

I told myself. Get the show on the road. Today will be spent checking all aspects of the event: food; bar; wines; glassware without spots; silverware polished; employees well-groomed, no noticeable jewelry on the ears, around the neck, or fingers; boys clean-shaven and smelling fresh; shoes polished; preparations for the Pirates dinner; equipment for the TV taping being delivered.

"Where to, sir?"

"Go there in the lobby."

Lights are set up, moved to leave room for food and beverage service, projecting calm in front of employees, a word of confidence, a little compliment, and answering questions with a firm voice all become components of a successful show.

Now the search for any pitfalls! Playing the devil's advocate, putting everything to the test in my mind only, not getting any other people involved, staying out of the way of workers doing their assignments.

I recalled working as a Chef when asked, "Can I help you?" "Yes, stay out of my way!" Practice what you preach.

It is not easy not to mix in the process; it comes naturally when the skills are there.

One last check while the ribbon cutting began, a couple of short speeches, and thank you to key persons involved in this project. The ceremony breaks, and champagne is offered in tall flute glasses.

Pretty girls with big smiles offer the bubbly wine to the guest, while others pass little selected snacks.

The dinner tables are set for the banquet, all exactly symmetric, measured with tape, and servers on standby.

The servers are dressed in black and white and feel the professional pride, ready to go on a snap from the banquet Maître d' service.

When the guests arrived and searched for their place, card, and table assigned, the chairs were pulled for the ladies and gently pushed in as they lowered their bodies to sit.

The aperitif cocktail created for this occasion to premier was now being served, a toast to the host and glasses ringing, then the first sip, the surprised look, and then quickly a second sip. Talk among the tablemates now floated all about this great drink.

A conch ceviche in lime and scotch bonnet stood for the appetizer course. The part is served in a martini glass and decorated with a thin lengthwise slice of plantain fried crispy.

A robust Italian Barolo in a balloon glass, following the plates carrying a slice of beef tenderloin Wellington. Beef filet browned, then enveloped in a mushroom duxelles. The usual bacon had been substituted with prosciutto. A wine follows preceding the main course.

Puff pastry enveloped the noble cut of beef and baked it to a golden-brown color.

Steam rising from the layers of the puff pastry, flaky, crisp, and aromatic butter steaming from this creation.

A brown sauce with chopped truffle is added, then garnished with various calabaza squash harvested as melon balls, tender peapods, fresh and green, all placed on a fried slice of breadfruit to form a cup.

Croquette potatoes with almond breading, also known as Pommes Bernie, completed the plate. Special care had been placed to supply an array of colors, flavors, and textures for a taste sensation.

The wine would stand up to all this competition on the plate.

Then we departed from the traditional order and served the salad after the main course.

Unexpectedly, it raised questions. The server supplied a valid reason before anyone had raised the question aloud.

We are serving you lamb lettuce that had been grown in Holland and flown in. The leaves take three months to mature in a cold climate but are not frozen, usually in a hotbed. The dressing is made with aged balsamic vinegar, a tiny touch of garlic, finely chopped sweet Vidalia onions from right here, and avocado oil harvested at our neighborhood island, Saint Lucia.

"The benefit of serving the salad after the main meal, a heavy beef dish, is to help digest the meal by adding the acidic elements of the dressing and the enzymes of the lettuce. You notice that the dressing has been mixed with the lettuce."

There were oohs and ahhs and acknowledgments.

Dessert came on a large glass plate, a molded vital lime mousse with leaf gelatin to firm it in a mold and then remove it with the upside-down motion. A crunchy wafer made with cornstarch, agar-agar, almonds, and sugar baked crispy and rolled into a cigar while hot. A chocolate triangle pointing to the stars and a mango rum coulis are painted on the plate to finish this kaleidoscope plate.

To finish this dessert, a sherry with a hint of sweetness and walnut aroma!

The guests had been blown away, speechless. They called for the kitchen crew to come to the dining hall. Rousing applause broke out with the jokester calling, "Encore, encore."

Humor comes in different forms.

There is a German proverb, "Humor ist wenn man trozdem lacht" (Humor is when one laughs in any case). Not a good translation. Something gets lost in the double meaning.

Now to the Pirate's dinner. Television was set up and the releases printed, given to all internal staff members supplying permission to be shown in a television program, the same for all attending guests.

The General Manager and corporate dignitaries, including the CEO, attend the dinner. The actors performing this "premiere" without a red carpet are listed as performers on the playbill hanging on the wall and being part of the menu.

Priscilla, a bit nervous, had all her ducks in a row, ready to go. The Executive Chef aided her, plus the food production manager was assigned to get her started. She looked radiant; I gave her a little hug and the assurance that all would go as planned.

The appetizer had been preset simple but was delicious seafood from the restaurant menu. Then an in-between course of a curried vegetable dish with custard was served.

On to the main course, but wait, the pirate was making his appearance. In full captain's dress uniform, triangular hat, a wooden leg pounding on the parquet floor with every step, he appeared like a ghost from behind a foggy entrance. Once cleared, the strong baritone voice took command of the room.

"Greetings to my honored guests. I am coming from my dark world to which I have been condemned. It has been a long time since I could host a table like this fine table. Still the very same from my past, I am Captain Samuel Lord! I created this castle from the planks of my shipwrecked schooner, a fine ship, I might add.

"This has been my paradise until my death. I had entertained dignitaries, men, and ladies, of course. The ladies had the majority, for I have a soft heart for them. Courtesans had pleasured my body, despite my crippled leg.

"To reaffirm my honor, I must tell you and assure with my heart that none had been taken advantage of. All of them left after my passing with a healthy dowry and a broad smile.

"I plundered the rich merchant ships and then gave most to the poor. The people of this Island have the deepest affection for me.

"I will tell you a secret now. Few people know of it. Only one family has any idea. The family supplying tonight's dinner food is a descendant of one of my favorite courtesans.

"Love goes through the stomach. She was a terrific cook then, passed it on to the children, grandchildren, and now to this girl." He pointed to Priscilla watching at the lobby entrance!

"My real name is Henry O'Shaughnessy. I took a nobleman's name to elevate my status and gain the respect of this island population. I

*escaped a monastery in Ireland, took a job on the ship, and landed her
with the shipwreck on the reef below there on the beach.*

*"I must say to the Castle owners that you have done a brilliant job
preserving it, and the added commerce does not hurt at all. No more
shipwrecks, no more plundering, only the history of it. Now I must go.
My time is limited, and I am out of it. Enjoy your meal. It carries my
account in this pretty girl right there.*

"Farewell to you, and may the captain bless you!"

With this, he left back into the fog.

Priscilla was all red, blushing, and surprised by this revelation she had
not known. Her cousin, the taxi driver, had told me the lineage of this
bloodline.

Proud and confused all at once, she finished the last touches of the
main course while wenches filled the tankards of the guests while bending
generously to the men, allowing peeks into the cleavage.

The guests now ate with a new distinction to the food from her
mother's recipe that, in all likelihood, had its roots right here at the Castle.

Flaming bananas with lime rind and juice, brown sugar, molasses, and
fine rum finished as the dessert.

When Priscilla saw me after the meal, she ran to me and pounded her
fist on my chest. "Why did you keep this a secret?"

"Ask your cousin. He was telling me the secret, and a secret between
two persons is, in fact, no longer a secret. Are you angry?"

"No, not at all. Just too much for a little girl to digest, you understand."

Yes, I do. We have put you through so much, and you are still able to
smile?" Smiling, she did again, and all was forgiven.

After an event with highlights and being onstage follows a
decompression period. Satisfied with the results and performances, it was
time to face daily life.

* * * * * * *

The flight to JFK and National Airport, then the shuttle bus to fetch
the car. I told the driver that I get out on lot number 2. Grabbing the two
suitcases, one with wheels and the other with a shoulder strap, I went to
the parking area by instinct to fetch my car,

Where is my car? I looked up and dowl the row and did not see my car.

I finally set down the luggage and ventured further in to the next rows. Still no sight of my car.

Returning to my luggage, I thought of a way to call home and have me picked up, Could the car have been stolen?

Another last look around and now, I realized that I had taken my wife's blue car and failed to recognize it. A had been searching for a white car.

Is it stupidity, or mental fatigue?

* * * * * * *

The home the turf was quiet. Nothing had happened. There was a brief mention in the local newspaper listing the police activities She had been watching it. There was also mention of the breakup of a sex slave rink and the later arrest of the principals, the three men's names listed among others and no mention of her name or how this was detected.

Good, we do not need this kind of notoriety. Bond had been set in the millions for reasons of flight risk.

* * * * * * *

The office had a surprise waiting for me. The RVP was moving the office to New York, setting up shop in the condominium tower. That meant moving to New York City, Charles Baker informed me.

He knew at once, that the move was not pleasing me. A transfer to the Mid Atlantic Reagon was now arranged replacing the Regional Donald who was going to retire.

Chapter 18

The summer was filled with a hotel opening in South Carolina.

They had strange liquor laws. All alcohol had to be mini bottles, 1.75 ounces. "At least they get a good shot. The lawmakers must be alcoholics and locked the part in with this regulation.

I almost did not make it through security at National."

I greeted Rob at his arrival in the hotel lobby.

What happened? He showed me a square bag and an array of makeup and lipstick. Are you okay Rob?

He was laughing. "They got the wrong impression too, so I told them I am a makeup artist going to a photo shoot at the beach.

I will teach the cocktail servers how to put on makeup, which I must do as if they are in front of the camera. The light in the lounge always makes them look sickly unless the makeup is good. You will see.

Donald arrives tomorrow. He is, as I am, told a wild animal at these openings.

Donald will split up the duties to phase me in the region and an opening procedure.

He will manage the supply distribution. I handle the task force and corporate support staff. Then practice meals and eventually the handover. He is also committing to keep the GM in check, if not checkmate."

"Good plan. Can we also have a practice run in the lounge? A bunch of new programs get introduced, which he would block. On the other hand, you have programs running in the NY region, Kumar told me."

The kitchen will be routine, not too many new things, but Willy wants to put his signature on the food offering. Menus are written and printed.

He said with a lingering question, "Oh yes, he plans to create specials from local products, seafood, and typical Southern dishes."

The menu was supposed to have these items listed but while I was busy in Barbados, they had pulled a fast one and rushed the printing. Too late, there is always another way to skin a cat. Glad to have Willi on board.

Crabmeat, the famous Southern fried chicken, and we have others in mind. I do not want to be laughed out of town by the locals.

Catering will to be off to a late start. The construction workers, in particular these cats that put up the finishing touches, the wood trims, crown moldings, and the guy working on this built-in cabinet in the bar, are forever measuring, trying, measuring, and cutting a new piece, simply no progress in a day's work.

"I have an idea. These guys are a very particular breed. The tools they work with call for precision and expensive staff, yet they all leave them at the place they last worked on."

"We must move these tools into one location under the auspices of securing them, near the security guard. This worries them in the morning, and the work will go much faster. I learned this trick at my last job."

Let us start in the ballroom. The room is the first one we will need.

When delivery is sent from the warehouse, the distribution of equipment, tools, and supplies must be staged in the ballroom. Then when the cabinet guy goes to lunch or toilet, we move his tools. It will drive up blood pressure.

The IT department sent Genny. She is the one with the extra healthy body.

"You mean the extra pounds?"

"She is much nicer than the other Ginny doing the menus. Tracy is also kind. I got to know them well; their workspace is next to mine."

I carpool with them!

"Now I understand why you are in their discussions so often!"

Jointly we went to see the GM Magnus, safety in numbers! He was very low-key but had little praise for the construction quality and speed, and now it had come to a standstill.

"These bumps are milking time. After this job, they likely all get laid off."

We could see the blood pressure rising. Time to cool him off. We can help this along.

"How so? Are you woodworkers, cabinet makers, or furniture specialists? That is what the union is sending. Union, I see, you had dealings with unions in New York," he chimed in!

Did they tell you? If they did, I better leave right now before they do a fitting for new shoes!

"Cement, you mean.?" Yes!

"No, I heard this from your former RVP. We are good friends and much impressed how you handled this."

"There are no secrets in this company; no, there are not! We are both foodies, you will get no hustle from me. Done this too long, and I have compassion for this field of work. Hard to get out of it. I know firsthand."

Good old country boy fits right into the landscape as we left, but not the threat with which he is labeled. He may have been a hard ass while running corporate F&B.

* * * * * * *

I checked in on the home front. Everything okay. Sonny is working hard, takes in any overtime he can get, time plus half again," he explained. "He is scraping every penny together, even picking up change he finds on the ground.

"Good, he is motivated. He likes painting and comes home to tell me all he learned about keeping brushes, good brushes, and it is terrible to buy cheap brushed, he emphasized but must keep them clean. And here is a trick, put them in warm water after cleaning and add hair conditioner to keep them smooth and soft.

He will hold me to my commitment of matching every penny he is earning with the summer job.

He want a car! It is motivating him to work hard and make the most of it.

"We need to push back the Germany trip since he wants to make max money."

Fine, but I have a window that fits my schedule before the next opening in Tampa. Talk to him and find out the average pay he gets plus overtime. Tell him to stop two weeks earlier. I will add this amount to his earnings and the other half.

He now has a bank account with my cosigning, keeps the booklet hidden, and asks for a debit card. Good move: this way, the cash is not lying around for temptation. He receives a check by the book with FICA deduction, social security number, and honest official. He picked a good company, and they love him to death. Already had dinner with the family: a high-school-age girl and a six-year-old boy, but he does not seem to take to her."

* * * * * * *

The opening was now in full swing; a task force from hotels on the East Coast had arrived and was bunking together in pairs at a nearby motel!

The ballroom received all hotel supplies from the warehouse which had been the collection point of the various shipments. Not a minute too soon had the woodworkers collected the tools and been chased out with their choices of Southern power expressions? Work completed, except the punch list, had to be followed up.

The training folks collected all task force staff, issued name tags, and preceded with a Train the Trainer class. "The Task Force employees who had been chosen will arrive for training duty tomorrow.

Who has done this before?" One-third raised their hands. "Okay, we will go through the process for all to inform you of the sequence and define your role? All task force will attend a training and orientation, a refresher, and information about the aims for this property.

Innovations will be introduced, all of which you may take home with you and present to your manager. Those managers from this group pay attention and ask us for backup material."

With that, a short video covered all the subjects. You can be proud to be chosen for the task force.

It will be hard work, sometimes long days, and we will arrange for fun. All work and no play make for a dull person! We want you happy and motivated." At that moment, I was introduced as the overall task force director.

"Good-looking group," the trainers mentioned, we knew from past openings, all strong leaders.

We are off to a good start. "Welcome to this necessary process, and I introduced myself as the task force commander.

303

Each trainer took the members in the department they would lead the training.

Beware that it is still a construction zone. Do not touch any wires. Beware of nails on the floor, wet paint, ladders standing, and overhead material; let these workers do their job. We need to get these rooms turned over and completed.

The cleanup would start right after this class. Pick up everything that resembles trash but ask the worker to confirm. "Tools must find a safe corner with the toolbox, ladders not in use get folded, then laid sideways against a wall.

This being under control, we should see the speed of the workers increase. The comfort zone of construction debris is what they are used to. Now we make them uncomfortable. A clean surface with no debris will be left clean, too obvious to make them look sloppy.

Wet dusting and carpet cleaning will follow. We do this first, and when the employees are here, they will be trained in this and take over the task,

Employees arrived in their street clothes, jeans, others in cutoffs with a tank top reflecting the daytime temperature. The air-conditioning had just been started and tested, chilling the public areas to sixty °F.

Too cold for tank tops, very obvious signs of goosebumps skin and blue lips pointed to it. The type of girls had the most challenging time since nothing was available to cover the different body reactions. The test was completed, and the temperature climbed to 72 °F.

Now the real training could begin. Orientation did not need to be done as the HR department helped this at the recruitment center of the property. My role now changed to seeing the action, the individual paying attention or disrupting others in the group. Name tags provided identification for a follow-up with these individuals.

Donald had completed the inventory and announced to disburse the equipment and supplies to the various departments in the following order.

Kitchen first, for it was delivered at the end and easiest accessible, followed by a restaurant, then room service, bar, lounge, and banquets at the end. Any odds and ends, we would advise.

Gather the troops in an organized fashion; Aisle space becomes available when we get stuff out and gained air. This took the entire day, until late in the evening.

Mealtime was announced catered by an outside deli, eating on available chairs and paper plates, soft drinks, and a simple meal this time. Everybody would sleep well.

The next day is set to organize each area,

Everything into the designated place; all must find a home on the directions of the managers.

The trainers met with the task force to prioritize the day's action.

After that, we will get the first food delivery. There will be assigned tasks to do in the storeroom to put away the frozen food, meats, produce, dry goods, and Produce last.

Tomorrow you receive your uniform, and grooming standards are enforced. Cleaning and sanitizing procedures are described, and a thorough cleanup is underway. This is your domain, your workplace. Be proud of it.

Now about workplace safety! As you know, we work with intense heat, hot water, grease, slippery floors, sharp knives, heavy lifting, food crates with wire closures or stapled boxes, metal objects finding their way into food, and hair entering the food.

"Guys, girls, control your hair. We recommend a short haircut for the men, certainly no ponytails. Buns are good. The girls need to tie it neat. Use hairpins and or clamps in addition. Simply spoken, no hair can be loose.

You will use the process we call *clean as you go*. Any work area must be cleaned and sanitized after the individual task is completed.

Wash your hands often, and every time you start to touch and handle food and at the completion, of course. You cannot do this too often, understood?

We use gloves when you are handling the finished product to place it on the dish for service. This being done, the gloves are discarded. Important, the most important, are temperatures. Look at this chart. It tells the safe temperature zones for cold, frozen, and hot food. It also refers to the time it takes to consider a product unsafe.

Then there are the so-called dangerous food items. This chart lists raw fish, poultry, eggs, cream, milk, cottage cheese, and more. Learn this, grab a copy, and study it. There will be a quiz tomorrow morning. The health department will check and ask you individual questions.

"Now, let us do some commissary work."

And so, the food preparation began for an employee meal tonight.

The restaurant folks had a precise script to follow. When a guest sets foot in a service outlet, these procedures must be followed. From the greeting by the hostess, no cliché you may have used elsewhere, we are greeting the guest with a good morning or other time of day. "Will anyone be joining you?

These service procedures make a difference, and we ask that you follow all of them.

Beverage sales are also explained in detail. We will do roles play and teach you the proper handling of wine and champagne.

"After the food is served, you must go back within five minutes to see if they are happy with the food. Again, the cliché used, *is everywhere okay*, '*How is everything*; is asking as if you don't wish to know. The opportunity to set a mistake right is at this very moment. Please try and find out specifics about the food on the plate, is it tasing good, food temperature, texture, and cooking temperature with steaks,

Do not congregate in the back of the restaurant or the kitchen. Stay nearby the side station. Stay moderately busy but do keep an eye on your tables. Train yourself to see motions, body language, and facial expressions. All this will tell you the status of satisfaction."

The bar-headed up by Rob had a different tone. Here the focus was on selling, knowing the drinks. Wines, seeing the customer's condition, speech, body posture, and eyes to decide a cutoff.

When a customer reached his or her limit of alcohol consumption, a redirection of the beverage may result in a mocktail, alcohol-free wine, beer, soft drink, sweet tea, or an invitation to get a taxi for the journey home.

Alcoholic beverage laws are strictly enforced and followed up with consequences.

Let's talk grooming and makeup. Rob asked for a volunteer and pulled out his makeup case to show the correct type of makeup to look their best in dimmed lights.

Bartenders were reminded of the control procedures of the par-control system, the cash handling. The danger of being over in your count of your bank when reading is done on the register, and the bank will be audited.

Technology has replaced the old NCR machines. A reading with the manager's key brings the current sales up and the basis for the audit. Violations may not only be the loss of a job, but they may also involve the long arm of the law.

Promotions like happy hour and two for one are prohibited.

This lounge was set up to facilitate games, checkerboards, backgammon, and cards. These were available. Guests are encouraged to use them. You extend the stay to keep them engaged and increase the sale. Of course, the drink needed a refill at one-third from the bottom with the customer's agreement.

While seeing the group, I realized that all the bar employees were looking sharp and attractive. Being engaged in the training and cheerfulness brings the right attitude to the job.

We will provide the employees with meals from the hotel kitchen in two days. Training meals will be scheduled with the employees to begin, then expanded to a bigger audience.

A couple of days more, employees' meals helped the kitchen crew to get a head start and be ready for practice meals. The first practice includes all the hotel employees in the restaurant.

The next day, we expand with housekeeping and selected guests associated with the hotel.

Then comes the serving of aa small banquet meal.

The lounge will pick them up after dinner for two-hour free drinks.

Critics, after every meal, served as self-critique to find flaws for correction. The next morning, tis a breakfast service to the employees, followed by lunch as the employee meal and a view visitor.

Soft opening in two days allowed for a review of all aspects of training, and then the mentor role was explained with the gradual pullback.

Donald let me do all training activities and checked the progress only once.

In the evening, he usually disappeared into the nearby town, no doubt to interact with the locals of the same blood as him.

The GM received his periodic briefing in great detail. He is from the old guard and kept comparing to his time in the VP position.

"Boy, we sure have come a long way."

The Foundation was set during your reign, just not that intense and for a different product those days. We needed to adapt to the standards a customer is expecting today. We have a complete book for your reference that will be left with the property.

I have three weeks to prepare for Tampa, hardly time for a family visit to Germany. I had just realized the time constraint.

The GM had been on his best behavior from the start. We did not surface any issues that would involve him, and he received daily briefings on the progress.

Donald must have had a verbal exchanges with him at one time in his former position. There was an uneasy relationship between them.

One night, the hotel received a call from the police saying that Mr. Donald had been arrested and he needed to post bail. The police officer had asked if the hotel would handle this since he named himself as a director in a high-level position.

The Resident managers drove to the police and assured the officer that he would not be a flight risk and would appear in front of the judge. He was released on that promise duly recorded and signed, witnessed with a copy to the hotel and the individual.

The tavern owner later confirmed his story, that he had shots of Wild Turkey Whisky, and the alcohol had influenced a conversation about Southern politics. Disagreements escalated into a shouting match and, finally, name-calling.

Off came the gloves, and a fight was in full force. Others joined on both sides, and it turned into a full brawl! Damaged barstools, broken beer bottles, and glasses were minimal; it was a messy place and made it look so much worse.

The out-of-town big shot from this fancy place became his label.

Local workers had been pushed out of their job early; this was the real reason for the fight.

Donald assured the bar owner that he would pay for the damage as soon as the handcuffs were off.

Just now, this would hit the paper. The GM got the full-blown story in the morning, but as a Southerner, he expressed sympathy for Donald. He could ask the paper to minimize the news and list the story with all police activities and bury it on the lesser read page.

The home office was another story.

A watered-down version had now been agreed to pass the incident to corporate.

The employees got ahold of the story from being at that bar and had seen the ugly side. With them telling the actual events, the story got ugly.

Donald paid the bar damages and returned home. My handover was now completed with a bang!

The same night, trainers and managers had a campfire and beverages, mostly beer plus a bottle of tequila, the original one with the worm. The challenge to get me drunk was on, but I had experience in camouflaging this.

Genny from the IT department had finished her work and went home the next day. Her participation in the tequila shots took its toll and made her slightly drunk.

She was still coherent, knowing the action surrounding her.

One girl from the hotel front desk had had her fill as she reacted to a challenge to jump into the pond. She appeared from the muddy cesspool and was hosed down before going to her room for a shower.

Now the last sip of tequila with the worm, a challenge for me, which I took. I did it and left enough of the liquid to swallow this worm as one did a large pill. What could be so bad as consuming an animal preserved in alcohol Nothing could come of it, but if I declined, I would lose face.

There you have it, Applause; then the party was over.

Genny asked me to help her get back to the hotel. "Too drunk? "Please get me to the door."

We navigated the elevator and then down the hallway, the same hallway I had in my room. I found her room number, and she gave me the door key. She entered the room and pulled me inside.

'I have been waiting for this opportunity to make love to you since our first carpool rides!"

She disrobed quickly, then took off my clothes, and now we are both butt naked.

She flashed her sexy and voluptuous curves, then expertly processed to arouse me. "I want you so bad inside me."

The effect of the alcohol only inflamed her desire as she went on with the controlling position to bring the activity into full force. She is a tigress, hungry for the flesh and satisfaction of the chase. The appetite seemed to grow with every peak; she needed it bad and had been starved for affection. I gave it my all and spared no effort to bring her to exhaustion.

When I reached the point of no return, she whispered, "Don't worry, I am on the pill." Sweet words, relief, and taking a deep breath to recover from this marathon session.

She cuddled close to me and softly confessed having a poor or almost no sex life with her husband, no children as he did not want any; "A boring life was it not for the stimulating conversations you give us, girls when driving to work and home. All in good taste and fun!"

She was sober now and ready for one more activity.

Back at the office, neither of us gave away anything, just a smile when it was safe' She wrote me a short note inside an envelope marked "For your eyes only," name, and title to make it official but mysterious.

Tin a wanted to know, what the message was inside. Since it had been labeled, "For your eyes only," with my name on, it drew extra curiosity. There was no way she could risk it and open it. She would have taken it home to steam it open over the teakettle if I had been out of town.

Inside was a big thank-you, a lipstick impression of a kiss, and a tagline, "Best sex ever!"

Chapter 19

Flying to Europe with three adults costs a bundle of money. The bonus would be paid out within a month, making me financially secure to meet the travel cost and rental car.

She had still not found a job; not looking at all would be the honest answer; it frustrated me again. Any contribution to fund the flight from her wages would help. It would keep her out of trouble.

The son was working every day during his summer school vacation. Even on weekends, he wanted to maximize his savings for the car; Papa would match the savings. The more I can save to more significant the contribution. He was on fire and, in real terms, set an example for his mother. I had hoped it would shame her and move her to get a job.

The opposite was why she again had the run of the wild while Martin was working, and I was a distance away with my duties. Suspicion was surfacing, yet I had nothing to go on.

Arriving in Zurich, we boarded the train and visited her cousin in Luzern. I had met them only once, and the kid not since he was a baby. Look how big he had gotten, the usual small talk of women admiring a young man. Her husband was more substantive, talked about the current events in Switzerland, was interested in my work, and was astounded at the scope of work.

I left Europe for better opportunities; in the old country, one had to reach the late fifties to make it to midlevel management.

On to Austria, I wanted to get these in-law visits done to go home to my town in Germany.

The same took place there, just more women, The husbands either lost in the war or died from war-related illness. Only one man had survived this terrible time. The youngest in the bunch spoke to my son as an adult.

He had been assigned to the mountain unit and survived without getting into significant confrontations. The Americans did not have mountain-trained units on the skies nor the Brits.

He spoke to Sonny about it and made a massive impression as a young guy who almost worshipped the army, guns, and all that stuff. These two bonded rapidly, lasting for years into his adulthood.

Then off to Germany in a rental car. The car ride took 2.5 hours only and took us along the shores of the biggest lake forming the borders of Austria, Switzerland, and Germany.

Hillsides growing grapes for the famous Riesling, A castle on the hill, pristine houses, windows decorated with geranium in flower boxes, and the occasional manure pile in front of a farmhouse. We are home; this is my home turf.

Mom had been expecting us, had fresh-baked bread, a flat bread pulled from fresh bread dough and sprinkled with coarse salt and thin-sliced onions, then baked nice and crisp. It was still oven warm when we arrived.

She knew how to get our favors as we sliced cold-smoked belly bacon into chewable pieces and washed it down with a half-liter size bottle of beer. Margo chose sausage and liverwurst just made that day, smoked and not even chilled; it filled the room with its aroma.

My older brother Paul and his wife, Emily, joined quickly while my father drank generously from his favorite local wine. Mom begged for a sip of beer; a whole bottle was always too much. Despite resealable bottles with a snap top, one did not leave leftovers of beverages or food. "You must finish. Think of all the poor people that do not get enough food."

My younger brother and his wife will be arriving tomorrow from Stuttgart.

This was home for so many years, this town where everybody knew one another and the valley where fruit trees dominated the landscape.

A panoramic view of the Swiss Mountains will be rewarded when the weather conditions provide it.

It was my playground as it was for Martin. He used it to his fullest enjoyment during his school vacations years ago.

Urgently, he left to visit with his friends from that time, but sad news overshadowed it; his best friend had committed suicide.

He came back shaking and crying; he just could not understand it.

No substance was discussed except the work I was engaged in. My relatives did not understand the scope, and for that reason, they ignored it.

Despite the efforts to downplay it, they received it as bragging and grandstanding. Their world had not changed, but mine had gone through metamorphism in proportions they would not understand unless they could see my work.

Dad casually touched the Black Forest Hotel, labeling it as a chance of a lifetime. A visit had been planned, and we were all *Vorangemeldet*, preannounced by appointment as it was called here.

Then a good night's sleep. Sleeping late here meant 7:00 a.m., It was 9:00 am., so we had bridged a good part of the jet lag.

I showed for breakfast, but we let the wife and son sleep longer. Breakfast would have to wait for an exception.

Excellent coffee was always a highlight in Europe no matter where one went; liverwurst, fresh-baked country bread, butter, soft-ripened cheese like a Brie running out of its crust, homemade marmalade, what more could one wish to start the day?

Dad joined us and took up the hotel's subject and location, describing the building and sitting on high-level grounds.

The owners were getting older and motivated to sell since no heirs existed. Properties like this do not come on the market often, if at all.

Usually, the rundown places only make it on the real estate market; this one was in excellent condition. He pulled out all the stops and even said the asking price and that there was negotiating room. His financial help would also be assured, no details on that.

Well, this would be something we could run, being a distance away and a hotel, not a drinking Gasthaus only. The economics with guest rooms and vacationers staying two weeks or longer made good business sense.

It was indeed a business model I could now relate to and apply my experience and creativity in the culinary field. It motivated me to see it with an open mind and motivation. It would be a family business and, in time, proved an existence for our son to continue.

"There is nothing that compares to self-employment," he hammered at me. "Working for someone like you do now, you make them rich. It is to their benefit, and they will always keep you a little hungry to assure that you stay, not become independent."

He said, "We must talk about Hans He is on his way now, and you must hear this before he gets here.

He is involved with some strange people. He talks enthusiastically about what they can do for a man like him. The entire movement is built on psychological stuff I do not understand, but it sounds not too kosher. They are based in America. You must find all you can get so we can protect ourselves from them. When I hear what they all own, there has to be money involved. Not paying taxes is another suspicious thing; they call themselves having status as a church. He is trying to recruit Paul into it. Tell them you are thinking and checking on it. It is over there, so no problem for you to obtain information."

I have heard of them on the news. Prominent actors are in on it, and major corporate big shots claim to be members. It is hard to get out once you're in. So far, I have not paid much interest to it, but I can find out more.

Just as we finished, Hans walked in with his wife. We greeted, and when I greeted his wife, Gertrude, I was shocked. She was breathing hard, and blue and red on her face.

Is this from walking up one flight of stairs? Are you not feeling well?

"Oh, it's only for a short moment. I need to catch my breath; I will be okay in a minute."

She sat down in the comfortable chair I had vacated. I offered her a glass of water that she gladly took, then on to the usual catching up on the lives of family members.

My son had joined, greeted all, and told the group about his best friend's suicide. My mother knew the story from the neighbors being so close to her.

Hans bragged about having two manufacturing plants in his name, one that cleaned up metal parts from the casting, polished them, and sold them to the car factories. The other one was a high-precision mold-cutting process where lasers cut into metal blocks to create the form to inject liquid plastic for the creation of forms "Like this." He too

Showed us a plastic kitchen container as an example.

Mother had been busy and cooked the main meal in the meantime. It was now ready for consumption as the main meal of the day. Everybody pitches in to set the table, and the feast begins.

Roasted veal shank pan gravy or "Jus" homemade noodles called Spätzle. Her vegetables, as predicted, the peas and carrots from her garden, were overcooked as usual The meal was delicious; the meat had to be roasted at first, then finished braising in juice and mirepoix, herbs, and peppercorn and cooked until fork tender.

My dad's favorite.

After the midday meal, everybody was ready for a nap. It was my opportunity to catch up on jet lag.

After napping, coffee and apple cake are now served on the terrace. She had made it yesterday, and that was emphasized. A walk with Hans allowed him to talk my head off about this organization. Hammering away on how they would elevate my position in the company I worked.

I waved him off, saying that I was my own man, always had been, and would continue to make my own future. Help was neither needed nor wanted. I did not want to be controlled by anyone else. The bank holding the mortgage on the house was enough to handle.

With this, I had taken the wind out of his sale and shut him down.

I did find out the name of the organization. Now I had enough to pursue information on them.

The next day, they left.

I visited my cousins, drove to the lake, and spent the day in the town where I had done my cooks apprenticeship.

At the harbor's edge, I told my son that one winter, I had walked from the other side. "You can walk on water.?" Yes, but it has to be frozen.

He laughed; "Good joke, Dad!"

It was the case when that particular winter produced a steady freezing temperature to cause the entire lake to freeze; it was an event of the century. I had been in a school during my apprenticeship to get the theoretical education for my new profession. It gave me the once-in-a-hundred-year opportunity to walk on water. My wife was amazed, remembered it from the news, yet had not known of my experience until that day.

The trip to the Black Forest was shorter than I had expected. Everything in Europe is so close together one forgets after getting accustomed to US distances.

The owners greeted us with a warm welcome, a juice or coffee offering, then a chat directed to hear my professional history.

'Last week, I finished the opening of a beach hotel in North Carolina. It captured the owners' attention and also my parents. The details that went into this and my role in the process I had to explained in great detail.

They are now comparing my experience to their hotel operation. Astonished, they said, "this is a toy for you!"

Then a tour of the front of the building with all the land, public rooms for guests breakfast and other meals, a library reading room, music in another room, and light, big windows. These all looked fine.

The back of the house never matched the front; I expected that much. A small closet served as Pantry, then a broom closet for various cleaning supplies, and a food pantry the size we have at home.

The kitchen is too small and not suitable for full meals.

It looked as if a private home had been converted to a hotel by adding guest rooms and leaving the back as is. That was a turn-off that I kept to myself.

I asked for sales records, cost, and profit statements. They were labeled as private and confidential.

Cost to run in terms of utility cost, maintenance, taxes, allowances and whatever, would eat away a profit, again it was not available.

With the roof's age, electrical supply upgrades, plumbing and types of pipes, and cost of water and sewer, we received no direct answers. It seems as if they either don't know it or simply wanted to hide it.

I thought to myself, *Do they want to sell, or are they looking for a sucker?*

It did surprise them to receive all these questions. Since no broker had been involved, it was conceivable that this was inherited and never had gone to a buy/sale procedure. For that reason, they were caught flat-footed.

They gave us no clue to set up operating projections and, of course, the basis for the actual value of this hotel. What was it worth, not just the building but the production of the business as it was today? Any buyer would want to know this to arrive at a feasibility study and run the numbers, if only using the averages of standard hotel cost's.

My father had bought a business at one time. I do not know if he was looking at data like this, for he was equally shocked and motioned to me to chill, "It is unreasonable to ask all these questions."

No, it is not. *One does not buy a cat hidden in a sack. Must see the beast first;* It is that simple, I stated with a firm voice. He had never heard me speaking to him in that tone.

On the way home, my wife said that she would not want to take part in this kind of business: never a day off, always there for the guests, and demanding service. You turn into a slave with this type of business.

Not having a job, she had her priorities made clear that her life of leisure was not to be interrupted.

There you have it; she did not want to take part, yet both had to pull on the same string in the same direction in this kind of business. Nothing came of it.

* * * * * * *

Back home in Virginia, she was supposed to look for a job, but now she acted defiantly "I will not be commanded like your mother is being made a slave-like your father does. It is a family trait, so I turned down this business, knowing that it can only work if the family takes part.

I want to live a normal life!"

I had an answer on my tongue but held back. School had just started, and the kid was now actively looking for a car.

His grandfather and my older brother both gave him money. He was now set to invest all his savings and matching dollars to get a good car. He still had money left for insurance and backup in his savings account. He knew that a vehicle was an ongoing expense, and the need for money was now like feeding a hungry animal. It took the fun out of having a car.

Meanwhile, I was again amidst a preview visit of the hotel in Tampa still under construction. The target date is delayed, and a new date is set thirty days later. A memo to announce the new schedule had to go out to all participating people. The hotels in the Southern states need to nominate taskforce candidates.

* * * * * * *

The call came to the Chairman from the owner of the Fort Lauderdale hotel. The owner is the man who had previously managed the franchise properties. He was now the proud owner of his first hotel with this own company and the brand name of the operating company's name on the roof.

"Things do not click; I have difficulties meeting the interest and principal payment to the lender. Get your regional team down here to fix the problem."

I had seen this hotel on my first go-around; I knew too well that the problem was with the top management.

He called the meeting and chaired it too.

"I propose to get this lounge on its feet. It will be the least investment with the highest return. This is a party town, and I want you all to go to these places and see for yourself and bring back ideas."

Meanwhile, the RVP and I will have a private meeting.

I knew the GM is a veteran in the company, but he is not cut out for this property. I need a young man, a progressive kind of manager. This one has fallen asleep and plays poker with the marketing and F&B director. The F&B is weak and must go. The marketing man can be salvaged after he gets a shake-up.

This occurred while the regional team was out individually and shopping a dozen hot lounges. Packed during happy hour, live bands later took over to drive the action.

In the morning, we began at 8:00 a.m. and went straight to the meat of the action that took place last night. The two men had been ended at 7:00 a.m., escorted out, and replacements were being contemplated.

This was a bang that woke up everybody. This owner did not take prisoners!

During the morning, a tentative plan had come into focus. A commitment from the owner to find and hire the best band in town without asking the price.

For the bar to be more efficient, minor modifications came into view, plus added beer coolers, ice bins, and a cocktail pouring station. "Think big" was his motto. "You guys in the kitchen will come up with an elaborate snack food bar, some substantial stuff, like this!"

318

He named items from the other places "Any more ideas, write them down and start cooking, guys."

" Happy hour at ninety-nine cents drinks, I made a bold proposal. I like to be bold; it would work.

Then we got the band going at 8:00 p.m., and now we needed something else that would draw the girls. "What is it?" He was thinking.

I said, "Diamonds are the girls' best friends!"

"What do You mean to give away diamonds?"

Yes, but only one in a bowl of fake ones. What are they called again? Cubic zircon We fill a bowl with fake stones, place one one-karat diamond mixed in with the fake stones and let them pick a stone during drawings at different times. We can have someone knowledgeable there with a jeweler's loupe.

"What a terrific idea Marketing will loosen the purse and go on radio to promote the hell out of it. No cover charge ever, no parking fees ever. That is the plan and you", pointing his index finger at me "you are the watchdog. If they make changes and the GM signs off, I need to hear from you. Here is my office number."

With the action plan enacted, we had an immediate response. The revenue before the promotion was in the low 20.000. One month later, it doubled.

No, not so fast; the numbers kept increasing by 60% until we maxed out at 300,000 per month. They had been overrun and no more parking places for the cars. People parked illegally on curbs, other business lots and inside was standing room only

The Beverage cost had dropped despite the low drink prices.

A Buffet filled with a variety of snack food filled the bellies so they could keep on drinking. It was working incredibly well.

The ridiculously low price during happy hour drove the boys to the bar, and the girls followed, not wanting to miss the chance for a diamond.

The payment was mostly cash, but those with a tab had the tab transferred to the night bartender and were ordered to buy out the tips. This way, the customer would not be reminded to go home.

Every trick we thought came into play. Boys to meet Girls. Breaking the ice between the sexes had proven successful. The hotel started to fill the rooms with business travelers on the reputation of meeting girls in the lounge.

The restaurant filled up with dinner customers and even banquets noticed a booking boost.

A happy owner, yes, a thrilled and grateful owner, acknowledged my contribution to the chairman.

One evening, I was in the lounge and noticed the sister of the Catering director in Miami with a young restaurant manager in the lounge. I was about to have dinner when I saw them and asked them to join me.

During dinner, we got more acquainted. She was talking about her sister's success and the personal meeting, which gave her the courage and ideas for her success.

The guy she came with had little to offer to the conversation. She dominated it and enjoyed the chance to converse with me. Her sisters had me checked out and found out personal details about me. She asked if we could go back to the lounge; she wanted to hear the band and dance.

"Oh, I do not dance," came from the guy. What an idiot?

We are not dancing the tango; what people call dancing is a simple hopping and rhythmic body movement, no skills required and nothing to worry about.

"I really want to go home; can you get a ride home?"

She looked at him with disbelief, then at me to see if I would bring her home since she had lost her ride. I confirmed; yes, I will give you a ride home.

With him gone, she was ready to go to the dance floor. She danced with me, fast once, and especially liked the slow dance while pushing her small frame into my groin. The move was not lost on me as I squeezed her arm and caressed her neck. The reaction was swift, recognized, and verified by brushing over it as if by accident. Oh yes, it was to size me up. She looked into my eyes with a sneaky smile, which said everything.

In my hotel room was no time lost to consummate this desire. She was small and tight. I had difficulties initially, and then we enjoyed each other's pleasures with added stimulation.

We made love into the early morning, and I took her home to her apartment.

My sleep never came; I had this girl on my mind. It was a forward move by her; she had to have a plan for it. As luck would have it, it worked out well and formed the start of a lengthy relationship.

* * * * * * *

With the opening of the Tampa hotel at the doorstep, preparation kicked in high gear. It was a standard city hotel near the airport designed for the typical business traveler. A family restaurant to serve three meal periods, banquet facilities for small to midsize groups, a bunch of meeting rooms, a soundproofed board room, and a lounge right off the main entry. It would be a routine opening; therefore, the trainers will carry the torch and bring the employees to their full productivity.

The bar, however, received special attention.

The success in Fort Lauderdale had gone through the company and hotels all over the country like wildfire. Everyone wanted to copy this success.

Not every city is the same, and we checked out Tampa and found that we can have an excellent chance to apply promotions. The town has a Snowbird population from the Midwest during the Winter month. We also found a young customer base in other bars, but none offered any activities or entertainment. Just loud recorded music.

Rob and I agreed on a plan, got the nod from the VP, then the General Manager who was hesitant. It is her first hotel, yes we understand.

The F&B director is an experienced company manager. He showed great enthusiasm for it and would certainly do his part to succeed.

I need to bring numbers; she understands that with her accounting experience.

This will be an easy opening. The task force showed good, experienced employees from sister hotels in the South. I knew many personally from my hotel visits.

The restaurant and kitchen will not require much of my time. It had now started, and I left the work to the trainers.

Ron and I concentrated on the lounge setup. He knew the steps we took in FTL, and he built it into his training agenda.

The search was on fora promotions equal to the lounge in Fort Lauderdale. The revenue would not support a one-karat diamond. The price was too rich for a smaller lounge.

We searched for attractions and smaller prices that could be drawn like a lottery. Then the greatest price would be Disney World ticket, Bush Garden or the Daytona car race, something big and popular.

Give people freedom and leisure time. We added hotel rooms which can be purchased from sister hotels at the employees rate, dinner for two for Valentine's Day; just let your creative juices flow.

Music must be produced from a disco table with an DJ personality. From this position, the price drawings will be started. Rob made a list.

We will go with a happy hour and a premium wine-by-the-glass program.

Since the lounge's name is Sadie's, we added a Sadie Hawkins night, allowing the girls to go aggressively after the chosen boys and drag them on the dance floor.

The lounge has now a list of attractions to offer that the competition does not have.

The F&B director embraced it. We will have a successful lounge with a short build-up with marketing support and radio ads.

The GM was still on the fence and asked me to go to dinner to discuss it privately. She knew a small, classy restaurant, not a noisy one where we can talk, and it also is known for delicious food. She would give her undivided attention and the opportunity to sell her.

We ordered wine for the cocktail, then the dinner, and now the time to talk without interruption.

I had asked her if she had seen the FTL action. "No, there was no time to break away. It is my first opening, and I want to get it right. Aside from my brother, a GM in the company, I do not have a source from whom I can get good advice. Yes, the RVP is kind to me, but perhaps because I am a woman."

She is a numbers girl with controller experience so the numbers would sell her. I went through the progression of the East Coast sister hotel numbers. I started the iconic increases, the corresponding profits, and the effect on room occupancy, the restaurant, and event catering.

She took the bait, agreed full-heartedly, and squeezed my arm, reaching across the table. That was followed by a warm and fuzzy smile with eyes speaking loud and clear about her intention for the rest of the evening.

We finished the food and wine, she paid the bill, and then she proposed a nightcap at her house. "I have to sell you on something also!" No comment from me. I knew too well the female seduction game was directed toward a willing participant.

In the morning she dropped me off early a block distance from the hotel, made a few more rounds around the city block and went to work.

Ron knew that I would make every effort to get her on board with our concept.

I used the numbers to convince her. She was a controller before getting a resident's assignment in Maryland, and the job had the RVP's blessing. Eyebrows were rising, and a smile affirmed his sharing this suspicion.

"You are up early, An early riser by nature?"

Yes, much on my mind. The situation at home is not going the way I wish. She is not honest. Any attempts to have an open and indiscriminate debate have become impossible and end in a shouting match. My son is the victim of this infighting. He shuts his door or gets out of the house.

"Why can't you two children get along? Make peace." The child is calling his parents children, and he is right.

"I know this situation, been through it with devastating results. Do not care to talk details. The wounds are too deep."

The F&B was relieved to have the GM's backing and hired a stunning female DJ. She is promotion-oriented! "How did you get her?"

"Stole her from a shady place. She was trying to make it a go with a solo efforts and ended up frustrated. When I told her the efforts, experience, and backing from the top, she was ready to quit on the spot."

Ron pulled all registers, pricing tiers, product selections, and wines by the glass with higher quality and corresponding rates.

It was a home run with absolutely no price resistance. The wine-drinking had become fashionable, the choice had to expand, and a range of quality levels was in order. "I am so glad to hear this You got this ball rolling and now going full speed. If nobody ever thanked you, accept my deepest gratitude right now."

Employees were arriving for the training and the practice sessions. The routine had taken over; my involvement was relegated to looking at the fringes that may be overlooked. Catering had a shaky start; the service was based on temporary staff. That must change; we cannot work on that basis. The GM had this idea saving on labor cost in an area where good profits are realized. I needs to ramp up the sales and it will come with a little growing pain.

It took a corporate order to change this to a regular staffing guide.

While in the shower, I heard a knock at the door. I slowly opened the door in a robe, only to see who wanted to see me.

It was the girl with the question, "You never gave me the answer I have come to 'find out.' You do remember, the joke, for me to know, and then you dropped the second part,

I have come *to find out*, and with this, she pulled out a measuring tape. You can't be serious! Yes, I am I want to know; you cannot just tease a girl and get away with it."

With that, she pushed the door open and locked it behind her. Quickly, she had me disrobed and offered to do the same to her. She took measurements as soon as the full size was ready for the truth. She took full advantage of the situation and made it to the top.

"I have some unfinished work now."

"What?" she wanted to know.

"A man that does not give a woman total satisfaction has not performed like a man.

There was no resistance to an encore performance.

She was ticklish until arousal took over. Her small but firm breast, topped with perky nipples, responded instantly until the hunger took over. Yes, it is the right way and the noble task to do.

To see the satisfaction on a woman's face is as rewarding as having a climax.

Then the smile and warm and fuzzy cuddling caressing the body, she is now a happy girl.

Before she left, "Tomorrow an encore? I cannot. I have business commitments.

The day's training was primarily routine. The briefing to the GM on the lounge took place in the morning. "You are getting it together; I am curious to see it come to the finish line.

Busy tonight? Sorry, I must prepare the paperwork with deadlines.

Sorry!

I booked my return flight one day earlier and called my house from the airport. Martin answered the call and started to tell me that Mom had left food for him to reheat, and she would be late. Do you know where she went?

"I do not know, with certainty. She told me not to wait up for her."

Okay, I will be back home shortly.

How is your car?

"Runs great I am happy with it. It makes it easier with her being so unreliable?"

Does this occur often?

"A couple of times a week?"

Chapter 20

When I had entered the house, I found an almost grown-up boy in tears and worried about death.

Oh boy.

"Yes, I know, he said, something fishy. Should I snoop around to see if there is any stuff around that may give a clue?"

If it is obvious, but do not go and disturb drawers, papers, that sort of stuff that raises suspicion. I have to think of something.

He told me that he had seen the same car cruising by the house.

The same old game is on again. Will she ever learn?

You go to bed and get a rest. I will wait up. Then we should learn something. In any case, she will be shocked to see me home already; The body language will give away secrets.

The same old game was on again. She must be a willing participant, for otherwise, she could have called the neighbor or the FBI agent.

We prepared a meal together; my son is willing to learn cooking. I will be on my own soon and needed to feed myself. I was also spoiled with good food; I better get on the stick.

He had already learned procedures and was good at handling a sharp knife. He knew his meats from the times spent with Grandmother and was familiar with cooking procedures.

Only the more refined finishing touches had been missing. With practice and long-distance tutoring, he would get it together. Dinner was good. We drank a glass of wine his grandfather had introduced him to, and he now really enjoyed it.

After that, he excused himself to his room, wanted a head start, and fell asleep before she got home. "If it comes to a fight, I will not hear it with earplugs. Just try to keep it down."

She got home by 10:30. I was waiting in the family room and not visible from the front door; only when I stood up did she realizes she had been caught in the act. "You are early!"

When I called in, you had still been out. Our son is now seeing your infidelity since he had seen these coons snooping around the house.

What has come of you? Risking your family life. The son is now in grave danger. No wonder he will enlist as soon as school is out.

"It is your travel. You are never home."

So many of my colleagues do the same and manage to keep it together. You have one more shot at it. You are running out of excuses now.

This time, you have to do it alone. I will not dirty my hands on these creepy characters. Do it to last forever. Everybody has choices in life. This was spoken with a soft voice, never reached any high notes, and received her full attention. Then I went to sleep on the couch in the family room.

"Why aren't you coming to bed?"

I do not want to soil myself, not knowing what hellhole you came back from.

I heard her cry half the night. Serves you right.

In the morning, I took my son to a breakfast place. At his age, the amount a boy consumes requires substantial food. Dennis did an excellent job in this.

With our bellies full, we returned home, started one of his projects, and ignored mother altogether. That punishment was torture and most effective to get her to come out with the details.

By the evening, she was ready to do so in private. "Our son must not know this and hear me telling you."

We took a walk around the reservoir, and now she confessed, half crying and coughing. "They forced it on me, held me tight with one man, while the other raped me, then they took turns again and again until I could no longer go on."

Why did you not call the police when they came here?

"They forced their way in the first time, fucked me on the floor, then used strong language to disclose it to me if I did not submit again."

Blackmail?

"Yes."

I am still missing something! How did this all get started? And don't tell me this innocent story I already know. There is more to it, is there?

Reluctantly, she confessed, "During the church activity, a handsome young guy poured on the charm and eventually got me to go to bed with him."

That was consensual?

"Yes, I was turned on and really wanted him for sex and only sex. It was fun and exciting, and it made me feel young again, like a young girl in London when I lost my virginity."

"Then the pressure started to expand the pool of men to take part as a three-party, which I rejected. Then, these people showed up here, and you gave them the third degree.

As soon as they received the release early for good behaviors and are ready to join society as a good human being, the action started all over again. For a while, they had seen your car in the driveway. That kept them away, but as soon as my blue car was there again, it was the green light for them."

This means you have been violated several times.

"Yes."

Did they use condoms to prevent venereal infection?

"No, they found out I could not get pregnant from the first guy and then spilled it inside."

I want you to go to the doctor, tell her everything, and get a preventive medicine injection. You could have contracted AIDS, God forbid!

I will not have intercourse with you for a while until I am certain there is nothing contagious.

"I understand."

What is your game plan to get these goons out of your life?

"I do not know. I am not good at bluffing, and you have all this experience."

No, I will not do it for you this time. I told you that the last time, and I keep my word.

However, I will be on standby with a baseball bat, and so will the boy.

We can hide in the basement and upstairs to attack them from two sides if necessary. I can park my white car at Tracy's house and take off from work like the last time.

I think they will be snooping out the house for my car at night, staking it out to get the time of departure and return, then the action will begin.

You will receive them, let them in, and quietly lock the door behind you.

If they want to come upstairs, I will be ready. We will listen to the talking with these radios, then move in as soon as violence starts.

The violence will start just as soon as you tell them it is all over, and their blackmail is invalid since you confessed it to me. They will try to hit you. Now you have outplayed them, and they do not like this.

They may even try to rape you again for good old sake. Scratch them, go for the balls, fingernails into the eyes. Suppose you can rip them out, the better. It has to look like a fight for your life. Yes, there will be hits to your face and bruises afterward, but before it gets out of hand, the baseball bats will be hitting them on the heads, knocking them unconscious, and then we tie them up with electrical cable ties and call the police.

Now you will have to testify about the whole mess at the police precinct and later in court in front of a judge and jury. That will be your punishment! Are you ready for this?

"Yes, I want to come clean once and for good." She was crying on my shoulder. "I do not know what I will do without you."

Just do not push your luck too far!

* * * * * * *

Maggie called me at the office and invited me to be a monitor at the final training session; "Do you remember the game played between two groups in different rooms. I need you for your judgment and people's knowledge to be an observer."

Okay, I remember that game; it was fun, especially from the observer's point of view.

"Then Friday at 7 pm at the Dallas airport motel." It's a date; "oh, I like that! "

I told Margo that I would be late from my experience from the time I attended as a newly hired manager.

329

All the students of the seminar are eating dinner. Wine is served to the delight of who took advantage of this free service.

When I passed the rooms to glance at the young people, I noticed familiar faces. Can that be? Priscilla and Maya? They saw me and came running into the hallway, hugs, and kisses to no end. Teary eyes and neither could bring any words out. We stood there and broke out laughing. "What a coincidence and a huge surprise. Did you know this?"

I saw Maggie from the corner of my eye, smiling and saying that she had asked for me because she knows Priscilla. But she never met Maya, and now you tell me you are also roommates? Yes, it must be Karma paying us back.

Priscilla wiped her tears while Maya wiped mine first and followed up on her face.

Oh, a word of advice, speak softly and negotiate. You must get back; we'll meet after the seminar. I will wait for you.

You will catch on to it., Later Okay?

At the end of the dinner, a count of two was taken, splitting the group into A and B, and going to the marked room now.

Round tables accommodated the entire group in the two different rooms.

Maya and Priscilla had been together in room B.

A brief explanation and the groups need to prepare an opening statement for the other room.

Room A was boisterous, loud voices dominated the discussions, and aggressive language was put on paper. The few girls in the room never had a chance to get a word in on this statement.

Room B started initially the same way, but the women in this room would not allow dominance. We are part of this group and want our voices heard. Buy nature, a woman's voice is softer and a pitch higher, which made up for being loud.

The men held back and acknowledged that this must be a group decision. The instructions are pointing to it. With this, a statement was formulated around how best to enter negotiations. Yes, in talks like people in business do.

These papers are now in the room opposite and read.

Room B received an aggressive statement hinting at starting a fight. Only through a good argument can a winner be awarded. We challenge you to this.

Room B's note was received with laughter and ridiculed. What are these people over there? No courage, no guts, and no backbone. The same loud men continue to bully the entire group. Any attempts by the others had been squashed, "What do you know about this men's world? We will show them, leave it to us.

Room B took a soft approach and discussed the content. We received a challenge for a fight. Should we respond in kind? The girls had now formed a coalition and spoke as one. Priscilla and Maya are taking the lead and are whispering. We do not want them to hear us over there, but we stand our ground and propose formal negotiations. We ask them for points of importance to form a base and see what we get back.

Rom A continued with the aggression and challenged the opponents to a fight. We do not agree to negotiations; it shows weakness, and he will only respond through war-like confrontation.

Notes again get exchanged.

Meanwhile, all observers followed this battle with interest. Maggie took me over to room B and noted how my two girls had taken the lead and involved the entire group to form a consensus. Her proud eyes told me everything.

Room B took the paper from A and tore it up to be returned as such.

Room B followed with a note to challenge them to a hearty negotiation session and bring up substantive issues.

Room A read this, and now the mouthy guys had run out of arguments, and the women had finally a say in the matter.

Don't you see the strategy of the others? They will not show up for a fight. You will be fighting with yourself. In its place, they show reason and common sense and have taken the wind out of our sails. We lost this game.

The winners are in room B, congratulation.

Maya and Priscilla came running out to the hallway, and our reunion continued.

I want to show you around town and the headquarters buildings. I invited the girls to stay over the weekend and, if possible, all week. I have no travel on my calendar.

That will be fun, and I have been waiting to see you. I miss you. Life is not the same with the replacement. He is a bully and discriminatory. Is he Indian or Asian? He is all of the above. I know him all too well.

Then we have two houseguest. I look so much forward to this; I will be a breath of fresh air in our house.

I will pick you up tomorrow morning. Go and celebrate your victory.

Priscilla came to my side as she had done so many times and squeezed my arm affectionately. Then Maya took the other arm; I wanted to do this all the time, he is a rock for comfort and security, and I feel the same way. You always give good advice.

When I returned, I told Margo we would have friends as house guests. She was shocked initially, but when she heard the names, her eyes lit up. I know, these girls. I also treasure the support they have given to you. It will bring a fresh breeze into the house, and Martin can play host.

We told Martin in the morning. His eyes lit up; you mean your most favorite girls you spoke to us on so many occasions?

Let us make plans, food, a celebration, tours, take them places.

You get a head start while I pick them up from the Motel.

Maya was instantly recognized from the time in Hartford, while photos from the restaurant opening in Barbados had previously introduced Priscilla.

Martin made every effort to look and behave maturely; a gentleman is an image he wanted to project. But in time, the guards came down as he took them around the house, the neighborhood, and the reservoir.

Priscilla was at ahh, so many trees, how tall are they, and what's the name. This is an Oak, see the leaves shape, and this is a Maple, again, a different form, like the Canadian flag. Then we have Birch; you can see the white rind and Beachwood. The rest I must look up in a book.

Martin did his best to name the easy once. The day went fast, catching up on our past, and now we have a home-cooked Swiss meal.

But first, a celebration is in order. Martin popped a bottle of champagne as we all toasted to Karma, the good one which brought us together.

Dinner was exquisite. Yes, she is an excellent cook.

The girls shared the King size bed in the guest room.

In the morning we decided on a tour of the city, monuments, museums and with chance a white house tour.

My wife and Martin acted as tour guides while I went to work for a short day.

I had asked permission to bring them to the office, and obtained visitor passes for the next day.

In the evening, we went to Duck Cheng, a restaurant that serves Pecking Duck as their menu feature, and a pre-order was not required.

It was our son's favorite place, and now the girls are experiencing something of a surprise.

Martin explained the order of service; the skin comes first, and it is crispy, then roll it into these little pancakes and add this sauce. Ready to enjoy.

Cautiously at first, Maya tried it, while Priscilla went straight for it.

Oh, so good, uuhs and ahhs, the girls liked this surprise. Martin was proud, having made this his choice for the evening.

Back home, we talked into the late night. These talks engage three people and years in between, then the parallels and hick-ups. There is just so much to cover.

Today I will show you our company headquarters.

With a bit of luck, we may meet the owner. This gets me nervous! Don't be. he is a down-to-earth man who enjoys meeting young talents, knows me, and he remembers you, Priscilla. Remember the Pirates first dinner?

I took them to the second floor and introduced them to my secretary.

Now I can put faces to the voices. Welcome to this department. I am showing them around now. On tour, they met Rob, the IT people, and the service training people. Then Andrea and the boss.

He asked them to come and sit for a minute." I remember your voice, Maya. It has been a while, and now you have joined us. This is grand. You two had been a super team. I respect this.

Priscilla, you stole the show in Barbados, and what a show it was,

People are still reminiscing about the food and the Pirate's dinner."

Then to my office, the pile that never went away.

Look at this; it never gets read anymore; my secretary is sorting the important papers for action, and the rest finds a parking place. We throw it away from the bottom when it is getting too large. That's how we manage this.

The girls were getting an education on the functions of a large company.

The test kitchen was already familiar to both from the food school. Now we go to the cafeteria and get lunch.

"Who cooks this food, Priscilla is asking?" I don't know for sure, but the company has an industrial catering branch that services cafeterias, even nursing homes, and other medical facilities. This may be them; I must say, they do a great job. Employees must contribute a co-pay, then the company covers the rest.

Everybody eats here, including the most senior executives. "Even the CEO?" This may be why this food is so tremendous and consistent.

The girls picked on salads and fruit; "we are still stuffed from last night's exotic food."

I looked over the urgent papers that needed my signature. Then the question to the secretary, can I have the rest of the day off? She laughed, "you have never asked for that, but since you are asking so nicely, permission was granted. Suppose something comes this way and needs an answer. I will call you."

"Give these women a good look around town and countryside."

At home, we made plans to go to our favorite French restaurant.

Martin at once started to describe another of his favorite eating places. "I will do the driving.

The reservation is for eight PM, and it will take us forty minutes to reach this country setting in Maryland."

We drove out along the Potomac and showed the girls the countryside. For Maya, it was a routine.

Priscilla was amazed; hills, trees, so green, cows in the field grazing, horses playing in the paddock and chasing each other, chickens running around the farmhouses, this scenery was entirely new for Priscilla. She had her mouth open in astonishment and hardly spoke—just the sounds of amazement.

This is soooo beautiful. She emphasized the soooo to make her point.

It was a different world for her.

The season is at its prime now and the next three months. Then the leaves turn color, and trees shed them in preparation for winter.

"Winter, you mean snow?" Yes, dear, it does get cold here, and nature takes a good nap until Spring comes around.

She had to process this and compare it to her island's vegetation. "I suppose, we have something like it also. It is not so sudden, but a change of season is visible when you are alert to nature. We call it a rainy season and a dry season. Winter is the dry season with cooler temperatures. Then the summer brings the rain."

Martin took over at the door to the restaurant. He made the reservation in his name and wanted to impress our guests. " Martin spoke to the hostess about being a regular, and today we bring you guest's from faraway places.

We look forward to your fine cuisine again."

He mustered every ounce of maturity to make this statement. It sounded rehearsed. I gave him a little eye signal; cool it, boy, they love you already. There is no need to get stuffy.

The server passed the menu and quickly referred to the day's special, a delicious seasonal item. She described it with every detail; one could believe she had it for her dinner.

The girls and Martin opted for the special item, my wife had her favorite sweetbread in a dill and gin sauce, and I ordered the fresh rainbow trout, just poached and hollandaise on the side.

Everybody shared a small appetizer.

We ate with full enjoyment. Then the Main plates came to the table. Three women first, and I received mine after everybody had been served. The server went back to the kitchen and delivered my trout.

"Why is this fish blue, and why is it looking at me with the head and eyes still on?"

Maya was taken back; she had never seen a trout that had been alive minutes ago. I needed to explain this.

The fish is kept alive in a chilled water basin until an order comes to the kitchen. The cook takes a net, gives a little knock on the head, and places the fish straight into seasoned gently boiling water, which is just at the boiling point. Minutes later, the outside of the fish turns blue.

The whole fish is served because the head has the most precious morsel, the cheeks. It is the protective layer and serves as a defense. It is a very slippery substance. I pulled off to show her; She declined the offer to taste it.

Their food was enjoyed with a cautious approach. The mushrooms had them guessing. Neither Priscilla not Maya had ever tasted these. "is your food good, the server was asking." It is terrific; we are treated to new food items and want to go slow to get the full flavors.

Selecting dessert was left to Martin. I knew he would pick creme Brulé, his favorite.

Again, the cautious approach to the sugar crust in caramel color, then the soft, rich cream and vanilla aroma, you have chosen well.

The girls are paying Martin compliments. He glowed and thanked them. I asked him if he would pick up the check since he is playing the big shot host.

"If I could, I gladly would do that. But these guests relate to you, and I will accept the gracious generosity." The mother wanted to know where he picked up such polished language. I am learning it from Television shows; these swollen British talks are rubbing off on me.

Priscilla started to laugh; she could relate to it from her home.

On the drive home, it was dark now, and questions needed to be answered. Tell me what kind of mushrooms garnished our plates.

We call them Chanterelles. They show up in the forest during the season. It made this veal chop so much a special presentation. We were able to pinpoint the herbs and all other items. I have learned another trick: integrating a little smoked bacon into delicate meat.

I had to explain that it works in small quantities, but it can be overpowering, just like herbs do.

At home, Priscilla got noticeably quiet. Does she think about her departure, but she is staying two more days?

I looked her in the eyes, "I know I am unsociable, but it occurred to me that I have been missing my father. Seeing Martin and the bond you two have, I wished to have this bond with my father. Can I ask you now;?"

"Will you be my father?"

I will treasure such a relationship for the rest of my life."

I said yes, and everybody applauded. We embraced, and I kissed on the mouth; you are a great addition to this family. We wished for a girl, a sister to Martin, and now, we have the most precious gift we could ever expect.

Not a single eye was dry. "Maya was referring to her dad, he is there for me, but we do not have a bond. A girl does need a father!"

The next day May had to return home; she was destined to hand over her job to a newly hired girl. This is Maya; even with the job, she will not cut corners in the end. She could not be talked into staying longer.

I took her to the airport, and she was quiet. Aside from the courteous thank you and how much she enjoyed this reunion. I could see that she was thinking back in time. "Is anything troubling you? Yes, she came out at once; "Do you remember the lecture I received about *sins of omission?'* This is bothering me now; I finally realized that I am a sinner in this context.

I wish I had been more assertive when we worked together. I wanted you desperately, yet the job, company rules, and social restrictions made me hold off on it.

The day we meet alone, be ready for a tigress. I have much energy bottled up inside me."

I reached over to take her hand and squeezed it. "This is therapy for me. " To feel and touch you goes a long way. Thank you for being a great man to work with and a terrific friend. I love you in my way."

I will treasure this and remember that it goes both ways.

Martin took Priscilla and his Mom on a country ride into the mountains. Martin drove, and while going, he had ample time to explain how these mountains had been formed. The geological process he had learned in part in school and more so on public television programs. Again, Priscilla had never seen mountains.

Priscilla took the front passenger seat, and Mom could see how attempts had been made to hold hands,

These two youngsters are connecting.

The drive was another education for Priscilla. The scenery and steep inclines had her a bit uneasy. Martin impressed her that all these forests are, in fact, government facilities. Training grounds for the FBI, others are safe houses to secure people of considerable interests, and office buildings, testing laboratories and administration.

The day arrived for Priscilla to return home to Barbados. The mood was subdued. Are we losing a daughter and a best friend?

All of us have bonded with this girl; she is so lovely and easy to be with. I wished nothing more than to keep her at my house and live with us.

But life has its agenda.

The farewell was kept short and therefore minimizing the pain. I drove her to the airport. She was quiet, but inside I sensed that she was crying.

Suddenly she broke the silence: "Please stay in touch; I need you, much more than you can imagine. Please, I beg you, never leave me; you are my father now, be at my side when I call."

She was openly sobbing, tears rolling down her eyes, and I was at the point of being forced to stop on the side. I took her hand and squeezed it. She responded the same way; it was painful to see her emotions exposed.

I gave her my solemn promise. This is a commitment. I will hold to it. You are precious to all of us and especially to me, and this is from the beginning. I could feel this bond growing from the first moment we met. Just like a lightning bolt, it struck my heart to reserve a permanent space for you.

These are the sweetest words ever; I love you, Papa."

With this, she went to the security check and the last wave, and now I could no longer see her.

I went to the observation room and waited to see the plane take off safely. My eyes stayed wet until I reached my house.

Chapter 21

The new hotel was being built in the tri-city of North Carolina universities, famous basketball teams, and an endless list of technology companies. It seems a perfect location for a business hotel, but why so small?

My preview was routine but for a friendly, cute car rental agent. "Southern charm is still alive," I told myself.

The agent gave direction with every detail; this girl must enjoy the job.

She asks me my purpose for a visit. "Marketing research," she claimed.

"We are new and want to get a customer profile." How does my profile look?

As I turned sideways, laughing, and getting teased, she said, "Excellent to me!"

At the construction site, I was now much more comfortable reading blueprints, could make out the finishing detail descriptions, and now the South Carolina hotel with the slow finishers flared up.

I asked the project manager, Is it going to be like there? I am explaining my reason for asking.

"No, I will be on top of them. We have another large project already on the books and approved. We will be pulling them off as soon as they are done. The concrete guys are already there, and framers are sharpening the saws. It will be quick and professional."

Then I told them the method we used to speed up the work. "That will do it every time. When I worked these jobs, I hated when anyone came close to my tools. It is an investment, each worker with their own, for otherwise, the tools would disappear, and the wife selling them at home out of the garage. How are you doing it with the cooks? Knives are over one hundred apiece!"

We issue them two knives by the type of work. They have to sign for it, which is recorded in the employee file; then, if they quit or get fired, the knives must be returned before the last paycheck is issued. They pay for it twice the cost. The reason is that we are not a charity. If they lost it, broke it, that would be impossible.

The business model is for profit, all signed with the acceptance of the knife, not even small print. It will be the first professional knife with which they had ever worked. You know the difference in buying quality.

"Yes, I do."

The French have a saying; *You must be rich to buy cheap.*

"Now that I have to remember. It is so true. That is a good procedure in our situation."

"Right you are."

A true Southern gentleman, I could easily see him on a plantation in the countryside growing rice and cotton.

"We have a specialty restaurant. I was pointed to the location. Just off the kitchen with an outside entrance. Any idea what the concept it will be?"

Not yet.

"But we have a name already."

"Yes, after the developer's grandfather, the old money source. He wants to honor him with his name and set a living memorial in a way. The old boy liked his food. It will be Sigi's."

Catchy name. Did he have any favorites? We can incorporate into the menu selection, and names of his daughters are always an eye-catcher on the menu.

"You are willing to do this?"

Of course, we will. The local flavor brings a homey feeling, a comfort zone. What better place when homemade food is served and no dishes to wash.

"Yes, you are right."

I had planned to stay over at a nearby Red Roof to give me time for research. Crab, he had mentioned, and a strangely named soup, creamy, oh so delicious as his mouth started watering. Crab cakes for sure, but also something like a soufflé or baked to a crust, in a pastry crust.

I visited restaurants and noticed the she-crab soup everywhere and catfish in cornmeal and baked or pan-fried. A recipe would be in a cookbook and easily attainable.

Southern food was just the greatest. I had to make the server understand the reasons for ordering multiple dishes. The grazing method we used in Barbados came to mind.

Driving through the city, I could see only car dealers. Conversion packages are advertised to prepare a car for racing. Oversized tires, manifold above the hood, and noisy as hell. This is Nascar country. One dealer had a DeLorean in the showroom, with a big sign inviting the would-be buyer to a test drive!

I worked through menus and noticed the dignified atmosphere in all places. The old South is still alive. We must follow through on the menu with this, for we will make a fool out of it.

Armed with pages of notations on food, beverages, the points I picked up from the server, and the Southern charm, we must be selective and find the right people. It makes the dining experience so much more authentic.

By noon, off to the airport, returning the car at the car rental station. I dropped the key on the counter and thanked the agent for her service. The same cute girl was once again at the service desk.

"Y'all be coming back soon?"

In about two weeks, I will then need the car for two weeks minimum.

"I will put one aside for you. I will upgrade you at no additional charge."

How nice of you. Fine Southern service!

"Yes, sir. Have a safe trip."

I took her business card and would call her when the date was firm.

* * * * * * *

Off to Fort Lauderdale to take the pulse on the lounge.

A management change is always a time when new blood wants to make changes. The greeting was professional, a big change from my first visit; the hotel looked busy, with million-dollar yachts tied up at the Intracoastal Waterway and every slip taken inside the marina.

The outdoor bar had a new supervisor or assistant manager with a perky personality. She made one feel at home and chatted freely about life, the kind of small talk the customer gets engaged in until serious staff surfaced, like, "How is the fishing? any luck with a sailfish?"

"No, just marlins."

I introduced myself to this new employee, and the familiar girl came to us simultaneously. Her big smile is still her trademark. She had picked me up at the airport in the limo.

"Meet Carol. She is now in charge of the deck by the yachts, the outside only. Since we expanded to create more seating space in the lounge, especially for these prominent people, it needed to be looked after.

The inside staff is no longer able to cover the outside.

It has gotten so crazy that we are running out of parking. People park on the side of the road to the bridge and get tickets; it's not a good situation. We must do something."

Now I had upfront info. I must see how the upper ranks were seeing it.

The GM from the Middle East seemed nice but wait a minute; I knew this face. It took a minute to place him. Yes, Springfield, MA. That was it. I wondered if he recognized me.

The F&B director was recruited from the outside, a German man.. The girls did not reveal anything about the new management team.

They are new and must learn the marketplace. That was all I could squeeze out of the girls. A smirky smile added to the mystery and a hint of displeasure.

Off to meet them at the executive offices. Both of them are in the office and greeted me. The GM instantly connected with the training I had done in Springfield, wanting to know how I landed this job. He had heard rumbling in NYC.

The F&B man, yes, German, native language, but a distinct northern Austrian dialect came across real thick.

After telling the GM the short story on New York, he referred to a union hotel he had difficulties with previously in another company. "I could have used a smart fellow like you to win my case, but without backing, alone, one does not stand a chance. God be blessed this company is union-free, and this NY hotel is offered for sale now."

I just spoke to Tracy and Carol and learned about the parking issue.

"Yes, we are thinking of doing something dramatic. Daily we are violating the fire code. The people are rowdy, and a cover charge will sort out the rowdy patrons." And on it went.

After they had finished, I asked them if they had met the owner of the hotel?

"No, not yet. We are scheduled for a meeting at his office in a week."

Okay, then let me prepare you a little. A former VP of franchise hotels for this company, this is his first hotel project.

Since the beginning, this hotel did poorly, primarily due to management neglect.

The lounge project was implemented to secure cash flow and save his skin from creditors. This is the beginning of this success. We, as a regional team, signed on to keep this lounge's success. I was given the task of being the *Gatekeeper.* Yes, that is what he did, pointing directly at me.

Since then, he bought a beach site to build an ultra-luxury hotel. He is facing stiff opposition from the zoning board and the homeowners association.

A bundle of money is by now into this project before breaking ground. He is a determined man. Now the details of how we arrived at this lounge concept and the results.

By telling the gory details in a step-by-step detail fashion, the faces had now changed. It became clear that they had a mission to secure continued success. The money this lounge generates is too large to take this on the soft shoulder.

A sudden change will affect the room's occupancy, the restaurant, and the catering since all are profiting from the new reputation. All I could see were blank faces.

To drive the final nail into the coffin, I said, You are settling into a **readymade nest**. Never forget this. It is the reason for my visit today. I am the Gatekeeper and must report to him personally any action that may jeopardize the success.

I realize there are problems, and there will always be problems. Our job as managers is to solve the problem without hurting the cash flow. Every problem has a solution. I challenge you to find this solution. The

GM agreed with me in principle. The F&F director showed me the longest face I had ever seen.

Look around for parking spaces that can be rented at night. The attraction down the road and then there is an art school, shopping, and the port across the causeway. Something can be contracted for a cost but look at the volume this place produces. A parking cost and valet staff will not break the bank.

No parking fee is in the doctrines, as are the drink prices, the serving times, and promotions. The same goes for the band. Don't fix what isn't broken. I would like to hear something from you so I can brief him on my purpose for this trip.

I will be spending the evening to assess the customers' conduct, make a report on it, and if needed, I will make recommendations to solving issues.

We are managers. Let's never forget this! With this, I excused myself.

When I ran across the F&B director Emil a little later, he invited me to dinner, but I declined. I must experience this lounge as a customer, food, drink, service, and entertainment. Some other time when we have to show for the zoning hearing.

"This hearing has now been postponed."

The owner appreciated the briefing, the prompt encounter to stop any devastating changes, and an update on the hotel at the beach.

"I want a first-class seafood restaurant there. Think about it. No rush, just planting the seed. I know your background. There is stuff in that head of yours."

Thanks for the vote of confidence.

* * * * * * *

Back home, the day of reckoning was approaching; she was worried but had rehearsed her poker face and the words she would be using. We had switched the cars and parked my car in front of the house to keep them at bay. This had worked before and did the same again. With my car out of the way and her blue car parked again, it would lure them once again to their old game.

During the daytime, I was hiding in the guest room with a view of the front of the house. The boy was excited about the potential arrest and, releasing his bottled-up anger at them He took up camp in his room on the lower level, with a good view from the ground up to the front.

Monday passed without any contact, likely to check a day if the pattern was normal. In the evening, still no car. He must be traveling again. Better yet, keeping him at the greatest distance was preferred. Then Tuesday at 10:00 am, the two goons walked towards the door.

We had made a signal to alarm the three of us without making noticeable noise.

Coming with total confidence and an air of intimidation, they did not waste time threatening her and grabbed her to teach her a lesson.

At once, the one man took both of her hands, and she started to scream. They stuffed her mouth with a cloth; the other man grabbed her legs to lay her on the floor. They bent over her to remove her clothes while she was biting, freeing one hand, scratching his face across the nose, the knee finding the other men's groin, which made him loosen his grip. And just as he was getting back to ripping her clothes off, the baseball bat from my son hit him point-blank in the middle of his skull. The other looked up as he saw my bat driving at his face, breaking his nose, and raising his eyebrows. A second hit which put him to sleep.

"You waited long enough to show up. Timing is everything," I said to my son, who smiled and agreed. "You made your mark on his face"

If we had come earlier, they could have seen us from the corner of their eyes. This way, they felt to have the upper hand, a fine line for us to time the assault. Let's get them secured.

My son had the cable ties handy in his pocket, expertly pulled the zipper, then followed up with pliers to cause pain.

They may wake before the police arrive. Then Martin called the police and gave them the details of the assault. It took three minutes, a quiet night at the station, took the story down, and asked her to come with them to file the assault.

Charges will be filed; they got locked up with good wishes from her.

"I hope they lose the key on you. Burn in hell, for sure."

She came home after the police station had recorded her testimony. Peaceful once again

I returned to work a day ahead. "Is all okay," my secretary, Tina, wanted to know. I did not tip her off but let her in on the big picture. When the cat's away, the mice play!

I thought the visit from Maya and Priscilla had contributed to making Margo realize what she has at home. Life at home had now settled down to normalcy once again. A son, a husband, comfortable living, and too much time on her hands. She promised again to try to secure work, if only to keep her busy and out of trouble.

* * * * * * *

Now off to North Carolina! As planned, I made the rental car reservation myself, and the call was answered by the same voice I had gotten to know. "I have your car waiting for you, a brand-new BMW, so be good to your country's product."

Sweet as ever, she had a brand-new car ready, a special treat; she must have pulled her father's favor for that. Papers signed and no more directions needed, she asked me if she would be allowed to see the hotel at any time. I want you to see it like a guest when we are in full operation. This way, you can describe it to your clients if they seek your advice.

"That will be even better. You mean I will be invited to dinner by you?"

I will arrange this, of course. After all the excitement is settled, I always visit to check on the operation. That will be the time to do the invitation.

At the hotel, all seemed calm and normal, the managers are all in their job, the trainers arriving tomorrow, preparation is on track. What could go wrong?

The Chef transferred from Tampa had taken his girlfriend from the Tampa hotel with him. Initially, this did not sit right, but kindness had to prevail when they were in love. We assigned her the assistant restaurant manager position.

She was a supervisor in her earlier job, has been proven to be groomed for the management position, and now she received the assistant manager title.

The bar was small and didn't have a place for a dance floor, nor set up for games.. We needed a new idea.

346

The specialty restaurant had suffered a setback. Another region had failed to do their homework, and their efforts had failed. Enough reasons to deny our request.

"Let's just do a steak house and do it well. Steaks are always a good seller. There are no arguments; except the hotel's reputation is at stake in this demanding market.

While the area is unknown to people, it may look like the countryside in the South, with Baptist churches on every street corner.

Stock cars are ruling the streets, and cowboy boots with horse manure on the heels are the norm. This is far from that kind of a place.

High-paid jobs are here. Just look at this list of companies, schools' laboratories es. Does this not tell you anything, and further, when have I failed you?

"*No*, no deal. There is always a first time."

I was ashamed to bring this decision to the General Manager and the project manager, who was eager to view the choices. In his mind, he was going to be the very first customer.

Secretly I had prepared a menu at home and on the road, looked up recipes in Southern cookbooks, copied them, and had a good but small menu ready. The denial did not sit right with me. Southern food was too good to be ignored.

I had asked Tony to get expensive stationery and print the Sigi's name on the top, address, and phone number without any reference to the hotel for the image of a freestanding restaurant. This would serve as the daily menu in small quantities, giving an exclusive appearance.

Then I had to let the GM, F&B, and Executive Chef in on the plan.

To start for training, we would go with the steak menu; then, when the dust settled, we will give this a try. The Chef had to test-cook the recipe and feed it to the task force as lunch and dinner.

Test meals would be done with the corporate menu. Counting on keeping it a secret was wishful thinking.

A secret between two people is no longer a secret unless they become accomplices.

The food coordinator the VP had appointed for this opening turned out to be a stumbling block. It was her first opening, and she thought she had to prove her worth. She started digging around every food purchase. The secret was leaked to her, and she made a scene and called the headquarters office to have the VP intervene.

I was alone and without a defense. The plan had to be put on ice.

The opening took place without a hitch; my apologies to the project manager for failing him with the menu.

This girl acted maliciously and caused interference. Once I caught her violating protocol, I sent her back home. There is always another opportunity; the documentation would stay under lock for now.

During this turmoil, the assistant restaurant manager asked me to meet with her off the property, a personal issue involving the Chef.

She drove me to an apartment building where she had a room rented.

A small, suitable unit and right for one person with no men's clothing gave me a clue. They two had a fallout and broke up. She would stick it out on the job and get over him, it would not affect the work. He was now dating the GM's secretary openly and said that I should not intervene on her behalf. It's over!.

There was trouble on the horizon.

The secretary was a gorgeous girl; if not for her height, she could easily be on the cover of *Vogue*.

I noticed that the secretary was a flirt, she used her attractive looks to manipulate the male gender and gained their favors in this way.

This young asst manager started to cry and hugged me to find comfort. My shirt is wet from tears and mascara. She fumbled on my belt, then pulled down the zipper. "Make love to me, please. I need this the most right now." She had since shed her clothes, stood butt naked in front of me, and dropped to her knees for the most obvious. That was followed by my giving back to a final crescendo to complete the act. "Now I feel like a woman again. I will be okay now. Thank you so much. I know I was using you, but you gave me a great service."

That was a first, and again I became the prey. What had changed?

Six-month time later, I found out from task force personnel that they had gotten back together; the secretary had dumped him in the worst way.

Chapter 22

Martin, Alexander! I realized that our son had grown to be a man. Soon he would serve in the navy, and we were still calling him by all kinds of names, first baby, then child, then the nickname Sonny, which had stuck through his young life. He does have a name, and we must make every effort to call him by his name. We took great care to match a name that would project his personality.

Martin because he is the patron saint of my hometown, known for being charitable, a strong knight fighting with the sword for human dignity. The second name is Alexander from the famous King Alexander of Macedonia. Courage, intelligence, strong personality, a natural leader, and visionary. Martin likes his name and is proud of it. Also, it is challenging to disfigure this name. Not like Richard becomes Dicky, or William turns into Billie. I shake my head at these variations.

No, I will never be a Marti or Billie. I will defend my name.

In the Southern German dialect, names get the added "le" attached while being a child.

Only his favorite aunt was allowed this privilege. My Martin'le is what she called him.

My wife, greeting me for a change with affection. It assured me that this past criminal action had finally ended.

Her court date was not yet set, but forthcoming was a mental burden. It will make you stronger and give you self-confidence. Do you think people in a leading position sometimes do not face the same pressure? They prepare, fight through it, and go on with a more vital self-belief.

Do your homework. Showing emotions is okay but be very sharp on the facts. Think of the way you will present this without crying. You will gain credibility, and you are the only one that can do this.

They may want to hear from me about the final act and the scare at an earlier date. Answer only the question. Do not add to it unless encouraged by the DA. They are your friends.

The defense attorneys will be asking leading questions conducive to blabbering on and saying something they will use against you or in support of the defendant. If you do not understand the question, ask for it to be rephrased. Remind them that English is your second language.

The assistant DA should object to questions that become too personal and intimate. Otherwise, play as if you did not understand it. I don't understand or I don't have an answer, can you explain?

It can get testy when the judge is pressing for an answer. At this time, you need to cry. Ask for time to collect yourself. You may get a short recess out of it. I will be an opportunity to get advice from the DA.

Keep your vocabulary primitive and build in errors that are typical for Europeans. Think of someone new in this country. Words they use and parts of a sentence omitted.

"How do you know all this?"

Partly from TV shows with court and jury and DA versus attorney arguments. It is fictitious but has to resemble the real world. I am sure they hire legal experts to guide these dialogues.

Three to four weeks is enough time to be super prepared.

Martin followed this talk with great interest. "If I were here, I would be with you for support. Just hanging around in the audience, displaying that there is a son in the play, and it caused him harm too. I would slide this in at the best opportunity in your situation.

****

Back at the office, I was summoned to Charles's office.

"We are restructuring your region. You will have too many hotels since a whole bunch more are in the pipeline within a year. Additionally, we are negotiating to buy a resort on the gulf coast in Alabama. S well-established golf resort, tennis, marina, huge swimming pool, fitness center, lawn games, and shuffleboard. Fishing and on and on.

The staff has been there for twenty to thirty years, and while this is good for continuity, they do not subject themselves easy to changes.

The guests are loyal Southern families spending the vacation as a family for generations on end. It is common to see four generations on the dinner table, all neatly lined up by age and rank.

I want you to go there and check it out and see what you can learn about the operating procedures and controls in the kitchen. Size up the Chef and look around for disrepairs, equipment, and that sort of stuff. I must give a budget request to bring it up to snuff.

"Now the other issue! I do not have a candidate for the new region from Florida to South America. None of these guys want to bite. I know that your time in this region is young, but I have a replacement for it from an F&B that has earned his laurels. Are you interested?

I will tell you the name, but first, the placement for Florida. All Florida hotels are already in your domain."

I have a strong interest in Florida. It should not be a problem. We had lived in Florida before and the hotels already in the region will be an easy transition. I always had a soft heart for Florida.

I want to run it by the wife. She also knows the terrain, and the son, Martin, is going into the Navy in two weeks.

"Great, I will count on it and feed this to the new RVP. He is the GM from the mega hotel downtown Chicago. A nice, experienced man. He will be at the Alabama property to look around for the big picture.

We should coordinate your trips to meet there. His name is Harry Parker!"

Traveling to Mobile via Atlanta requires navigating this vast airport with an underground rail shuttle and up the mile-long walks to the gate.

L.A. is the abbreviation of Lower Alabama. It gives one a false anticipation of LA, California.

It is redneck countryside; pickup trucks with the gun in the gun rack, trash on the truck's bed, twelve-packs of beer and empty bottles everywhere, and the smell of the yeast makes you vomit.

The drive took about one hour; arriving at the guarded entrance gate and after asking the name and purpose of the visit, one was granted entry to the parking lot. Vans and minibuses dominated the scene.

The Check-in was met with cautio and Southern charm, *y'all* rolling over the tongue with every sentence.

I was escorted to the room by the bellman, an older man of brown color or a mixed blood. In Brazil, he would be called a Creole.

It was evening yet too early for dinner. Proper attire was expected from a hostess stand sign and a display menu. A glance gave me an idea of the menu choice. I see Steak Diane, Shrimp de Jong, and relics from the 60's times. The time has stood still in this resort.

Then the bartender or barkeeper, Buddy, greeted me with Southern respect, calling me "Sir" at every opportunity in his greeting.

"My specialty is Mint Julep, got to have it, Sir! Good bourbon and molasses with the fresh mint made this special. He must have ownership of a particular recipe.

He left to the bar inside, then stepped outside into the landscape to pick fresh mint.

"Do I have the right to reproduce it at home?"

"Yes, sir, you may do so with my permission. I developed the ingredients on my own because the bartender's guide showed them differently, and there was something else in it. I will not tell you."

I tasted it, then told him I had already found the secret. "Oh, yes? Let me hear it."

Will you confirm it if I am right?

"Yes, sir, I will do so."

Angostura bitters!

"Bingo, you have a sensitive tongue. What is your profession?"

I gave him a ten-dollar tip. This is for your honesty, Buddy.

"Was not necessary, but nice to get it. Will buy my Missus something she likes, and then with a little luck, I get the favor returned." He was laughing loud. "You know what I am talking about." I nodded my head.

"Now tell me, what brings you here? I know everybody that comes here for the last thirty years, remember the names, and call them respectfully by their last name and then Sir.

Everybody knows Buddy."

I am here for a mission from this company. Sad-faced, he acknowledged to know of the pending sale. "Supposed they will change it all around, and an old horse like Buddy would be retired.

Do not know what I do being around the old lady at home driving her crazy."

I assured him that the company had a reputation for recognizing valuable employees and wanted to keep them on.

If they so desire, so do not prejudge it.

"Is that right? Suppose you are already making notes or carry a recording machine, those little ones that fit in the breast pocket?"

Not so fast. See, the pocket is empty.

"You know, from talking to you, I see you're an honest man, and I like you already."

I finished the drink; he offered a refill. "Still have the mint in there."

Thank you, Buddy. I am a wine drinker. That hard stuff hits me in the head quickly.

"Well, have a good dinner, Sir."

The dining room, capable of holding two hundred plus dinner guests, was half full. I was seated at one of the very few deuce tables, and by sitting alone, I was the object of intense scrutiny.

Finally, the man sitting with his large family of three generations asked me, "May I ask you a question, Sir? Sitting here all by yourself, you are not here on vacation, are you?"

No, I am not, was my reply, and I was not going to volunteer anymore.

"Are you from this company buying this property to ruin it?"

Now being put on the spot, I had to reply.

I would not characterize this company as a destructive force. On the contrary, it will do this place good. The architects have a neck to preserve the character of a business, enhance and embellish its physical attributes and improve the product.

"This fancy talking does not get you off the hook from delivering a stern message to the owner. We as customers since the 1930s and are not pleased if we see massive changes and will leave, and so are the families that come here time and time again."

I shall do so as your messenger, and with pleasure, I am sure he will want to hear this.

"Very well, Sir, what is your name? Y'all have an accent. Where is this from?"

Germany!

"I served the army and was stationed in this wonderful city Heidelberg, even brought back a present to my parents. This woman here is my wife; she was German, or still is. She is a US citizen but has this temperamental German blood rolling in her veins. Boy, can she cook. It must be in the bloodline. Do you know how to cook?"

Yes, sir, I have been an executive Chef worldwide for years.

"Now, how do you do that?" I have had jobs in other countries.

"Now, that is very impressive. Don't think so, Gertrud? Lovely to meet you. Do not let us spoil your dinner. Go and eat; your food is getting cold from all this yakking."

Dinner was good and wholesome, with the old-fashioned presentation. The service by the young server turned out very professional with formal distance as these folks here like still playing the master; speak only when you are asked or told! It was difficult for me to get her to open up and relax.

When she learned about my heritage from the talk, she started to talk like an ordinary relaxed girl, all too willing to speak about this management. I must be cautious; the management is structured with family members, and as an outsider, I am vulnerable. Can we talk after I finish my shift? We can meet by the parking area to have privacy.

I finished my meal and was offered a dessert, Pecan pie with a lacing of Bourbon.

She came out and took a deep breath; relieved to be alone, we started to walk.

I had waited for her near the parking area until her duty ended.

She described the working condition and all the discrepancies she had found.

"It is high time we get structured management here, it's all nepotism. If you are not related, there is no chance to get out of the gutter. Tips are built into the American plan and paid out after the owner has skimmed the bulk off the top. The pay is below minimum wage."

"My name is Bekki, but it is my middle name. I have a first name, but here I am, Bekki. Avoiding duplication. You know, family!"

She took my hand and made it look like we were close friends.

"It makes them think we are family. "Very smart of you and I do not mind holding hands with a pretty girl.

She squeezed my hand, signaling equal enjoyment. "Then she picked up from before; this was a family mafia. Jobs are not plentiful here in the sticks, so one is forced to accept whatever is offered."

"The law is the local sheriff, an elected man, and all are kept in the family. No place to turn to, and even if there was, it goes all the way up the legal system.

Take it and shut up. I was hoping for a long time to meet an outsider to get all this off my chest, you understand. I can trust you, can I?"

Of course, you can. The only people that hear about this are the ones that will decide the course of the purchase.

Our Human Resources department wants to hear this also. Fair pay, regular performance reviews with automatic pay raises based on performance. Nepotism is banned. I presume that this will come to a quick end.

"That is so encouraging. Do I have to fear for my job?"

No. On the contrary, the information I am getting from you I would never know until long into the absorption of all employees, only to find out piece by piece what all is rotten in Denmark.

"Denmark?"

Figure of speech, meaning here!

"I will personally speak to the human resource department."

Human?

"Personal!"

"Okay, I understand what you are saying."

Yes, they will get your name from me and hold it in strict confidence. For that reason, I cannot include it in my report, for this one gets to so many people.

"You must be an important person!"

Still holding on to me, she was now squeezing hard.

"Forgive me. Am I hurting you?"

Not at all. I am not getting my hand squeezed unless a strong handshake does it. Your squeezing is different. It is with good feelings.

"I think so too."

She carried on with details about how the pay was handed out. "Sometimes in cash, no check, no deductions, they claimed, but the total showed the deduction taken off the top.

Health insurance is nothing; you must co-pay 80 percent of it. It is only to show on paper that they offer insurance to attract outside help. Family does not cover the low-paying positions, and all family is coded as management under a different benefits plan. I have seen a paycheck once."

"I take accounting in college and can read the numbers well. They do everything to avoid paying taxes, and oh, the suppliers have to kick back from the invoices to the family. Figure that this way, they inflate the cost, show no profit or a loss, but the money ends up in the private bank account, again a cousin, you got it, kissing cousins."

"So much inbreeding I am surprised there are not more dummies."

There must be, I commented.

"Rumor has it that outside the family are these kids that die of created circumstances and never make it past two years of age.

You have to be careful; they are friendly to the face, but the dagger in hand, ready to stab you in the back."

I think I will not have to deal with since my territory is realigned. I will be in Florida and all that is south of it. I will lose Barbados.

"Barbados? You have been there."

Yes, and figuratively speaking, I have a daughter there.

"How so?"

I told her the story to divert from the horror of this place.

We must have walked two miles by now in the moonlit warm Southern breeze. She listened intensely like a child getting a bedtime story for the first time, looked at me with her warm brown eyes, and forever squeezed my hands. she would not let go of it and had tears in her eyes.

At that moment, the hand released mine to find the other hand to lock around my neck, and a long kiss sealed what became a long friendship for years to come.

"Can you get me a transfer to one of your hotels?"

I can see, but I want it to be the right hotel with the proper management. Not all hotels are created equal. Leadership sets the tone.

I will give you my card. This will change because I have to move to a new location and do not know where the office is. Call me at the work number there. The secretary will give you my unique number. I will provide her with the instruction. She must do so for every call until the new number is known.

"It has been a long time since I met a nice person like you." She turned toward me and said, "I love you," and planted a hot kiss on my lips.

Returning, she hopped into her car and drove off in the moonlight without the headlights on. Confirmation that she had to be careful, for termination is the easiest but usually not the preferred choice by management to punish an employee.

The South is certainly a different cup of tea! I was glad that a good old boy was getting the region. It would be another hard lesson for me.

I met my designated new boss, Harry, that morning while eating breakfast. We had a short interview if one could call it that.

His wife with him being elated to make the transfer from the Windy City riddled with gangs and murders and finally settle to where they always wanted to retire. He was a golfer, and so was she, but not on his level. He had stronger hands and much bigger ones. His nickname was Paws, have a look!

Smiles and a timetable of approximate timing to have the office open were discussed.! "I have the office address, and it is now getting set up. I estimate it to be ready in two weeks.."

What is your timing? I told him I had a family issue ending with a separation agreement as the wife flatly refused to move. She had never done this, but other circumstances were involved. No more for now.

"Okay, let me know once you have a moving date to set you up for temp housing at the hotel in Fort Lauderdale."

The introduction turned out as promised by the boss; it was all coming together now.

On the way back, I still felt the warmth of Becki's hand. I could not get her out of my mind. She was a beautiful girl inside, good-looking, and easy on the eyes outside, but I felt bad for the treatment she had to endure.

I knew too well that this was all illegal stuff. Then the kiss, two times: "Sins of omission!"

The indebt report made waves all across the departments and set a change of directions in motion. The folks in finance got hold of it, then called me to ensure the accuracy and source of information. No doubt this would come into the negotiating phase, squeeze the price, or move the seller from a holdout position on sensitive issues. The tax info could be checked and compared to like resorts, then thrown on the table as a chess move, if not checkmate.

"You never come empty-handed," Charles said. "I do not know how you do it repeatedly."

* * * * * * *

The change in the region also prompted a move to Florida. Presenting this proposal to the family and the next action, I was confident that Margo would accept it. Our son has since enlisted and will be in the navy.

The wife had a week to think about her decision.

And a final choice must be made. We must move, sell the house, and buy a smaller home and a house with a pool.

She responded, "NO; I will not move again and not to Florida."

I am committed and motivated to settle in Florida. If you refuse, we have no other alternative but to agree to a separation. Then we will have a split, a breakup of the marriage. It supplies time to think it over and decide at a later time to get back in Florida or file for a divorce.

We divide the assets down the middle and negotiate an agreement ourselves. I do not want to engage an attorney. They only create more problems before any are resolved. All this only helps them by increasing the fees.

My wife agreed to this method, and we managed to keep the emotions in control to have an orderly discussion.

We settled on her keeping the house for safety and comfort, no sale, and Martin had a home to come to when on leave or ending his Navy tour of duty.

Ten days later, with patience and frayed nerves, we had it written out, ready for a legal professional to write a formal separation agreement.

While she received the real estate and the lion's share, it gave me a start in Florida. I have a job and opportunities to recover. Her having a roof over her head and a home for Martin meant more to me than a fair split. I could not throw her out on the street; a breakup was hard enough on her and me despite the motive.

The thought entered my mind once more and spawned great suspicion for her reason, but no straight answer confirmed that there was something once more! With Martin in the navy, she had all the time in the world, and since the separation agreement called for alimony payment plus child support, it supplied a comfortable lifestyle.

I volunteered to pay while Martin was in the navy. A nest egg will be beneficial when he returns to civilian life.

Sailors don't make money; they need a care package for a fresh start and go to college.

It was the mother's duty to set up a safe harbor account and accumulate the money.

* * * * * * *

Leaving home is challenging and an emotional moment. I felt uprooted and uncertain, not knowing where I would be living. The change in personnel had its effects on my mood.

The Fort Lauderdale hotel had a room reserved for two weeks. I hope to secure a condo by then.

"Well, if longer, let us know. For the hotel, it is a sale. The Company is paying the full rate for relocation."

I took a ride out to the office address about ten miles inland. Alligator alley to a new town. The office was still locked but seemed ready to move in.

Staying at this hotel gave me time to look at the lounge situation.

Running into Mark, the new F&B director, enthusiastically reported the solution to the parking situation. "The nearby attraction offered the best rate. We are set for now. Nothing was changed since the last meeting. Sales were still robust, and this town was the place to have fun. "

Good to hear. I will be living in the hotel temporarily and checking out the clientele. The bad apples need to be weeded out and replaced. A delicate process, you understand.

A realtor found a suitable condominium for me, and my credit rating helped settle the sales within a two-week time limit.

It is a new beginning.

Being single had given me hope of finding a girlfriend for a stable relationship. I had become the prey and the hunted. It was not a satisfying reward. Sex is essential to support a healthy prostate, all good and pleasing; a relationship with a caring person has much more to offer.

At the lounge, I saw a different crowd now. Bully-type guys had made themselves known and tried to dominate the scene. Girls sometimes felt uneasy as they approached them for sex and in a very straightforward way.

Something must be done quickly. Didn't these managers see this?

I spent the night at the bar keeping tabs on control; all seemed clean unless there was a new trick. For now, the female bartender who took over at 7:00 p.m. knew me and started talking.

"See what I see?" she had asked and pointed to the rough boys making their way to the bar.

Yes, I had seen it and will have to fix it.

Do you ever see Marco in here?

"Very seldom. He is a morning person, married, and on a short leash!"

Okay, I suppose the GM is out of the question too?

"Never do I see him; I was told he is a room's person and leaves this area to the F&B man. I saw the owner with his partner having drinks and left. He is busy with the new beach project."

"Yes, I am familiar; I must go to have a look."

"Not much to see yet. Construction is still putting the floors on top of another."

What is selling now?

"Mostly the low-end domestic beer."

That fits this crowd; I am not surprised. We seemed to have lost the upper end. Is there a new place that is attracting these people?

"No, none that I can point to."

What would you do if this were your own?

"A doorman, a bouncer to control who is allowed, keeps the numbers in check and enables the staff to give service.

A security man in the lounge mingling with customers to hear and see the action should a bully guy have slipped past the doorman, then be on him at once."

This girl had all the correct answers; if only management would perform the people program and talk to them.

You are lovely, Tracy. You just solved the problem.

A new promotion has to come in now. The classy girls must be lured back, and an image advertising must be enacted.

I made notes for the following day's meeting to be at the lounge with Continental breakfast waiting.

These new hotel managers must come with me to the owner's briefing. The warning signs had to be revealed, and a dip in the revenue must be expected while we flush out the bullies. A copy must be printed for the owner's briefing.

But what about a promotion?

I will also push for a change in bar manager, rename the title, and rewrite the job description. Better management and visibility on the floor will have an impact. Be at the front line; there is too much money at stake."

Dinner at the Polynesian restaurant gives me time to rehash my thoughts and check on food and service.

The restaurant had good food but competed with the Mai Tai, which features a massive Polynesian show.

Back at the lounge, I spent time seeing and listening to the band. Suzanne the singer of the band was still doing her magic, flashing her body and sexy moves to the public, but few made it to the dance floor. It was certainly not the music; it was the customer.

I let my impressions mature and looked beyond the surface, which looked fine. Yet the need for more vital management was the ultimate solution. Manage on your feet, not from the reports, hearsay, and the office chair.

A good kick up the butt now will do good!. It would be delivered tomorrow morning on an empty stomach.

Thanks to Tracy, I had my action plan ready, and if I did not have any promotion ideas. Can they rake their brain for a change and produce something clever?

The strategy was to lead them to the idea, leading them to ideas and then make it their own. It would then be guaranteed to succeed. They will not fail their own ideas. I had the missing pieces for my plan and was ready for the meeting.

Half-awake at 7:00 a.m., they dragged themselves to the lounge for this meeting. It must be difficult for Nine-to-fivers, arrive alert, and become productive! I thought the subject and my plan would make it much more dramatic.

The defense was building at once when I told them all the information I had learned from the bartender. The observation from this base employee received an even stronger negative body language.

The GM opened up with a statement directed to his position's authority.

"Why do you listen to a bartender? They are not managing this place. We are in charge."

I countered that a bartender is in the room and sees this action every night, and as a long-term employee, there was a basis for comparison. You cannot see this yourself unless you spend time in the room.

Are you spending time in the lounge to see for yourself?

I did not get a reply; I thought so. You cannot see the action unless quality time is spent to make these observations.

Their livelihood depends on a good volume and healthy clientele! Do you think the employees are stupid? Think again. They are your eyes and ears. You better listen to them, all of them.

Long faces and now the solution to solve this issue.

First, we need to weed out the bad apples by putting a doorman to control and select the desired people. He must understand the profile and have people knowledge of our preferred customer. Think of someone in-house that has seen the good times, a part-time job until eleven p.m.

Then a young security guy with muscles in the right places to mingle with the customers. He has to look like a customer. The employee will point to when a rowdy troublemaker is getting out of line. He may have looked too deep into the glass and began to harass the girls.

Then he will pick a fight with a guy. At this time, the security man will spring into action and begins to remove him discreetly.

At one point, the security office will take over and call his home. Pick him up; he cannot drive.

Smiles appeared on the manager's faces; they were ready to leave. Hold, not so fast; we are not finished.

"What more?"

Just sit and listen. We need to rebuild the business and attract our old clientele back.

"Right. Well, yes, what do you propose?"

A marketing campaign. Yes, the marketing guy has to loosen his purse-string now; later, he will do more to prop up the revenues, and you can forget the bonus!

That hit home like a snap off the bat.

But he must have a message, namely, a new program, a change in enticement. I think the diamond has had its run and needs a break. Later, it can be part of the choice.

"Anything you have in mind?"

My treasure chest is empty, so I look to you for ideas.

Long faces again, blank looks, nothing, just silence.

Have a look around and think of high value at an affordable cost. It may be right at your doorstep or across the road!"

The GM opened up. "You mean a cruise? That would fit the ticket. In that line, everyone wants to go on a vacation once a year.

Rooms at a resort or right here or to an event, the Formula One race in Miami, NASCAR in Daytona. We have hotels everywhere. You can get employee rates It's not at a big expense.

He listed now methodically and started to show enthusiasm.

"You have fantastic ideas. The band can do it as a lottery drawing. Marketing has a message to go on the radio and spread the word. This method of advertising had worked at the beginning. Let's go with it."

Can you summarize the action steps for the meeting with the owner? We will come to him with the solutions to the problems.

I am sure he is aware of them. Do it as a draught with low-budget stuff, a gift card, a bottle of champagne, and then a big-value ticket.

We can talk to the cruise line for trade with our rooms for open cabin space.

Now bright smiles from the GM Omar and a forced smile from Marco.

To soften the revenue dip, I have a strategy for you, Marco."

He was all ears, not knowing what came next, and it had just popped up.

I told him the price tier during entertainment hour could be spread. "Keep the low level but tell the servers to pour call brands for generic drink orders at the call brand rate. A customer would have to request a house brand at the lowest price. There are those that know and don't care, but very few.

Upselling to the next tier will bring added revenue. Business travelers will not know and be grateful for better quality. Salesmanship needs to be sharpened, and you have your mandate there. "What can I get you from the bar?' and not the routine 'Can I get you a drink?' Get specific!

"Last but not least, the bar manager's job description and the lounge manager title must be revised.

His job is in this lounge and not in his office.

"Are you always that well prepared?"

I opened my eyes and listened, and all the answers were in front of your nose, Mark.

'Inspect what you expect,' a famous proverb from our fearless leader in food and beverage, Mr. Charles Brown."

* * * * * * *

My apartment is settled, and I have a pause with opening new hotels until Miami on Biscayne Bay comes on the horizon.

I took part in college recruitment at FIU. Graduating students signed up for the interview. Rooms with privacy had been filled quickly and left me with the outside as the choice.

I asked the candidate *from New York State* if he would mind if we went outside into the fresh air.

I stood him in a position where I did not have to look into the sun but unfortunately, the sun was now facing him.

He was in a white dress shirt and jacket, expecting quick questions.

My style departed from the routine questions they had prepared to answer.

I tell you a story; what else does a storyteller do? Here is a scenario.

Picture yourself in an outdoor café on a nice summer day. You are the server. A man sits down in your station. You ask him what you can get him.

"I want a pot of coffee, not just a cup."

You go inside and prepare for a delivery of a cake to another table, and now you are passing this person with the pending coffee order.

He called you and asked, "can I have a cake instead."

Gladly Sir, and you get the cake and serve it.

You follow so far? "Yes, I do!"

He looked confused, not knowing what the point of this was.

Now the man who was ordering coffee first is asking for the check. You present the bill for the cake.

Are with me, yes? Then okay.

He calls you back, telling you there is a mistake with the check.

"Your reply, this is what you had asked me!

No, that is incorrect. I had asked you for coffee but did not receive coffee. I received cake instead.

Are you confused?' 'Yes"

Well, he said, since I ordered coffee, never consumed coffee, and got the cake instead, I am not paying this bill!

What do you do in this situation?

Profoundly confused, the kid did not think logically or segregate the dialogue and produced the oddest answers.

I did this to all the applicants. They were shaking their heads and gave up.

The customer walks out without paying. This is an actual occurrence, and there is an answer to it!

If the server had stated the price of the coffee since he ordered without a menu/price list and again when he accepted the change order for the cake and stating the upcharge for the cake, the customer would have known the cost and be obligated to pay.

In this scenario the customer has the legal right to refuse to pay! It is that simple.

For this reason, all sales outlets must have price lists.

* * * * * * *

Going back to the lounge at the hotel, I saw that all action steps had been executed. The promotions had the room buzzing once more. "Thank you, sir. We love it here!"

A cocktail server delivered my wine and casually brushed up on me. It did not look conspicuous. She and I noticed it and confirmed it with a passing smile.

The bartender had passed the information she had a hand in and was proud of. The same inconspicuous brush-up was noticeable every time she passed.

The lounge was packed, with limited space to pass; it was all innocent. Then as the night reached midnight, she whispered in my ear, "I want you. Come to my house. I will drive. Just follow me. Mine is a red top-down car. Just flash your light once you are in reach, then you can follow. It is not far."

At once, I thought, *Is she a hooker and does this with other guests?* The only way to find out was to go with her! She does know me and my position.

Her apartment complex only a few blocks from the hotel.

She kept the apartment neat and clean and tastefully decorated, just an efficiency with a bed!

"It is only me living here' I had enough from roommates, better to be on my own and nobody to interfere with my life."

She offered me a glass of chardonnay, Kendall Jackson. "I got hooked on this when we learned about wine selling, and you let us taste it too. Us girls make a ton of money and thank you for all you have done once again. We are in love with you."

We got undressed and had a fun night on a waterbed.

Wow! she got out of heavy breathing, *which is a first for me. I must stick to the experienced men and avoid the wham-bam, thank you, madam boys.*

* * * * * * *

By a special invitation, I attended an exclusive wine tasting. It was an evening to present the premier wineries and champagne houses with various red wine vintages. Wine store owners, beverage distributors from multiple Florida markets, and wine buyers from high-end restaurants were present for this introduction.

I was elated when I received the invitation. I am not a buyer. The answer came when they had noticed that a specific price grouping of wine sales had been traced to me.

To my surprise, I was introduced and asked to stand up to be recognized. They were running short on products. The success in sales had generated this dilemma. Selling it in an upscale establishment as wine by the glass had shown movement in large volume.

As a result, the winery will resort to re-allocate distributing the supply to the premium wine by the glass sales locations. None of these wines will be on a supermarket shelf, never, ever.

Applause and a humble bow by me, I sat and started to sip the first wine.

* * * * * * *

Tampa was due for a follow-up visit and on my way back, driving my new sports car, I planned a quick visit to the resort near Naples.

I had just bought a Mazda RX& by trading my ageing VW

Fire engine red with the rotary engine, the car had great reviews and the "looks to kill.

Besides, my life needed uplift from all-work-and-no-play life.

The lounge in Tampa, I was told, was doing great, with the right profile and female-male mix, the thirtysomething and younger generation.

367

Servers were carefully selected, and the bar staff, primarily females and bar back boys were doing the heavy lifting.

"The restaurant is my biggest concern," Brian was telling me. The typical hotel restaurant syndrome. "The food is excellent, well prepared, consistent. Yes, this young Chef is great. I love him; he follows through on all decisions we make jointly; he is just a great guy. It gives me time to keep an eye on this beverage sales source of income.

"Late surprise checks on pars, register banks, and reading have not yet surfaced any funny business. They make so much money the legal way. Why risk the best job in town?"

You are so right. When the sales are not there, they look for profit sharing."

Brian was fun.

"Banquets are progressing nicely. The usual bouts about space protections get solved with the GM and me playing referee."

I am glad to hear she is involved in operations. As a former bean counter, her comfort zone is in the office. "She is excellent."

Now for the restaurant, I have an idea!

"I knew it. You always produce crazy stuff. I am sorry, I meant creative stuff!"

That's better. Here comes the long story. I know the procedure. You can take a horse to water but cannot make him drink. "Show me the water. I am thirsty!"

Breakfast is busy with business travelers, and occupancy runs in the high eighty. The business traveler eat their breakfast at the hotel for convenience.

It will be our target.

With this, I described what I had done before and earned great success.

We start with coffee. Find a local coffee roaster.

"I know just the right one."

This coffee becomes the exclusive product for the restaurant, room service. Get three small coffee brewers and produce coffee in small quantities, just enough to keep pace with the volume. Then get a small burner, raw coffee beans, and roast coffee by the hostess stand to bring the aroma into the lobby.

The aroma infiltrating the lobby will be a pleasant aroma, may even bring more guests in that otherwise grab Danish and coffee to go.

The lure is this coffee as the exclusive for the restaurant.

A menu revision bringing lighter foods for the female guest, the yogurts, cottage cheese, berries, Crepes, fruits, exotic selections, make it colorful and fresh looking. I have a sample menu with me.

Okay, the office will bug you until you give in and let them have the coffee, and that is okay for peace's sake.

We briefed the GM on the plan and made Brian the presenter this idea! "I like it?"

"It is a wonderful plan and should work."

"Didn't you not do this in a hotel up north?" I said, New Jersey!

"No, not that one, not a company hotel."

Hartford! That was my pilot program.

I know it, I was at the Travelers' Hotel as controller, still young and green behind the ears, but I got tipped off by the chamber of commerce.

"My all-time favorite person to plan banquet events.

"I remember the balloon deal in the arena, creative."

I said it was a collaborative effort.

"Born in your head!"

You know too much about me!

"You have a knotty side too!"

Smiles. Brian interjected, "Keeps life interesting!"

****

We rode to the airport hotel for the rest of the afternoon Only accessible from the terminal elevator.

A woman about twenty-eight years is running two outlets and the bar as the manager.

She gladly showed us around.

"You are going to buy this!"

No, not us two. The company is in negotiations to buy.

I don't like this term *buy,* meaning a clean sweep and all-new management. That may have been the case ten years ago. The need for proven talents is now to the point when experienced managers are integrated. New operating procedures and service changes are always going to be introduced.

"Will you be involved?" she asked me.

Yes, that falls into my domain.

"He is great to work with." Brian added, "Easy if you follow through, but watch out if you go against him. See New York!"

I will never live that down!

"How can you? It was bigger than Nagasaki!"

She looked perplexed, but Brian assured her it was the best thing for this hotel since sliced bread. It had to do with a union!

"No union in this hotel," she remarked.

"I want you to come over for breakfast in about two weeks. Am going to do something terrific. You will receive help for it, and since we will be sister-and-brother hotels," saying it with a smirk, "you get a head start. Working together and being in the same marketplace can only help to increase our share."

We had made the introduction and received a warm welcome. The ice is broken and will be a foundation for the handover.

Off to the room to make notes on the airport hotel while Isit in my underwear, I suddenly heard a knock on the door. What is it, problems?

I quickly slipping back into my pants and opened the door.

"Please let me in. I'll tell you!"

Pulling her in to avoid any commotion in the doorway, she said, "I need you. Really, I need you," making motions for sex!

You are taking a risk?

"Not really. I sometimes inspect rooms before arrival to ensure all is okay."

In no time, she had me butt naked and herself following. There was no way to deny her wish; she needed it right now.

Time passed fast, and she left with a smile on her face.

A kiss and hug, and out she was on her way home.

Are you wondering who that was?

* * * * * * *

The drive to the resort took longer than I expected. An interstate was being built within the next few years, actually already started but far from completion. Arriving midday left me just the remaining day, evening, and a short morning meeting if needed.

A classic resort property with huge banquet space, still doing MAP plans in the dining room with breakfast and dinner included in the room's package.

Large insurance groups held awards dinners and preceding pep talks to the agencies, while the wives were entertained with shopping trips to Naples, golf, tennis lessons, or beach time.

The beach restaurant could easily fit on a Caribbean island. Always full of hungry customers seeking a snack and a tropical drink.

This F&B from Europe had his act together, proper schooling, and was brilliant. A pleasure to see it function. The tour revealed nothing I would change myself; the kitchen showed good organization.

The one area I took a hard look at was the storeroom. Inventory levels were high; is there a reason?

"Yes, we must get the shipment from Miami once a week. No supplemental deliveries except the stone crabs. If we run out, we are out of luck, and must do without it."

Thank you for your time. Stay out of trouble!

I went to the coffee shop for breakfast the following day but decided against it. The door had a waiting line, and the volume was overwhelming inside.

Everybody had shown up at the same time. I had flashbacks of San Diego, and it gave me goosebumps. I needed to think about this!

Observing the traffic flow of servers, I could see that everybody did their best.

A female manager took great care of the guests and communicated as best she could with the servers and bussers to free up tables. It was not a staffing or training issue it was simply too small a room and too many hungry guest for too little space.

When I met with Chris, he was apologizing. He told me he had a plan, but the room's guy was blocking it.

A large Continental buffet in the lobby as a self-service at a fixed price will require minimal staffing and can be set up and removed with little interruptions. We don't do the hotel or guest a favor by ignoring this issue.

It almost looked to me that the room's manager was dwelling on the food department's demise, thinking it made him look that much better. The problem was that he had the GM's ear!

I committed to him to take this up with the Regional Vice President. We share the same boss. He will be hearing back from him.

On the way back, I took the road to stop in Miami at the Airport hotel to look for any progress. I knew catering was doing well since I had met Angie. As the catering director's sister, she was well informed.

I owed that girl a dinner date.

The executive office was empty except for Angie. A perfect time to propose the dinner. Can I call you at home to set the time and date?

"Sure." She handed me her phone number!

I have a mission now. Tell you later. Any progress in food and beverage?

"Nothing. The foodie is openly defiant in your back, upfront the nice face and answers for everything, just not the right ones. I overheard you talking the last time. Virtually he wants to prove you wrong."

I like nothing better than that. I am always game to learn something new.

I bought a new car, considered buying a better house, and looked at townhouses. "Call me tonight, please. I want to know!"

Chapter 23

That evening, I called Angela and told her I must visit seafood restaurants and would like to have her with me.

The plan was to hit two or three fish restaurants and sample the food. It will be a research project, offering her free food and eating out on company expenses.

She yelled into the phone, "yes, how wonderful," and wanted to hug and kiss me if I was with her right then.

I'll give you the date and time for this. The other thing was tasting the finest champagne of France. "Moet Chandon?" No one stepped up, and we would get every types to taste as the invitation was hinting.

"Goody, wow, this is getting better by the minute."

With it comes selected food, which you may have never tasted. I should wait to tell you all this to capitalize on all the hugs and kisses!

One more, and with this, you have to choose yes or no. It is a cognac tasting with vintages, quality grades from VS to XO, and even one more notch, Louis 13th. With food, of course. "If I do not have to drink the entire tasting part, I will be okay. Just do not count on me to be the designated driver."

Tomorrow, the first fish places.

Yes, meet me here at my new place. Here are the address and directions.

* * * * * * *

Any calls?

"Yes, a man from Miami wants to show you bread. French bread," she knew I wanted specific messages to save time with a return call.

There were about thirty seafood restaurants to Pick from.

I had no idea where to begin. The choice fell on the alphabet first, working the way up and keeping them in the same town to save travel time.

Angela arrived in a light summer dress, full of colorful flowers, lovely and airy; a strong wind would make it fly above the panty line.

She had to check out the car first, then inspect the apartment. Not bad for the price, got a pool and a clubhouse for parties, similar to mine.

Off to the task. "Now, tell me why you are doing this?"

The new hotel under construction will have a specialty restaurant, a high-class seafood restaurant. The owner said it would have to be innovative. Right now, this city does not have anything he would find acceptable.

I have to report to him in time, and he has become my second boss on two properties."

The food was bland, very much the run-of-the-mill, and so was the second one; then I stopped, It was enough mediocracy for one night. A single girl living with a roommate, and neither one cooked, I could imagine this to be a treat. She ate indiscriminately and must have been hungry.

Somehow, I had a good feeling about her, to have as a friend, with benefits on both ends. In time, her taste would be more discriminatory. Hopefully, this will change. Let the good life begin.

At the apartment, romance entered the air. She wanted to kiss, had too much wine, and felt romantic. "This will be our second time," she announced. "Can we take the time to warm up? I wish to reach a climax. It has been a long time." She stopped and kissed me again. Then the slow disrobing and the lovemaking begun.

"Can I stay with you tonight?" The aftermath of lovemaking is as pleasurable as the act itself. She cuddled up close to me, staying naked; she fell asleep with soft breathing until the morning. Today was Saturday, no work, no duty. "Do you have to go in?"

No, just write down my notes and lay out a format so we can judge these places on the same criteria.

"You said we."

Yes, I meant we are doing this together. I will see so many restaurants I would never get to see on my own. Want to go to the beach? If we get a parking space near that Sheraton Hotel, we can walk the beach to our new hotel we are now working for."

"Working, you call this?"

Yes.

"Then what is my pay?" she said kiddingly!

Free food, all the ice cream you can eat, and all the loving you can handle. Is that good?

"More than I expected."

That night, I stopped at a fish store to pick up fresh fish and stone crabs. I was not clear what was available. Grouper fillet was my choice, plus four large stone crabs. She knew both by name but never tasted any.

I prepared both with flair, not going crazy, but different with a sauce for the grouper and a cold dip for the stone crabs.

She ate with such a hunger I should have bought more. "I had never tasted such a good meal," she proclaimed! Now you have a direction of what I am searching for.

The high-protein meal had a profound effect on her appetite for sex. Time is on our side to use as needed. I prepared her like I had done a couple of times before. Caressing with the hands at first, probing all sensitive areas with a soft breath, a little air blow to the wet spots by now, the tongue doing its teasing. The effects rewarded her with a highlight and a big smile.

By midweek, we visited more fish restaurants. The same boring menu and bland fish, broiled with paprika sprinkled on top and the so-called lemon butter, meaning melted butter with lemon wedges.

The very least they could do is heat the butter to brown it; at least it is better tasting.

Tired of this type, we first looked at the posted menu outside and decided if we would go or pass on to the next.

On the weekend, we found a Bahamian food stand with conch chowder. A sizable island woman served the chowder. Let us check it out."

It's like the one of Priscilla's.

"Who is Priscilla?"

She is my daughter in Barbados, I said with a wicked smile!

"You are teasing me. You are pulling my leg;"

I told her the short story, promising the extended version another time.

We have work to do! We choose this one for the menu. I already have the recipe.

Another dive bar smelled of beer yeast. However, everybody was eating oysters. Oyster orders are shucked in the open at the end of the bar.

Ever had oysters?

"No, I don't even know what they are."

Here right here, you, see?

"These ugly things, they are not even cooked."

That is the way to eat them. I suppose you'll pass.

"Yes," with the nose pulled up.

Have a glass of wine. Make it two. Got something decent?

"Yes, Mondavi Chardonnay."

Good.

While Angela went to the restroom, I asked the bartender, Who sells these oysters?

"Apalachicola. You know?"

Oh yes. Mobile Bay, right?

"This Atlantic Fishery sells them, always fresh, not the cheapest, but no waste, clean, and reliably fresh, got to come closed." I told him I was in the business like him, just a little larger.

"What is the name?" When he heard the company's name, he at once connected to the Intercostals property lounge name.

"Some business you have there!"

I know. I am the watchdog to keep it that way. "Is she is your wife?"

"Occasionally!"

He got it and laughed. "Benefits, yes, my kind of too."

Just then, Angela returned, "Talking about me. "Would not do that. Just a boy's joke, not fit for tender ears.

As a bartender, you know this town. Who or which restaurant has the best seafood?

"Right down this street, go to the Intercostals. There is the best, strange name, called Fresh Fishery."

Need a reservation?

"Yes, advisable for a nice table. Otherwise, get to wash the dishes."

"What do you mean by this?" she asked him.

"You know, the table by the kitchen entrance."

I smiled. I have been there, done this! "Just wait till the early birders are done. Cannot get in and smaller portions."

"He gives a deal but got to be there at five, cause by five-thirty he closes the door for this deal."

A notation to my memory as I put my finger to my temple!

"Why did you do this?" She wanted to know.

This way, I remember it better. Who knows what else we get into tonight? The night is young.

Another kick on the shin bone!

She would change her mind after another glass of wine and a half dozen. "Thanks, a mill for the tip. We will look him up soon.

Oysters are an aphrodisiac; I am told to test it tonight.

It proved to help, and it put lead in the pencil again. The night was filled with heavenly sounds, a time I refer to as being at church since she called on God.

* * * * * * *

I announced another visit to Miami as an official inspection. I had briefed the boss in advance. The F&B director had been given the time to react. If he had not done at least half of it, we had to make a change and replace him.

The market was competitive, and the rooftop restaurant received a total renovation. A steak house for a man's hotel will work.

Grilling great meat will make the aroma noticeable in hallways and stimulate the appetite.

I told Angela not to say anything, not even her sister. The GM knew it and is a logical person and a seasoned manager. His impeccable reputation preceded him. It turned out that he made a similar list and received no results either. His cup was running over by now.

He had kept my visit a secret. The element of surprise had a profound effect. It caught the F&B by surprise.

377

The inspection revealed a clean kitchen but a tired Chef. It did not look right.

I went ahead with the people program, saying hello to dishwashers, calling them by name, and inquired if the treatment was good. "Are you getting a fresh uniform? And are you paid for all the time worked?

All questions received a "Yes, sir," but when it came to paying, there was a slight hesitation.

I repeated the same dialogue with other employees, the same reaction, not a complaint, not a *no*, just the hesitation to say, yes. I touched my temple to brush back the hair; there was a rat. I could smell it.

Then the to-do list. Update me on these issues please?

"No, I cannot do it." And here came the list of excuses.

How is it that all the other hotels find it easy to implement? What would you do if I transferred you to one of these? Will you dismantle and sabotage the business?

"Well, no, but"

Let me say it this way. We have solid numbers to back up the success of all these initiatives. Your refusal to enact these programs is, in effect damaging the business.

You are standing still, meaning falling behind. You have become ineffective, making yourself obsolete. Do I make my point clear?

"I want a transfer. I cannot work with you, just way too many demanding. You foreigners, are turning this company upside down."

I will relate your request to Mr. Brown, but he must find a taker! My reference to your performance will be in my following report to him and also go to my RVP.

Do not put your hopes up too high. No matter the years you served in this company, get your pencil sharpened and update your résumé while there is still time!

The briefing with Hector was no surprise to him. "If you did not do it today, I would have done so myself"

I do not see a transfer unless he has a friend amongst the other regionals. The company is very loyal to a guy with twenty-plus years. I will put him up for grabs and minimize the stubborn behavior.

He may have something against me, too aggressive or prejudiced being a foreigner.

We have good old boys from the South. He could take over the existing hotel in the Carolinas and promote a good one to a new opening. This way, he can serve out his time to retirement.

There is, however, something I cannot put my fingers on. When I walked and talked to cooks and dishwashers, every question was returned with an affirmative 'Yes, sir.' Only when it came to paying did I notice an ever so slight hesitation. Could there be something?

Is the overtime not recorded but worked to keep the payroll in line? It is all about his bonus.

"I will put an accountant on the trail in a confidential way. I have just the guy for this job."

Good, I leave it in your hands. It always ends up with the GM anyway. He laughed.

****

Angela, my partner in crime, and I took another search for a high-quality seafood restaurant. The restaurant on the Intercoastal Waterway was recommended and indeed a fine place. The owner by the name of James, was an active on-the-floor manager. He held it together and had an excellent fish choice on his menu, something I had not found elsewhere. We ordered appetizers to graze and the same with entrées. James took notice of this unusual order. Two people and all these orders. "Who are these people?"

"Restaurant critics?"

"I thought I knew all of them, travel writers; I must find out."

While we were tasting and sharing, James approached the table.

He said, "my name is James, and I am the proprietor. You are enjoying the appetizers and still, have main plates coming. May I ask for the purpose?"

I did not want to put him in suspense. I gave him my card and said the mission we were pursuing. Sorry, it will become a competition.

"I welcome it; the level of quality seafood restaurants will increase. Competition breeds excellence, and in time we will earn a reputation for it, much like in New Orleans."

"I teach this philosophy, marketing and food and beverage at FIY. "

"I know this school from interviewing prospecting employees!

"Would you be the manager from? Forget it. I just had a thought."

Spell it out, please.

"I had a student in my class that told me about an unusual interview. The man had him face the sun outside for lack of privacy inside. Then instead of asking me the tough questions for which I studied, he started telling me this story."

My smile gave it away.

"This is you?"

"I know the whole story; It took me a minute to come to the right answer, for he would not tell me to test me. But in the end, I nailed it with the sales price laws."

"Tell me too," Angela asked!

Later. For now, we must talk business.

Would you mind revealing your source of fresh fish, or do you buy direct from the boats?

"I could have them coming here to offer the catch, but fish is finicky. It must be fresh. It must be inspected to be free of parasites. The waters are no longer clean, and the quality must be consistent. The customer will always judge you for your worst performance. With fluctuations, you cannot keep a loyal clientele".

"A great seafood restaurant must start with the best available fish and continuity of supply."

"Go and see Michael at Atlantic Fisheries the next town up. He is a fisherman, has his fleet, and does something no other is doing. He is in the phone book. I do not have his address in my head. But I let him tell you not to steal his thunder ahead."

"I have a thought. I teach two classes at FIU weekly. My business takes me to Japan to learn from them the sushi stuff. I will be gone one week and need to fill the teaching spot. So far, I have not found anyone I would trust. But you look like the perfect candidate. Judging from your interview methods, you think outside the box; that is a lecture they need right now. Would you do the honors?"

I do not have a teaching degree. I don't have any degree. Will the faculty allow this?

"I will vouch for you and assume responsibility. There will not be a problem. The school will adopt your interview method in the HR course.

Besides, a fresh approach to whatever you wish to pick will significantly interest them.

"Here is the date, two classes. The first is in an auditorium, we do not need mandatory attendance, but I expect a full room. The second class is more like a classroom, to be close to the students and encourage questions and answers dialogs."

"You choose the subjects and roll with the punches; the initial nervous stage will be gone in a minute."

Okay, James. Deal!

"Dinner is on me. You just lifted a rock off my shoulders. Thank you. Come again soon. Good night."

Now that was what I would call a fruitful evening. We have now concluded this search; I have what I need to continue with the planning.

"No more dinner at restaurants?"

Not the fish kind, but others are on my shopping list, namely, the May Kai with the show.

"Oh, I love you. You are the best that ever happened in my life."

* * * * * * *

My son announced a visit; he is driving to Florida to take in the sunrays and spring break. A navy friend is coming with him.

My new townhouse with the extra second bedroom for one guest and a couch in the den will work. I will have enough beer and a ton of food. He will expect meals cooked by his father, Navy chow, as they refer to is not cutting it with his taste of food.

He had paid cash for his car and received a well-maintained used vehicle. Good gas mileage and reliability were foremost among his criteria. The car performed to his satisfaction on this fourteen-hour drive,

The young men spent the day on the beach, watching and wishful thinking while sizing up the bikini-clad girls.

On one of the days during their visit, I was attending a cocktail party at the hotel when the PBX placed a call to the meeting room phone.

"This is for you; says he is your son. Sounds like trouble to me," Larry announced! I took the receiver and learned that there had been an accident.

Tell me how it happened and where?

"I had stopped for a red light at that intersection near the Ice cream place. A pickup truck hit me at an angle. The rear fender and bumper are damaged. No one is hurt except the car."

"He told me to follow him; his friend has a body shop and will set it straight. It does not look like a big job. My friend took down the license plate but gave no name or phone number. We followed him and realized that the car was pulling to the right. I had to go slow to make it back. He just took off and was gone."

Stand by. I will leave now, and then we take it to the next step.

I called the police to report a hit-and-run. We have a witness and need to file a report. The officer came at once, took the information, and left to visit the pickup truck driver.

Withing the hours we received the call that the man was charged with the violation and to pick up the report.

"Take this to the insurance office here in the next town. It is right next to my office."

We have the man in custody for fleeing the site of a collision. He will be standing trial for this offense.

The Insurance company has an office next to where I work. You take the car there and deal with the adjuster. If you meet difficulties, call me, and I will come over there.

Okay? Yes, but I had hoped that you would come with us to be there in case. I am, but not holding your hand. You will learn from it.

The adjuster took the report, took pictures, and looked halfway under the car with a mirror, but did not get a close look. He pulled out his chart and offered the blue book value for the vehicle. "We pay you $800.00."

Martin was shocked for it would not replace his beloved car.

He called, in tears and pleading, "please come over."

I walked over and told Martin, you ask him to drive the car; it must come from you, stern and firm like a drill sergeant.

When the adjuster drove, he turned around and took another look at his chart. "Total loss, $2800.""

He issued a check and handed it to Martin who was now all smiles.

Wait, how will you get back? Are you buying a car here in Florida?" I did not plan, but how?"

The adjuster overheard this and looked at me. You have to make it right, sir!

"I did not realize and neglected to look at the license plate. Of course, we must get them back; I will issue two airline vouchers to fly them back".

Jubilantly he proclaimed, "This is more than I paid for."

Then I took them to the beach for the remaining visiting days.

Call when you have had enough sun, and if you get lucky, bargain the lift home into the arrangement.

I called his mother and told her what had happened, the settlement, and the flight details. Can you fit this into your busy schedule to pick them up at the airport? I said with a sarcastic tone!

* * * * * * *

Martin had checked out Mom's house to see if he could learn and pick up evidence. He felt out of place. Something was not right again. He could sense it but had not found out who or what it was. He told me the information that he was able to find out about her. He confirmed that the child support had never made it to a separate bank account; she looked sick, had hollow eyes, had lost weight, and acted strangely.

I assured him that it is and will remain his home for as long as the house is in our name. I am still on the deed and have control over it.

The navy fiend quickly diagnosed her situation. She must be taking drugs and heavy narcotics and addicted to them.

The money is spent to obtain these drugs; she is in a deadly spiral unless she gets professional help.

A guy must live with her like a bloodsucker and provide her with narcotics. This way, he can keep her dependency and suck the money out of her.

"We noticed a car driving by the house, slow and looking."

"The neighbor informed us with most of the information."

"He was the slimy guy that lured her into this sex gang, but he managed to stay clean, or shall we say, he did not get caught."

The money belongs to you giving you a start after the navy.

She cannot be trusted. I need pictures of this guy going in and out at different times.

Can ask the neighbor. Will he do it?

"I am sure. He is a former navy man and will do anything for his navy friends. We are a tight fraternity!"

Give him my address. She is about to learn a harsh lesson.

"What do you have in mind?"

"For starters, the money appointed for you will go into a bank account downstairs. I bank here also. The child support, which I am still paying, will stop. She has no legal right to this since your eighteenth birthday.

These payments should help you.

All gone, I am sure it will get a little tight in the purse.

It will hurt.

Then there is the alimony. She has a legal claim for herself to support her lifestyle alone.

If necessary, I will use the pictures and statements from the neighbor to support my petition to the court to stop or reduce the amount of alimony. If successful, she will have no money coming any longer.

"What will she live off?"

Like anyone living alone, get a job, and earn your living. The guy will be taking a hike. No money, no drugs, and his comfortable nest has lost his favor.

"Harsh reality, but fair," his navy friend said to him.

She has sucked me dry now for over one year. Had she planned it intelligent and conservative, she would have a nest egg now!

I just wish I could teach this bastard a harsh lesson too.

"Me too. In a way, he stole my money."

Yes, in a roundabout way, but legally he is still in the clear unless she files extortion charges.

Look around in the house when she runs errands if we can get his name, address, and phone number if you find the address book.

He must have something, a drifter, of course, with little or no papers to himself.

He has a car; the license plate is valuable.

"Also, ask her if you can take your money Papa has given for safekeeping to add to the car purchase. No doubt the prices have gone up, and new insurance for the time you use it here.

Call me when you have something and use a pay phone, call collect!

I stopped every auto pay to her account the next day.

Now comes the homework on the alimony! It would make it all that much easier if I had dirt on this man.

The action was within my rights. She could not run to court and get an injunction. I paid it out of my goodness for the son's welfare.

Funny how life goes around. Like they say in India, karma will set it right.

Nothing came from the neighbor's effort. I must plan a stakeout when I go to the next meeting.

The license plate number is the key, and once I have a good photo, I can go to the FBI man who had promised to take the case.

I will stay over on Saturday after the meeting and hope to complete it by Monday morning. Should this plan fail, I will visit the house for a surprise visit. She will then have to confess to me and surrender the information. I can see now that nothing good will come of it. A final solution must be planned.

Leaving her penniless is not a good solution. She is the mother of our son; I must keep this in mind.

Chapter 24

I knew it if you want something done, sometimes one has to take it on himself. Such was the case; I planned it and finally got two good license plate exposure.

I went to see her and inform her of all that was now going to face her. The photos are going to our trusted FBI agent, and the money situation will be like a noose around her neck.

She turned pale and was about to faint.

You could be in a comfortable home with me in Florida. But you blew your chance, and this is no longer a choice. Sorry, but you abused your privileges and became a victim of your weakness.

Lost and grabbing for straws to find a defense for her situation, but she knew that she had fallen into a trap. Crying, pleading, and promises will bring no resolution, and she knew it. Too many broken promises, it cannot carry on any longer.

You are the mother of my son, my grown-up son. Soon he will start to manage his own life and start a family. He does not need us anymore but for moral support and the family bond.

Do you want to take this away from him too? Has he not already lost the help of his mother? How much more are you going to hurt him?'

That shook her to her bone, and she realized the dire situation she had created.

"I must take responsibility for it; I am clear on this."

"'What am I going to do?"

You need professional help to get off this stuff and, in a center, where they keep you safe from yourself and the dealers.

A gradual withdrawal is a method with medication to protect your organs and rebuild your inner machinery and the brain. You are gravely ill; you cannot do it without medical treatment.'

'I will help find a place like this and decide.

Meanwhile, you will put the house on the market. The sales proceeds will bring a chunk of money. I will set you up in another state. You must move into a gated condominium with security and an alarm system.

I will have an attorney watch over this, for you still need my signature. My name is still on the deed, and since you never recorded it as the sole owner, it gives me control over the money.

The money will go to the institution unless we get insurance to pay for at least a part of it.

When you are ready, and we decide on the location, I will arrange the move and the living space, and the rest of the money will be placed into a trust account in our son's name.

You will receive startup money when the drug treatment is completed. Then everyday life begins with a job to earn your living.

Divorce papers are being prepared now and are mailed to you. Fait accompli.'

* * * * * * *

The inner city are full of gangs, and the women there are abused like animals. I discussed this with my secretary, who had done social work in Chicago, Michigan. "I will give you places to call for drug treatment. These institutions are in part sponsored by large corporations as a charitable contribution. Also, the state they are in is paying a part, and her or your share is 20 percent. Then they do rehabilitation like it is done for criminals, getting them into a skill and job. When they get released, job opportunities are waiting.

Employers know that in most cases, the individual cannot afford to screw up again.:

"She will look her best after treatments and good food, rest, and peace. She should go into social work, nursing home care, and anything to help the needy.

It will give her a sense of purpose and set up self-esteem. Study it on a fast track while she is in detox and finish a degree for instant employment. There is so much need for these people.

They will grab her before she gets her diploma. one hundred percent sponsorship by the state with the commitment to remain in that state."

Thank you, Lina. Now my plan is airtight. No multiple choices anymore,

✱ ✱ ✱ ✱ ✱ ✱ ✱

Angela went with me to this fancy cognac tasting. She bought a new dress for it, something semiformal. "You take me to these fancy places. I must look the part."

You look loveliest naked to me.

"Stop it."

The event took place in a four-star hotel in Coconut Grove.

The food was impeccable, and the spirits received the right temperature and proper glasses.

Snifters and small tulip-shaped glasses all had the Remy Martin logo.

The explanations that described the care and methods which made these cognacs, were lost on Angela.

the alcohol consumed while tasting had made an impact on her.

I received prominent recognition from the leading man for my wine sales efforts. A bottle of Louis XIII was presented without fanfare.

"Take this home and share it with special friends."

I almost blushed.

It followed up with a proposal to introduce their entire line of spirits and the Pommery champagne at the new hotel in Fort Lauderdale. Consideration of the price will be extended since the state law disallows donations. Thank you for your kind proposal. I will present this to senior management.

"Thank you very much for attending, and your beautiful lady has good taste in clothing."

Angie was pleased and blushed just a little, such a refined gentleman! "You come in touch with the crème de la crème."

Let us take a walk along South Bay shore to work off the alcohol. It will do us good.

"I am not drunk."

We walked into the village, looking at art studios and crafts in the windows. The bikini shops with the latest style from Brazil; are called

388

tanga. The effects of the alcohol did intensify as it made it into the bloodstream."

"I could not wear this. My ass is too big!"

Don't kid yourself. You will see these on bigger derrieres than yours. Besides, your buns are perfect, especially seeing them from the overhead view. That earned me a punch into the groin.

We had a double ice cream cone with mango and persimmon ice cream at the gelateria.

Finally, my head had cleared enough to drive. I took care not to attract the attention of highway patrol. The back road served us well that night.

Loving would have to wait for the morning.

My appointment with Atlantic Fisheries was set at 9:00 a.m.

Alex looked like a fisherman that would fit the cover of an outdoor magazine. He took me to the dock; "Our quality control starts right here." I saw the unloading and noticed that every fish was carried as if it were a baby. "We don't throw any fish. They bruise and lose texture. This is precious cargo from the sea."

"To maintain the freshness, we installed saltwater ice machines on every boat; this way, there is always plenty of ice, and we can stay out until the hull is filled. These machines work with ocean salt water; the engine generates electricity. Only when we run out of diesel are we forced to come in.

The ice freezes at 28 °F into powder snow. It serves a perfect purpose since it works everywhere and does not freeze the fish."

He showed me a tuna fish that had been on a boat for a week and was landed this morning. Gills were still blood red, with no odor and firm texture, as they took them off the hook. Yes, we do long lines and target our catch. Nets bring in everything, and most is too small. We would also have to deal with endangered turtles or other fish varieties.

Workers kept their space immaculately clean, with no bones, gills, scales, or skin remnants anywhere. I could not detect an odor, none, nada, despite the age of the building. Alex showed his pride and pointed to how each fish filet was handled. The care carried through as each fillet received careful, gentle handling.

Impressive.

At the office, he introduced a business partner. "He handles marketing and promotions. The fisherman knows how to catch fish but has no business sense."

He took two pieces of fresh tuna, the thickness of an eight-ounce filet mignon part.

"Now watch me." He had a spice mix all dry, a plate with a bit of corn oil, a cast-iron skillet heating up dry, and when that skillet reached the point to turn red, he dipped the tuna lightly onto the dry spice mix, both top and bottom, leaving the sides untouched. Then a quick dip on the oil, one side on the outside of the spices, and into the cast-iron skillet.

Smoke gave us cause to cough and an aroma that resembled a pepper steak was being transformed with the intense heat.. Black on one side, turned the other side and again the same reaction, and when this side was black he took it from the skillet.

Cutting it open resembled a filet mignon and it was medium rare, then the taste revealed a miracle has just happened, I called out.

I was impressed by the taste. It was so tender, and the flavor, I just could not believe how a piece of fish had turned into a filet mignon of beef.

He smiled. "Can you turn water into wine?" Laughing, we had a glass of wine with it. Then he gave me the product list, emphasizing the availability, varying with what the boats brought in.

"We have our boats and more under contract that we do not own, and generally, we always have fish, for otherwise, we are out of business."

He added, "If you can stay away from the New England fish types, it will help him, for these guys in Boston are Mafia. We will deal with them or New York on special occasions or for a banquet."

"Who will do the buying?" It was something I had to clarify and push for a variance. If corporate procurement got involved, it would be about the price; they did not know the word *quality*.

On the way back to the office, I briefed my boss. I had an ace up my sleeve since the owner was charging me personally to run with this concept. I could use his name, and he had the chairman's ear. I will be in touch as soon as this is completed.

"You are putting a lot of effort into this project."

I got to. If I leave this to the menu people, you get what happened in Irvine, California.

＊＊＊＊＊＊

By lunchtime, this bread man was scheduled for his presentation.

Andre arrived punctually like a European, I thought. "I am from Canada, Quebec, but my business is here in Florida.

Please take a look at these baguettes that have been in my freezer for three months; they come from France by sea container and are par baked. All one needs to do is to pop it into a 375 °F oven for five minutes, and this is what you get."

The aroma from the bread had by now filled the office, and since it was lunchtime, everybody was starving. "Starving a misused term."

Andre started to break off pieces and distributed pieces to the "starving" office staff.

My boss smelled it. "What is going on, something to eat?"

Come on over and have a look.

As he devoured half a loaf with great satisfaction, he asked, "Can we get this into our hotels?"

"It is available now. I have supplies and more floating across the Atlantic. The cost: no more than what you pay for these soft banquet rolls! But you will have more volume in the consumption. That is a compliment. "

"What do you think of it, troops?"

"Oh yes, very good from all sides to me now."

"Make it happen. I am so tired of the bread we have in the hotels."

With that, I finally found a long-overdue solution to inferior bread.

We will get with the hotels to obtain an estimate consumption.

＊＊＊＊＊＊

Irvine, California, invites you to the first corporate Food and Beverage conference. It came by special invitation to introduce a new aera of standards and ideas to upgrade the catering and other food and beverage services.

391

A ballroom set up with new serving dishes, glassware, unbreakable pool drinking ware, food displays, and tasting tables with Chefs tending to explain the items, bar service, and wines by the glass.

It was to be a kick off to a new generation of luxury hotels. Eyes wide open, catering managers and foodies made their way through the exhibits. A schedule of seminars and presentations is posted for the three-day affair.

I looked it over and found that Rob had volunteered me to help him with the wines. At that moment, he caught up with me.

"I should have called. I apologize for springing this on you without advance notice. I want you there, if only for a backup if I get stuck."

Not a problem, we are both old war horses, and we will wing it. If only I had known my bread man a week earlier. I would serve them freshly baked French baguettes right in here. "Who is that?" I will tell you later.

Yes, we can have fun with these stuck-up Food and Beverage directors. I said it with a sarcastic undertone.

We could have introduced this excellent French bread at this time.

All this commotion and meetings to gather the disciplines together was a long day and called for recreation.

"Anyone game for tennis?" Three people raised their hands. "What about you?" He was pointing to me. "I know you had some private lessons in Barbados from Maggie. Come on. We need a fourth person. It does not matter how good anyone plays. It is just for fun."

An audience had already assembly. I was already dressed in shorts, a casual shirt and in sneakers as I was handed a racquet and assigned to a partner.

"Let us review the rules. First, a gentle warmup and hit to the opposite player. That improves accuracy. The serve, the first service that makes it into the service area, will kick the game in motion.

The other side won the toss and opted to serve first.

"Think, eye on the ball, move the feet, stay on the toes, get into the strike zone, read the opponents' body position, strike with the sweet spot, turn the body, topspin to get the power and speed, but bring the ball back down within the court with topspin. Follow through to the shoulder blade, get back into position, and keep your racquet up in both hands."

All these pointers came to mind again. Thank you Maggie!

I must remember all of them. Concentrate was the last word, and the match was underway.

The backhand ritual rehearsed and some selected shots if conditions are right.

The first server hit the ball into the net, then out, and wide long was the call. "Has to find his range," my partner whispered. Finally, a soft serve, bounce up, eye on the ball, racquet back, and topspin return crosscourt to the corner. Love–15!

Applause from the audience! I looked up and noticed Andrea, the corporate F&B secretary, smile at me and wither my boss's secretary, Helen, next to her. Thumbs up for encouragement.

My partner moved back, gave me a pat on my back, and prepared to receive. I was near the net. He missed the first, now the second serve. The service counted as a fault this time or made it out.. The second serve came in gently, returned by the partner with a top spin and force, a counter shot, and again the ball ended down the line for love 30

Now is my turn to receive. This time, he found his range and hit a strong serve. I was not fast enough to reach the strike zone and hit back with a weak shot to his partner, but I caught him flat-footed. He was counting on me missing the return. Applause, name-calling, go, go! Love–40.

I noticed that the next serve scored the opponents a point, an unforced error. He nodded. 15–40. Now is my turn to receive. Again, the second serve but right down the centerline, an attempt for an ace, and a strong return, I can dish it out too, a recovery shot came back high, and my partner returned the overhead smash. Game: 0–1.

The match was repeated for games two and three, A good part of luck had been on our side, and audience support was growing. With four games in the win column, we stopped to make room for the waiting team.

"You tricked us. "You played like a pro!"

Beginners' luck!

"It was fun. We want a revanche!"

Time allowing, we still have a conference to attend. Rob asked me to copresent the premium wine by the glass at an assembly.

Helen and Andrea made it a point to see me after the match. "You played very well," Helen said.

It was a fluke. I have never played doubles. I surprised myself. I mean it. The only explanation I can give is that I am a good learner by observation.

"Must have been the instructor." Now fishing which it was! From Andrea.

I watched a match. up close at the Madison Square Garden, observing the professionals how they prepare before the ball strike and of course the footwork to get them in the strike position.

"Oh yes," from Helen.

Do you play tennis?

"Yes, we must do it someday in Florida! "How did you manage to get such a premium ticket?"

Maggie, she is dating an official that organized this tournament.

"Did she teach you?"

Yes, with ample patience, and she also instructed strategy, which is why we won.

"Plus, the footwork," she said.

"Let us have a glass of wine!" From Andrea! "You said that you are a good learner from just seeing? I want to hear that story!"

A follow-up on the strategy to win: a lot of luck, concentration, footwork to get in place to strike back with the sweet spot, and my partner was powerful, so the matchup was the strongest with the weakest against the equal-matched partners.

"Well analyzed,"

"Yes, she is into tennis, will whip my ass in Florida."

"Mr. Brown always commented on you as being special, a talent I cannot put my fingers on in how he does it."

Now the cat is out of the bag, but there is more. This was the beginning only. But that story is for a rainy day. You have to wait a long time for a rainy day.

"Not me," Andrea said. "I just have to hijack you when you are up there."

I went to my room to prepare for the presentation tomorrow. I'm just unsure which way Rob would take it, so be ready for anything, have your numbers ready, and illustrate the Tampa effect backed up with numbers plus customer testimony.

I was about to undress when I heard a soft knock at the door. Andrea!

"I came to celebrate your victory today."

She lifted a Chandon Blanc de Noir champagne and two champagne flutes.

"Are you game for that too?"

Come on in before we have a busload joining. She opened it expertly, tilting the bottle to let the bubbles travel along the neck and not spill over, and poured three-fourths of the glass. A toast to my favorite regional. With this, I almost won too, but to reach the finish line, I need your help."

She undressed, kissed, seduced me with every trick, and we made passionate love half the night. "Now I am the winner."

I had forgotten the former talk, but now she explained that the two secretaries who had worked at headquarters together for VPs had a bet, which would get me into bed first. See, I won. If I did not have a natural attraction to her from day 1, I would have felt like a pawn in a chess game, the king, chess mate by the queen.

She was a very compassionate woman, easy to talk to, warm, understanding, and with a type of "I serve you" mentality. Her romantic skills had been a teaching moment for me, and as I asked her if this was from girlhood up to marriage, she confirmed my hunch.

"In East Asia, girls do not have much value to our parents. Girls are only good for housework.

Mother makes every effort to prepare the girls for marriage, including sex education and skills that will please the man she later marries, for this is the essential skill to keep a man happy and healthy. They need it more than you, but you give it to them and do the best job. That was the daily lecture to girls."

"The other skill is cooking. 'A man's love goes through the stomach,' she would always say." This means you are a good cook. "You can count on this. I invite you to my house when the next meeting comes around or travel to the DC area anytime. I know you have unfinished business with your house, wife, or ex-wife?"

Soon, ex-wife, all in the making now! "I will give you my address, drive, or subway. Either way, it is easy to find."

"One good rumble deserves another."

"Okay." She sneaked out while I was sleeping, taking the empty bottle with her, her trophy! And so was another nighttime well spent.

Time in the morning must be at a higher speed. My presentation in front of all these people came up in no time, just a glance to refresh my memory on critical points. The rest, I would wing it as I had done at FIU just recently, be calm, roll with the punches.

In every crowd, small or large, are those that shoot their mouth off, whether substantive or not, mostly darn right stupid, but they must make themselves heard.

Right in the middle of explaining the benefits of this program for customers and the business, he interrupted. "I have to say something to this."

I put up my hand, showing him to stop, but he continued his argument. I let him empty his head, and as he stopped, I told him that there would be a question-and-answer session at the end of the presentation, at which time I would gladly address his issue.

"No, I want an answer right now. This is bull. It will not work. Why would we be so concerned about the benefit for the customer? He gets the wine, he orders. That makes us even. No benefits. We suck him dry if we get the chance."

While this rampage was going on, the observers noted and named him.

I said to the audience, "My apologies. This man does not want to play by the protocol. I will answer him right now.

If you have such strong feelings and arguments about this program, would you please come up to this podium, and you have five minutes to explain what you do in your property being so much superior to ours. Please state your name and the property you are working on here.

As he approached, the tension in the room could now be measured with the Richter scale.

"My name is Larry. I work at the best hotel chain in Kansas City, where we know our business."

"Go on," I said. Tell us your secrets.

"Ahhh, I do not know how to bring it to you. You have to see it."

Surely there are some points to share, a description, numbers, cost control, revenues, and profits.

"Yes, cost control. We have the best cost in the company!"

You mean the lowest?

"Yes, of course, the lowest. What else?"

A quick question, What's the average time a bar guest sits on the barstool?

"Do not know."

How many drinks does your clientele consume on average, one or two? It would be fair to assume that you have a customer on that stool fifteen minutes or say twenty? Long face. And what about the rotation of your customers? They come and go like in a railway station?

By now, the audience was smiling.

"No, we get them one after another with times in between."

"Thank you for your revelations."

Instead of following my script, I picked up from this guy's points. Then I continued where I left off before the interruption.

Anybody looking at the P&Ls?

All hands up except this guy. "You see that the business pays many bills: wages, FICA, uniforms, glassware, water, electricity, property tax and other business taxes, and on and so forth.

The beverage cost is but a measure! Now let me look at it from another angle.

You buy a bottle of wine for eight dollars. Then you get the opportunity to make a sale. We take the price at one-quarter of the bottle sales price times four portions sold brings you thirty-two dollars. Your cost of the full bottle starts at 100.

The first glass sold at eight dollars per price guideline, brings the cost 75% by the conventional formula.

But with the eight dollar sale you just paid for the bottle.

Zero beverage cost. Still no profit, but that comes with every added sale. You can even squeeze a fifth glass if pored accurately.

The revenue is either $32 or $40

I pointed to this guy; you with me?

The second glass is sold quickly to the same customer because he enjoyed it, and a third glass may sell in addition.

High-quality wine is consumed faster than jug wine.

Still with me?" Nodding head.

Another customer hears the name of this wine, and it amazes him to get this wine quality by the glass, for all the other times he needed to buy the entire bottle.

He orders the same and has two or three drinks. Profit is twenty-four dollars per bottle.

Still with me?" No shaking. "Let me explain this.

This Gallon wine does not go down easy. He would have consumed one glass if he had received your cheap wine. He would also spend double the time emptying the glass. The same with the second customer. Your revenue at $2.50 for each drink, a total of $5.00 in sales.

The cost % is whatever you brag about.

This premium wine took in $24 per bottle and a total of $48.00

The cost is $16.00 or 25%. Even if the bottle still had something left and the bartender decided to be generous and poured the remaining wine to top off these customers' glasses, he is still more successful for the house, and I guarantee they made a good tip on it.

He had made two customers happy and booked them for the future. He will also tell his friends and come back.

Applause from the audience and wide approval from their faces! This man stood up once more and tried to add to his speech, but an uproar from the audience demanded to give him the hook!

"You pulled this off like a magician pulling a rabbit out of his top hat."

"Not Rob. I did pull it out of the hat at the FIU presentation. Here is simple logic. Just look at it from a practical side. We get fixated on the cost percentage, and we forget the dollars. That's the money we take to the bank.

Yes," he said, "and it all makes a lot of sense.

His GM was in the audience, embarrassed." A surprise may be waiting for him at home.

Chapter 25

The first day back, I had Lina book an appointment with the owner of the new beach hotel. The briefing was due for an update on the lounge, and I wanted to pick his brains on other priorities.

At 11:00 a.m., The owner called me into his office. His partner was with him, and I started with a brief review of the competition. "I know all this. what do you have so far?"

Here are some of the fish dishes. I described it to make their mouth watery.

The sourcing of the product will come from the Atlantic fishery.

"Great choice. I did not mention this at the beginning. Carry on."

I have one concern. These penny-pinchers at corporate procurement like to undermine the efforts, talk the product down as too expensive and then make every effort to kill the concept. I will be accused of being in the vendor's pockets, and this story can get ugly. Then I get a nasty note to have gone outside the company directions

This hotel will be a four-star luxury resort. We do not have four-star hotels in the chain yet. A learning curve must be bridged, for I have more ideas that break the corporate mold.

"Go on."

The bread will be baked in France.

"What?"

Actually, yes, but it is shipped par-baked and frozen. All the kitchen needs to do is pop it in the oven for five to eight minutes, and oven-fresh bread is on the table, crusty and delicious.

More: I attended a cognac tasting from Remy Martin. We sampled VS, VSOP, and XO all the way to Louis XIII.

. After the tasting, they pulled me aside and made a proposal.

They want to introduce their Pommery champagne into the Florida market and offer a dirt-cheap price for the grand opening.

Added to this product line and bringing the fifty-plus year-aged Louis 13th to the hotel's bar, the first outside NYC. Again, a high cost, but at forty dollars a shot, it is a good margin. The glassware they will provide with their logo, of course.

Supply limits made it impossible to export it out of Europe. Any problems with that?

"You must be kidding with a blink of an eye. How do you get these kinds of invitations?"

I'll tell you, but I attended Krug vintage champagne tasting and a wine product line from this company on separate dates.

"I want to hang out with you!" The partner was blown away.

I am sticking my neck out for these programs and need your cover. When you get the owner's ear, it will help to cover my Ass!

Now I will tell you what prompted these invitations.

The premium wine by the glass sale we started at the causeway has made waves. The wines we chose came from their product line.

The wine sales are now in thirty hotels including the hotels in my former and current regions. It affected volume so much that they had almost run out of supplies.

The level of quality was not selling by the bottle. Once we started wine by the glass, we became so successful that it drew their attention.

They traced this sales action to me since I introduced it independently. I really stuck my neck out until Rob took it company wide and wrote the SOP.

They recognized me in front of the audience at a wine tasting and hailed me as the Messiah.

Thank you's, handshakes, kisses, I was almost embarrassed. (You know the French!)

Again, when I attended the cognac tasting, they called me aside afterward and made this proposal. You must know that you have solved a massive problem for us, we wish to show our gratitude. This way, we think it is the best method and will make you look good in front of your boss. Aside from this, please accept a token of our finest for you and friends' enjoyment. I opened the box home and discovered I had received a Louis XIII.

If you have the time, the lounge looks good so far, with concern about overloading and fire regulation violations. The parking is resolved with the overflow valet service for tips only; then the promotions are now reworked to award half dozens of drawings for a hotel room, dinner for the in-laws, (one can constantly improve the relationship) the grand price is a free cruise. Trades and barter will pay for it.

The band is happy that we now have an incognito security mingling and a doorman screening the *hoodlums*. The profile is back to our norm.

"Thank you. You have done it once again. Proud of you, and we will take care of the CYA."

Leaving the office, I overheard them talking, "He will make a great GM!"

"You think he falls for a boring job like that? He has an exciting life, way too much fun to give up. No way would I jump for a GM's job if I were him. He is single. We should hook him up with….."

"No, don't do it."

* * * * * * *

The boss had all his disciples in the office for a rare occasion. "Let us have a meeting and get me updated.

Every regional director reported their recent activities, visits, staffing needs, performances, and opinions.

My report centered on the conference in California and the briefing on the beach hotel to the owner.

It made him a bit jealous, but he did not comment negatively.

I will need your backing on this concept and am facing stiff opposition.

"Then the bread initiative. Where are we on this?"

Again, the fear of breaking away from the rigid rules.

I can give it another push.

" I am scheduling a meeting with that hotel. It will be good to meet with the management as a team. They feel the pressure from corporate visitors. All eyes are on this hotel.

Arrange a presentation at the bread; once they see, touch, and taste it, the sale will be secured."

Then in his usual fashion, he moved the meeting to a pub for the rest of the schedule.

"A couple of beers will do us all good now."

He reviewed his list of staffing changes. "We will take the GM from the causeway hotel to open up the new beach hotel. He is a sharp man with a vision and four-star experience. The GM from Miami airport will replace him, and a new hire will take over at the airport hotel. It will be good all around. We want experienced managers for this hotel. You have time but start the search."

"What you just told the owners is right up their alley. Good planning."

"Next up will be a team visit to Acapulco. Make yourself accessible for next week."

"Then comes Miami Biscayne Hotel in three weeks! How do you feel about your counterparts?"

I have a reservation. He is too close to the VP.

Corporate appointed him. I have to make it work.

Not much has been revealed.

I know that he lives in Miami and speaks fluent Spanish.

Dinner followed the meeting, and as usual, he made me use my credit card to pay the bill.

It gives him the authority to approve the expense report.

No complaints. I am building up my credit again.

The new president had come to visit on the day we had our meeting with the hotel management team at the causeway hotel. The GM, controller, and chief engineer from the beach hotel joined.

The new president was an addition to aid the CEO.

He joined our meeting and reiterated the importance of the future four-star goal for this beach resort.

The regional Vice President introduced everybody by name and rank.

"I have to repeat the words from the beach resort's owner about the importance of setting up that property as a shining star under this company name. Make it a showpiece; it will be the first.

The owner, with whom I met last night, has his eyes on it."

He looked at me and told me that any variance contributing to this four-star quality would be granted. "You have my backing!"

"The dust will settle soon."

I hoped that Charles was not part of this; I needed his backing.

He excused himself with a short side talk to the RVP and left.

We continued with the meeting. "You heard it from the horse's mouth. Big wheels are rolling in. Be on your toes. Keep it efficient. They will not expect an upgrade from this hotel, but efficiency, squeaky-clean, competent staff, your frontline staff can receive help from new uniforms.

The gut feeling is that this hotel will be sold soon to secure the financing for the beach.

* * * * * * *

A team visit to any hotel had always been a lively event.

Acapulco was no different.

The arrival in Acapulco was a real treat. We were ushered through immigration and customs and never touched our luggage when we arrived right off the planes jetway.

A limousine took us to the hotel. Management just took charge of the entire visit schedule.

Keys are handed out, and rooms are assigned on the top floors, facing the ocean. We will meet at 6:30 at the Palenque bar.

It was still early and time to dip the toes into the ocean. Tanned and slender bodies took in the last sun rays while beach vendors disrupted the tourists with efforts to peddle their ware.

I noticed a boy contacting a Gringo woman. He opened an attaché case and pulled out a necklace to show it to the woman. She was not excited about it; another chain came out. The boy described in his broken English and used body language; see, this is a perfect complement for your personality.

This boy knew how to say an open-ended statement to provoke a reply.

"How do you judge my personality?"

Understanding more than he could speak, he replied instantly; you have such a pleasant, kind, good-hearted personality, and you love children. I am still a child, only six years. Can you tell?

She was shocked at such a reply and started to have another look and mumbled. "How do you know all this at your young age?"

He placed the necklace around her neck, moving her long hair aside while complimenting her soft and wonderful-smelling hair. "You see, I am right, such a beautiful long neck with nothing to garnish. See, I have a mirror."

The sale is now agreed and no haggling on the price. He was pleased and smiling while he pulled out a bracelet.

"Now senorita, still young, we call you senorita, better than senora."

"Your slender arms, also so long and beautiful," as he took her hand and let his left-hand glide over her skin.

Boy, this kid was good. He used sensuous touches to stimulate the sexual senses, and seduction came.

The boy was at it, kept caressing her arm, then touched her neck, pretending to have another look at the necklace, then an accidental touch of her shoulder.

For the kill, he kissed her on the cheek. Hook, line, and sinker, she bought one for her and one to take home as a gift.

The woman pulled out twenty dollars and paid, but this kid would not give up until she showed her empty wallet.

* * * * * * *

It is Hora Feliz, the Mexican happy hour at the Palenque bar. The business was brisk and standing room only. A marimba band seduced the customers with popular songs.

Ignacio, the F&B director, ordered two shots of Tequila served with lime and a saltshaker. "Lick the salt from the skin of your hand, take the

Tequila as a shot, and suck on the lime. It is Mexican medicine against the cold." A Mexican welcome in earnest.

Juan, the GM, joined. "So, you *niños* are getting a head start. One for me and two more for the boys here. Cannot stand on one leg!"

Then the regional team members filed in and ordered a beer and snack food.

I started laughing to myself, but Richard took it that I was laughing about him. I said I have just seen a sale in action at the beach!

He looked at me with big eyes. "How so?"

"His name is Gonzalo, six or so years old with broken English. He sells jewelry out of a briefcase.

This kid pulled out every trick to make a sale on this woman. She tried to wave him off. He does not take a no for an answer.

You must see him in action.

Juan added: "Yes, this guy is doing great; he feeds the entire family." The kids are very dynamic. They learn early and use their youth to their advantage.

You will see this everywhere, the streets, at the airport, where they find tourist traffic."

This is real, genuine local food. Dinner was perfect, with a variety of Mexican food I had never experienced and served professionally by friendly servers of the male and female gender.

The Fiesta, with the choice of seafood, poultry, red meat, and desserts, had filled me with discomfort.

"Have a shot of Tequila; it helps and makes you feel better." Universal medicine did help me. Full stomach, we now show you the nightlife of Acapulco.

A discotheque filled with tourists and local girls who did their best to lure young Gringos on the dance floor.

"Are they hookers?" Richard asked.

"No, they do this to hook up and maybe get to marry a Gringo to go to the land where the gold lies on the streets?"

"Yes, there will be a few lucky guys tonight. Just hope they have condoms, for otherwise, the Mexican government will be looking them up and show the picture of a bambino."

"How does that work out?"

"They say that they live with the family and do not have a room with privacy, so they end up in his hotel room, and there she gets the information from the front desk on her way out.

While in the room, she works him over and then puts him to sleep. The wallet will be fair game, but not all; he will not need to go home. Taking all the money will get the police involved.

Breakfast at 10:00 a.m. is late for our timing, but when in Rome, you do as the Romans do.

We feasted on local tropical fruit and everything the Chef could imagine. Like the dinner, it was over the top but meant to impress the Gringos on the first team visit.

Richard came last to breakfast, eyes bloodshot and crabby looking. It provoked smiles on all faces.

The visit with Ignacio was planned like a ritual. A review of the Pesos' financials and confusion. Then a look into next year's projections, and the chronic problems with the city government and travel agencies left me disinterested.

Can I walk around, meet your employees, key personnel, and see the operation, please? He was surprised and tried to stir me in another direction.

I started in the receiving area, the goods arriving at the hotel, and then follow the product to the final destination, the dining room table!

"Take a look at the quality." I do not know the standards of meat grades here in your country. Can you give me an education on it?

"I know some, but our Chef is the specialist."

Please show me what you know, then we'll catch up with the Chef in the kitchen.

He did his best to point to a marking as we have in the US, prime or choice. The blue stamp showed choice to me, I said.

Then inside the storeroom, I looked for signs of rodents. Properties close to water usually have rodent problems but there was no evidence.

"How do you manage this?" He pointed to two cats, big black cats. That explains it, better than poison.

"Si, senor!"

We moved on to the kitchen. The coolers and freezers looked well organized and clean. "Do you have a commissary room?"

"Right this way." Three women were busy peeling potatoes, washing lettuce, and packing it into bins with cheesecloth lining.

"This keeps the lettuce crisp," one of them explained.

Excellent, nice work.

"Gracias, senor!"

Then the Chef joined us and proudly introduced me to the kitchen staff. "El Senor Jefe de Washington, *muy importante*." The Sous Chef did not speak English, but the cooks tried to show off their knowledge.

Between their English and my Spanish, we almost got a conversation going. Funny how this came together when the best efforts are made from both sides!

The Chef took me to the walk-in coolers, trays of ingredients stacked on carts, one on top of the other, meat portioned and marked with a paper appointing the party or restaurant with the date and number of portions. It shows organization and control.

Then on to the hot cooking area where I stopped watching the sauce cook put the finishing touches to a sauce for the banquet, a wedding. He looked at me and offered me a taste by handing me a small spoon.

"Muy Bien, my specialty," I commented. He smiled, and the Chef asked me if I was a Chef. I said I was glad he asked in the present time form.

Yes, I worked as a Chef, and once a Chef, always a Chef. He smiled and precisely knew my meaning of it.

The F&B director then wanted to know if I was still working as a Chef.

No, the meaning spoke to the knowledge of being with one for his life and coming to the surface whenever the need arises. Second, a Chef looks at food from a different angle. The waste and the love and care the product receives are visible.

"Now I understand, It's a noble profession. I should have gone this way, but my father signed me up for college; I need to be a manager with a better future.

The restaurant manager wanted to show me all stations and service procedures. She was truly kind, but I had witnessed the professional service at dinner and breakfast. I am assured that everything is in good order. She smiled, and Gracias Senior.

A large radio company owns this property. Renovations are overdue and are getting postponed again. Department managers had to use creative ways to keep equipment in functioning order, even if this resorted to Duct Tape. While they are super-rich, they are very stingy in supporting the hotel.

The visit had been scheduled to deliver the last warning and a date by which the renovation must be started; the RVP will give an ultimatum.

"God forbid to let this happen. Yes, this is serious, and the employees are getting hurt the most. Management will be looked after with reassignments in other hotels. It means disaster for all these employees."

After lunch, I went to the hair salon to cash in a coupon I received with the VIP presentation. Manicure, pedicure, massage with our compliments, it said, signed by Juan.

I knew why women hung around the nail salons while I received my first manicure.

This service was enjoyable; she put clear nail polish on before I could stop her. "It will not shine after this dry," she remarked.

Other women took my feet and soaked them; they needed work badly. Walking barefooted had created calluses. They scrubbed the hard skin with a rough scouring pad, then more soaking while the other foot received the same care. We can take care of the nails." An application of a lotion and, "Good as new," she remarked and pointed me to the massage room.

A woman in her thirties told me to get undressed.

"All, please," pointing to the buttocks.

"Turn around." Facedown in an opening lined with a small towel, she started to work the muscles until they yielded to the treatments. Nothing was left out with the feet and the toes, arms, and hands stretching.

"Not finished yet. More work is needed for the neck, shoulder, face, skull, arms, and fingers."

She pulled each finger and gently massaged it as if a girlfriend had given her hand.

The leg muscles up front, the upper thighs' lower shin bone muscles from underneath, feet and toes, and the same pull on each toe received help from this expert care.

Working her way up the legs, she moved the legs apart. On each side and pushed her hands on the stomach in gentle and soft circles.

The circular movements reached my pubic area and then back to the upper thigh muscles. She concentrates on the inner part and is close to the family jewels.

At first, an incidental brush on the underside and back to the leg, returning a bit more, finally taking hold of the entire package.

Like marbles in her hand, she expertly moved me to the arousal.

The blood was now rushing to this area and pumping into the muscle. Hands took over and finished the massage to final satisfaction.

Not yet, un poco más.

She raised me once more for another treatment, only this time she had pulled off her panties, mounted me, and worked me to a climax. Mass Grande. Gracias senior!

Best VIP presentation to date!

* * * * * * *

At home, my message recorder had an urgent message from my secretary. "You must call the realtor as soon as you get this message. She needs your decision on a good offer."

"The offer just came in, and I have not spoken to your wife, knowing her emotional status. Please tell her. These people love your place and are willing to buy the furniture for extra money. The offer is two percent under the asking price. Will you accept? "

They have enough money to settle in cash, no bank involved, and no appraisal to prolong the closing date, as in no contingencies. This deal could not be better."

You are right. Thank you for your great work. Please fax the papers to my office. Here is the number. I will call at once and help her understand. She is resolved to make a change. Too much has gone sour for her there.

When I reached the wife on the phone and explained the deal, she understood and was willing to go ahead.

Yes, this is a good deal, and it will serve as your security as your safety net. Are you going to sign it?

"Yes," I will have her drop by. "I am now resolved to make the change, already get the feeling of a calm coming upon me. What a fool I am."

Stop the self-pity. It brings only negative feelings. You enter a new chapter in your life and the hope to be happy.

I called the realtor to get her signature before her negative elements again took control.

"I will organize the move from here and negotiate the furniture price on her behalf. Thank you!"

At the office, the secretary wanted to hear the outcome and was pleased that this was finally going in the right direction. She updated me on searching for a suitable institution to get her off the dependency.

Until now, the family doctor kept her stable with small doses and slowly reduced it to the beginning of the end.

"There is a beautiful place in New Mexico serving the Indian population as they have a big problem.

It is primarily financed by federal funds and specializes in rehabilitation to get these people into a productive life again. They will take her. I made a tentative reservation. I call to confirm if this suits you."

Excellent, Lina; what would I have done without you?

"Just the job. You know we have to support the boss."

* * * * * * *

With a reservation booked, I called Angela to take her to the Mai Kai restaurant. A hula show, excellent Hawaiian music, and exciting food with an Asian flavor. It would be fun.

I found the drink menu of great interest and slipped one into Angela's purse.

410

The show featured twelve girls in grass skirts moving hips in a circular motion in the gentle rhythm of the music. Then guys in loincloths are doing acrobatic and fire dances!

"What if the skirt catches fire?" I asked Angela.

"Wouldn't you like to see this? I am sure they wear panties under the skirts.."

Do you think, when the ship of Captain Cook discovered these people, did they wear panties then?

"Do not know. Why?"

It served a purpose not wearing panties then.

"Why not?"

It deals with the insect population.

It was meant as a choke; instead, it earned me a punch into my chest.

The house closed in two weeks, and the move had been planned to the last detail. All she needed was to drive her to the address. Once there, she will be in good hands. God bless this realtor, and my secretary.

****

Martin called and told me that he wanted to go to Colorado. He found a small community college to make his associate degree in preparation for the university to study Architecture. Good. It was within driving distance to visit his Mom and stay connected.

****

Another regional meeting at the headquarters served to select the F&B director and executive chef and, with luck, also the catering director. That will appoint the critical professionals for the Beach resort.

Andrea had showed that she had a great evening planned. I booked the morning flight under a pretense for added time. But an excellent Asian dinner and later TLC were on my mind.

She had left work early since the boss was not expected to return to the office that evening.

The aromas from her cooking reached the front entrance. She wasted no time engaging in pleasures and working every angle again to keep me engaged. "Stay overnight and give me a ride in the morning. Do not worry, so many new people are there now. We are busting out of our seam's. Nobody will pay attention."

The meeting produced a candidate of my choice; he had been groomed for it and is still single. I have the perfect candidate for the F&B director's job. The Chef came from another region with excellent credentials.

Catering directors did not make it on the schedule; we do not have any available that fit the criteria. Look outside and secure a quality candidate from a reputable resort.

I wanted to deliver the proposal in person. A drive across Florida will complete the process. The GM may become an obstacle.

I showed the candidate for the F&B director to my boss and the beach resorts General manager. He is French and has a culinary education and a college degree in hotel management. A first class man who knows the finer things in life.

"Can I get him here for the final interview? Thank you. We do it on Monday."

I do not know the Chef personally.

Do you want to see him? "I will leave this to the F&B."

The catering is still a genuine concern; the available candidates do not fit the requirements, and we must look to the outside to fill this position.

Now the premium beverage offering from Remy Martin!

"Yes, I know about it by now. All sounds great; the details must be nailed down once the F&B is on board. I want to see if I can get him ahead of schedule."

Yes, I agree, there is work to be completed.

"I am glad we are on the same page. How do you do all this? I mean, keep it in order and stay on top?"

Multitasking is the operative word, and a good secretary here and at corporate.

"You have two?"

Not in that sense, but someone looking out for me there is helpful.

"I wonder who that may be."

Smiles. Have a wonderful day!

I drove to see this man; his life was about to take a turn for the better. He received a thorough briefing on the goals, restaurant concepts, and the premium beverage proposal. "Yes, I know this great champagne; how did you pull this off?"

We need a rainy day to cover this story.

The owner has a pet project with the pool. It will be a very ornate pool like an oasis with waterfalls and caves.

There will be cabanas as a club facility, a buffet service, bars, and children's facilities to provide privacy; I want you to be involved with it.

By chance, do you know of a super DOC?"

"I do. Not sure if he will move. He has a great job now, but one can never tell. The money has to be right. He is creative, works at a high-end place, and thinks outside the box."

Good. We are off to a good start. Will your girlfriend follow you? How do you know of her? It is written all over her face when she sees you!"

Chapter 26

My son had returned from his tour on the aircraft carrier and landed in Jacksonville. He stayed with me to get his civilian bearing and fill up on dad's cooking.

We received a phone call from Barbados. "It's Priscilla. She called me. She has good news for us. We are invited to her wedding. Wants to talk to you!"

Hi, darling. Tell me, who is the lucky man? "He is the third son of the Appleton family, the youngest, and he's going into business for himself. He purchased the food distributorship, the one we were getting our deliveries."

"The American is now too old to carry the burden and finally ready for retirement. Alex, my fiancé, has received a buyout from the company to release him from any inheritance claims. This purchase will set him up in this business."

"Do not worry about Priscilla's restaurant. My sister took over. I always check up on a restaurant with my name. Are you coming to the wedding? I need my daddy to walk me to the altar! And my little brother will be the best man? Say yes, please."

Of course, we are booking a flight right after. "You can stay at the house."

We, I mean you and I, are going to Barbados. You will be the best man. Get your speech ready now. We fly there on Thursday and back on Sunday. The wedding takes place at the Castle.

The groom arranged for us to receive an upgrade to business class for the roundtrip flight.

"An excellent way to travel beats these military no-frill flights on cargo planes with a dozen seats along the fuselage."

Our arrival was a celebration on its own. It touched the emotions of Priscilla and us. Martin had taken to her on her visit and adored her ever since. Seeing and hugging her surrogate father and brother coming to her wedding is the best wedding present.

Her fiancée Alex was introduced and may have been a little jealous.

"I was delighted in how this girl matured, a self-assured woman with a radiant personality. Her popularity on the island can only be helpful.

Alex was all business.

"This island has to become a world-class resort, a destination, not just for one, but we must increase the size of the pie to have plenty to share in."

He spoke with a vision. His family had promoted business and awareness in the tourist trade. We have a golden opportunity to follow in these footsteps with the food."

Priscilla took her brother around, holding hands like siblings, showing him around the estate and the countryside. Together we visit the Castle and the restaurant while looking if we find familiar faces.

Staff changes are inevitable. The ones that stay are the pillars of the business.

We dressed in tropical white without a necktie for the wedding ceremony I took my place to escort the bride with the veil over her face. She hooked her arm into mine, and we walked progressively more precisely towards the groom. The music played a romantic song; it was touching. I had to hold my tears when I handed her over. She did not want to let go. Ready?

Dearly beloved, the priest began his standard litany, and the wows followed and concluded with: I pronounce you Spouses, God bless you and your future children.

May I introduce to you "Mr. and Ms. Appleton."

Mama sat next to me in the front row. She took my hand and squeezed it so hard during this ceremony, and then the tears of joy. "Job well done," I told her. Raising her precious Priscilla has been carried out.

"Thank you for your help."

The party was in full motion, the first toast offered by the best man, who recited a short poem on how he became her brother and how he had treasured this all his young life. But now, while he would hand over the protective duties to her husband, it would remain his duty.

A committed to a home for her if she ever fell on hard times remained in effect as a solemn promise.

A toast, prosit, cheers, santé, every language that came out of the audience, but not the English version. "To the queen."

On the flight home, Martin was quiet. Why should we consider a person of particular affection lost to a marriage? We should celebrate the union and continue close connections.

He had tears in his eyes; it falls to us to keep the connection. A new chapter begins for Priscilla. Don't take offense if you do not hear from her. These small gestures are essential for frequent phone calls or cards or sending flowers for her birthday. They will be treasured as much as you keep her in your heart.

Martin was ready to embark on his trip to a small town in the Colorado Mountains. A small prep school appealed to him.

While he packed his car, the same emotions had taken hold of me. Am I losing a son? It was the same feeling he expressed about Priscilla's wedding. Time to let go, they will find their path in life.

He had matured into a self-confident man, knew what he wanted, and was destined to become successful. Satisfaction took over, and I was okay.

* * * * * * *

Now full speed to get this Miami hotel opened. The task force accommodations at the nearby Omni Hotel had been arranged and assigned me a room. I could have driven from home, but I was not complaining. Late nights could present a danger. The driving distance was taking an hour with normal traffic.

The need for a standard city hotel will be routine and Deja vu. The employees looked good, and management was carefully selected. Only the F&B director gave me concerns.

His close association with the VP, "his personal friend" Charles he kept on boasting about. He was a handful to guide and keep in line. A fast talker, he cozied up to me and made every attempt to become friends, especially since we were both Germans. He often switched to the German language while in the company of Americans. It provoked an adverse reaction, and I had to remind him not to continue.

He was not engaged with the training and did not follow up on assignments. It made this opening a challenge. I had hoped for a routine; however, it had turned into a babysitting job to keep this man in line with the opening process.

The GM knew the situation but said, "He is your man. I did not have a say in the choice. Take it up the chain of command."

Not a good situation. I was concerned and had to find an angle to reach this man without crying wolf to the VP.

I took him out for a drink at a tiki bar and let him have a clear text ultimatum.

You can throw your friend's name around for as much as you wish, but, in the end, it will do you no good. My RVP will decide your future. His boss is the same as your friend is reporting, The EVP. Do not forget this, please.

Right now, you are your own worst enemy with your behavior. You best concentrate on bringing this hotel to a successful opening and take the credit for it. I do not need this credit, and it does not serve me any purpose. I give this to you as advice; you make your future for yourself.

He settled down and complied, cooperated, and stayed to himself.

That night, I received a phone call from another room. Tracy from Fort Lauderdale was on the line asking me to come to her room for a question. She had the door ajar and was waiting inside, dressed in a bathrobe.

I just got out of the shower as she walked beside me, ensuring her legs became visible. The robe's parting in front, supplying a peek of her legs. The handwriting was on the wall; now I knew what these looks meant; she wanted to have a tête-à-tête.

On the bed, she opened the robe further, showing the entire naked body. Aggressively she grabbed my pants and tore them off with expert skills. There was no need for preparation. She had to have me and score this conquest. She has been starved for love, a confession she made at the conclusion.

Gratefulness serves both parties, I felt the need for a release after my confrontation with the F&B man, and her need for great bodily satisfaction had come at the opportune time.

Another happy woman had been neglected by her husband. She may be single soon unless the lazy husband shapes up.

****

The grand opening was a must-attend. I made my way around the guests and employees.

The GM's secretary had transferred from Tampa, and we had known each other since that hotel's opening.

Dark-brown hair and big dark eyes made her an attractive woman.

She engaged me with the latest news from Tampa, the lounge, and the crazy F&B director. We moved around as if we were a couple; she would not leave my side. At the close of the party, she invited me to her pad. "Just follow my car. It is a blue Toyota. I know yours, ensuring I will not lose you to the traffic. Just up the I-95 to this address."

A boy was asleep in the adjacent area. "Just stay quiet. He sleeps deep. We will not wake him." She had achieved her obvious goal. She stripped off her cloth while I was taking off the tuxedo.

"I was told you are incredibly blessed, and now I get to see and taste it.

She went at it as if it would be her last time. Keeping the sound level down became the biggest challenge.

When she calmed, she said, "She was not kidding!"

"Who?"

"Cannot tell? Please do not ask me again, but I shall name him now. For being famous, he needs a name! *Big Mo.*"

Another round of twenty minutes had satisfied her, and she released me from the Big Mo duty.

****

Martin had settled into this mountain town. A rented room from a woman that fed him and cared for him like a mother served him well.

He drove to Santa Fee to see his mother. She had completed her treatment and settled into an apartment. Working as a social worker with Indian tribe alcoholics and the ever-increasing drug problem gave her work and esteem. She felt a sense of accomplishment again.

She talked about the work and illustrated how she got to these people. The satisfaction to see improvement, if only very marginal, gave her great pride.

Martin was now pleased to see her putting her life together again. She put on weight. She looked healthy once again,

"Keep in touch. I am here for you now!"

While getting ready for university studies in Boulder, guys told him how hard it was to find work in architecture.

"You will be starving; there is not enough work," and they planted a seed in his head.

****

The property could not release Bekki from the Alabama resort to serve on the task force in Miami. A promise to release her for the next opening had been made. A message from her personally was left with the office. No need to call back.

The beach resort will be a better fit for her.

Preparation at the beach had now reached a feverish pace. Silverware for the specialty restaurant, glassware, serving utensils, all these four-star quality had fallen into the hands of the hotel. So many duties had fallen on the property to handle locally.

Corporate procurement took a hands-off approach.

The family restaurant was set up to feed the masses, with added seats on the terrace. The trainers knew how to get this done.

The Catering director candidate was still negotiating his terms.

The corporate trainers are here in full force; Specialty restaurants have me in the grips. I spent enormous time clarifying the concept and setting the wheels in motion. This opening will demand every last drop of energy from me. It became clear that I must do my best to pull this off. All eyes are on the F&B director and me.

This time, I commuted from my home to the hotel, a twenty-minute drive at its worst time, and the comfort of the house had its appeal.

Amanda, formerly called by her middle name Bekki, was assigned to the task force; it pleased me to fulfill her request at last.

The F&B was on top of most activities, but when he needed help, he felt comfortable engaging me to fill in on his behalf.

419

The GM had his battles to fight, and the restaurant manager's position was filled by a senior trainer, an experienced woman in her late twenties. She was good and would be an icon on the team.

The Executive Chef came from another region. German culinary training and years of experience gave us confidence in him. Two Sous Chefs and two specialty restaurant Chefs on the level just below the sous chef had needed personal guidance to get it right.

He had once received the step-by-step instruction on the intricacy of getting the blackened tuna right. It has to be drilled twelve times to get into his brain! Habit tends to take over, and this goes against the conventional grain.

The purchasing staff had a tour of the fish plant, met with the owner personally, and was instructed to place the order on specific days. The fish will be shipped packed in saltwater ice flakes. This method keeps a 28 °F."

"With all these details in place, what can go wrong? "

Murphy's law!" I stated this to the F&B, but he did not catch on to my remark.

What can go wrong will go wrong is Murphy's law.

Be proactive; if we catch mistakes early, we have a better chance of ingraining them into their habits.

Catering got off to a fast start. This man we hired for a high price had shown us a new way to deliver in his department. He took the department and hotel to another level. He received permission to buy props, which became a stage production with every event. We had never seen elaborate parties in this company.

The pool had its own kitchen crew, running independently from the central kitchen: A creative food production man and the girl we took from the sister hotel across the intercoastal waterway took charge. A Mediterranean buffet was the result of their joint efforts.

Tracy understood the delicate need for privacy and confidentiality to service the cabana club members.

She started service procedures on her own initiative, taking the chance to be reprimanded. Her territory was overlooked as unimportant by the corporate trainers. She made the best out of this neglect.

When she had a chance to show me her work, I was impressed. I did not expect this level of fine work beforehand. Outstanding work: we need more like you. Do you have sisters? I said it kiddingly. I owe you one!

"How else would I land a dream job like this?" Indeed, fired up, and she was on the right track.

Meanwhile, I coordinated the wine program and assured the delivery of these wines. I showed Tracy how to open a bottle of champagne safely and. "When will I be able to taste this champagne?"

All in good time, soon! She smiled with that wicked grin on her face, speaking volumes.

I did have a bottle of Pommery at home for special occasions, compliments of Remy Martin. I did not tell her, but I was sure she was thinking of it.

The French specialty restaurant had very selected wines from the Burgundy, Bordeaux region, Loire, Rhone, and Alsace, and others mixed in from the Napa, Sonoma, and Santa Barbara regions.

Personalized training by the F&B director took care of this; how nice is it when knowledgeable professionals are available?

The lobby bar and the casual lounge shared the same clientele. Premium brands, the full compliments from Remi Martin, are proudly displayed and offered at the right price. The same concept is carried to the choice of wine by the glass. Rob from corporate had fun setting up these bars. He was in his element.

A dual product and service concept had to be set up. We have the adults at the pool, and we cannot forget the children.

Our bartender had seen a market with the children. His idea came to me for approval. "Can we offer kiddy cocktails? I will take a combination of juices, grenadine, or other syrups and shaved ice and place it in a metal shaker. We will allow the child to shake their cocktail. I had seen the children making big eyes when they saw me shaking an adult cocktail. Do you like this idea?"

Why didn't I think of this? Yes, an excellent idea. Run with this idea. I will brief the brass.

All areas are in full gear and firing on all cylinders. It is now a matter to keep the machine running and lubricated.

The corporate trainers came with smiling faces and a good part of relief. We pulled it off, thanks to you and the hotel team.

Amanda cornered me to tell me how grateful she was to be on this team. It had been a learning curve for her and will continue. "This is a different world than LA." Yes, dear, it worked out for the better with you having to cancel Miami. You are at a unique hotel. It will be a pillar in the company's hotel portfolio. Can we have a drink outside this evening?"

We stopped at the coco bar, an outdoor restaurant with a bar on the water's edge. They have a reputation for fresh and well-prepared seafood. She ordered wine and appetizers. "That is all I need. I need to relax first."

"Something troubling you?"

"No, it is not that, just I had hoped to be seeing you a lot more, but this project has us all so busy. There is hardly any time to sleep, and I have to share a room. I had hoped for privacy," as she squeezed my arm. Do you live nearby and go home at night. Do you mind if I tag along and spend the night at your house? No obligation. Understood? Just need the feel of a home once to keep me sane."

As we entered my townhome, she was elated and checked all the rooms, saw the waterbed, and at once requested to sleep on this. "I know it is yours."

"I do not mind sharing!"

Your generosity is overwhelming!

"Oh yes, I think we get along just fine."

Another glass of wine, and she crawled into bed butt naked. "That is how I sleep."

We have something in common.

"More than that, I will now show you what real Southern hospitality is all about!"

There goes another sleepless night!

The Southern hospitality came close to the Asian hospitality. The same concept when Mother getting the daughter ready for marriage. She did not disappoint and erased *a sin of omission!*

The executive office accommodated the GM and F&B director, sharing the secretary, Nina, who had transferred from Miami. Nina had been eyeing me at every opportunity.

Seldom did I need to visit the office; everybody was on their feet and all over the property. Only confidential meetings with the top made me go up there.

In time, when the dust had settled, everybody can now take a breather. Nina lived in the same direction and knew my address.

A soft knock at my door late at night had me wonder. Nina pushed her way inside and kissed me passionately. We spent the rest of the night with quality time. "I had to see big Mo again."

It is getting heavy. Soon I'll have a waiting list?

Never mind the morals. I got to make hay when the sun shines.

The specialty seafood restaurant staff assembled at my request. All of them were seated in the chairs and were in full attention.

I wanted to impress the delicate nature of the concept and the fine line that either made it a trademark for the hotel or turned into failure.

Starting with the fish, the meticulous attention to detail this fishery was paying attention to preserve the integrity of this tender flesh.

Look at this product's care, which is delivered in frozen seawater.

We will buy short and want to run out. That will be the epitome of fish house marketing. It signals to the customers that the fish is impeccably fresh, like just off the hook from this morning's catch. Do you follow?

"The filets will be handled as they are at the filleting table at the fishery. Carefully taken from the ice tray and with kid gloves, the filet makes it to the preparation, and as soon it is finished, this plate must leave the kitchen.

I want to see simple but colorful garnish. The fish is the main attraction!

I do not want to see any plates under the heat lamps. The plates are hot, and the fish will continue to cook.

Cooks: you cook the fish to 90% only; the time it takes to serve it will be perfect.

Any available Servers must take the plate to the table, no matter who's station the plate belongs. You set up the order slip to find the customer by seating location. I know this is a break from the corporate standard to serve the table at once with all orders. We break another mold as we have done so far. The fish gets the priority in this restaurant. Make it work and write up an SOP for the property.

"If by chance the guest will return it for more fire, the manager must interact and explain the reason for this process. Yes, we will cook it more. However, we cannot take responsibility for the result.

This restaurant is a high-profile request from the owner. I had spent four-month in researching and developing it.

We must pull this off. It will be a feather in everybody's cap.

The next critical item is the blackened tuna.

I took off my jacket, rolled up the sleeves, and took an apron, ready for a hands-on demonstration.

"First, the spice mix. Ground black pepper and all other spices are carefully measured here. A dry mix will serve as the outside crust of a thick tuna fillet. We are receiving unique cuts from the fishery. He is intensely interested in getting this correct since he entrusted me with his recipe.

Notice the thickness; it looks like a filet of beef. With this, I proved the need for the cast iron pan to be red hot, the spices dipped directly on the flesh.

Then a light oil coating and the cooking process with the intense heat will burn the spices and turn it black. The flavor transforms into a sirloin.

I repeated it verbally; yes, we cook it medium. Well done; orders will be given other options.

I know this sounds snobbish, yet the integrity of this recipe requires strict adherence. There is no room to deviate.

Taste it, please.

The servers took my message to heart and followed it to the point.

The test meals had issues and messed up two orders of blackened tuna.

I took it to the cook and made him eat it. The intense burning in his mouth cured the man; he will remember the procedure in his sleep.

"Tough lesson," I know; remember, my neck is on the line.

We have a test luncheon scheduled for about sixty persons. The catering director was planning extra service to show off his skills.

He staged the service like a parade, precise and like a showman; he glowed in his glory.

When Charles showed up and had a good look around, he was in Ahh.

Pleased, he told me "You had pulled off a master plan and proven all the corporate brass wrong. The fighting to get the exceptions had paid off."

I thanked him for his support in this fight.

A long and stressful day came to an end. I made it home to relax with a glass of wine and watch the news.

The phone rang. "Hi, how are you? You looked stressed. Care if I come over? I am at the door outside. Can I come?"

Nina stood at the entrance and walked in, giving me a hug and a deep kiss. "I thought to provide you with some stress release.

While sipping on wine from my glass, I had the opportunity to explore this naked surprise further. Here." As she took my hand to shove it under the miniskirt, she whispered, "I have shaved. Feel!" No panties, this girl came prepared to play. Oh, so smooth, my instant reaction was not lost her.

She pulled me into the bedroom and undressed me to expose her naked and shaved body. She looked so young. She wasted no time heating up the action in the bedroom.

Something was going right with this girl. "Now I know a place where I can get my nookie. You don't mind, do you?"

****

Charles had dinner with the F&B director and me. "You do a lot of interesting new things, bending the corporate rules, but all in the contents of the new initiative.

"The corporate problem was that they could not keep up with you, therefore the resistance and mostly envy. When all is set and done, spend some quality time to write it all down, please."

I promise. Yes, sir, I understand!

* * * * * * *

The first night alone in bed was a treat. Eight hours of desperate sleep did me good.

With the action winding down, I was looking for this party of six that found their way to the newly opened hotels.

As by the clock, here they are. I knew the scope, first an expensive wine, then appetizers across the menu, all on the high-priced list, then the main plates. Halfway through eating, the call to the complaint.

Frustrated over it, it was a scam, yet they ended up with a free meal.

"This is not good."

"I am sorry, the server replied as being trained. "Can you please tell me what you do not like?"

"This is simply not good."

"Yes, you have told me that, but you are not telling me any specifics."

The voice raised to alert the other guests was all part of the play as they listened and stopped to see what this commotion was about.

"I told you this is not good. Can't you hear or do something about it?"

I will call the manager. You do not want any correction done to it.

The manager arrived, being briefed by the server. Sir, if you do not want to tell me the reason, we are at a loss, for you do not allow us to correct or replace these dishes. All of them?

"Yes, no good, we are leaving now."

Not so fast. I have to do something first. the manager knew this scam and produced a plan.

I will bring the server back. Come here, please. Tally up the check. Add 20 percent service charge, and now we will collect the payment.

They were protesting and threatening to leave. The manager said very calmly, if you leave, we will have the police come to arrest you. I am sure you must know the law for shoplifting.

We call it theft of services. It carries the same legal violation and will end you in jail. Would you like to spend the night in jail?

Security had since been called and arrived with handcuffs on the belt. The uniform had the looks of a police officer.

The group paid, mouthing off the restaurant. "What a lousy place and rude."

Security escorted them outside with best wishes and advice. "Do not return here; you will be refused service everywhere on this property.

* * * * * * *

With this resort on its feet, the laurels had to be earned from this day forward. Most everything moved forward as planned; minor hiccups in the kitchen needed to be addressed by senior management.

My time had to give priority to visiting all existing hotels.

Follow up, check the pulse, and assure controls had been on track. Although the numbers looked good, examining the employees may reveal any hidden problems.

Inspect what you expect, stuck in my mind.

Tampa was doing well. The acquisition of the airport hotel was on automatic handled by senior and experienced management; a follow-up visit in a month would be good.

The problem from the start at the Miami Biscayne hotel could not shake off the routine conflicts.

The GM had aired a complaint about my counterpart. Was it unfounded or simply a personality clash?

When I looked at the accusation, I found that both elements had taken it to a boiling point. It is a time bomb; the GM just lit the fuse. The fact that this man was pushed on to him never left the bad taste in his mouth.

* * * * * * *

Another Acapulco trip was scheduled on a short-term notice. "Bring extra empty suitcases. It will get ugly if the owners play dirty. We are pulling out.

A clear message and an ugly job will be ahead to shut down this hotel.

"The GM and all executive committee members will receive other assignments in Mexico."

"Puerto Vallarta and Las Hadas are in negotiations.

The EVP will join me to negotiate and hopefully close a deal.

427

Angela was going to be disappointed to cancel our weekend plans.

Amanda from LA, Lower Alabama, managed to get a transfer to Fort Lauderdale Beach and now works as the restaurant manager. She became instrumental in holding the fish restaurant together while replacing management.

She came for a visit one day to the office and wanted to talk. I took her to my home at the end of the day. I need your advice." At the house, she wanted sex. "Just one more time, and then I will leave you alone. My mom also recommended not to pursue you. "Learn from him. Stay friends. Keep him in your heart. He is a good man."

"I realize the motivation for a family will not materialize with you. My mom wants grandchildren. One last time for goodness sake. It has been an education for me, and now I feel ready for a serious relationship."

"We will stay friends, promise, a special place in my heart. Yes, friends, trustworthy friends when in need. Yes, always!"

* * * * * * *

Acapulco was like a funeral. Sad faces, tears everywhere, every employee is hanging on us, begging yet understanding the reason! Everybody knew the reason for this dramatic action.

"You will get all your benefits paid out and a severance package. It will hold you over for several months." Options had been laid out. The alternative to keeping a dying hotel from falling to its demise would not supply all this. As per the separation agreement, money was held back from sales receipts to fund all this.

The General Manager distributed documents of a sensitive nature. Every team member had a package to carry back to the regional office. The remaining paperwork was shredded.

A final farewell party brought out smiles. This company had been good to the employees.

A final cleaning and the doors closed.

The key was hand-delivered to the owner's office.

Something had just died!

We felt the pain as a team; the flight home resembled a funeral.

* * * * * *

The weekend was saved after all, and that made Angela happy. She had wanted to go to Orlando but opted to stay home and spend the time closely together.

Puerto Vallarta and Las Hadas never came to any agreement. The time and efforts ended as a big zero. But there is more! Is there?

Yes, Volume II